**Industrial
Policies for
Growth and
Competitiveness**

The Wharton Econometric Studies Series

Wharton Econometric Forecasting Associates and
Economics Research Unit
The University of Pennsylvania
F. Gerard Adams and Lawrence R. Klein, Coordinators

Econometric Forecasting Studies

Stabilizing World Commodity Markets
   Edited by F. Gerard Adams and Sonia A. Klein
Econometric Modeling of World Commodity Policy
   Edited by F. Gerard Adams and Jere Behrman
An Introduction to Econometric Forecasting and Forecasting Models
   Lawrence R. Klein and Richard M. Young
Modeling the Multiregional Economic System
   Edited by F. Gerard Adams and Norman J. Glickman

Studies on Export Instability and Economic Growth

Coffee and the Ivory Coast: An Econometric Study
   Theophilos Priovolos
The Copper Industry in the Chilean Economy: An Econometric Analysis
   Manuel Lasaga
Copper and Zambia
   Chukwuma F. Obidegwu and Mudziviri Nziramasanga
Commodity Exports and Economic Development
   F. Gerard Adams and Jere Behrman
El Salvador and Economic Integration in Central America:
An Econometric Study
   Gabriel Siri

Industrial Policy Studies

Industrial Policies for Growth and Competitiveness:
An Economic Perspective
   Edited by F. Gerard Adams and Lawrence R. Klein

Industrial Policies for Growth and Competitiveness

An Economic Perspective

Edited by
F. Gerard Adams
Lawrence R. Klein
University of Pennsylvania

LexingtonBooks
D.C. Heath and Company
Lexington, Massachusetts
Toronto

Library of Congress Cataloging in Publication Data

Main entry under title:

Industrial policies for growth and competitiveness.

Includes index.
1. Industry and state—Addresses, essays, lectures.   I. Adams, F. Gerard (Francis Gerard), 1929-   . II. Klein, Lawrence Robert.
HD3611.I38   1982   338.9   81-48557
ISBN 0-669-05412-7

Copyright © 1983 by D.C. Heath and Company

All rights reserved. No part of this publication may be reproduced or transmitted in any form or by any means, electronic or mechanical, including photocopy, recording, or any information storage or retrieval system, without permission in writing from the publisher.

Published simultaneously in Canada

Printed in the United States of America

International Standard Book Number: 0-669-05412-7

Library of Congress Catalog Card Number: 81-48557

Contents

	Tables and Figures	vii
	Preface and Acknowledgments	ix
Part I	*Economic Considerations*	1
Chapter 1	**Economic Evaluation of Industrial Policies for Growth and Competitiveness: Overview** *F. Gerard Adams* and *Lawrence R. Klein*	3
Chapter 2	**Meaning of Industrial Policy** *F. Gerard Adams* and *C. Andrea Bollino*	13
Chapter 3	**Theoretical Justifications for Industrial Policy** *Peter Urban*	21
Chapter 4	**Innovation, Technical Progress, and Industrial Policy: A Survey** *F. Gerard Adams, Martin Cherkes,* and *Robert Wescott*	41
Chapter 5	**Industrial Policy: A Review of European Approaches** *C. Andrea Bollino*	49
Chapter 6	**U.S. Approaches to Industrial Policy** *Robert F. Wescott*	87
Chapter 7	**Developing-Country Perspective on Industrial Policy** *Jere R. Behrman*	153
Part II	*Country Studies*	187
Chapter 8	**Recent Approaches to Industrial Policy in Australia** *Peter Urban*	189
Chapter 9	**Industrial Policy in Canada: A Survey** *William J. Milne*	205
Chapter 10	**French Industrial Policy from 1945–1981: An Assessment** *Francois DeWitt*	221

Chapter 11	**Industrial Policy in the Federal Republic of Germany: A Survey** *Gerhard Wagenhals*	247
Chapter 12	**Industrial Policy in Italy: A Survey** *C. Andrea Bollino*	263
Chapter 13	**Industrial Policy in Japan** *F. Gerard Adams* and *Shinichi Ichimura*	305
Chapter 14	**Industrial Policy in the United Kingdom** *Michael Davenport*	331
Chapter 15	**Developing-Country Experience with Industrial Policy: Korea, Venezuela, India, and Brazil** *F. Gerard Adams, Jere Behrman, Jaime Marquez, Brian Pinto,* and *Theophilos Priovolos*	359
Part III	*Criteria*	391
Chapter 16	**Criteria for U.S. Industrial-Policy Strategies** *F. Gerard Adams*	393
	Index	421
	List of Contributors	435
	About the Editors	437

Figures and Tables

Figures

3–1	The Ricardian Model	27
3–2	Production-Possibility Frontiers for Countries	28
3–3	The Product Cycle	29
3–4	Labor and Technology Immobility	30
3–5	The Hierarchy of Policies	34

Tables

2–1	IP Matrix: The Decision-Making Process	17
5–1	Instruments of Industrial Policy	54
5–2	Assignment Matrix of Industrial Policy	55
5–3	Selectivity Nature of Instruments	58
6–1	U.S. Government Support of Research and Development	106
6–2	U.S. Industrial Research-and-Development Expenditures in 1977	108
6–3	Research and Development as a Percent of GNP in 1963, 1973, and 1978	109
6–4	Percent of Government Research and Development Allocated to National Defense	110
6–5	Tax Incentives for Exports	122
6–6	U.S. Tariff Rates, 1979	136
6–7	Export-Promotion Intensity, Major Industrial Countries	138
7–1	Growth and Structural Change in GNP, Manufacturing, and Exports in High-Growth Developing Countries and Industrialized Countries, 1960–1978	155

7-2	Multivariate Regression Estimates of Impact of Variance in Effective Protection Rates on Quinquennial Developing-Country Growth Rates	175
10-1	Examples of Industrial Priorities Given to or Determined by the Ministry of Industry	225
10-2	Industrial Sectors Most Heavily Supported by Government	226
10-3	Direct Aid to Industry	239
11-1	Government Research-and-Development Expenditures as Percent of the Total Sources of Funds for Research and Development in the United States and West Germany, 1975	251
11-2	Federal Research-and-Development Expenditures by Industry	252
12-1	Areas of Public Enterprise Intervention, 1980	266
12-2	The Italian Planning Experience	272
12-3	Italian Industrial Policy Matrix	275
12-4	Intervention in Mezzogiorno	282
12-5	Investment of Public Enterprises in Mezzogiorno as Percent of Total Public Enterprises Investment in Each Industry	284
12-6	Government Transfers to Industrial Sector, 1973-1977	286
12-7	Preferential Loans Granted by Special Financial Institutions, 1973-1977	287
13-1	Changes in Industrial Composition	308
13-2	Annual Increase in Labor Productivity	320
15-1	Percent Average Annual Growth Rate of Manufacturing Under the Four Five-Year Industrialization Plans	369
15-2	Diversification Achievement	370
16-1	Growth of Productivity, Leading Industrial Countries	395
16-2	Employment and Unemployment, U.S. Economy	396
16-3	Inflation	396
16-4	International Data	397

Preface and Acknowledgments

This book is based on studies of industrial policy (IP) carried out at the University of Pennsylvania Economics Research Unit under sponsorship of the U.S. Departments of Labor and Commerce during 1980–1982. The studies were to a large extent a group project, entailing considerable collaboration among authors in producing many chapters. The work is intended as an overview of the issues of IP: the definition of the concept of industrial-incentive policy, the underlying economic theory, and philosophy and experience with respect to IPs and their implementation in the United States and abroad. The aim was to set the stage for further studies of general and industry-specific incentives in the framework of models of the macroeconomy—domestic and international—and with respect to particular industries. Thus the book seeks to draw conclusions about the IP experience that relate to understanding unanswered questions and the need for further research.

The authors wish to thank Arnold Packer, who helped initiate this study, and Nancy Barrett, Roland Droitsch, Samuel Woods, Warren Farb, and Allen Olsen for the helpful suggestions and support. Thanks also go to Lynnmarie Costello for valiant typing, and to Judith Lachterman for her editing of this complex material. The information presented in this book is, however, entirely the responsibility of the authors and in no way represents the view of past or present staffs of the Departments of Labor and Commerce.

Part I:
Economic Considerations

1 Economic Evaluation of Industrial Policies for Growth and Competitiveness: Overview

F. Gerard Adams and
Lawrence R. Klein

The 1970s were disappointing years for the United States and for many other industrial economies. The decade saw declining economic performance and increasing economic interdependence, even dependence. The OPEC experience left the United States, as it did many other industrial countries, with higher unemployment and higher inflation and with low growth rates of real income and productivity. The sharp change in the prices of inputs of energy relative to capital and labor and the shift in the relations between developed and developing countries require far-reaching changes in the industrial structures and the production technologies of the United States. Only in this way can the United States return to the successful pattern of macroeconomic performance recorded in the 1950s and 1960s.

Although new technologies may go a long way toward redressing industrial-world problems, there is no assurance that market processes will automatically effect the required structural changes. It has become widely recognized, as a consequence, that explicit policies will be needed if a continuation and even worsening of this situation is to be avoided in the 1980s. Such policies include those aimed at increasing the economy's supply potential (that is, increasing resources, and labor supply and capital stock), developing technology, fostering industrial development, and improving mobility and structural adaptation, et cetera. Frequently these policies have been called industry policies (IPs) or structural policies. But the association of policies or even political administrations with certain labels tends to make words such as *reindustrialization* or *supply side* a focus for spirited political debate. We intend to use the term *industrial policy* without preconceptions or biases. We are concerned with all measures that will improve the economy's supply potential: anything that will improve growth, productivity, and competitiveness.

One of the central debates of the industry-policy question is whether policies should be broadly general, leaving the structural readjustments needed at the industry level to free market forces, or whether industry-specific policies (ISPs) are required.

The traditional approach underlying U.S. policy has been to operate principally at the macroeconomic level, seeking to stimulate or to reduce demand in accord with cyclical stabilization objectives and occasionally seeking to stimulate supply—again, largely through economy-wide fiscal or monetary measures. The objective claimed for much U.S. policy (for example, antitrust and trade negotiations) has been to seek reductions in impediments to entrepreneurship and domestic and international trade. In principle, industrial development and change have been left largely to market forces. However, in practice, even in the United States and particularly in the 1970s, important market interventions have appeared as regulations aimed at pollution, health, and energy use. Also there has been a tradition of government aid to agriculture, transportation, and to the defense industries, which has affected U.S. industrial structure.

In sharp contrast to the U.S. approach, a number of leading industrial nations and advanced developing countries have relied heavily during the postwar period and, particularly in the 1970s, on explicit industrial-development strategies. Such policies frequently have aimed at assisting export-oriented or import-substituting industries. In many cases these policies have focused on developing capability in high-technology industries (the Japanese and French efforts with computers, and the Concorde and Airbus projects, for example), although with doubtful success. Frequently, they have been targeted on declining industries, sometimes providing protection and financial support and in other cases easing the transition from a sector in the down phase to another on the threshold of expansion. Various countries have used myriad planning and implementation methods, including overall industrial planning of varying degrees of detail and stringency. Specific tools have also included measures such as direct subsidies, government corporations, public-sector purchases, loan guarantees, interest subsidies, aid to research and development, specific tax and credit advantages, write-offs, and so on. Although the mechanics have varied, these approaches often involve decisions to stimulate specific industries rather than to use broadly based economy-wide policies designed to stimulate business and industry in general. Consequently, these avenues require policymakers to choose among the appropriate industries to aid and the appropriate instruments with which to bring about the desired developments.

There is an urgent need to evaluate U.S. IP as a means of increasing productivity and competitiveness for the U.S. Principal questions involved are:

1. Can IP have desirable effects on U.S. economic performance, on per-capita income growth, productivity, employment, inflation, exchange-rate stability, balance of trade, and so on? While numerous studies have examined various specific elements of IPs, there has so far been little effort to evaluate the overall impact of such policies in a compre-

hensive macroeconomic framework. In particular, do such policies lead to higher productivity and real income on an economy-wide basis?
2. What are the advantages and disadvantages of general industrial policies (GIPs), that is, policies that lack a specific industry target, compared to policies that are industry specific? This question is central to the policy debate concerning the optimal strategy for growth and competitiveness. Can general policies improving the operation of the market, or stimulating investment and research and development, effect the changes required? Or will it be necessary to pick the winners, providing assistance specifically to the industries that have the greatest potential? Or should transitional aid be provided to the specific enterprises that bear the impact of changes in demand and of foreign competition?
3. If ISPs do have beneficial effects, what industries should be chosen and how do the impacts of alternative industry-specific measures compare? Potential policy options include a broad range of alternatives such as tax-and-depreciation write-off incentives, direct financing, research-and-development policies, guaranteed markets, revisions in the treatment of policies on pollution, protectionism and other aspects of trade policy, and so on. The issue here centers on how policymakers should select appropriate industries and appropriate methods of assistance. What specific criteria should be used?
4. Focusing on the international aspect, what would the impact of U.S. industrial policy be on the world economy? What will the impact be on the U.S. economy of industrial-development strategies being implemented by other countries? In particular, what are the implications for the U.S. share of selected markets, and should the United States adopt similar policies or should it retaliate? What will the impact be of retaliation by other countries?

The issue of whether to employ IP and, if so, what form it should take, covers a broad spectrum of issues. Our work has involved many of these concerns—protectionism and trade policy, tax incentives to investment, research and product innovation, economies of scale in existing and new products, and international division of labor and multinational corporations, for example. This book explores many of these issues insofar as they are relevant to the question of IP and aims to establish guides for the formulation of U.S. policy for growth and competitiveness.

Research Program: Overview

This book represents part of a broad study of IPs for growth and competitiveness carried on at the Economics Research Unit of the University of Pennsylvania during 1980–1982.

The IP study has four phases. First, an initial phase comprised a review of theory and experience. This is the objective of this book. Second, IP scenarios were examined on the macroeconomic level to evaluate their implications on growth, inflation, and employment in the U.S. economy and on its relations with its trade partners. The third phase, a series of industry studies, focused on a range of industries to which ISPs may be applied and considered alternative policy instruments. Finally, the industry studies and the macro-simulations were intended to serve as the basis for generalizations and policy recommendations on IP strategies for the United States.

State of Knowledge on Industrial Policy:
Theory, Philosophy, and Experience

To establish the appropriate background for the study, we first review in this book the state of knowledge on IP on a worldwide basis. First, the survey summarizes the considerable theoretical research on the topics relevant to IP (for example, theory of comparative advantage, product cycle, innovation, impact of market size, entrepreneurship and risk, and so on). Second, we carry out a survey of the main literature focused more specifically on discussions of IP in Europe, the United States, and Japan. This analysis seeks to disentangle the rationale for the policy initiatives that have been carried out in many countries. Third, we review the IP experiences of the major industrial countries and of key developing economies. Many of these countries—for example, Japan and France—have experimented with ISPs, but others have used more general development strategies or have avoided IP. The successes and failures are important to gain an overall perspective on the potentials of IP for the United States. We pay special attention to the justifications for policy, the methods used to select target industries, the mechanisms utilized to influence industrial development (for example, free-market incentives versus government initiatives) and particularly, the strategies adopted to restructure older industries phasing out noncompetitive product lines in favor of new and more competitive products.

An important objective of these surveys is to establish criteria for policy selection, for choosing the target industries and, ultimately, for evaluation of IP recommendations.

Macroeconomic Analysis of Industry Policy

The second phase of the study consisted of the evaluation of the impact of various IPs in a macroeconomic framework.[1] This work examined how the performance of the economy, from the perspective of various measures of economic performance, such as growth of gross national product (GNP), inflation, productivity, and balance of trade, would be affected by various industry policies. The emphasis was on comparing general industry incentives, without specific industry focus, with targeted alternatives. We examined a number of industry-policy scenarios. For example: What would be the macroeconomic impact of stimulating the growth of U.S. high-technology industries? What would be the payout from a basic-industry scenario? We also compared strategies based on alternative approaches to investment incentives. For example: What would be the impact of changes in depreciation guidelines or investment-tax credits as compared to reductions in the corporate income tax or in interest rates?

To assess the impact of policies from an economy-wide perspective, a broad macroeconometric model and substantial industrial detail was used. It is essential for evaluating the impact of such policies on particular industries to be able to recognize, for example, to what extent industry-specific incentives will shift capital and labor among industries and to what extent such shifts affect the level of costs, prices, and relative competitiveness of the entire economy. Simulation exercises of alternative policy scenarios were carried out with the Wharton Long Term Industry model. This is a large-scale (over 2,000-equation) macroeconomic model of the U.S. economy with an embedded flexible input-output matrix and numerous appropriate policy handles. The policy scenarios provide a wide view of the likely impact of the alternative policies on U.S. economic prospects.

The simulation studies show that investment-incentive policies can be effective in improving overall economic performance. ISPs, targeted broadly at the metal-using and high-technology industries appear to be more effective than general policies. Among the policy instruments, the investment-tax credit appears to have more impact than alternative policy strategies. Regionalization of the results to the nine Census Regions of the United States shows that the policies have differential impacts among the various parts of the country.[2]

In order to introduce an international perspective, some simulations were also made with an international linkage model, Project LINK.[3] This model of the international economy provides a framework for measuring trade impacts and for evaluating the possible responses of other countries to U.S. policies. Since international trade issues are key to the IP issue, LINK simulations provide an important alternative perspective on the policy issues, particularly the impact of a separate U.S. IP as compared to the effects of coordinated IP with our trade partners.

The international simulations show that an international coordinated IP would be considerably more effective than a separate U.S. policy.

Industry Studies

The evaluation of the potentials of IP requires detailed analysis of policies, actual and potential, at the industry level. A broad range of industries and a wide variety of policies must be considered. To recognize a variety of possibilities and approaches, the industry studies fell into three categories as follows:

1. the general-industry studies
2. the international-competitiveness studies
3. the high-technology studies

All of the studies aimed at defining past experience in particular industries and determining potentials of IPs for development of particular industries. The philosophy and methodology of approach differed among the various studies, reflecting differences in the industries and in the critical issues. The general-industry studies focused largely on econometric and quantitative approaches. The international-competitiveness studies drew substantially on industry and firm data, whereas the new-technology studies emphasized the process of research and innovation.[4]

General-Industry Studies. The basic framework of the general-industry studies was comprehensive quantitative analysis of industry performance largely, though not entirely, in econometric terms. The studies were qualitative as well as quantitative and sought to explain the relation between policy (or the absence of policy) and the past and future developments in the industry. The questions addressed included the following:

1. What has been the growth, competitiveness, technological dynamics, profitability, investment, and so on in the domestic industry and its world competitors?
2. To what extent can these developments in the industry be explained in terms of U.S. government policy (or the absence of policy) directed specifically at the industry or at the economy in general?
3. How might the industry have developed had alternative approaches to policy been taken in the United States? and abroad?

These studies focus primarily on the U.S. industry in an international framework.

The studies that comprise this set are the following:

1. Econometric-model study of the U.S. steel industry
2. Production-function study of the chemical industry
3. Econometric-policy-simulation study of wheat
4. Econometric-simulation study of electrical equipment (transformers)
5. Linear-programming study of trade in coal.

International-Competitiveness Studies. The international-competitiveness studies were more product- and firm-oriented than the general-industry studies. The international-competitiveness studies focused on evaluation of the world market for specific products and on establishing what policies may be necessary to improve the competitiveness of U.S. industries in the world market. We carried out an evaluation of the current policies of the U.S. government toward the domestic industry and the effects of these policies and other potential policy strategies on the competitiveness of the U.S. industry.

Various international-competition studies were carried out.

1. To consider the role of U.S. industry in providing for health and learning on a world scale, studies are carried out for medical equipment with special emphasis on pacemakers, and on the training industry.
2. To examine competition in a product requiring basic resources a study of the paper industry was undertaken.
3. To focus on the international role of machinery, additional studies covered machine tools and agricultural machinery.
4. To evaluate the U.S. role in an industry where it had achieved dominance in the world market, a study of the commercial aircraft industry was conducted.

High-Technology Industries. The focus of the high-technology-industry studies was on the process of research and development and technical innovation. Many of the success industries in the United States have been the result of high-technology research brought to application and developed into major industrial products in world markets. Some striking examples are the computer and microelectronics industries, the copier industry, and the pharmaceutical industries. Currently at the threshold of this stage of development is the bioengineering industry. Among the issues considered in these studies are: (1) the role of government in providing the initial research and development support; (2) the influence of government policies—both financial policies and regulations such as patent law—to foster innovation and application of the new developments; and (3) the nature of the process by which new products find a place on the world market. This work focused on the study of industrial innovation contrasting the development of various high-technology industries.

Evaluation and Implications for U.S. Industrial-Development Policy

IP studies aim to evaluate the potential effectiveness of alternative industrial-development strategies. This phase of the study appraised the previous phases of the work and what they imply overall and in particular. That is,

1. Can IP be justified on macroeconomic grounds?
2. Should IPs be general or industry-specific?
3. What are the implications of such policies for specific industries?
4. Under what circumstances (and in what industries) are they likely to work and where will they not be useful?
5. What criteria might influence the type of policy tools used?

Outline

This book comprises the review of the present state of knowledge and experience on IP.

Chapter 2 is concerned with the definition of IP and the policy mechanisms. Does IP encompass general policies as well as ISPs? What are the mechanisms of IP?

In chapters 3 and 4, we consider the theoretical justifications of IP. These chapters focus on the justifications for intervention in the operation of the free market, the interrelationships between development strategies and the theory of comparative advantage, and the theory of innovation and the product cycle.

Chapters 5 and 6 are concerned with the main literature and philosophy that underlie IP in Europe and the United States.

Chapter 7 considers the role of IP in the less-developed economies.

Chapters 8 through 14 comprise studies on IP in each of the principal industrial countries (that is, Germany, Canada, Australia, Italy, France, United Kingdom, and Japan).[5] Chapter 15 concerns the experience in developing countries. In each case we consider the principal thinking on IP, the major policy initiatives and their background, and we attempt a broad evaluation of the success or failures of these policies.

Chapter 16 represents an evaluation of the criteria that can guide the development of IPs. This chapter wraps up the experience and analysis surveyed in the earlier chapters.

Notes

1. This work is summarized in Adams and Duggal (1982).
2. The regional study is summarized in Glickman (1982) and Del Rocilli and others (1981).
3. These are described in Klein, Bollino, and Fardoust (1982).
4. The studies are available as reports at the Economics Research Unit of the University of Pennsylvania. Selected studies will appear in a forthcoming volume of the Wharton Econometric Studies Series.
5. The country study for the United States is incorporated in chapter 6.

References

Adams, F. Gerard, and Vijaya G. Duggal. "General Versus Industry-Specific Industrial Policy Incentives." *Journal of Policy Modeling* vol. 4, no. 2, June 1982, pp. 161–174.

Del Rocilli, Colin J. Loxley, and P. Luce. "A Regionalized Analysis of Industrial Policy Issues." Study prepared by Wharton EFA Inc. for the Economic Development Administration, U.S. Department of Commerce, 1981.

Glickman, Norman J. "Regional and Industrial Policy." Study prepared for the Economic Development Administration, U.S. Department of Commerce, 1982.

Klein, L.R., C.A. Bollino, and S. Fardoust. "Industrial Policy in the World Economy: Medium Term Simulations." *Journal of Policy Modeling,* vol. 4, no. 2, June 1982, pp. 175–189.

2

Meaning of Industrial Policy

F. Gerard Adams and
C. Andrea Bollino

Widespread recognition that the U.S. economy has lost momentum in the 1970s with respect to growth, productivity, and international competitiveness has been accompanied by a variety of recommendations for remedial policy. These proposals, which are broadly aimed at increasing and improving the nation's productivity potential, have gone under many labels—supply side, structural policies, IP, reindustrialization, for example—and have a variety of features. But there is as yet little consensus on what the content of an acceptable and viable policy might be. Indeed there is not general agreement about the meaning of the term *IP* nor about the range of policy tools that it comprises. In this chapter we will consider the meaning and mechanisms of IP.

Industrial Policy: A Broad Interpretation

Our concept of IP is broad. IP has been defined to include only policies aimed at specific industries. Diverse approaches, however—some industry-specific and others in general—can be used to improve growth and the competitive performance of the U.S. economy. In our discussion, we will include any measure, policy, or program aimed toward these ends among the potential IP strategies to be considered.[1] But we restrict the discussion to policies that have a direct focus on the supply side, that is, on shifting production functions and the composition of factor inputs. This eliminates from the IP concept policies that are oriented primarily toward the stimulation of demand, even though some of these policies have impacts on supply indirectly.

While the targets of policy lie in the broad dimensions of economic performance, the IPs themselves are likely to be oriented somewhat more focally at the sources of the nation's productive power—that is productivity and competitiveness, the factors that lie behind the growth of productive power; the operation of competitive markets; investment in productive capital; research and development and technical change; and so on. Thus while the policymaker's concern is ultimately with the broadly defined goals of economic performance with an economy-wide perspective, the immediate focus of IPs may be with issues that are closer to the performance of the industrial and service sectors themselves. This may or may not call for policies that are industry-specific.

The strategy of selecting particular fields for public subsidy obviously must be industry-specific. Aid to declining industries or transitional assistance will generally be directed toward specific industries or even specific firms, but nonspecific IPs are also possible. Policies to improve the operation of the market—investments in infrastructure, contributions toward research-and-development spending, tax incentives, across-the-board tariff measures, for example—can be quite general. But these policies are likely to have industry-specific (and often region-specific) impact even when they are framed in nonspecific terms.

A Taxonomic Discussion of Industrial Policy

The problem of defining what refers to IP and what does not is not a trivial one. This is so partially because this concept is rarely clearly defined in the literature and partially because its meaning has changed through time and is perceived differently by various countries. For instance, according to the proceedings of a symposium held in 1974 (see Machlup 1976), IP in Western Europe is often conceived of as an attempt to determine, in advance of the market competition process, the likely success of new technologies. In the centrally planned economies, IP corresponds to planning and plan implementation. In less-developed countries (LDCs) it means industrialization and development strategy and trade policy. In the United States, IP has often been considered as industry-specific policy though much U.S. IP has been of a nonspecific nature.

We have adopted definitions of IP which will be used throughout this book. The objective is to classify the behavior of the decision maker so as to reveal the underlying philosophy. This classification will offer a convenient device to reinterpret, in economic terms, a vast body of political, sociological, and technical literature.

The first step is to take into account the characteristics of IP actions, according to their scope, time, and intensity dimensions. With regard to scope, we distinguish the policy actions in descending order of generality as follows:

> *Industrial policies in general.* This includes all types of IPs, both general and specific. The broadness of this definition reflects our previous discussion of the numerous possibilities. We do not want to unnecessarily restrict this concept.

Meaning of Industrial Policy

General or nonselective industrial policies (GIPs). GIPs are intended to be available on equal terms to all industries of the economy. These may include broad policies aimed at improving, in general, the resource-allocation mechanism as well as encouragement of investment expenditures or technology. These policies have also been referred to as "horizontal industrial policies" (Stoffaes 1981).

Activity-specific policies (ASPs). This concept is a subcategory of GIP. We refer here to policies that are nonspecific with respect to a particular sector (all industries are eligible) but the policies are selective with respect to particular activities of the production process. For instance, as noted previously, we have encouragement of research and development or investment. Although these policies have sometimes been labeled "input policies" (Prodi 1980), we prefer the ASP definition for it naturally encompasses concepts such as positive spillovers and externalities.

Region-specific policies (RSPs). These may overlap with the previous two categories, for regional policies may not be targeted to a particular industry or activity. At the same time, there may also be an intersection with industry-specific categories (see the following discussion) since regional policies are oriented toward development of particular sectors or even industrial projects. For instance, infrastructure development in a selected area of the country could be considered an RSP and an SSP. Moreover, an ISP may have consequences in the regional dimension if the targeted industry is heavily concentrated in one area, and a project-specific policy obviously has localized impacts.[2]

Sector-specific policies (SSPs). These are policies directed at specific but broad sectors of the economy, for example, manufacturing as a whole in contrast to agriculture, policies of import substitution, export-industry promotion, and so on.

Industry-specific policies (ISPs). These are policies directed at specific industries, defined broadly or narrowly. Among these are policies aimed at developing high-technology winner industries (for example, microelectronics) as well as policies intended to assist industries in trouble, such as autos and steel.

Firm-specific policies (FSPs) or *project-specific policies* (PSPs) are policies designed to benefit particular firms. Much direct government investment in industrial efforts and public enterprises and most infrastructure projects fall into this category as do assistance directed toward specific firms (those in financial difficulty) or aid in the development of particular technologies or products.

IPs may be (1) transitional or temporary or (2) long-term or endless. The length of time must be determined on a case-by-case basis in view of technology and other considerations. The important point is whether the policy is intended to be transitional, permanent, or semipermanent. All too often temporary aid evolves into long-term assistance. The decision maker's degree of commitment and influence may increase or decrease over time. Temporary policies may call for gradual phasing out whereas permanent ones may even require expansion.

Further, we consider a three-level hierarchy of policy actions as follows:

1. At the most narrow level, a measure is the simplest IP action—a specific regulation, for example.
2. A program embraces a set of measures which appear to be coordinated among themselves by the decision maker.[3]
3. An industrial strategy is defined at the broadest level, in turn, as a set of coordinated interventions.

The concept of coordination is important for two reasons. First, a broadly defined IP should not lose its specific content. This is accomplished with the concept of the measure as the building block. Second, we want to characterize important policy actions such as ASPs or RSPs discussed earlier. The terms program and strategy seem suitable for this purpose.

Finally, we shall consider an origin/destination scheme of the decision-making process, as depicted in table 2-1.

A variety of institutional bodies can engage in IPs. The potentials in this regard are closely linked to the organization of a country's economic institutions. Generally, policy can be made by government bodies on national, regional, state or community levels. With the advent of supranational authorities, the European Community (EC), GATT, ECSC, for example, supranational industrial policies must be considered. Finally, within each country we may visualize policies carried out by public enterprises or by private companies in cooperation with government authorities as happens frequently in Japan, for example.

Each of these bodies may direct its policies to various policy foci. Several classifications of the principal areas of economic interest, which are the focus of IP, are possible. We discuss in particular four issues in industrial policymaking, summarized in table 2-1.

1. Improving market characteristics. Such policies are aimed at encouraging competition, to prevent the formation of monopoly or oligopolies (U.S. antitrust) or, on the contrary, to promote mergers and concentration, as in France. We have labeled these competition, antimonopoly, and concentration objectives.
2. Stimulating innovation. These policies actively promote research and

Meaning of Industrial Policy

Table 2-1
IP Matrix: The Decision-Making Process

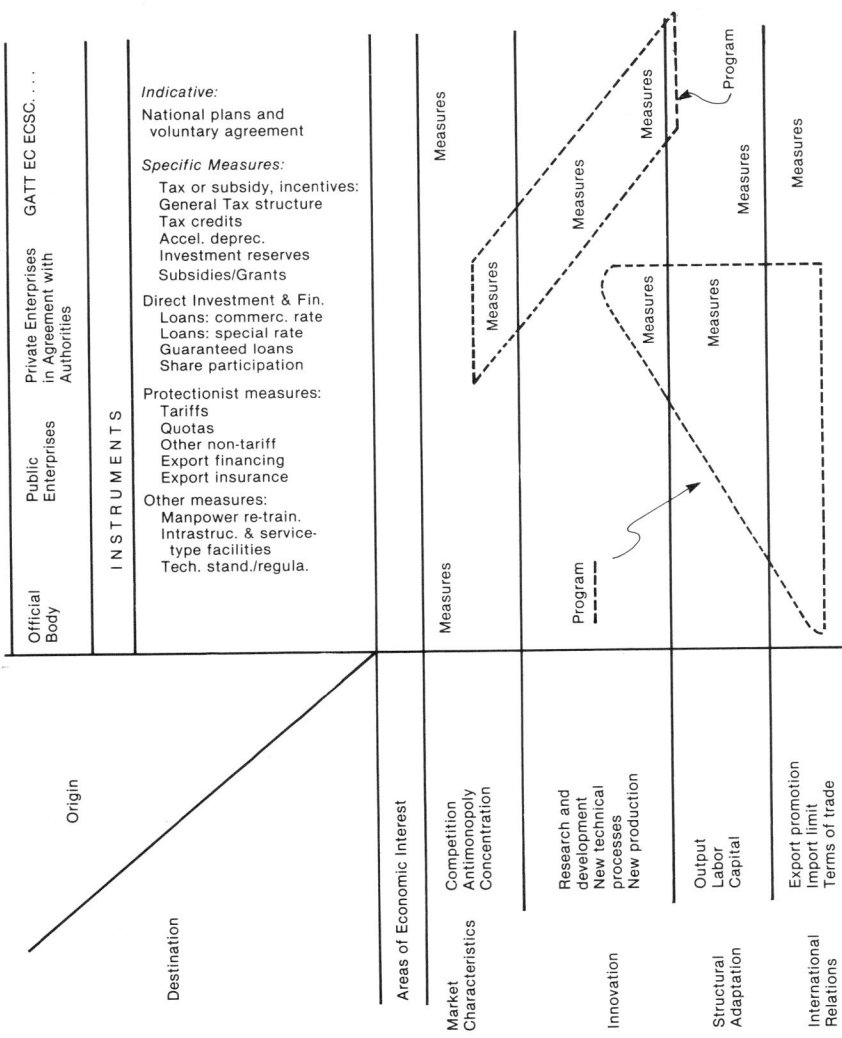

development programs, public procurement, specialized assistance to technological development, commercialization, and development of new products. Moreover, some environmental regulations and technical-standards legislation may have an indirect effect on innovation. We have labeled these R&D, new-technological-processes, and new-productions objectives.
3. Smooth structural adaptation. These policies are specifically designed for adapting industry to changed conditions. These policies could facilitate the assistance given to producers to overcome temporary disruption of the market for their output or assistance given to workers or to industrial plants facing a declining demand for their services. We have labeled these output adaptation, labor adaptation, and capital-adaptation objectives.
4. Restructuring international economic relations. Under this heading, we will include trade-creating and trade-diverting policies such as export promotion, import limitation and management of terms of trade and exchange rates.[4]

The vertical dimension of table 2-1 is made of the range of instruments used for implementing the desired policies. We have highlighted two main groups of instruments according to whether they are indicative or whether they call for specific actions.

The first group comprises national plans or voluntary agreements between the authorities and private concerns. As subsequent chapters will show, many European countries as well as Japan have traditionally had vast planning experience, but voluntary agreements have not been so rare either.

The second group is constituted of all measures affecting the decision-making process of the production unit. Some, such as price regulation, are coercive in nature. Others provide incentives (for instance, subsidies) that may or may not be used by firms.

Among specific measures we include traditional fiscal tools, such as tax credits and accelerated depreciation, together with more sophisticated financial tools, such as custom-tailored loans at preferential rates, share participation, and complex schemes of public purchases and development contracts.

Obviously the problem of measuring the impact of instruments on the economy arises.[5] In fact, tariffs or quota restrictions are easily measured in absolute percentage or physical terms, while the effect of subsidies to research and development, of technical- and manpower-regulation policies would be more difficult to measure in a precise, meaningful way.

A typical cell of table 2-1 represents a measure of IP, that is, the application of an instrument toward an area of economic interest for the decision-making center. A collection of cells in table 2-1 is depicted as a program (by a dotted line) if it has a common underlying strategy. It appears from table 2-1 that a program might embrace many foci using several instruments at the same time, and it might involve more than one decision-making center.

Table 2-1 should be seen as a conceptual framework in order to clarify the interpretation of such a complex issue. For instance, we shall see in the following chapters that the simultaneous assignment of several instruments to several targets poses the problem of analyzing their degree of complementary or substitutability. In addition, there may be the problem of consistency between different instruments, which may, at the extreme, cancel each other out.

IP encompasses diverse instruments, institutional structures, and targets. Even the classification proposed in this chapter occasionally fails to do justice to the range of possibilities.

Notes

1. Such a broad perception of IP is also taken by Diebold (1981).

2. The Italian experience in Southern Italy development efforts constitutes an extensive example of this type of policy. A more refined analysis of the relationship between IP and regional policy is conducted in Glickman (1981).

3. It is understood that, if it is not possible to define a common strategy for a specific set of measures, we will refer to it simply as a list or collection of measures.

4. Others have proposed alternative classifications of IP objectives. For instance, Prodi (1980) stresses the distinction between output policies and input policies. In this classification support for research and development is distinguished from labor- and capital-adaptation policies and output adaptation is distinguished from development of new products, because there are (especially in Europe) different underlying philosophies, as discussed in chapter 5.

5. In this respect, chapter 3 will discuss a hierarchy of different policy instruments.

References

Diebold, William. "Thinking Structurally about the American Economy." Working Paper prepared for the Study Group on United States Industrial Policy, New York Council on Foreign Relations. Mimeographed. 1981.

Glickman, Norman. "Regionalized Industrial Policy Impacts," preliminary draft. Philadelphia: Economics Research Unit, University of Pennsylvania, 1981.

Machlup, F. *Economic Integration: Worldwide, Regional, Sectoral.* Proceedings of the Fourth Congress of I.E.A., McMillan, London, 1976.

Prodi, Romano. "The Italian Experience as Regards Public Sector Intervention in the Economy." *International Symposium on Industrial Policies for the 80's,* Madrid, May 1980.

Stoffaes, Christian. "The Rise of Industrial Policies," paper presented at the meeting of Wharton EFA in Oslo, May 29, 1981.

3 Theoretical Justifications for Industrial Policy

Peter Urban

Economic theory should provide a major part of the underpinnings of any analysis of IP. Obviously the policymaker must consider a variety of social and political, as well as economic, issues. The importance of the economic calculus is that it focuses directly on costs and benefits. Is the economy better off on balance with or without the IP intervention? The social or political questions cannot be ignored; indeed they may often dominate. But emphasis on the underlying economics means that in most, if not all, cases the costs of taking account of the social and political aims can be evaluated.

In this study, we begin with a simple economic model of a market economy and then proceed to outline how failures of the real economy to meet the assumptions of the model may serve as justifications for IP interventions. We begin the discussion in the context of a single, static economy, and then progress to a dynamic multicountry context.

In choosing to begin with what may be viewed as an *idealized norm,* we risk portraying this abstract theoretical construct as in some way achievable, to be sought through policy action. This is not our intention. Rather, we take the position that perfection is unattainable and that the role of policy is to improve the *performance of the economy* as much as *possible,* bearing in mind that all actions involve an associated cost.[1]

The next section outlines the general theoretical model of a simple competitive economy. The key assumptions of this model are then evaluated in terms of their implications for public intervention in the marketplace. This model is then extended to the international context. Following this is a discussion of the implications of the analysis for choosing appropriate policies. The final section summarizes the discussion.

A Model of the Economy

The fundamental model of the competitive economy is that of Arrow, Debreu, and McKenzie (A-D-M) (Arrow and Debreu 1954, Debreu 1959, McKenzie 1959).[2] In this model, the market consists of an array of consumers and firms, each attempting independently to maximize welfare and profits respectively. *This economy will achieve a (Pareto) optimum without government intervention.* However, the assumptions of this paradigm are restrictive. In particular, the model assumes explicitly the following:

1. there are no public goods, that is, goods whose benefits or costs are not confinable to those producing or paying for them. Examples include defense, police forces, air pollution, street lighting, and so on.
2. there are no nonconvexities in consumption preferences or production possibilities (for example, scale economies in production).
3. information and adjustment are perfect and costless. In fact, the model is essentially timeless or static insofar as there is a finite number of markets.
4. markets are complete in the sense that all goods entering an individual's utility are traded. (For example, noisy neighbors cannot be a problem in the A-D-M model, since noise, if it affects anyone's preference, must have an associated market.)

The model implicitly assumes that:

5. there is equality of social and private discount rates,
6. there are no policy-induced rigidities in the system (for example, there are no minimum wages, and so on).
7. there are no questions concerning the distribution of wealth. This issue is treated on two levels. First, it notes that any Pareto optimum may be achieved through taxes and subsidies (Varian 1978). Second, the more fundamental issue of aggregatability of preferences is questionable (Arrow 1963).

Breaches of these assumptions provide a possible cause of nonoptimal behavior and, hence, form a basis for government intervention. These *divergences* between nonoptimal actual market outcomes and outcomes possible through intervention are, given the pervasive possibility of breaches of the assumptions, likely to be common. This conclusion ignores any costs associated with intervention and, hence, must be viewed a priori as only a normative basis for policy.

Divergences from the Arrow-Debreu-McKenzie Model

Divergences from the A-D-M model which provide a basis for IP usually involve at least one of the following factors:

1. creation of new information, products, or technologies
2. development of work-force skills

Theoretical Justifications

3. learning by doing
4. risk
5. government intervention

All of these factors have both domestic and international aspects. In this section, we will restrict the discussion to the domestic context.

New Information, Product, or Technology

Any firm developing new products or techniques faces the risk that its innovation will be copied before its gains can be fully exploited. Clearly, this justification underlies the idea of granting patent rights to inventors. However, with the acceleration in the rate at which knowledge is acquired and new ideas become obsolete, patent rights may no longer be completely satisfactory in guaranteeing profits to the firm responsible for major breakthroughs.

Nevertheless, such inventions are a major source of economic growth. Examples of industries where these considerations apply include computers, microelectronics, and agricultural chemicals and plant research.[3]

Work-Force Skills

In most industries, there is generally an initial period during which new workers undergo a settling-in or training process. For some industries this training is particularly important, but once skills are acquired, the worker can move freely between firms in that industry without further training.

Examples include shipbuilding, electronics, automotive design, and the aerospace industries. Therefore these industries are commonly concentrated in a particular region or country where firms may hire from a large pool of highly skilled workers. The advantages of such a skilled work force, once established, form a barrier to entry of new regions into the industry and can have a snowballing effect on growth of the industry in established areas.

From the firm's viewpoint, expenditure on extensive training programs poses the risk that trained staff may be lured to competing firms that do not need to invest in any training costs. Again, government intervention may be justified insofar as the expansion of the work-force skills contributes to productivity growth and industry expansion.

Learning by Doing

In some industries new firms find they have a higher cost of production than existing firms, but after a "learning" period they can reduce their costs below those of their competitors.⁴ However, it may not be profitable for these new firms to bear the initial losses since by reducing costs, they may reduce the prices for which output is sold below the point at which they can recover their initial losses. A similar situation occurs with firms that can reduce average costs by expanding output (for example, where there are significant production-run economies). In both these cases, while production may not be profitable for individual firms, the community as a whole benefits from lower prices. Thus there may again be a case for government intervention.

Each of the discussed cases, (namely, new information, skills, and learning by doing) have a public good element in that investment in any of them produces benefits for the community at large that are not restricted to the actual firms or individuals directly involved. There is presently substantial government intervention designed to promote research, education, and research and development. Obviously, the question to be answered is whether these policies encourage the appropriate level and pattern of these activities.

For our purposes, the existence of these problems as a possible source of divergence is of greatest relevance. It may be noted that such important programs as the space program are unlikely to have been undertaken in the absence of substantial government subvention. These programs provide knowledge both directly and indirectly useful in diverse applications and, hence, they must be viewed as public goods.

Risk

In the A-D-M model, uncertainty is either ignored or it is assumed that markets are complete in that commodities are differentiated by state of nature as well as type of good and time. This problem of uncertainty (or incomplete markets) raises problems insofar as individuals are normally risk-averse—that is, they prefer a dollar with certainty to a gamble with the same expected outcome. The implication of this is that, even in the absence of any other source of divergence, firms may be unwilling to invest in a particular venture because of uncertainty. This problem may be exacerbated where the investment involves research that produces new information.

The problem of uncertainty and risk aversion has two basic dimensions:

1. Firms may *spread* the risk associated with any venture across many small shareholders, or across many diverse activities. Thus larger firms are likely to be less risk averse than smaller firms which have fewer opportunities to spread risk. (Large firms, however, may exhibit risk-averse behavior. Management structure may emphasize divisional per-

formance without regard to overall firm objectives; hence, division managers will make risk-averse decisions.)
2. Policy intervention undertaken to reduce private risks may not necessarily reduce social risks; thus such an action may simply transfer risks from firms to taxpayers. An example is the case of public investment in synfuels projects. Obviously, such funding lessens private risks; however, because of the *size* of the funding required, it is not at all clear that society is risk neutral (Arrow 1971).

Government Intervention

A very common cause of divergence between private and social costs and benefits may arise as a result of government intervention. Regulations and policy measures have effects beyond the point or problem at which they are directed.

An obvious example is the effect of minimum-wage legislation. The primary purpose of such a measure is to raise the income level of unskilled workers. However, a major indirect effect is to reduce the competitiveness (domestically and internationally) of industries that are major employers of unskilled workers, thus reducing the employment prospects of workers and, through possible effects on the balance of trade, altering the profitability of a wide range of industries.

Other examples include the impact of protection measures: Import quotas on steel would benefit domestic steel producers; however, domestic industries using steel as an input (for example, autos) would face higher costs and, hence, reduced competitiveness.

The argument that government intervention justifies further intervention seems contradictory. However, it is important to consider this case in detail because of the pervasiveness of distortions arising as a result of government action.

First, one may note that such a case for government intervention is indirect in that more direct measures are available for removing the distortion (for example, removal of steel quotas or repeal of minimum-wage legislation and replacement with direct subsidies in the previously discussed examples). Second, the case relies on measures having unintended or secondary effects.

The issue of secondary effects highlights the interdependencies in the economic system and the importance of considering government actions in a general framework. In view of these considerations, appropriate policies are likely to involve a review stage before any actions are implemented to offset the effects of policy-induced distortions and may result—not in additional government intervention—but in modifying existing government intervention.

A separate, but in many ways related, case for intervention concerns the action of foreign governments to assist their industries. This situation generally involves claims of unfair competition. However, the basis of government action is not the fairness of the foreign competition, but rather whether the actions are viewed as short term, being aimed at gaining some measure of future market power. This international aspect of government intervention is discussed in the next section.

Employment

Another general case for industry assistance involves what may be termed the *employment argument*. Economic change, as a result of shifts in tastes, new technology, demographic shifts, or the policies of overseas governments, frequently leads to declining competitiveness of existing industries in particular countries. Although adapting to change is essential to economic growth, it may, in the short term, impose severe hardship on the affected industries. The policy dilemma, in these circumstances, is to assimilate the gains from change while minimizing the (unemployment) costs of adjustment.

The arguments discussed thus far have, to a significant extent, ignored the international trade aspect of IP, although it is this aspect that most often serves as its underlying motivation. In the next section, the various models of trade are reviewed within the IP framework.

Trade, Models, Comparative Advantage, and Industrial Policy

The A-D-M model, although serving as a useful model of the competitive economy, has many limitations in the international context. The model essentially views the economy as a single entity. Samuelson (1949) points out how the traditional competitive-economy model may be cast in the broader international context; however, breaches of the assumptions of the model, of which the A-D-M model is a formalization—particularly the assumptions of timelessness and no convexities—are important factors determining the pattern of international competitiveness.

The Heckscher-Ohlin Model of Trade

Early explanations of the pattern of trade were based on the Ricardian-Torrens concept of comparative advantage whereby countries specialized in (that is, exported) those goods in whose production they held a relative advantage. (As figure 3-1 shows, country X has a relative production advantage in good A.) However, the classic theory provides no explanation of divergences in production functions between countries apart from climatic differences[5] and implies specialization.

In the Heckscher-Ohlin (H-O) model, (the two factors, two countries, two goods or $2 \times 2 \times 2$ case), tastes and production function are similar in both countries, with the production function being homogenous of degree one.[6] (See figure 3-2.) Within this model, the pattern of trade results from differences between countries in factor endowments, with each country exporting that good whose production uses (relatively) intensively its (relatively) abundant factor.

In early tests of the H-O model,[7] notably Leontief's, explanations of the divergence between predicted and actual patterns of trade (in terms of factor intensity) relied heavily on differences in labor-force skills and on endowments of natural resources (see, for example, the study by Baldwin 1971). These explanations do not contradict the H-O model; rather they relate to the importance of careful factor definition to retain factor homogeneity. This view is supported by the results of more recent studies (for example, see Harkness 1978) supporting early views that the United States has a comparative advantage in capital-intensive industries.

Also important in explaining the shortcomings of the H-O model are

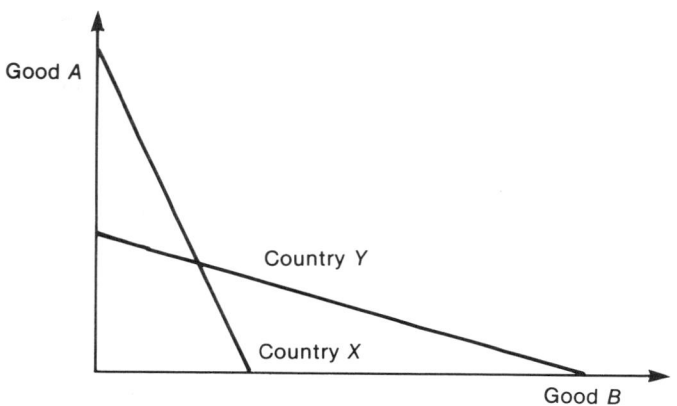

Figure 3-1. The Ricardian Model (Fixed-Coefficient Technology)

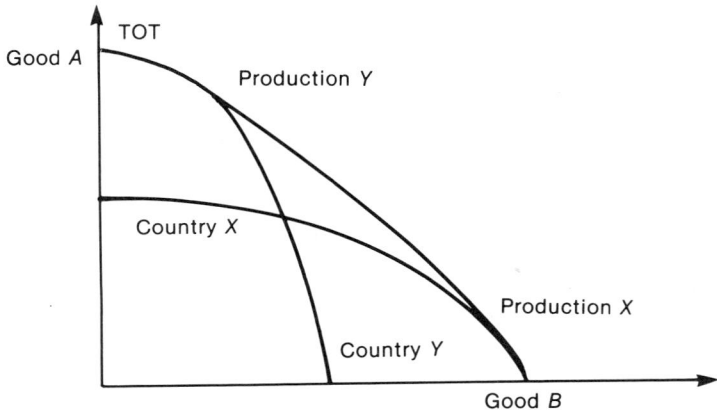

Figure 3-2. Production-Possibility Frontiers for Countries

the assumptions underlying the model. As pointed out by Chipman (1966) in a survey paper, these limitations arise as a result of the following factors:

1. international disparities in production functions
2. increasing returns to scale
3. trade in intermediate products
4. nontraded goods
5. variable factor supplies
6. international mobility of capital

Within the context of IP, the key limitations are likely to be differences in production techniques, increasing returns to scale, and mobility of new technologies. These limitations may be viewed in a static and dynamic context.

In the case of increasing returns to scale, the limitation is similar to that arising from nonconvexities in the A-D-M model, namely that intervention may lead to a result preferable to that arising from the market forces.

The *nature* of economies of size is also related to their *existence*. Traditionally, these economies have been discussed in the context of an industry or country. However, as pointed out by Ethier (1979), economies may be explained largely by the division of production (or of labor in the case of Adam Smith's famous example of pin production) within or between countries. In the alternative explanation of the traditional static external-economies case, recourse has generally been made to the existence of some unpaid factors or the creation of atmosphere.

Theoretical Justifications

In both static explanations, the existence of economies provides an *endogenous* explanation of comparative advantage in that *trade,* once begun, determines the direction of comparative advantage (Negishi 1969). However, the *initial* pattern of trade is indeterminate. Thus the question of some underlying dynamic considerations applies.

The importance of technology transfer and differences in production techniques in a static context seems less than that of returns to scale, which Ethier (1979) has proposed as a major explanation of trade patterns. Clearly, differences in techniques do exist as a result of incomplete information. Similarly, market imperfections may lead to slow diffusion of new technologies. However, the rapid improvement in communications technology would be expected to reduce these limitations.

Dynamic Considerations, Product Cycles, and Alternative Models of Trade

In some recent models of trade, economists have stressed the role of dynamic considerations such as technological change, development of new products, or dynamic economies (arising from learning by doing whether internal or external to the firm) in affecting the pattern of trade.

Early writers in this area generally emphasized the development of new technologies, associated with new products, as determining the pattern of trade. Thus Vernon (1966) and Hirsch (1974) have argued that there is a product cycle whereby a new product or technology results in the innovating country initially dominating trade in the good. Eventually, the production technology becomes more widely understood and simplified. Then production passes from innovating (advanced) countries to low-wage economies (see figure 3-3).

Two related but separately treated views are the Linder model (Linder 1961), where differences in tastes enter the explanation, and the Posner model (1961), where technological change, by resulting in factor augmentation, underlies the explanation of trade.

Key to all of these models is the immobility of technology, capital, or some other factor or the existence of learning-by-doing-related economies. This view may be strengthened by closer scrutiny of the product model as outlined by Finger (1975). Finger argues that a major determinant of trade is the introduction of *new* products. As an example, he cites women's fashion; it is not, he argues, economies associated with production runs or new technology. However, unless there is some immobile factor, it is indeterminant whether *new* fashions will be produced (or even designed) in, say, Paris or Milan. A similar argument can be given in the case of the Linder model.

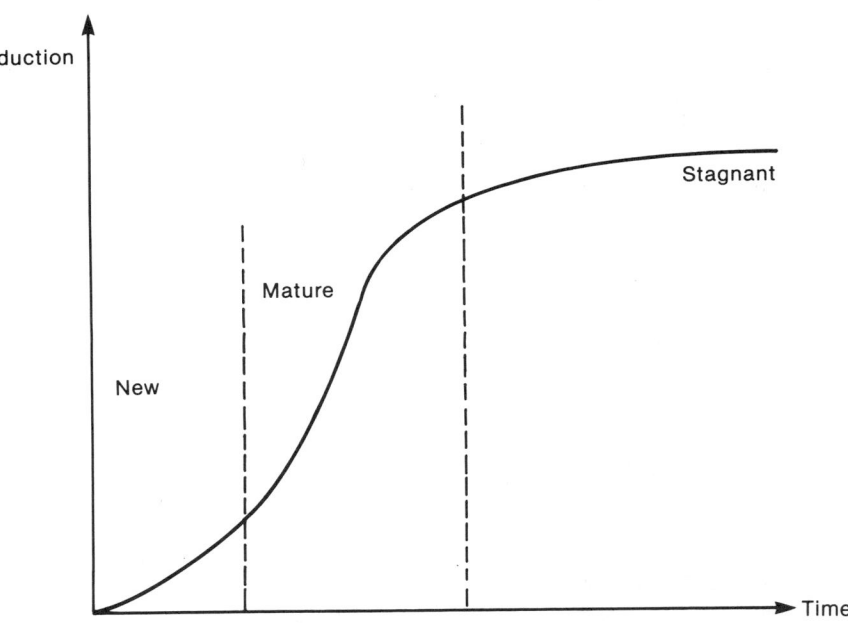

Figure 3-3. The Product Cycle

Clearly, differences in tastes alone are insufficient to explain the pattern of trade. Otherwise, cars favored by Australians would be produced where they could most efficiently be produced (that is, not necessarily in Australia).

This view was implicit in Hirsch's discussion of the H-O and technology-based explanations of trade (see Hirsch 1974). In the H-O model, the central determinant of the pattern of trade is the existence of fixed-factor-endowment differences. This is the case in the technology model, where technology is the fixed factor. As figure 3-4 shows, X will tend to specialize in (export) the labor-intensive good and conversely Y will tend to specialize in (export) the technology-intensive good.

The stability of this pattern of trade is related to the mobility of technology. Clearly, if technological developments were perfectly immobile, the pattern of trade would depend solely on the development of factor-augmenting technology. On the other hand, if the new technology were perfectly mobile, then technological change would be shared simultaneously by

Theoretical Justifications

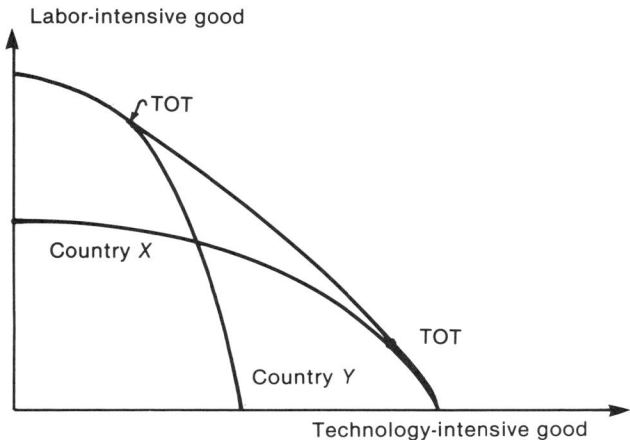

Figure 3-4. Labor and Technology Immobility

all countries (regardless of innovating country) and would not influence the pattern of trade.

An interesting example relevant to these issues is discussed by Majumdar (1979). In this case study of trade in electronic calculators, Majumdar finds that technological developments, by creating new products and simplifying the production process, confers a competitive advantage. However, these advantages are generally short-lived as competitors quickly imitate the development.

The issue of learning by doing is, in many ways, intertwined with immobility of technological developments. It may be that technological developments are transferred internationally very rapidly. However, the innovating country may retain a competitive advantage through greater (and increasing) familiarity with the new technology. This factor seems to have been relevant in the calculator example previously cited. While Japan was initially an imitator, once having captured a substantial market share as a result of its low wage advantage, it became in turn, an important innovator.

Learning by doing thus may be regarded as providing economies and generating technological developments. Although the relative importance of this influence may seem vague, it appears difficult to overestimate. As noted earlier, learning by doing underscores what may be viewed as the *dynamic* nature of external economies and, thus, is likely to underlie the Linder model, in which differences in tastes provide the basis of *initial* patterns of production, but learning related economies provide a basis for stability of this pattern of production. Similarly, it is likely to explain why particular countries, for example, the United States, United Kingdom, and now Japan are major innovators in a number of industries.

Overall, it appears that we can integrate the more recent, dynamic explanations of trade with the H-O framework, depending on the importance of learning by doing and mobility of technology. With the trend to multinationalization, international mobility of capital and technology has been enhanced. Thus it appears that in the future the pattern of trade is likely to be influenced more by wage costs and the existence of learning-by-doing-associated economies rather than by differences in tastes, production methods, or factor endowments. This is so even in the case of substantial (static) economies related to the division of production.

The Infant-Industry Model and Extensions

The infant-industry argument is generally viewed as the main case for protection in developing economies (Corden 1965). The argument has a long history dating back to Alexander Hamilton in 1791. Nevertheless, the model has undergone substantial refinement with two essential features being identified as underpinning this case for government intervention.[8]

In this section, these essential features will be discussed to outline the more general applicability of a wider version of this argument in the case for government intervention.

A main feature of the infant-industry model is that time must enter the argument in some essential way. The effect of time may be internal or external to the firm. For an example, an individual firm may benefit from learning-by-doing in the production of particular goods. Alternatively, experience gained from production in a single firm may benefit the entire industry and, hence, the benefits may be external to the firm.

These time-related benefits are, in many ways, related to the externalities or divergences discussed earlier. They may be based on knowledge, training, or atmosphere. These benefits accrue in virtually any industry and in this sense provide only a prima facie case for government intervention.

A second essential feature of the argument is that there must be *a divergence* between social and private benefits from the effect of the time-related experience. If the benefit of experience is entirely internal to the firm and there are no imperfections in the capital market, we could treat the benefit of experience as a form of capital (albeit in invisible form) and would not, in the absence of any *pecuniary* externalities, expect any need for intervention.

However, the assumption of a perfect capital market is questionable in many cases. A good example is that of training, which may be viewed as the creation of human capital. As noted earlier, the benefits of training are usually external to the firm providing it. This is not in itself a basis for assisting the firm insofar as the workers themselves would, as the beneficiaries of the increase in human capital, be expected to finance the investment (for example through lower wages during the apprenticeship).

Yet this is not always possible. The wage reduction may require the worker to borrow against his human capital. Given the problem of moral hazard associated with such loans, the capital market may apply a higher discount to such loans than is socially desirable.

The case of pecuniary externalities was proposed by Negishi (1968). The main point of this case is that some of the benefits of the increased experience accrued to consumers and factor-input suppliers as well as the firm (or industry). Pecuniary externalities are likely to be critical in the case of microelectronics (for example, where a major benefit of experience has been a substantial fall in the price of these goods). This is also true in certain other industries (poultry and plant breeding, for example).

The infant-industry argument has general applications, at least insofar as it is an economic basis for government intervention. The general applicability of the case also extends to the industries for which the argument is applicable. When first proposed, the argument was applied to import-competing industries. However, Corden (1974) and Johnson (1969) both point out that it may be applied to export- and nontraded-goods industries and, insofar as the external benefit arises through creation of atmosphere, to broad sectoral complexes. An important case in point is the training of scientists, technicians, and other researchers in research and development. These skills are usually widely applicable and, insofar as they may be considered public goods, contribute to raise productivity in general.

The major conclusion here is that there is a general framework in which to consider the economic basis of IP—namely, through analysis of divergences between social and private costs and benefits. This framework applies to all industries, whether import-competing, export, or nontraded. However, this framework only forms a prima facie basis for intervention.

Appropriate Policy Measures

The literature on optimal policy in the presence of domestic distortions is largely centered on trade policy. Given the emphasis of much IP on export- and import-competing industries, this orientation reduces any questions of special assumptions or a case-by-case application of the underlying concepts and ideas. However, as Corden (1974) points out, the methodology is not restricted to the analysis of trade policy, but has much broader application.

The essential issue discussed here is that of policy choice in the presence of distortions between social and private costs and benefits. In the literature, these distortions are related to the Pareto optimality conditions. As noted in the previous sections, it is the existence of such distortions that provides the basis for policy actions.

The question of the choice of appropriate policy measures has only been considered briefly. To paraphrase Corden, for any divergence between private and social costs or benefits, there is a hierarchy of policies. It is always true that as one goes down the list, the appropriateness (in a welfare sense) declines and the correction of the problem at which the policy is directed also declines (see figure 3-5).

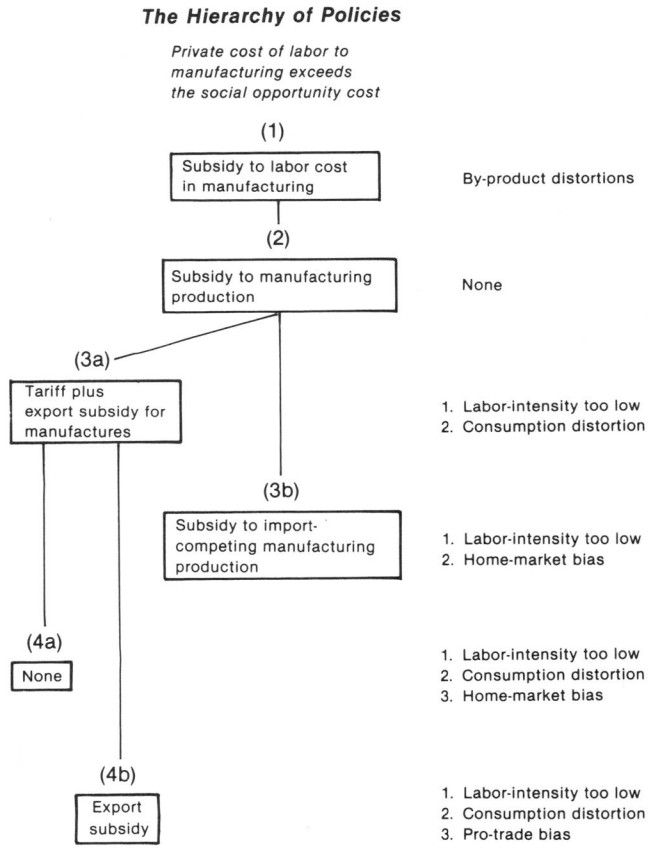

Source: Corden (1974) p. 29, chart 2.1.

Figure 3-5. The Hierarchy of Policies

Theoretical Justifications

The original work in this area is largely based on a paper by Johnson (1969), which is an extension of the theory of the second best (Lipsey and Lancaster (1956)). The essence of Johnson's analysis may be summarized in two propositions: namely, (1) The correction of domestic distortions does not require taxes (tariffs) on international trade; and (2) Taxes on international trade designed to correct domestic distortions will not necessarily improve welfare by comparison with the free-trade situation.

Corden (1974) considers the question of policy ranking in detail. In his schema for ranking distortion-correcting policies, he emphasizes the importance of recognizing the side-effects of policies. In this framework, the most appropriate (or first-best) policy is the one that deals with the problem most directly.

The problem with this approach is that, as noted by Corden, it assumes that costless nondistorting tax instruments are available to policymakers and that any income-distribution effects of correcting the distortion may be ignored. Removal of these assumptions leads to a modification of the hierarchy given in figure 3-5. Nevertheless, as both Corden and Johnson note, there is an efficient tax-collection and disbursement system in most developed economies. This explains the widespread use in many countries of exemptions and other special taxation provisions as an instrument of IP. Overall, it appears that the assumptions are not too restrictive. Lloyd (1975) points out that the informational requirements for empirically evaluating alternative policies are very substantial.[9] The limitations these requirements impose are likely to mean that, in the absence of a consistent, general equilibrium framework for evaluating policy, prima facie evidence for or against particular policies will be weighted heavily.

In this context, it seems reasonable to assume that, in the absence of strong contrary arguments, policies that deal with the distortion directly are preferable to more general policies. Thus in the case of the infant-industry model, if the distortion results from insufficient private investment in training or research and development, then government policies that subsidize these activities directly would be more appropriate than subsidizing output of the industry.

Conclusions

This chapter has identified several factors likely to be significant contributors to the pattern of international trade, namely:
1. technological innovation
2. increasing returns
3. learning by doing

These factors are interdependent. As noted in the calculator example, innovation and learning by doing can interact. Similarly, many technological developments often result in scale economies, and size, in the Schumpeterian view, contributes to a faster rate of technological innovation.

We also noted that these three factors, as well as uncertainty, can be associated with a divergence between social and private costs and benefits. Thus they may also serve as a justification for IP. However, certain questions persist.

1. Just how important are these factors in determining international competitiveness?
2. What are the policy measures appropriate to reduce any negative (or increase any positive) effects of these factors on national income and competitiveness?

In the first case, many writers (for example, Ethier 1979) have argued the importance of increasing returns in determining the pattern of trade. Similarly, the prima facie evidence suggests that innovation and learning by doing exert substantial influence on international competitiveness.

The importance of uncertainty as a determinant of international competitiveness remains ambiguous. Agent actions may be influenced by uncertainty. However, whether particular countries are adversely affected by uncertainty is a more complex question. It would be expected to influence the level of investment in research and development and in industries associated with learning by doing. Thus uncertainty may have an indirect effect on international competitiveness insofar as it results in underinvestment in research and development and innovations. Also, it may result in a general misallocation of resources that, if corrected, will result in a rise in incomes generally.

Thus it appears that each factor already noted is important as a possible basis for IP. Nevertheless, specific industry studies will be necessary to test this general conclusion in particular industries.

The question of appropriate policies is more complex. In the case of innovation, and, to some extent, learning by doing, the cause of the divergence is the public-good nature or knowledge. Thus the first-best policy appears to be the introduction of subsidies to stimulate such investment in the industries concerned. For example, taxation provisions oriented to increasing cash-flow retentions by firms in the industry affected would likely be appropriate. However, in the absence of measures to restrict the mobility of technological developments, such a policy may only result in development of the technology in the United States with the refined process being transferred to other countries without any net benefits accruing to U.S. industry (see Borkakoti 1975). Thus slower technological growth may have contributed to the declining competitive position of the United States, government measures to stimulate research and development may not contribute substantially to a reversal of this situation.

In the case of increasing returns, the situation seems more hopeful. The substantial part of world trade in manufactures accounted for by intra-industry trade is, according to Ethier (1979) a result of what he calls "international" economies.

If this view is correct, then policymakers face a dilemma. Efficiency considerations may require that firms be large or that a number of firms in an industry integrate their activities. Obviously, the firms concerned are likely to influence the market and, hence, may raise antitrust considerations. Compounding this is the fact that it may indeed be in the national interest if the U.S. firms do exert this market power in foreign markets. Overall, a review of the U.S. attitude to antitrust policy seems relevant. The French attitude of flexibility has much to recommend it. (See Hough 1979). At the same time, it will be important to differentiate between economies arising from technical considerations and those achieved through the exercise of monopoly power. This consideration is not important in the case of export- and import-competing industries insofar as foreign competition acts as a barrier to monopoly. In the case of tertiary industries, however, it may be important.

When the various factors underlying the theoretical rationale for industry policy are reviewed, it is apparent that they can be significant in a large number of industries. Thus IP could take the form of a detailed set of industry-specific measures. However, it may be more appropriate for policies not to be of an industry-specific form, dealing instead with the factor underlying the need for intervention in a general context. This approach would, for example, encourage research and innovation generally rather than approaching the problem with policies directed to encouraging specific research areas or research in specific industries. These policies may be viewed as picking the winners. However, as with any such approach, picking the winner requires considerable information (which may be costly to collect), involves risks, and may be administratively demanding.

This conclusion ignores what may be termed *second-best arguments* for IP. These arguments center on the assumption in A-D-M model of no policy-induced distortions. In a complex, mixed economy such as that in the U.S., this assumption is clearly unrealistic. Again, the first-best approach would be to remove the distortion directly. This may not be possible because of political considerations. Thus the second-best approach may be to provide measures that reduce the undesired effects of the distortion. An example quoted in the analysis was minimum-wage legislation. If the legislation cannot be repealed, it may be appropriate to provide subsidies to the low-wage, labor-intensive industries that are most affected.

The important consideration in second-best arguments for protection is the unfeasibility of first-best measures. In the just given example, the first-best policy would be elimination of the minimum wage, with the welfare problem being handled by direct income support. In practice, second-best arguments are generally difficult to evaluate, involving subjective judgments on welfare and feasibility.

In conclusion, although imperfections in the simplified market model, divergences between public and private objectives, and dynamics provide many ways to rationalize IP, it is wise not to lose sight of the risks associated with government intervention. As the discussion of national practices in the following chapters illustrates, political considerations have often dominated economic ones in the policymaking process. All too often policies that originally had a sound basis, justified on grounds of economic theory, have been maintained long after their original justifications have disappeared. Theoretical rationalizations for IP are no substitute for repeated reappraisal of the benefits and costs of such measures in the framework of the entire economy.

Notes

1. This chapter is concerned with the resource-allocation aspects of public intervention rather than income-distribution questions. Clearly, income distribution is a major concern of economic policy. However, in this chapter, we take the view that these questions may be considered separately from questions of IP.

2. For a detailed discussion, see Debreu (1959).

3. See chapter 4 for a detailed discussion of issues related to technical change, inventions, and innovations.

4. Most discussion of "learning by doing" has been in the international context, for example, Corden (1974). However, the argument is relevant in the domestic context as well.

5. For a more detailed review of the Ricardian-Torrens model, see Chacholiades (1978).

6. In the following, problems associated with factor intensity reversals are ignored. While this issue is important in the literature, it is not very relevant to our concerns.

7. For some examples of these tests, see Roskamp and McMeekin (1968).

8. For a detailed discussion of the infant industry argument, see Corden (1974). The approach used here essentially follows this treatment. For a discussion of this material in relation to development policy in LDCs see chapter 7.

9. There have been several recent theoretical contributions in the area

of optimal policy in the presence of domestic distortions. (See Lloyd (1974), for example). They highlight the complexity of this problem.

References

Arrow, K.J. *Essays in the Theory of Risk-Bearing.* Chicago: Markham Publishing Co., 1971.
——. *Social Choice and Industrial Values.* New York: Wiley, 1963.
Arrow, K.J., and G. Debreu. "Existence of an Equilibrium for a Competitive Economy." *Econometrica* 22, No. 3, 1954.
Baldwin, R.E. "Determinants of the Commodity Structure of U.S. Trade." *American Economic Review* 61(March 1971).
Borkakoti, J. "Some Welfare Implications of the Neotechnology Hypothesis of the Pattern of International Trade." *Oxford Economic Papers* 27(November 1975).
Chacholiades, M. *International Trade Theory and Policy.* New York: McGraw-Hill, 1978.
Chipman, J.S. "A Survey of International Trade: Part 3, The Modern Theory." *Econometrica* 34(January 1966).
Corden, W.M. "Recent Developments in the Theory of International Trade." Special Papers in International Economics, Princeton University, 1965.
——. "Monopoly, Tariffs, and Subsidies." *Econometrica* 34(February 1967).
——. *Trade Policy and Economic Welfare.* Oxford: Clarendon Press, 1974.
Debreu, G. *Theory of Value.* New York: Wiley, 1959.
Ethier, W. "Internationally Decreasing Costs and World Trade." *Journal of International Economics* 9(February 1979).
Finger, J.M. "A New View of the Product Cycle Theory." *Weltwirtschaftliches Archive* 3, No. 1 (1975).
Harkness, R. "Factor Abundance and Comparative Advantage." *American Economic Review* 68(1978).
Hirsch, S. "Capital or Technology? Confronting the Neo-Factor and Neo-Technology Accounts of International Trade." *Weltwirtschaftliches Archive* 110, No. 4(1974).
Hough, J.R. "Government Intervention in the Economy of France," in *Government Intervention in the Developed Economy,* ed. P. Maunder (London: Croom Helm, 1979).
Johnson, H.G. "Optimal Trade Intervention in the Presence of Domestic Distortions," in *International Trade,* Bhagwati, J. ed. (Penguin Modern Economics, 1969).

Linder, S.B. *An Essay on Trade and Transformation.* Stockholm: Almqvist and Wiksell, 1961.

Lipsey, R.G., and K. Lancaster. "The General Theory of the Second-Best." *Review of Economic Studies* 63:11-32(1956-1957).

Lloyd, P.J. "A More General Theory of Price Distortions in Open Economies." *Journal of International Economies* 19:365-386(1974).

———. "Tariff Compensation: An Undesirable Policy." *Australian Journal of Agricultural Economics,* (1975):146-153.

Majumdar, B.A. "Innovations and International Trade, An Industry Study of Dynamic Competitive Advantage." *Kyklos* 32(1979):559-570.

McKenzie, L.W. "On the Existence of General Equilibrium for a Competitive Market." *Econometrica* 27(1959).

Negishi, T. "Protection of the Infant Industry and Dynamic Internal Economies." *Economic Record* 44, No. 105(1968).

———. "Marshallian External Economies and Gains from Grade Between Similar Countries." *Review of Economic Studies* (1969):131-315.

Posner, M.V. "International Trade and Technical Change." *Oxford Economic Papers* 13:323-341(1961).

Roskamp, K.N., and G.C. McMeekin. "Factor Proportions, Human Capital and Foreign Trade." *Quarterly Journal of Economics* (February 1968).

Samuelson, P. "The Gains from International Trade," in *Readings in the Theory of International Trade,* eds. Ellis and Metzler, 1949.

Varian, H.R. *Microeconomic Analysis.* New York: W.W. Norton, 1978.

Vernon, R. "International Investment and International Trade in the Product Cycle." *Quarterly Journal of Economics* 80(May 1966).

4 Innovation, Technical Progress, and Industrial Policy: A Survey

F. Gerard Adams, Martin Cherkes, and *Robert Wescott*

IP and the innovation process are closely linked. There are strong theoretical arguments that suggest why market failures in the innovation process occur and why a public-sector response might be proposed. On a more practical level these factors are linked because a frequent goal of IP is the encouragement of technological progress in order to promote leading sectors and improve international competitiveness. This chapter focuses on questions of technological change and innovation. Our main objectives are: (1) to analyze the theoretical justifications for public-sector policy in the area of innovation, and (2) to explore relevant innovation issues and study their implications for IP.

Definition of Innovation and the Dynamics of the Innovation Process

The frequently used term *innovation* has various definitions in economics literature. The meaning of innovation used here is very broad, ranging from scientific invention through research and development to commercial realization and diffusion of the invention. Methodologically, one can divide the process into six stages as follows:

1. research (basic)
2. invention
3. entrepreneurship
4. investment
5. development
6. diffusion.

Research precedes invention but is often purpose oriented and profit motivated. The *invention* represents the discovery of a new process or product. *Entrepreneurship* is the process of deciding to take advantage of a known (usually) invention or idea. *Investment* is understood mainly as the stage of mobilizing resources, whereas *development* is the stage of technical development. It calls for additional research of an applied nature and involves commercial utilization of the idea. *Diffusion* is the stage of massive penetration of the new tool or technology into industrial practice and into the marketplace.

From an IP perspective, the dynamics of the innovation process are most interesting. What causes the development of a particular industry? Why do some inventions attract investment capital while others languish? How do the capital and skilled-labor requirements of certain industries change as they experience technological growth? How do these changes affect production and competitiveness? In an attempt to shed light on such questions, W.J. Abernathy (1978) presents a general approach to the process of innovation[1] by describing the innovation process in concrete terms and organizing his observations into a theoretical framework. He suggests that there are two types of innovation: *main* and *incremental*.

A main innovation appears with the identification of emerging needs or a new way to meet an existing need (for example, automobile, airplane, television, semiconductors). Main innovations are performance-maximizing and not cost-minimizing. They are often introduced by small, new enterprises. Incremental innovation—product and process improvements—is concentrated on cost reduction. This kind of innovation usually occurs in price-competing industries where economies of scale are important. Production is generally capital-intensive and equipment is highly specialized. Each change in product (or product performance) is very expensive.

Main innovation usually emerges in a skilled-labor-intensive, cost-inefficient industry with general-purpose equipment and without a standard product design. Users can ask for changes in the product and will get them. Examples include the computer industry twenty-five years ago, and the aircraft industry sixty years ago. A main innovation is not very likely to emerge in a large, established firm that is efficient and looking for more productivity and efficiency.

Abernathy sees the process of technological progress in an industry as moving from the main-innovation stage to the incremental-innovation stage. He sees this as a shift from main-innovation characteristics such as highly skilled labor, general-purpose equipment, the maximization of product-performance, product-design diversification, and informal cooperation among employees to the characteristics of incremental innovation such as capital-intensive, highly specialized equipment, the minimization of production costs, and the emergence of one main product design, and a strong interfirm hierarchy.

The main-innovation period gives performance-maximizing products that are made with inefficient production processes. Efficiency in production dictates special equipment and standardization, for example, and this cannot be achieved if the design changes frequently. In a rapidly changing industry, it is risky to develop a highly specialized production process because the product might soon become obsolete. When the industry achieves one main design, the innovation activity switches to incremental innovation with emphasis on reducing production costs by standardization, specialization, and so forth—in other words, to what has also been termed *process innovation*. This can cause difficulties, however. Eventually this process may lead to total identification between the product and the production line. Thus there is no incentive to change the product because it is too expensive to make changes. The result is a trade-off between efficiency and innovation.

From a social point of view, the importance of incremental investment should not be underestimated. Some studies show that more than half of the gains of technological progress are due to incremental innovations (Maier 1979). Other social and economic differences between main and incremental innovations are sometimes possible. With a main innovation the risk of failure is usually greater, the possible gap between social gains and private returns is bigger, and the possibility of monopolization of a successful innovation is stronger than in the case of incremental innovation.

Issues on Technical Progress—Implications for Industrial Policy

The theoretical and empirical literature on technical progress focuses on a number of questions which have implications for industrial policy. This section considers some of these questions.

Investment in Research and Development

The question of whether the quantity and direction of investment in research and development is optimal in a regime of free competitive markets has been raised in chapter 3. We have concluded that the inability of the investor to capture all the possible gains represents significant externalities that are likely to reduce research and development expenditures below the socially optimal choice.[2] Mansfield (1968) concludes that investment in research and development depends on expected average profitability, the research-and-development projects at hand, the profitability of alternative uses of funds, and its size. The notion that economic considerations govern these decisions is not unanticipated but does not assure, in view of the earlier theoretical discussion, that sufficient investment in research and development will be carried out.

A prima facie case for government assistance remains, though the magnitude of such support and the form it should take are not easily determined. In fact, once a decision that government support is advisable has been made, serious questions about the amount of such aid and the processes for its allocation remain. Economic theory indicates the need for a social benefit-social cost calculation that incorporates the benefits and costs as perceived by the individual economic agent with the externalities involved. Such a calculation is not difficult to visualize in theory, but its implementation in practice is considerably more problematical.

Another question is the degree to which the public sector should intervene in making the choices about resource allocation. This is a central question since it focuses directly on whether assistance should be industry- or project-selective—that is, pick the winners—or whether it should be general. The theory of innovation is suggestive in two respects. First, there is a large degree of uncertainty about research and innovation expenditures. One of the problems in private-sector activity in research and innovation is the limited ability of private enterprise to spread the risks. A second point is the options nature of technological research and development. The development of one stage of research provides a setting for more advanced stages to follow. Investment in research and development represents investment in options for future technological development. Both of these arguments suggest that a broad approach to research and development support has advantages over a selective approach. Whether it is possible to make realistic choices among the potential winner technologies—and to do so without limiting the options of future technological development—is a question which needs further study.

Role of Industrial Organization and Size of Firms

While the theoretical concepts of optimization typically presuppose competitive markets, there are grounds both in economic theory and, as we shall note further, in the practice of some countries (France) to favor noncompetitive market structures for advancing technical change. The hypothesis that monopolies are the "engine of technological progress" arises in the work of Schumpeter (1939) and Galbraith (1952). Consequently the issue of optimal industrial structure for technical advancement is important and involves such questions as the following:

1. What is the relationship between industrial concentration and technical progress?
2. Does the size of the firm influence its approach and contributions to research and development?
3. Does the organization of the industry influence the rate at which technical developments are translated to new products and processes?

Quantitative evidence does not provide a simple answer to these questions. The quantitative results do show a small positive correlation between concentration and technical progress. Greer (1976-1977), for example, found a small improvement in productivity was related to a large increase in the concentration of sales among the largest firms in an industry. With respect to research and development, a small correlation was found between research-and-development expenditures as a percent of sales and an index of market concentration.[3] A possible explanation for these findings might be that, as Scherer (1980) puts it, the atmosphere for innovation is better in concentrated than atomistic industries.

On the other hand, the belief that bigger firms contribute relatively more to the process of innovation than smaller firms is not supported by empirical evidence. In summarizing his findings on this question, Mansfield (1968) points out that only in certain limited cases are the largest firms in an industry responsible for a large proportion of the innovations. Exceptions occurred mainly in cases where the investment required to innovate was large relative to the size of the potential users, when the minimum size of the firm required for profitable use of an innovation was relatively large, or when the size of the largest firm was much larger than the average size of the potential users of the innovation. In other words, the largest firms accounted for a disproportionate share of innovation when economies of scale attached to the innovation were large.

Big firms do not invest relatively more in research and development (Scherer 1980), and their results are not generally more efficient. Of the seventy most important inventions of the twentieth century in Jewkes, et al., (1958), only twenty-four came from the industrial laboratories of the giant firms. In fact, it is frequently thought that small firms are more likely to develop new products (Abernathy 1978). One argument is that high entry barriers insulate an industry or a firm from outsiders and perhaps from new ideas and initiatives. But Comanor (1967) found that industries with moderate barriers to new entry have much higher research-and-development employment relative to their size. Atomistic industries, which by definition have very low entry barriers and are obviously highly competitive, are likely to have few incentives for big investments in research and development. This point derives directly from our previous discussion of the inability of small firms to fully internalize the benefits of the investments in research and development.

What, then, is the meaning of these conflicting results for IP? The answer is far from clear. IPs to advance innovation cannot ignore the organizational structure of the industry, nor can they ignore the technical requirements of the anticipated innovation, its scale, or scientific sophistication. These, for example, will affect the optimal environment for and approach to advancing the innovation process. Thus there may be some justice on both sides—on the advantages of small-scale competitive research-

and-development and innovation initiatives and on the gains from large-scale systematized-research efforts in large firms. Consequently there is no clear answer on an optimal industrial structure from the point of view of innovation toward which IPs can be aimed. These questions will also have to be considered in making the choices among GIPs and ISPs to advance technical progress and in the selection of the policy instruments.

Industrial Policy and Innovation

In theory, market failures with respect to the socially optimal rate of innovation can be corrected by appropriate policy. In practice, there may be significant obstacles to this goal. The most direct and obvious response is to internalize economic externalities of innovation through a system of patents. A prima facie theoretical case can be made for patent protection as an important feature of IP on technology. If financial incentives could be perfectly protected, the problem would disappear; then the bias against innovation could be reduced. Unfortunately, this solution carries its own problems. First, the flow of information can never be perfectly bottled up under patent protection. A second criticism is more fundamental: Patent protection may be used to restrict the use of new technologies and may well stimulate the owners of the patents to continue to use or license a patented technology even after new, more effective techniques have been developed. Although patent protection is an important component of public policy on innovation, it cannot fully reconcile private and social interests.

Other policy options include general public support of basic and applied scientific research, tax advantages and subsidies for firms engaging in research-and-development activities, government-guaranteed procurement contracts for new products, and government bounties for new products or processes. As we have noted earlier, a critical question is whether government support should be general or specific.

From an IP perspective, it is probably desirable to keep public support untargeted or aimed at broad targets in the early stages of the innovation process. This approach might be termed *keeping the options open* and would allow time for policymakers to see which projects come to fruition. In terms of the stages of innovation given earlier, this might be desirable in the first, second, and third stages.

In later stages, the justification for public support is not as clear. More is known about the likelihood that the new technological development will be a winner, its probable costs, market, timing—in short, its prospects for becoming an economically viable innovation—so that the gains can be captured to a large extent by the innovator. Under these circumstances, IP support is much less justifiable than at earlier stages in the process of technical innovation. Nevertheless, the additional available information also makes a policy of picking the winners more feasible. Such policies could be directed toward projects that have good chances of economic and technical success and that fit in with long-run national, technical, and economic objectives. This has been the approach in France and Japan and, to some extent, in West Germany.

Notes

1. Also see Maier (1979).
2. See Arrow (1971).
3. Also see Horowitz (1961-1962).

References

Abernathy, W. *The Productivity Dilemma.* Baltimore and London: Johns Hopkins University Press, (1978).
Arrow, K.J. "Economic Welfare and the Allocation of Resources to Invention," in *Essays in the Theory of Risk Bearing,* Markham Publishing, 1971.
Comanor, W.S. "Market Structure, Product Differentiation and Industrial Research." *QJE* 85 (November 1967).
Galbraith, J. *American Capitalism.* Boston: Houghton Mifflin, 1952.
Greer, Rhoades D. "Concentration and Productivity Changes in the Long and Short Run." *Southern Economic Journal* 43 (1976-1977).
Horowitz, I. "Firm Size and Research Activity." *Southern Economic Journal* 28 (1961-1962).
Jewkes, J., et al. *The Sources of Invention.* New York: St. Martin's Press, 1958.
Maier, H. "New Problems and Opportunities of Government Innovation Policy and Firm Strategy." Laxenberg, Austria: IIASA. Unpublished, 1979.
Mansfield, E. *Industrial Research and Technological Change.* New Haven: Yale University: Cowles Foundation for Research in Economics, 1968.
Scherer, F.M. *Industrial Market Structure and Economic Performance.* New York: Rand McNally Publishing, 1980.
Schumpeter, J. *Business Cycles.* New York: McGraw-Hill, 1939.

5
Industrial Policy: A Review of European Approaches

C. Andrea Bollino

The purpose of this chapter is to survey the views that lie behind IP developments in Western Europe during the last two decades.

First, an extensive review of the literature is presented to identify relevant studies and the main centers and agencies that have conducted research on this issue in this period. Second, this survey aims at consolidating the empirical evidence about IP experiences in order to characterize the underlying philosophies adopted by European policymakers.

Given the social and cultural differences existing across countries, it is not always meaningful to treat Europe as a homogeneous area. In fact, there are at least three perspectives from which one can analyze the European IP experience.

1. One can look at the common features of national approaches as an outsider, generalizing across Europe.
2. One can borrow the European Economic Community (EC) viewpoint, considering European IP in the sense of a European supranational organization.
3. One can look at the national level, reviewing individual countries separately.

In this chapter the first two approaches are used to shed light on European IP; a more detailed analysis for each country will be taken up in the following chapters.

As we saw in the previous chapters, the main economic justification for IP is to supplement the market in case of failure, and its ultimate goal is to increase the society's level of welfare. This latter concept is multidimensional. It can be interpreted to mean a stable rate of growth; an increase in production potentials, in productivity, and employment; and also an improvement in international competitiveness and in the balance of payments. Obviously, these various considerations are not equally weighted. Indeed, priorities among them are likely to differ not only between countries but also between different times within specific countries.

Often, the literature on IP is not written in the precise language of economic theory. Therefore, the problem is this: In reviewing objectives and instruments of IP, is it possible to disentangle social and political considerations from economic ones? In doing so, is it possible to clarify the main features of European thought about IP?

Given the time span covered, it may not be entirely legitimate to discuss IP without knowing the main characteristics of industrial development that occurred in Europe through time. We have distinguished three periods in the postwar history of economic growth in Europe: (1) the Reconstruction Period, from the Marshall Plan to the creation of the EEC, (2) the Rapid Growth Period (1960-1973), covering the consolidation of the Common Market until the oil crisis, and (3) the Post-Crisis Period of rethinking from 1973 to the present.

This chapter is structured as follows: The following section presents a taxonomic discussion of goals and instruments, explaining their interaction and highlighting a crucial issue common to all countries: the selectivity of intervention. The third section sketches some important structural changes that occurred in the European economies during the 1960s and the 1970s and the relationship between IP and historic developments. The next section offers two interpretations of the philosophies underlying the IP responses in terms of the empirical evidence and reviews in some detail the IP experience in Europe with respect to the use of the instruments for specific policy objectives. The fifth section provides some insight of the role performed by the European Communities in shaping IP. The major findings of the analysis are summarized in the concluding section.

Goals And Instruments of Industrial Policy

What Is Industrial Policy in Europe?

In discussing European IP experience, some authors state that IP does not have a clear meaning because it is virtually all the legal, financial and fiscal framework of business (Ohlin and Hesselborn 1977). Others see it as an overly broad concept, embracing any policy that might aid industry (Warnecke 1975) and define IP as the "government intervention which attempts to modify industrial patterns of resource allocation" (Komiya 1976) or as interventions to supplement the market when it is not fast enough to adjust to changing conditions (Ekstrom 1969). Alternatively, IP is conceived of as a collection of measures aimed at saving jobs in order to alleviate massive dislocations of workers (Suleiman 1975). From a nationalistic point of view, IP is defined as government intervention that will enable firms to match other Western firms on the basis of indicators such as research and development, productivity, profits, and so forth (Young and Lowe 1974). A somewhat cynical viewpoint sees IP as the (Italian) solutions for regional depression in the "Mezzogiorno" (Prodi 1974). Finally, on the pessimistic side, "much of what governments do in the name of IP is simply to continue old-fashioned protectionism by more sophisticated means" (Pinder, et al. 1979, p. 9).

During the last two decades, a vast body of literature concerning IP has developed in Europe, peaking during the early years of the 1970s and declining afterward. Two key elements appear to be common to most of the early writings: first, the increasing concern about the degree of coordination of decision makers' interventions, and second, the increasing awareness that the decision-making center was moving from national to supranational entities (Cooper and Denton 1976).

The first issue appears to be the consequence of the structural changes that occurred during the period of rapid growth throughout the 1960s. In fact, structural imbalances, changes in welfare distribution, rising integration of markets, and bottlenecks induced a rethinking of the prevailing philosophy of intervention. The concept of IP, initially a mere inventory of actions and ad hoc measures, started to become what may be defined *industrial strategy*.

The second issue is obviously the result of the creation of the EC and the increased importance of transnational enterprises. The establishment of an effective common market, the integration of capital markets, and the increased mobility of labor forces have been simultaneously the cause and the effect of the reduced effectiveness of national policies. Consequently, the various bodies of the EC have experienced a de facto increase in their sphere of influence upon various aspects of IP, both at indicative and prescriptive levels. This fact has fueled a wave of interest in international cooperation.

Ironically, there is evidence in the debate following the oil crisis that worsening structural problems, inflation, unemployment, and exchange-rate instability reduced the enthusiasm for supranational cooperation. In fact, individual national authorities tried to cope with domestic crises, often resurrecting particularistic measures bordering on a new beggar-thy-neighbor attitude.

All this suggests that there is an intimate relationship between IP and historical economic developments. The rest of this chapter is aimed at analyzing this issue in depth.

Main Goals

A variety of goals have characterized European IPs during the postwar period. In fact, the objectives pursued by the authorities have changed in response to developments of economic structure. This section reviews briefly the historical developments of IP goals in Europe. The relationship between IP and economic developments will be discussed later.

During the 1950s and until the early 1960s, IP was generally conceived at most as an instrument for achieving broad macroeconomic goals (Vernon 1974) such as full employment (West Germany, United Kingdom, and the Netherlands), the stabilization of investment (Italy), the achievement of national unification (between French- and Dutch-speaking regions in Belgium), price stability (West Germany and the Netherlands), the maximization of growth of national product (France and also Japan), and the target of balance of payment equilibrium (Europe and also Japan). France, with its long tradition of national planning, the so-called *économie concertée* (that is, coordinated strategy between big business and government) was the first country moving toward more specific goals.

Early in the 1960s the increased openness of the economies following the creation of the EC had a substantial impact in the formulation of IP, as shown by the French example. In 1960, the export: production and import: consumption ratios were lower in France than in partner countries, and in designing the Fourth National Plan government authorities thought that the national growth spark was inside the economy. On the contrary, the outside forces (opening up of international markets) unexpectedly took over, weakening state control over the economy. As a consequence, French IP was increasingly directed toward firms competing in international markets, attempting to encourage the development of large industrial conglomerates to resist the U.S. challenge and to acquire international prestige (Suleiman 1975).[1]

During the mid-1960s the debate about assistance to industry in the United Kingdom was centered on the controversy between the Industrial Reorganization Corporations (IRC) constituted in 1966 seeking the most efficient firm within a given industry and merging all others into it, and the monopoly commission trying to prevent concentration (Smith 1974) and (Maunder 1979).

Meanwhile, Italian decision makers were arguing that stimulating private industrial investment during downturn periods was like pushing on a string and that, consequently, state-owned enterprises had to fulfill the role of stabilizer in the national interest (Holland 1974) and (Franko 1978).

There were no doubts among the German decision makers about a laissez-faire policy. From the 1950s until the end of the 1960s, the West German government explicitly wanted to rely only on market forces (Balassa 1975). The Act for Promotion of Stability and Economic Growth of 1967 still gave priority to macro instruments in order to achieve price stability and high employment and only in 1968 the federal government issued policy guidelines recommending that entrepreneurs be responsible for structural adaptation and that government roles be confined to temporary, declining measures (Kuester 1974).[2]

The most recent period—the post-oil-crisis period—was marked by a paradox: On the one side, major problems were affecting European economies (presumably, requiring government intervention), and on the other side, IPs became increasingly impotent because of the conflicts of interest pervading the European societies. The French debate was stagnating among three positions: (1) those in favor of the picking-the-winner approach (Cotta 1977 and Stoffaes 1978), (2) those who refused such specific policies in favor of a general policy guideline allowing industry to pursue its own structural transformation (Balassa 1979), and (3) those who charged that the authorities behaved inconsistently, promoting at the same time both concentration and antimonopoly legislation (Jenny and Weber 1976). In the United Kingdom, an increasing feeling of mistrust of IP has developed since the beginning of the 1970s because of alternate changes in government philosophy. Between 1970 and 1974, the conservative government attempted to dismantle the IP efforts of the previous administration and the labor government tried to resort to IP afterward, thus impairing the confidence of private business (Franko 1979). In Italy, the decisions taken by the government are not based on a plan to achieve the best level of industrial development but are only motivated by political and social considerations (Prodi 1980, p. 6).

Instruments

If the goals of IP have been myriad, we can say that the instruments used have also been varied, differing across countries as well as over time.

In reviewing the most important instruments, we have classified them according to their indicative or coercive nature. Roughly speaking, the former consist of, for instance, the Long Term National Plans (Belgium, France, Netherlands, and Sweden in the late 1950s and the United Kingdom and Italy in the early 1960s), the voluntary restrictive agreements (for example, cigarette advertising, and oil imports in West Germany in 1966), or any national specific program (such as the Buy British campaign to limit imports), while the latter are all measures affecting the decision-making process of the productive unit, either passively (for example, subsidies, preferential credit, and so on) or actively (for example, specific taxes, capital controls, and so on).[3]

The main instruments used at all three decision levels are listed in table 5-1 (see also table 2-1); it is not surprising that the instrument range is widest at the government level whereas it is basically confined to financial instruments at the other two levels.

Table 5-1
Instruments of Industrial Policy

	Official Body	Public Enterprises	Private Agreements
Active Measurable	Indicative (national plans)	Voluntary agreement	Voluntary agreement
	Tax structure		
	Tariffs, quotas		
	Capital controls		
	Exchange-rate policy		
	Price controls		
	Share participation	Share participation (state holding companies)	Share participation (joint ventures)
More difficult to measure	Nontariff barriers		
	Technical standards		
	Regulations		
	Development contracts	Development contracts	Development contracts
	Public purchases	Public purchases	
	Manpower retraining		Manpower retraining
	Service-type facilities	Service-type facilities	
Passive	Tax credits		
	Accelerated depreciation		
	Subsidies	Subsidies	
	Loans (special rates)	Loans (special/normal rates) by special institutions	Loans (normal rates) and export financial/insurance with state guarantee
	Grants		
	Export financial/insurance		

In order to characterize the use and function of the instruments of IP it would theoretically be desirable to analyze their assignment to specific objectives. This is a difficult task, however. First, the assignment is not always made explicit by the decision-making center. Second, even if this is the case, there might be a multiplicity of objectives for the same instrument, or vice versa, and it is difficult to track down the priorities. Finally, most of the instruments were modified through time as regards both the way in which they were applied and the objectives they were intended to pursue (OECD 1978a).

Table 5-2 attempts to sketch an assignment matrix according to the European experience, where the major economic areas of interest have been subdivided into twelve different objectives, thus providing a magnification of table 2-1.

First, we note that suggestive or indicative instruments have been used for practically all the objectives, given their nonbinding nature. Second, we note that some instruments have been widely used for different objectives,

Table 5-2
Assignment Matrix of Industrial Policy

INSTRUMENTS	Market Characteristics			Innovation			Structural Adaptation			International Relations		
	Competition	Antimonopoly	Concentration	Research and development	New technical processes	New products	Output	Labor	Capital	Export promotion	Import limitation	Terms of trade
Indicative:												
National Plans and voluntary agreements	*	*	*	*	*	*	*	*	*	*	*	*
Specific Measures:												
Price control		*				*	*					
Exchange-rate control												*
General tax structure	*	*	*		*		*	*				
Tax credits			*			*	*	*	*			
Accelerated depreciation					*		*	*	*			
Investment reserves												*
Subsidies/grants			*	*	*		*	*	*			
Loans: commercial rate			*				*					
Loans: special rate			*	*		*	*		*			
Guaranteed loans			*	*		*	*		*			
Share participation		*	*	*		*	*					
Manpower retraining								*				
Development contracts			*		*		*				*	
Public purchases			*	*	*		*			*		
Service-type facilities			*	*	*		*			*		
Technical standards/regulations			*		*	*		*				
Tariffs											*	
Quotas											*	
Other nontariff											*	
Export financing										*		
Export insurance										*		

OBJECTIVES

as is the case of fiscal and financial measures and promotion of infrastructural facilities (service-type assistance) while others have been assigned only to specific objectives such as manpower-retraining programs, development contracts, and, obviously, tariffs and other barriers to trade. Third, table 5-2 should be interpreted as the direct or immediate link between instruments and objectives, as generally stated by the decision maker. Given its qualitative nature, I have not attempted to attach a weight to each asterisk in the array. Therefore, nothing is said about spillover or external effects of the policies.

In conclusion, three observations can be drawn from table 5-2. First, we see that many instruments have been assigned to each target, thus posing the problem of analyzing their degree of complementarity or substitutability according to the authorities' strategy. For instance, preferential fiscal treatment could have been used as a (partial) alternative to direct subscription of new capital shares in order to promote concentration and mergers, while at the same time these instruments could have been used in tandem in order to assist research-and-development activities. Second, there is a problem of coherence between different instruments as subsidization of certain production inputs may act as a disincentive to technological innovation that is to be promoted by technical standard policy. Third, possible conflicts may arise between objectives as is extensively documented by the debate concerning promoting competition or encouraging concentration.

A Crucial Issue: the Selectivity of Intervention

The picture of European IP presented so far is still incomplete, for nothing has been said about the distinction between nonselective and selective policies, that is, GIP versus ISP, FSP, PSP.

Based on the present survey, we can say that, historically, the choice of the level of intervention has been discussed in terms of the debate between *dirigisme* and liberalism in the marketplace. In the early 1960s, the debate was centered on the West German versus the French position. On the one side, those in favor of letting the free market operate (for example, West German and Scandinavian governments) have advocated nonselective measures in order to minimize the disturbance of the resource allocation mechanism (EEC 1962). On the other side, advocates of the vital role of government intervention (for example, the Commisariat du Plan in France) have been in favor of selective measures in order to influence (or shape) production and investment decisions (Denton 1967).

The government-intervention viewpoint gradually spread over continental Europe and the United Kingdom. As a result, in the late 1970s it was difficult to identify a country's IP according to its position in the debate because selective intervention had become a common practice. However, disagreement still exists about the practical implementation of selective measures, both within and across countries. The disagreement within a country has typically been the result of a conflict of interest among political or social forces, whereas the disagreement across countries has typically been centered on international cooperation and the role of the EC.[4]

The results of the review of European experience with selective policies are summarized in table 5-3.[5] In principle, it would be desirable to group the instruments used into two mutually exclusive sets and discuss the selective and the nonselective measures separately. As the table shows, however, this is not the case.

The main information provided by table 5-3 is that there is no clear-cut distinction among instruments. In particular, some fiscal- and trade-related instruments have been used both in a nonselective manner and at a sectoral level, whereas the financial instruments have been used, not only at the sectoral level, but also at the firm level.

Table 5-3 does not, however, provide information regarding the crucial difference in the process of designing a selective or a nonselective measure of IP. In fact, in both cases, there is the problem of consistency of the instrument with the objective; but in setting up a selective measure, there is the additional problem of choosing the appropriate industry (or firm).

Structural Changes and Industrial Policy

The European economies entered the 1980s with increased awareness of the fact that a number of problems affecting their economic performance and welfare can no longer be attributed solely to cyclical factors nor can they be handled satisfactorily with traditional macroeconomic policies. Persistent low rates of economic growth coupled with high rates of inflation and unemployment may be explained in part by structural causes due to economic, political, and social changes.

Although a discussion of the direction of the cause-effect relationship between IP and structural changes is beyond the scope of this chapter, it is crucial to recognize that IP has been responsive to economic conditions. The development of IP goals during the postwar period and, specifically, the main changes that occurred after the oil crisis have been discussed. In the next sections, we shall analyze some of the economic structural changes that have been faced by IP decision makers in the last two decades.[6] The objective is to provide some evidence about industrial performance in Europe (which sometimes is missing in the literature reviewing IP experiences) and to characterize some implications of these changes for European IP.

Table 5-3
The Selectivity Nature of Instruments

Instrument/Type	Nonselective	Industry-specific	Firm-specific
Indicative:			
National Plans and voluntary agreements	*	*	*
Coercive:			
Price control		*	
Exchange-rate control	*		
General tax structure	*		
Tax credits	*	*	
Accelerated depreciation	*	*	
Investment reserves	*		
Subsidies/grants		*	*
Loans: commercial rate		*	*
Loans: special rate		*	*
Guaranteed loans		*	*
Share participation		*	*
Manpower retraining	*	*	
Development contracts			*
Public purchases		*	*
Service-type facilities	*	*	
Technical standards/regulations		*	
Tariffs	*	*	
Quotas	*	*	
Other nontariff	*	*	
Export financing		*	*
Export insurance			*

Rapid Growth Period: 1960–1973

In this period the European countries experienced very rapid expansion. The GDP in volume of the six EC members increased at an average of 5 percent per year (United Kingdom, 3 percent per year), without any serious recession (lowest growth rate, 2.8 percent in 1967). The unemployment rate rose only from 1.5 percent in 1960 to 2.1 percent in 1973, confirming that this period was one of near full employment. Foreign-trade growth rate was high (export growth in volume, 9.7 percent per year), due in part to the creation of the Common Market.

This pattern of rapid growth was characterized by a significant change in the structure of GDP use—namely, an increase of the share of investment (coupled with a reduction of the share of private consumption both in nominal and real terms) and a structural surplus in the overall external balance. The common factors underlying the investment increase appear to have been:

1. fast growth of capital-intensive processes fueled by technological developments
2. changes in demand, shifting toward durables
3. rationalization and restructuring of certain industries

Analyses of structural changes that have occurred in GDP composition and trade specialization (for example, EEC 1978*a*) have pointed out remarkable differences across countries. This may reflect different strategies of growth. Nonetheless, a common pattern can be detected. First, for all EC countries the leading industries in terms of growth rate have been petroleum products, chemicals, plastics, electrical and electronic equipment, precision instruments, and communications. All these industries are characterized by higher exposure to international trade and higher productivity gains with respect to the rest of the economy. Second, among the slow-growth industries we find textile-leather-clothing, solid fuels, and agriculture, characterized by substantial decline in employment. Finally, the phenomenon of tertiary-sector growth is too well known to warrant discussion here.

Post-Crisis Period: 1973 to the Present

The overall GDP growth rate was 1.6 percent per year between 1973 and 1976 and 2.5 percent between 1976 and 1978. The unemployment rate which was slightly above 2 percent at the beginning of the 1970s rose sharply to 4 percent in the period 1974–1976 and to 5.4 percent in 1977–1978; the GDP deflator climbed to 12.3 percent per year in the period 1973–1976 and 9 percent in 1976–1978 for the EC as a whole.

Since 1971, the international economic environment has deteriorated due to the changes of the international monetary system,[7] as well as a fourfold increase in oil prices and a pattern of fluctuation of raw-material prices. After the general recession of 1974-1975 (one of the main characteristics of which was the synchronization of all major industrial economies), international trade slowed down and import restrictive measures were imposed after almost two decades of growing liberalization in trade.

Among the causes of the slowdown was that the intermediate-products industry—a pacesetter in the past—suffered from the crisis in the steel industry and from declining investment in residential building, overcompensating the fairly sustained growth rate of chemicals. Equipment-goods industries, on the contrary, have been sustained by export markets which experienced higher than average growth. Nondurable-goods industries (especially textiles and paper) declined more rapidly than earlier, due to both low demand and increased competition from the emerging countries.

The problem of increasing competition from the emerging countries has been widely debated (for example, EEC 1979*a*, 1979*b*). Analyzing the pattern of export specialization and import penetration shows that the relative position of the EC as a whole has not dramatically deteriorated in this period, although there have been perceptible differences across countries.[8]

Some Implications for Industrial Policy

There are important differences between the two periods that have had implications for IP requirements in Europe. The first (1960-1973) was characterized by a very low level of unemployment, a growth rate of foreign trade faster than GDP, and a sustained growth rate of capital-intensive industries. The second period was characterized by higher inflation (triggered by energy cost), higher unemployment, increased competition in international trade, and crises in consumption goods and some intermediate-goods industries.

During the first period, policymakers were facing labor-force migration from slow-growth sectors (mainly agriculture) into high-growth industries and tertiary activities and an overall positive contribution to growth of international trade. This has implied in general ad hoc intervention by the authorities, who have assisted restructuring of a few troubled industries without a total commitment to an overall industrial strategy. There have been exceptions (documented in the following discussion), but it is important to recognize that this has been the prevailing attitude.

During the second period, policymakers faced a slowdown of economic growth induced by adjustments to increased energy costs coupled with negative contribution of international trade. This has implied by and large an increased awareness of the need for more sophisticated industrial strategies in order to cope with unemployment and to foster international trade. Increasing attention has been devoted to policies aimed at developing technologies capable of absorbing higher energy costs and enhancing export competitiveness. Ad hoc policies, however, have continued to be used in the attempt to preserve employment in those industries most injured by new market conditions.

In conclusion, it appears that European IP has been responsive to economic developments. In some cases, however, differences among countries have been marked; the next section provides a more detailed discussion of the relationship between national philosophies and practical experiences with IP.

National Philosophies versus Practical Experiences

Is There a Common Philosophy behind Industrial Policy?

This question is not trivial since the thinking about IP has differed across countries and has changed in response to historical developments. Regarding the relationship between economic changes and IP in a recent study, it is stated that, "given these differences and divisions (among European countries), the making of Industrial Policy in Western Europe presents a complex and confusing picture." (Pinder, et al. 1979, p. 29).

In order to clarify the specific features of each country's philosophy, we shall interpret the thinking about IP in the light of the structural transformations that occurred in the last two decades. As a result, we could say that there is no common philosophy behind IP, for three main philosophies that have inspired the policies could be identified.

First, there is the principle that the task of the government authorities is limited to establishing favorable conditions for industrial development. The policies following this principle were aimed at providing maximum stability in the economic environment (for example, stable prices), effective competition in the marketplace, and sometimes undervaluation of the exchange rate (OECD 1976).

Second, there has been a stream of thought focusing on intervention aimed at stimulating innovation (sometimes labeled picking the winners or national-champion policies). The rationale seems to rely on the idea that public authorities could foresee a potential future demand for goods produced by certain industries—the winners, indeed—and therefore stimulating them is sufficient to ensure overall equilibrium and growth of the economy.

Third, there has been a school focusing on restructuring intervention. This approach seems to rely on the idea that "markets should clear." Restructuring the supply side, therefore, should respond to dynamic perturbations in a way that explicitly takes into account changes in the demand side as well as in other markets.⁹ In the mid-1960s government response to structural changes often meant simple ad hoc measures designed to cope with sudden crises. Throughout the 1970s intervention became more a coordinated design in order to assist and guide the transition phases of the market mechanism.

Although there has been a blend of all three approaches in each country's IP, it is useful to characterize some of the major European countries according to their prevailing philosophy. Anticipating the overall conclusion that can be drawn from the following pages, there is evidence that Germany and France have adopted an ex ante attitude of trying to lead the market whenever it was promising, whereas Italy and the United Kingdom have shown an ex post attitude of trying to salvage the market whenever it was failing.

West Germany. West Germany has been ideologically less predisposed to microeconomic intervention than most other European countries. In particular, until the mid-1960s, the main concern has been to ensure free competition in resource allocation. The law against Restraint of Competition has been the fundamental tool of this philosophy (OECD 1971).

Despite this image of free-market guardian, West Germany has conducted IP in a more extensive way than it may appear at first. In fact, one has to take into account the intervention of the Länder (regional entities of the Federal Republic of Germany) in order to promote regional development and the government trade policy granting protection to import-competing industries. According to a recent study (Hiemenz and Rabenau 1976), the rate of effective protection has been higher than the nominal one in raw-materials and labor-intensive industries.

During the second half of the 1960s, the government started to intervene in restructuring some of the slow-growth sectors (for example, coal mining) but concentrated its efforts in promoting innovation in industries such as aerospace and computers. It is especially interesting to recognize aerospace and computer industries as high-growth industries because this supports the view that German selective intervention has been conducted in a picking-the-winner spirit.

Moreover, between 1970 and 1977, Germany exhibited an increase in export performance of products basic to technological progress that include the targeted industries. This reinforced the conclusion that, in implementing selective policies, Germany had an eye on national champions.¹⁰

France. France is on the interventionist end of the spectrum in Western Europe, reflecting its mercantilist tradition dating back to the Colbert period. At the beginning of the 1960s, the inability of the national planning system to respond to international stimuli induced the French authorities to stress the need for resisting the U.S. challenge (OECD 1974 and Suleiman 1975) and strengthening the competitive position of French industry in Europe and throughout the world (for example, automobiles). Specifically, this means the achievement of dominant positions where there is not yet an international oligopolistic market (for example, aircraft and computer industries) (Stoffaes 1978).

During the 1960s, motor vehicles and computers were among the leading industries in French growth, whereas transportation equipment other than motor vehicles lagged behind. Moreover, there was increasing export specialization (as well as decreasing import dependence) for high-technology products during the 1970s. The question whether this happened because of IP or despite it is left unanswered here and will be discussed in chapter 10.

In conclusion, although the French approach has been more complex than merely supporting national champions (as suggested by the protection granted to textiles and steel—both slow-growth industries), this latter approach has constituted the prevailing philosophy behind the French IP.

United Kingdom. A crucial feature of British IP has been dicontinuity of intervention philosophy between successive governments. These governments have created and abolished through time several institutions and acts designed to inject public capital into private business environment.

The Industrial Reorganization Corporation promoted a series of mergers under the Labor government in the mid-1960s, suggesting the beginning of a national champion philosophy. The Industry Act, promoted by the government in 1972, instead stressed efficiency in the allocation mechanism. A new Labor government established the National Enterprise Board in 1974, the main function of which has become to support ailing industries and protect employment (for example, steel, automobiles, and shipbuilding), suggesting a peculiar restructuring philosophy that is occasionally labeled the rescue-the-loser approach.

This approach reflects the overall difficulty of achieving structural transformation in the British economy as well as the fact that steel and transportation equipment other than motor vehicles were slow-growth industries in the 1960s and experienced a further reduction in their GDP share in the 1970s.

In addition, the British performance in international markets has been generally characterized by a decrease in specialization of exports coupled with an increase in import dependence except for highly skilled labor-intensive activities. Among these exceptions has been the rescue of Rolls, which had acquired a position of long-term technological competitiveness (Pinder, et al. 1979).

In conclusion, the inconsistency of government behavior bears some responsibility for policy failures, but cultural attitudes, which have underestimated the role of industry in the economy, may constitute an additional explanation (Pinder, et al. 1979).

Italy. A crucial feature of Italian IP has been the extent of state ownership of industry. Government authorities wanted public enterprises both to stabilize investment in order to achieve steady growth and to promote regional development in the historically depressed Mezzogiorno area.

As already mentioned, however, Italian IP was motivated more by political than economic considerations. This was suggested, for instance, by the financial support granted to the Mezzogiorno, which perversely promoted capital-intensive activities in a labor-abundant region during the 1960s (Prodi 1974).

Among the countries analyzed, Italy is nevertheless the only one displaying high growth rates in the iron-and-steel industry and increasing specialization of intermediate-product exports. The issue of whether this is a result of IP will be discussed further in chapter 12. It suggests, however, some degree of success in the catch-up effort with respect to its northern neighbors during the 1960s. During the 1970s, however, the main IP result has been to preserve employment (Prodi 1980) by injecting public money into loss-making firms. In this respect, Italy shares with the United Kingdom a rescue-the-loser type of philosophy.[11]

Policies Affecting Market Characteristics

This section and the following ones review further the assignment of IP instruments to objectives, highlighting the distinction between specific and nonspecific intervention.

Policies Promoting Competition. It is quite difficult to find an exact definition of competition policy that would unify the main European approaches. In fact, promoting competition in itself is nonspecific in character and is aimed at establishing a fair environment for businesses in the society as a whole (through national plans and general tax structure). Procompetition instruments are classified at both nonselective and selective levels.

An example of the general tax structure as an IP instrument is the Value Added Tax (VAT) system. Around the beginning of the 1970s (although not simultaneously) most European Community members switched from a General Sales Tax system to the VAT system. The previous cascade system resulted in distortions of the final price structure because it was an increasing function of the number of transactions occurring between the manufacturer and the consumer and there is evidence that this encouraged vertical integration (for example, Saunders 1977). The new VAT system instead does not affect the organization of production and, in this respect, can be seen as a fiscal tool to promote competition. It seems important to recognize the long-term horizon and the ex ante attitude adopted by policymakers in designing this policy.

Among antimonopoly instruments, the control of market power and restrictive practices have been exercised actively both at industry and firm levels. The main instrument is constituted by antimonopoly commissions, which make recommendations if any practice is against the public interest (in the spirit of both national legislation and Articles 85, 86 of the Treaty of Rome). The pragmatic approach of the English legislator considers a monopolist as an enterprise that supplies at least 25 percent of a particular good, whereas the general West German and French approaches supervise cartels and mergers of a certain importance.[12]

Among other antimonopoly instruments there are voluntary agreements,[13] price controls (mainly used in Italy and France for antiinflationary purposes although de facto they have reduced the monopoly power in price-setting behavior) and share participation, ranging from partial control exercised by state holdings to 100 percent enterprises. (Unlike in the United States, airlines, railways, and electric-power plants are state-owned enterprises in Europe.)

In contrast with competition policy, antimonopoly intervention appears to have been mainly ex post in nature—that is, authorities have stepped into the market after a critical threshold has been reached.

Policies Promoting Concentration. The last type of policy aimed to influence market characteristics is the set of measures designed to promote concentration.[14] The economic rationale for this type of policy is the existence of economies of scale in the production process (and, therefore, long-run potentials to be exploited), but it is surprising how infrequently this argument has been explicitly recognized by the literature. Promoting concentration typically involves designing industry-specific measures in order to rationalize some sectors of the economy.[15]

For instance, the French government has provided tax holidays and long-term credit at favorable terms to mergers (Cotta 1977 and Balassa 1979) since the early 1960s in order to acquire international prestige and to resist the U.S. challenge (Suleiman 1975). Both the French and the Italian governments have managed many mergers and nationalizations. In the United Kingdom, the Cotton Act of 1959 and the intervention in the aircraft industry at the end of the 1950s as well as other more recent examples, were also aimed at promoting concentration, although their main objective was really to assist restructuring a troubled sector.

In addition, financial assistance to mergers has been provided all over Europe by the State Holding Corporations (Institute pour le Developpement Industriel [IDI] in France, Industrial Reorganization Corporation [IRC], in the United Kingdom, Vereinigte Industriewerke Aktien Gesellschaft [VIAG] in Germany) or by the Special Credit Institutions under direct government control (Istituto Mobiliare Italiano [IMI] in Italy). Finally, indirect aid has been provided through agencies specifically designed to assist small and medium enterprises; this aid is also promoted under the auspices of the EC.

Policies Affecting Innovation. In the present context, it is not necessary to enter into the debate about the Schumpeterian notion of innovation or to try to assess whether innovation is more demand-pulled or technology-pushed (see for example, Oppenlaender 1977 and Cazes 1977). According to the European experience, innovation policies can be conceived of as a set of means for inducing improvements in the production process and/or in the general welfare level of the society. Because of the value judgment implicit in the authorities' idea of improvement the distinction has been drawn between policies for innovation and those for structural adaptation (discussed in the next section), which imply the notion of change in the production process in response to some stimuli.

Research and Development and New Technological Processes. Europeans have been constantly trying to catch up with the U.S. example of promoting research and development. In statements issued by authorities there has been a common preoccupation with following the U.S. example in the nuclear, aerospace, and computer sectors.[16] As examples of outcomes of this approach, it is perhaps superfluous to cite the Anglo-French project, Concorde, the French-German Airbus, and the CII-Honeywell-Bull joint ventures. As an example of fiscal measures, we find the possibility of writing off substantial proportions of expenditures on the provision of scientific research equipment. Among financial instruments there are grants (United Kingdom and Germany) and special loans (France and Italy) where the financing share of government assistance cannot exceed a certain percentage (typically 50 percent of the total cost) and is repayable in case of success four to six years after marketing begins (OECD 1978*a*).

Government laboratories and the European Joint Research Center (EURATOM) provide examples of service-type facilities both at nonselective (basic research) and selective levels (nuclear-oriented research) (OECD 1978*c*).

It is difficult to separate policies promoting application of technology neatly from the previous policies. The main instruments have been grants and special agencies with the task of spreading information among small-

and medium-size enterprises (for example, the British Industrial Liaison Service). In addition, licensing aids and amendments to patent regulations (for example, in Germany and Sweden) and technical standards improvements have been used in this direction (OECD 1978*b*).

In conclusion, although many measures have been used for these objectives, it is difficult to qualify them as interventions (that is, as a strategically coordinated set of measures). In fact, it seems that the attempt to follow the U.S. example has sometimes lacked an economic rationale. Further discussion of each national case is deferred to the following chapters.

New Products. Finally we examine policies designed to encourage new products. The crucial feature of this type of intervention is that it has been conducted exclusively at the selective level.

Financial assistance, direct state participation, and development contracts have been the main instruments designed in Europe for developing the nuclear, electronic, information-processing, and aircraft industries, for example. Given the nature of the targeted industries (high growth rate and high exposure to international trade), it is straightforward to identify these policies with the picking-the-winner approach. This has been, par excellence, the ex ante policy in Europe—that is, authorities have tried to outguess free market forces in the development of new lines of products.

In order to characterize further this approach, it would be interesting to highlight the economic criteria that guided the French, German, and British authorities during the 1970s. Unfortunately, the available evidence is insufficient for a rigorous analysis. Some evidence exists in the literature that national-security considerations have inspired some of these policies. But, apart from moving toward products with greater value added, promoting advanced technology, and encouraging less use of energy more exact criteria are lacking. Even more skeptical is the position of some French economists, who suggest that we cannot expect economic studies to give indications as to which branches should be developed by means of IP (Jacquemin 1979*a*).

Nevertheless, there is additional evidence that the development of national champions may be seen as justifying government intervention to ensure proper resource allocation when the market fails (U.K. Department of Industry position: Rees 1973 and De Cormay 1978) or its size is inadequate (Vernon 1974). In both cases, the economic rationale seems to rely on the presence of externalities or economies of scale in high-technology activities.

Policies Affecting Structural Adaptation. The crucial issue underlying structural adaptation is the dynamics of adjustment. In fact, according to economic theory, the competitive adjustment that takes place in the long run is a normal phenomenon of the market mechanism. However, influencing the speed at which this occurs is a primary objective of structural adaptation policies. If market forces are not fast enough, the case for accelerating the transition period appears. On the contrary, if the same market forces are too fast—threatening market disruption or social costs such as long-term unemployment—there is the case for smoothing down the action in order to alleviate the social consequences of adjustment (Cairncross 1975).

Output Adaptation. Regarding output adaptation, a whole spectrum of policies have been pursued (OECD 1976*b*). In the earlier period, intervention ranged from merely rescuing individual firms to providing some assistance to declining sectors. It is interesting to note that often the intervention has been stimulated by changing conditions of international competition as in the case of a group of traditional sectors—namely, textile, clothing, leather, coal, iron and steel, and shipbuilding.[17] In addition, the automobile industry has been the objective of public assistance in order to remedy structural deficiencies or to maintain efficient production for domestic use or to improve international competitiveness.[18] In the 1970s increasing awareness of problems related to phasing out declining sectors (for example, Albrecht 1978 and Stoffaes 1980) led IP into the realm of restructuring debate (abandonment of ad hoc measures), sometimes colored by metaphysical tones about deindustrialization of the modern economies (Jacquemin 1979*b* and Blackaby 1979).

According to a recent study (EEC 1979*c*), IP is caught between Scylla—constituted by the international division of labor for which the liberalization of international trade is paving the way—and Charybdis—constituted by each country's preferred industrial structure, which is determined by reference to the pursuit of a complex system of economic and social objectives.[19] The crucial question is, therefore, whether the restructuring effort is aimed at adapting the economy to the pattern of international division of labor or whether it is motivated by the desire for preserving the present structure. This type of policy could be conceived of as ex-ante if authorities are able to forecast the pattern of comparative advantages. It is condemned to be ex-post, however, if authorities are merely responding to a sequence of external shocks.

Among nonselective instruments, we find fiscal measures aimed at promoting the mobility of productive resources and, hence, structural changes. In Germany, this is accomplished by making it easier to transfer hidden reserves,[20] and in Sweden, certain operations may be partially exempt from taxation of capital gains if taxes might inhibit structural adaptation. Examples of selective fiscal measures are special tax treatments instituted by acts concerned with specific industries of the economy. The purpose of financial incentives has generally been to ease the undertaking of structural changes often coupled with consultative services and preliminary studies at sectoral levels.

Among other instruments the most important is the share participation of public corporations. In 1968, the German Ruhrkohle Aktien Gesellschaft achieved a major concentration (merging twenty-six companies) in the coal industry in order to exploit only the most profitable mines. In Italy, the state holding companies (Istituto per la Ricostruzione Industriale [IRI], Ente Nazionale Idrocarburi [ENI] Societá per la Gestione di Parecipazioni Industriali [GEPI]) have engaged in rescue policy, subsidizing equity capital and providing loans otherwise denied by the private banking system, and often gaining control of the management, unlike the French state holding companies (IDI), which have sought to avoid explicit nationalization.

Labor Adaptation. The reason for distinguishing labor-adaptation policy from the previous one relies on the emphasis given to the employment problem. At the most general level, we can find agreements among social groups in order to define issues such as income policies and full-employment policies and general policies toward foreign workers.

Among fiscal instruments, there are social-security legislation (France and Italy), the Selective Employment Act (United Kingdom), and special tax credits for the location of new enterprises in depressed areas of high unemployment. In addition, minimum-wage legislation can be included under the general-tax-structure heading rather than under price controls because the latter are administrative in nature whereas the minimum wage can be conceived of as a general instrument for redistributing income.

Examples of industry-specific measures to promote recycling of manpower are subsidies in the form of unemployment compensation for workers displaced in particular industries by economic conditions. In addition, manpower-retraining programs have been designed to promote occupational mobility both from agriculture to industry and within industries.[21]

Finally, the Italian state holding company GEPI should be mentioned as an example of (perverse) use of the share-participation instrument. Although its main task was supposedly to speed up rescue operations, it has become merely a unit to guarantee everlasting employment (Prodi 1980).

Capital Adaptation. The main characteristic of capital-adaptation policy has been to provide incentives in order to promote capital intensity in the production process. Capital adaptation must be distinguished from policies promoting new technological processes (discussed under Innovation in the previous section) because it does not take into account innovation problems but rather focuses on capital markets.

A widely used instrument has been the management of depreciation rates in most countries when investment tends to slacken. In those industries needing massive undertaking of investment, public authorities have provided an incentive by allowing depreciation rates to accelerate or to differ. In Sweden, the investment-reserve mechanism allows enterprises to set aside (tax free) up to 40 percent of profits. In a period of recession, as defined by the government, the reserve may be drawn onto finance specified types of investment.

As far as financial instruments are concerned, assistance schemes have been designed to provide compensations for firms scrapping old plants and grants for reequipping programs in the United Kingdom (De Cormay 1978) and in Italy (Solustri 1975). Selective-investment policies have also been used in the United Kingdom (Regional Development Grants and Section 7 of Industry Act of 1972), in Germany (regional projects financed by the Länder), and in France (premiums for regional development) in order to promote regional development.

Policies Affecting International Relations. Encouraging domestic production in the form of restructuring existing capacity or developing new products is indeed a policy affecting a country's position vis-à-vis the rest of the world. In this section, we shall briefly review only those instruments that have been traditionally specific to international trade.

Regarding export promotion, apart from the emphasis given in national plans and some examples of export controls for national-security purposes (Bergsten 1975), the main instruments have been export financing and insurance (OECD 1976a).

The use of these instruments dates to the prewar period, and a complex network of private companies (for example, Hermes and Trewarbeit in Germany since 1919), bank consortia, and public companies (for example, the Compagnie Francaise pour l'Assurance du Commerce Exterieur since 1946) have managed public funds at special rates. In most European countries a special line of rediscount credit has been granted by central banks in order to finance claims abroad.

In addition, consultant activities and agencies for promoting exports (especially for small- and medium-size enterprises as shown by flourishing world-trade centers all over Europe) can be considered an instrument of IP.

Among policies aimed at limiting import penetration—apart from general objectives of balance-of-payments equilibrium and discrimination of public purchases against foreign goods and services[22]—we find tariffs, quotas, and other nontariff barriers. Intra-EEC trade policies must be distinguished from those dealing with trade between EC and the rest of the world (for example, Meyer 1978). The establishment of the Common Market (Treaty of Rome) has been the major example of the former, while the General Agreement on Trade and Tariffs negotiations (Kennedy Round and Tokyo Round), the implementation of the Generalized System of Preferences, the signing of Yaounde and Lome Conventions, and the Southern Mediterranean Cooperation Agreement (Maghreb and Mashrek countries) were examples of the latter. Both have been exerted at a nonselective level insofar as the aim has been to remove barriers to all trade flows.[23]

At the selective level, we find both Article 226 of Treaty of Rome and Article 19 of GATT allowing a member, respectively, to take protective measures in order to adapt a specific sector to general economic conditions of the Common Market and to suspend trade concessions temporarily for particular imports if they cause or threaten serious injury to the economy. Without reviewing these policies in detail, we shall remind the reader of the Cotton Textile Agreement (where the right to determine the threat of disruption was left to the importing country) and the Multi-fibre arrangements (designed to contribute to a more balanced distribution of imports within the EC (EEC 1977a). Despite the general tendency toward increasing liberalization of trade, many obstacles have remained (Balassa 1977), especially in those sectors suffering most from import competition.[24]

Finally, we shall mention the management of the exchange rate as a nonselective policy sometimes intended to affect the terms of trade and, hence, the international competitiveness. Although exchange-rate policy has been traditionally a macro tool of economic policy, there is some evidence that in specific situations there were IP implications (for example, French franc and British pound devaluations [Glynn 1976]). Especially since 1971, there has been increasing awareness of the effects of exchange rates on industries particularly exposed to international trade (Warnecke 1978). The attempt to reduce the volatility in prices of both imported inputs and exported outputs was one of the objectives of the creation of the European Monetary System in 1979.

Role of the European Communities

There is a fundamental reason for treating separately the intervention of the European Communities[25] in the realm of IP: The EC is a supranational entity with a certain degree of autonomy with respect to national governments in specific fields, yet it does not have any resemblance to a federal authority in the sense of the constitutional doctrine.

This section will not review in detail the myriad reports and resolutions of the European Communities. Instead, its aim is to provide some insights of the role performed by the EC in its interaction with the various national IP in Europe.

Spirit of the Treaties of the European Communities

The first step toward economic integration in Europe was the Treaty of Paris, signed in 1951 by Belgium, France, Germany, Holland, Italy, and Luxembourg. This treaty established the European Coal and Steel Community (ECSC) to promote free circulation of goods (coal, iron ore, and steel), manpower, capital, and to provide financial aid for retraining workers through Article 56 (Ellis 1978). Moreover, the ECSC was given the power to negotiate minimum prices or quota assignments among members to stabilize coal, iron, and steel markets during recessions. The main step, however, was undertaken on March 25, 1957, when these same countries signed the Treaty of Rome establishing the EC and another treaty establishing the European Atomic Energy Community (EURATOM).

The Treaty of Rome provides a general framework to guide national policymakers, and some of its implications for IP issue could be found in the following areas:

1. general integration and cooperation among members
2. competition policy
3. technology policy
4. free trade among members

Concerning integration, Article 2 of Treaty of Rome states that the task of the EC is to promote a harmonious development of economic activity among members, whereas Article 3 envisages the adoption of procedures permitting the coordination of economic policies of members. In addition, Article 58 envisages a European Company Law which is supposed to unify the juridical and fiscal treatment of European transnational enterprises. Article 100 calls for harmonization of national technical standards, establishing that all directives should be joint (except for railways, water, electricity, and small-size contracts).

Articles 85 and 86 assign a predominant role to competition in the Common Market, forbidding monopolies and restrictive practices. European law is applicable on a territorial basis to foreign enterprises affecting competition within the EC only if trade among member countries is hindered. Otherwise, national legislation will prevail (Schmitt 1974).

Regarding policies designed to promote innovation, a resolution of the Council of Ministers in 1974, unified the principles of scientific research and technological development policy of the EC (EEC 1972). The main objectives were reformulated in 1977 in communication from the Commission to the Council (EEC 1977*b*), focusing on the following directions: rationalization of efforts (for example, nuclear fusion); transnational nature of the research field (for example, transportation, telecommunications); supranational extension of the market (for example, data processing and

European Industrial Policy

aerospace); and common needs of member countries (for example, environment and urban planning, disposal of radioactive waste).

Regarding promotion of trade among members, the main EC guidelines have been to ban trade barriers and to open national markets for purchasing by public sectors. The principles for free circulation of goods can be found in Article 12 which forbids customs duties among members and Article 95 which regulates tariff equivalent measures such as VAT. Quota restrictions and equivalent measures are forbidden by Article 30 and controls of enfranchisement are regulated by Article 169. However, a handful of escape clauses are provided for reasons of public interest, security, and health (Article 36), for production and trade of ammunitions and weapons (Articles 222-223), in case of supply shortage of specific products (Article 103), in case of serious crisis of balance of payments (Articles 108-109), and in case of commodities originating outside the EC and covered by a free-circulation agreement with a member country if it can cause difficulties in another member (Article 115).

In addition, Articles 92 and 94 of the Treaty of Rome prohibit government aid that interferes with free trade, Article 30 of the Treaty of Rome forbids restrictions on public markets, Article 97 of EURATOM Treaty forbids discrimination based on nationality for nuclear settlements, Articles 4 and 63 of ECSC Treaty forbid discrimination of buyers with respect to suppliers, and finally, Article 177 of the Treaty of Rome forbids national monopolies (for example, the Italian Tobacco Monopoly abolished in 1971).

EC Experience with Industrial Policy

It was not until the second half of the 1960s that IP in the European Communities started to be developed parallel to national trends. In fact, the German veto had prevented until then any comprehensive action beyond the intervention in coal and steel industries. In 1964, a medium-term Policy Committee was constituted where each member country had a representative and in addition, the commission itself had a distinct representative. According to the program of the committee, the structural policy was supposed to be based on the principle of promoting employment, approving (temporary) national intervention to aid restructuring and adaptation, and pursuing common objectives in the spirit of the Treaty of Paris and the Treaty of Rome. The main objectives were agricultural and transportation policies and promotion of technical progress (Denton 1967). However, the third program issued in 1970 was the first one to call explicitly for harmonizing structural national policies.

The apotheosis of IP in the European Community took place in 1970, when the Colonna Memorandum (EEC 1970) was sent from the Commission to the council. It took three years of debate before the principles of European IP were formally adopted by the Council (Spinelli Report [EEC 1973]). On the eve of the oil crisis, these documents stressed the importance of harmonizing national policies toward the following goals: (1) removing of obstacles to mergers across frontiers (that is promoting concentration to face the competition of U.S. giants); (2) abolishing nontariff barriers to trade in manufactures; (3) removing the discrimination of public purchases against nonnational suppliers; and (4) establishing a common sectoral policy with respect to advanced-technology industries as well as industries in crisis.

Although this resolution constituted a major effort toward harmonizing national policies, it was argued that it has been the swan song of European IP (Venceslai 1975) caused by the resurgence of nationalistic behavior after the oil crisis. There is evidence, however, that even though European IP stagnated afterward, it has not disappeared completely from the scene. Let us turn our attention to some of the areas where EC has played a role.

Cooperation

First, in the field of harmonizing national technical standards, progress has been made. The EC Council and the Commission have adopted 115 directives between January 1973 and September 1978 relating to lifting machinery, pressure vessels, motor vehicles and motorcycles, agricultural tractors, measuring instruments, electrical equipment, fertilizers, dangerous substances, sulphur content of certain liquid fuels, cosmetic products, and crystal glass (EEC 1978*b*).

Second, in the fields of social and regional policies, cooperation has been promoted through numerous projects. The European Regional Development Fund has financed infrastructural development in depressed areas (EEC 1977*c*). In this respect, the EC is now conducting an extensive analysis of regional disparities. The European Social Fund has provided financial assistance for vocational training—the first guideline was issued in 1963 (EEC 1976*b*)—geographical mobility of workers and, in particular, the young unemployed (EEC 1977*d*). In addition, increasing unemployment after 1973 has induced tighter immigration policies.

Third, a Reorganization Program for the shipbuilding industry was issued in 1977 (EEC 1977*e*), aimed at reducing production overcapacity and redeploying the work force.[26] It also sought explicitly to ensure that national aids granted to undertakings not create disincentives for the recipients to modernize their production facilities. In addition, it envisaged European Investment Bank cooperation and European Regional Development Fund intervention specifically directed at creating new jobs in regions affected by reduced shipyard capacity and, hence, greater unemployment. In our terminology, this constitutes an interesting example of coordinated measures.

Finally, the ECSC has played an active role in the debate over restructuring steel and coal industries. According to Ruggiero (1978), ECSC policy has been the only IP of the EC. On the other side, Stoffaes (1978) argued that the ECSC has become a permanent protectionist measure encouraging overcapacity (for example, steel plants at Fos, France, and Taranto, Italy) and prolonging the agony of obsolete plants (for example, Lorraine, Belgium). In the field of technical-standards harmonization, the ECSC has adopted over one-hundred directives since 1955 about technical specifications of steel products: the EURONORM (Fame 1975). More recently, however, its restructuring efforts have been frustrated. In fact, although the ECSC succeeded in 1979 in establishing a floor price for steel imports (triggered by Japanese costs), the recent disagreement (Spring 1981) between Germany and other members about production quotas shows the limits of its power.

Competition

Observers have argued (Balassa 1975) that the same conflict between mergers[27] and antimonopoly policies affecting national policies has plagued the formation of EC competition policy. This is partially due to the lack of the European Company Law which is still under discussion. In addition, it is interesting to note that, on the one side, as trade expanded among member countries, European legislation became relevant for antitrust regulation. This is an example of the sliding of decision-making centers from national to supranational authorities. On the other side, the Council has adopted, among its IP goals, the promotion of concentration among a number of enterprises in order to improve international competitiveness.

Innovation

The following have been among the main instruments of EEC innovation policy adopted: research projects within the Joint Research Center (up to 50 percent of total expenditures), research contracts with member countries (50 percent EEC and 50 percent national government), coordination of projects entirely financed by member countries through the CERD (European Committee for Research and Development), and the CREST (Scientific and Technological Research Committee) (Bywater 1976 and EEC 1979*d*). In addition, financial support has been provided to encourage technological-development projects concerning hydrocarbons exploitation of alternative energy sources. In all cases, there is a reimbursement clause conditional on successful commercial exploitation (Moussis 1979).

Quantitative evidence about IP in the EC suggests the relatively small role of the EC in comparison to national IP efforts (EEC 1977*b*, 1978*d*) In 1976, EC expenditures for research and development represented only 1.3 percent of total expenditures undertaken by member governments for the same purpose. In addition, nearly three-quarters of EC budget is allocated to Common Agriculture Policy; the size of funds allocated to restructuring of industries in crisis (21 million EUR in 1978 and 13 in 1980) and to Research (212 million EUR in 1978 and 312 million EUR in 1980) should be compared to the size of funds granted by ECSC to the coal and steel industry alone (741.5 million EUR in 1977).

In conclusion, the EC has played an active role in European IP and has achieved positive results. Despite the richness of legislative instruments, however, the weakness of its institutions has often prevented the establishment of effective common policies. For example, observers have argued (Warnecke 1978) that the commission has not been able to coordinate EC trade policies with other national IPs, as shown by lowering tariffs to imports of pulp and paper from non-EC countries without designing measures to cope with competition of low-cost producers in North America and Scandinavia. Another example is represented by the recent disagreement (Spring 1981) on how to cope with the trade-account deficit of the EC with respect to Japan. Whether these remain exceptions or not will depend greatly on the success of strengthening the political ties among members after the direct election of the European Parliament (Pinder, et al. 1979).

Concluding Remarks

In this chapter we have summarized the main features of European experiences concerning public intervention in the marketplace and characterized underlying philosophies.

Following the tradition of the literature, we have referred to the term *IP,* recognizing the complexity of the issues associated with its definition. Disagreement still exists in the literature in regard to both the measuring and the prescriptive implications of IP. This disagreement is by and large unavoidable because it is caused by different traditions and economic developments across European countries, which have influenced writers of various nationalities. We have attempted to clarify the underlying rationale. As a result, we have gained better understanding of some common issues, but, more importantly, we have highlighted a striking diversity of policies among countries. In our opinion, therefore, there is really not a unique European IP.

The theoretical framework of nth-best hierarchy of policies was discussed in chapter 3; this chapter has reviewed in qualitative terms the instruments/objectives network fashioned by policymakers in Europe. Casting the analysis in such a way has been useful in order to clarify the economic rationale behind these policies and to characterize the various national approaches in terms of prevailing thinking.

We have identified four areas of economic interest that are common to all European IP decision makers: (1) market characteristics, (2) innovation, (3) structural adaptation, and (4) international relations. In the statements issued by European authorities, several objectives often overlap without a precise order of priority. Moreover, combinations of different instruments have been used in order to solve many problems at the same time.

There are, however, important differences among countries in regard to the use of instruments and to the objectives pursued. For instance, West Germany and the United Kingdom have pursued antimonopoly policies more extensively than have France and Italy. West Germany and, especially, France have pursued policies to promote innovation more openly than have Italy and the United Kingdom, whose IP has relied heavily indeed on restructuring interventions. Given these differences, our analysis leaves a question unanswered: that is, have these policies been designed in an optimal way? This problem deserves further analysis country by country and will be taken up in the following chapters.

As far as the decision-making center on IP are concerned, it appears from the analysis that in each country different centers, managing different instruments have dealt with different objectives of IP. If it is obvious for institutional reasons that taxation and regulation policies are originated by the government, this is not the case for financial instruments such as loans and grants, which have been managed by state holding companies, special credit institutions, or even private banking systems through some form of state guarantee.

The existence of many decision-making centers poses the problem of coordination among them, both within a country and across countries. This problem has been crucial for the intervention of the European Community, which has focused its effort on the attempt to establish cooperation and harmonization of national approaches in fields such as trade relations, structural adaptation of sectors of common concern, some research-and-development activities, and technical standards. However, the richness of the EC legislative instruments has not always been matched with effectiveness. We can conclude that both disagreement among members and limitation of available resources have prevented EC from performing a leading role in European IP.

As far as the level of intervention is concerned, a common pattern emerges because selective measures have been especially used to promote innovation, concentration, and structural adaptation throughout Europe.

In general, we can conclude that in the cases of innovation and concentration the French intervention shows that the selectivity nature of policies was desirable on the basis of considerations such as public goods, increasing returns, and technological externalities. In the case of structural adaptation, the Italian and British experiences show that more often than not, policies have been transformed from rescue to artificial respiration, thereby including distortions in the allocation mechanism. In this respect, a more refined analysis of the rationale behind the choice of target industries should be conducted on a country-by-country basis. This will be taken up in the next chapters.

Related to the previous issue is the problem of time horizon of policies. If it is quite obvious that correcting a market failure should be a permanent measure (as in the case of nationalization of a natural monopoly), this is not so in the case of infant-industry protection, fostering technological development, and restructuring an ailing sector. As examples of inappropriate time horizons of restructuring efforts we have already mentioned the case of temporary rescue operations that have become permanent.

However, permanent assistance may lead to an increasing resource commitment by the authorities along with the increasing divergence between market conditions and the specific situation of the industry in question. The Italian and British experiences should suffice to prove this point.

Moreover, the European experience in the so-called advanced sectors suggests that the problem of designing an optimal strategy to encourage technological development involves the determination of the relevant time horizon necessary for successful application in the market. In fact, a once-for-all injection of resources into research and development may be in vain if it is not accompanied by an increasing commitment of the authorities long enough to allow the takeoff of an independent productive activity. In this respect, the analysis of French experience in this field has left unsolved the question of whether such commitments have been successful. Chapter 8 discusses this issue further. On the contrary, the Italian experience—intermittent and insufficient flow of resources devoted to innovation—shows how the time-horizon issue is crucial; this issue is considered further in chapter 12.

Finally, in reviewing the European thinking about IP, we have identified three main philosophies that have inspired the authorities, and we have discussed their relationship with both policy experience and structural transformations that occurred in European economies.

In particular, there is evidence that the principle of establishing favorable conditions for industrial development has been chiefly associated with nonselective intervention throughout Europe. In fact, at a practical level, the notion of establishing favorable conditions has led to policies aimed at ensuring price stability and effective competition. Although not exclusively, this laissez-faire philosophy has been traditionally associated with the prevailing thinking in the Federal Republic of Germany and also in Sweden.

On the contrary, the other two philosophies have inspired selective interventions designed to guide the allocation mechanism in specific industries. The first of these two implies an ex-ante approach of the authorities who have tried to lead the market whenever it was promising. We have argued that, according to this approach, stimulating the supply side is sufficient to ensure equilibrium and growth. This is the case of the picking-the-winner or national-champion policies, tried in various degrees in most European countries. Albeit not without controversies, the French have been the leader in this field, followed at a distance by the United Kingdom and Germany.

The other philosophy implies an ex-post attitude of the authorities, who have tried to rescue industries when they were failing. We have argued that, according to this approach, both demand and supply conditions must be taken into account in order to achieve equilibrium. This is the case of restructuring or rescue-the-loser policies by injecting public money into firms making losses. The Italian and the British interventions have relied heavily on this type of approach in the last decade.

As a final comment, we reiterate that IP has been responsive to economic developments. This consideration, far from being trivial, has helped to clarify what view dominated where and why. In fact, during the 1960s—a period of low unemployment, high growth rate, and substantial structural changes—policies were typically ad hoc because authorities assisted restructuring of few troubled industries. During the 1970s, however—a period of higher unemployment, higher energy costs, and stiffer international competition—policies have evolved toward overall industrial strategies aimed at enhancing technological developments and export competitiveness, although ad hoc policies have continued to be used in the attempt to preserve employment.

The message for the policymaker stemming out of this survey should be clear. The crucial question is whether IP is aimed at adapting the economy to the pattern of technological and international developments or is motivated by the desire to preserve the present structure.

Notes

1. It is perhaps surprising to note that in doing so, the French authorities thought they were encouraging competition. Obviously, they were encouraging international competition, but not domestic competition.

2. It is interesting to note that in the West German business environ-

ment traditional commercial policy (tariffs, for example) was not perceived to be an active part of IP, as argued by Fels (1976).

3. From the economic-theory viewpoint, subsidies are equivalent to negative taxes. However, taxation is typically enforced by law (active behavior of the authorities), while a subsidy is only offered to the productive unit (passive behavior). This is especially relevant for the Italian case, where funds made available by law have sometimes not been used. This issue will be discussed in detail in chapter 12.

4. For instance, in the memorandum submitted by the West German government to the EC (EEC 1978c) the West German attachment to the principle of free market economy was reiterated, and it expressed concern about the growing number of protectionist EC measures in industries such as textiles, steel, and footwear. This statement of the foreign minister seems to contradict to some extent the chancellor's philosophy, denoting a divergence of opinions within the government itself.

5. Table 5-3 contrasts nonselective policies only with "industry-specific" policies, therefore neglecting "sector-specific" policies which are subsumed into the industry-specific ones.

6. The 1946-1960 period, from the Marshall Plan to the creation of the European Community has been characterized by a very rapid reconstruction; the recovery from the damage of the war has been undoubtedly determined by the aid provided by the Marshall Plan. However, due to the exceptional nature of this flow of resources into the European economies—which constitutes an example of IP in Europe—we shall not analyze this period in detail. Let us note, in passing, that during the 1950s each country pursued its own strategy of growth without coordination and there was still a relatively low degree of openness to international trade and substantial tariff protection at the end of the decade.

7. U.S. dollar devaluation in December 1971 of 7.9 percent, aborted "snake in the tunnel," Basel Agreement of April 1972; U.S. $ devaluation in February 1973 of 10 percent chaos in exchange markets in March 1973.

8. For instance, West Germany has a lead in exports of highly skilled labor-content products whereas Italy and the United Kingdom are more specialized in low-capital activities.

9. There is no agreement in the literature about the characterization of IP philosophies. For instance, in Krugman (1980) only the last approach seems to be considered as relevant for IP decision making.

10. This view appears to be out of line with Krugman (1980, p. 17), where it is stated that: "the workhorses of German growth (among which: automobiles) continued to perform well without special help." Actually, the German government has a share participation in Volkswagen.

11. Act 675 adopted in 1977 on "IP Coordination, Industrial Reconversion, Restructuring and Development" was supposed to reshape the whole Italian IP: however, the first financial layout under this act was granted in June 1980.

European Industrial Policy   81

12. In the period 1963-1973 out of eight hundred merger proposals in the United Kingdom, twenty have been deferred to the commission and six of those were given an unfavorable report. Also, in the period 1966-1973, the French Commission has examined forty-seven cases, deferring eight of them for further action (Saunders 1977 and Jenny and Weber 1976).

13. An example of the use of voluntary agreements as instruments of IP is provided by Germany. In 1966, the government convinced the big chains of department stores to refrain from suffocating the small retailers in the nonmetropolitan areas of the country in order to preserve local business. In the same year, cigarette manufactures agreed to limit advertisement (Kuester 1974).

14. Let us note in passing that, besides being an objective in itself, concentration may also be considered an instrument for achieving structural adaptation or promoting innovation. Because of this partial overlapping with other objectives discussed later, we shall focus only on those measures directly related with concentration of enterprises.

15. However, it has been argued (Jenny and Weber 1976, and Reid 1976) that the main result has been simply to encourage the "bigs to get bigger," incurring the risk of inefficient resource allocation.

16. Evidence of this approach can be found, for instance in Report V, of the Federal Ministry for Research and Technology in West Germany, in the various French National Plans and big sectoral plans, (for example, "Plan Calcul," "Plan Aeronatique," "Plan Composants" among others)(Michalet 1974), and in the Invention Act, Capital Allowances Act, and Science and Technology Act in the United Kingdom.

17. In the case of shipbuilding, reorganization of the sector before 1973 was motivated by technological conditions such as the need for large tanks and specialized vessels in the view of the growth of energy trade (for example, oil). After the oil crisis, a foreseen world excess capacity in oil transportation has rechanneled policies toward international cooperation to limit production capacity. Similar examples of international coordination policies are provided by the Multi-Fibre Agreement in the textile sector and the ECSC in the iron-and-steel sector.

18. Respectively, Alfa-Romeo in Italy; British Leyland in the United Kingdom; Volkswagen in Germany; Renault in France.

19. According to De Bandt (1977), structure preferences are the translation in terms of industrial structure of the hierarchy of collective values (that is, of the social objectives the pursuit of which the society has assigned to itself).

20. When shares result in realization of reserves and they are used for acquisition of new assets, these assets may qualify for special rates of depreciation subject to approval of the Ministry of Economic Affairs.

21. Federal Employment Bureau in West Germany; Fonds d'action sociale pour l'amelioration des structures agricoles in France; Vocational Training Centers in the United Kingdom, France, and Germany; the

Swedish program for assisting workers in relocation (housing, moving expenses, and so on). (Tautian 1975), (OECD 1978*a*), and (Miles 1975).

22. According to Maltzahn (1972), 99 percent of public purchases in the EEC are directed to national industry.

23. It is perhaps superfluous to point out that these policies had both a trade-creation and a trade-diversion impact on the productive structure of the EC (Balassa 1975).

24. However, a study about British protection structure shows no correlation whatsoever between tariff and nontariff policy and the vulnerability to import competition or labor intensity (Oulton 1976).

25. The European Communities (EC) embrace the EEC, the European Coal and Steel Community, and the European Atomic Energy Community. Among the organs of the EC are: the Commission, the Council of Ministers, and the Parliament. Members of EC have been: Belgium, France, West Germany, Holland, Italy, and Luxemburg since the foundation; United Kingdom, Ireland, and Denmark since 1973; Greece since 1981.

26. The estimated cost of conversion and restructuring schemes has been of the order of 4,650 million EUR over a period of five years from 1978.

27. As an example of instruments promoting mergers, recall the "Bureau de Marriage," an information center for small- and medium-size enterprises in Europe (Venceslai 1975).

References

Albrecht, D. "Subventionen; Problematik und Entwicklungen." *Schriftenreihe des Bundesministerium der Finanzen, H. 25,* Bonn, 1978.
Balassa, B., ed. *European Economic Integration.* Amsterdam, North Holland, N.Y.: America Elsevier, 1975.
———. "Effects of Commercial Policy on International Trade, the Location of Production and Factor Movements," in Ohlin and Hesselborn, 1977.
———. "L'Economie Francaise Sous La 5me Republique 1958-1978." *Revue Economique.* (November 1979), p. 339.
Bergsten, C. *Toward a New World Trade Policy: The Maidenhead Papers.* Lexington, Mass.: Lexington Books, D.C. Heath and Company, 1979.
Blackaby, F., ed. *Deindustrialization.* London: Heinemann, 1979.
Bywater, M. "La Politique Commune de Recherche," *Revue du Marché Commun* N. 195 (Avril 1976).
Cairncross, A. *Economic Policy for European Community: The Way Forward.* New York: Holmes and Meier, 1975.

Cazes, E. "Planning for Technological Innovation: The Case of France." in Saunders, 1977.
Coffey, P. *Economic Policy in the Common Market.* New York: St. Martin's Press, 1979.
Cooper, G., and J. Denton, eds. *European Economy Beyond the Crisis: From Stabilization to Structural Change, 1976 Bruges Week.* Bruges: De Tempel, 1976.
Corden, W., and G. Fels, eds., *Public Assistance to Industry: Protection and Subsidies in West Germany and the United Kingdom.* London: McMillan, 1976.
Cotta, A. "Reflexion sur la Politique Industrielle de la France. Le Redeploiment Industriel." *Etudes de Politique Industrielle N. 17,* Paris: Ministere de l'Industrie, 1977.
De Bandt, J. *Politiques Industrielles et Objectifs d'Industrialisation.* Paris: Cujas, 1977.
De Cormay, G. "Subsidy Policies in Britain, France and West Germany: An Overview." in Warnecke, 1978.
Denton, G. *Planning in the European Economic Community.* London: P.E.P. Chatman House, 1967.
EEC, Actes du Colloque de Rome. *Programmation Economique Europeene et Programmation Economique Nationale dans les Pays de la CEE.* Brussels, 1962.
―――. *Industrial Policy in the Community.* Memorandum from the Commission to the Council. Colonna Report. Brussels, 1970.
―――. "Objectives and Instruments of a Common Policy for Scientific Research and Technology Development." *Bulletin of the European Communities Supplement No. 6,* Brussels, 1972.
―――. "Toward the Establishment of a European Industrial Base." Spinelli Report. *Bulletin of the European Communities Supplement No. 7.* Brussels, 1973.
―――. "Action Program in Favor of Migrant Workers and Their Families." *Bulletin of the European Communities Supplement No. 3.* Brussels, 1976a.
―――. "From Education to Working Life." *Bulletin of the European Communities Supplement No. 12.* Brussels, 1976b.
―――. *Development of Cooperation Policies 1971-1976.* Brussels, 1977a.
―――. "Common Policy for Science and Technology." *Bulletin of the European Communities No. 3.* Brussels, 1977b.
―――. "Community Regional Policy. New Guidelines." *Bulletin of the European Communities Supplement, No. 2.* Brussels, 1977c.
―――. "Youth Unemployment." *Bulletin of the European Communities Supplement No. 4.* Brussels, 1977d.

———. "Shipbuilding, Reorganzation Program." *Bulletin of the European Communities Supplement No. 7.* Brussels, 1977e.

———. "Report of the Group of Experts on Sectoral Analyses." *Sectoral Change in the European Economies from 1960 to the Recession.* Brussels, 1978a.

———. *Directives Concerning the Elimination of Technical Barriers to Trade in Industrial Products.* Brussels, 1978b.

———. "Memorandum on EEC Structural Policy Submitted by the German Government to the Council of Ministers." Working translation by *European Report,* Brussels, May 1, 1978c.

———. *Preliminary Draft General Budget of the European Communities for the Financial Year 1979. General Introduction.* Bulletin of the E.C., Supplement No. 6, Brussels, 1978d.

———. *The European Community and Changes in the International Division of Labor.* Brussels, 1979c.

———. *Evaluation of Research and Development. Conference at Rungstedgaard.* Brussels, 1979d.

Ekstrom, J. *Changes in European Industry.* Louvain, Bruxelles: Vander, 1969.

Ellis, D. "European Industrial Policy." *Annals of American Academy of Political Science* (November 1978), p. 142.

Fame, J. "La Normalisation des Produits Siderurgiques dans la C.E." *Revue du Marché Commun* No. 189 (October 1975), p. 457.

Fels, G. "Overall Assistance to German Industry." in Corden and Fels, 1976.

Franco, G. "Sul Disegno di Legge per la Ristrutturazione e Riconversione Industriale." Rivista Internazionale di Scienze Economiche e Commerciali (Agosto 1977).

Franko, L. *The European Multinationals.* Stamford: Greylock, 1976.

———. "Industrial Policy in Western Europe: Solutions or Problems?" *World Economy, No. 2,* (January 1979), p. 31.

Glynn, D. "International Industrial Policy." *National Westminister Bank Quarterly Review* (November 1976), p. 59.

Hiemenz, U., and K. Rabenau. "Effective Protection of German Industry." in Corden and Fels, 1976.

Jacquemin, A. "European Industrial Policy and Competition," 1979a, in Coffey, 1979.

———. "Le Phenomene de Desindustrialisation et la C.E." *Revue Economique,* (November 1979b), p. 985.

Jenny, F., and A. Weber. "Strategie Industrielle et Raisonnement Economique." *Revue d'Economie Politique* No. 86 (1976):55.

Komiya, R. "Comment," in Machlup, 1976.

Krugman, P. "Foreign Experience with Industrial Policy A Critical Review." Mimeographed. Cambridge, Mass: MIT, July 1980.

Kuester, G. "Germany," in Vernon, 1974.
Machlup, F., *Economic Integration: Worldwide, Regional, Sectoral*. Proceedings of the Fourth Congress of the I.E.A.. London: McMillan, 1976.
Maltzahn, D. "Industrial Policy in the EEC." *Business Economics Oxford* (1972), p. 55.
Maunder, P., ed. *Government Intervention in Developed Economies*. London: Groom Helm, 1979*a*.
———. "Government Intervention in the U.K.," 1979*b*. in Maunder, 1979*a*.
Meyer, F. *International Trade Policy*. New York: St. Martin's Press, 1978.
Michalet, C.-A. "France," in Vernon, 1974.
Miles, P. "Adjustment Assistance Policies: A Survey," in OECD, 1975.
Moussis, N. "Un Nouvel Instrument de Politique Communautaire: Le Soutien Financier Reimbursable." *Revue du Marché Commun* (December 1979), p. 542.
OECD. *Industrial Policy of 14 Member Countries*. Paris, 1971.
———. *Industrial Policy of France*. Paris, 1974.
———. Development Centre Studies. *Adjustment for Trade*. Paris, 1975.
———. *Export Credit Financing System in Member Countries*. Paris, 1976.
———. *Policies for Promoting Industrial Adaptation*. Paris, 1979*b*.
———. *Selected Industrial Policy Instruments: Objectives and Scopes*. Paris, 1978*a*.
———. *Policies for Stimulation of Industrial Innovation*. Paris, 1978*c*.
Ohlin, B., and P. Hesselborn. *International Allocation of Economic Activities*. Nobel Symposium. New York: Holmes and Meier, 1977.
Oppenlaender, E. "The Role of Business and Government in the Promotion and Transfer of Technology: The Experience of the Federal Republic of Germany," in Saunders, 1977.
Oulton, N. "Effective Protection of British Industry," in Corden and Fels. 1976.
Owen-Smith, E. "Government Intervention in the Economy of the Federal Republic of Germany," in Maunder, 1979*a*.
Pinder, J.H., T. Hosomi, and W. Diebold. *Industrial Policy and the International Economy*. New York: The Trilateral Commission, 1979.
Prodi, R. "Italy," in Vernon, 1974.
———. "The Italian Experience as Regards Public Sector Intervention in the Economy." *International Symposium on Industrial Policies for the 80s*. Madrid, May 1980.
Rees, M. *The Public Sector in the Mixed Economy*. New York: Barnes and Noble, 1973.
Reid, S. *The New Industrial Order: Concentration, Regulation and Public Policy*. New York: McGraw-Hill, 1976.
Ruggiero, R. "Strumenti Finanziari della Comunita' per le Ristruttura-

zione e Riconversione Industriale." *Atti del Convegno AREL,* 8–9 May 1978.

Saunders, C., ed. *Industrial Policies and Technological Transfer Between East and West.* Wien, New York: Springer-Verlag, 1977.

———. "Concentration and Specialization in Western Industrial Countries," 1977, in Saunders, 1977.

Schmitt, P. "La Politique du Concurrence de la C.E.." *Rivista Internazionale di Rivista Internazionale di Scienze Economiche e Commerciali* (December 1974), p. 116.

Smith, T. "United Kingdom," in Vernon, 1974.

Solustri, A. "La Politica Industriale Italiana 1966–1970." *Rivista di Politica Economica* (April 1975), p. 445.

Stoffaes, C. *La Grande Menace Industrielle.* Paris: Calman-Levy, 1978.

———. "The French Experience of Industrial Policy." *International Symposium on Industrial Policies for the 80's.* Madrid, May 1980.

Suleiman, E. "Industrial Policy Formulation in France." in Warnecke and Suleiman, 1975.

Tavitian, R. "Problems of Employment Policy in EC Countries," in Warnecke and Suleiman, 1975.

Venceslai, S. "La Politica Industriale della CEE." *Rivista di Politica Economica* (December 1975), p. 1442.

Vernon, R. *Big Business and the State.* Cambridge, Mass: Harvard University Press, 1974.

———. "The E.C. and National Subsidy Policies," in Warnecke, ed., 1978.

Warnecke, S. "Industrial Policy of the E.C.," in Warnecke and Suleiman, 1975.

———. ed. *International Trade and Industrial Policies: Government Intervention and an Open World Economy.* New York: Holmes and Meier, 1978.

Warnecke, S., and E. Suleiman, eds., *Industrial Policy in Western Europe.* New York: Praeger, 1975.

Young, S., and A. Lowe. *Intervention in the Mixed Economy, Evolution of British Industrial Policy 1964–1972.* London: Croom Helm, 1974.

6

U.S. Approaches to Industrial Policy

Robert F. Wescott

U.S. Industrial-Policy Philosophy

In general terms, the expression *IP* represents a confluence of ideas about government policies designed to influence a country's productive processes. While many policies affect a nation's industries, the key element of IP is the degree to which interventions are systematized by policymakers as part of a conscious plan to achieve certain objectives. In a practical sense, IP is defined by what European and Japanese policymakers have done in its name. France, for example, has a very active IP that has included the widespread use of indicative planning, the encouragement of mergers, the creation of incentives for innovation, and even the rechanneling of national economic activity to give priority to industrial sectors. Japanese IP has been more informal, but its effects have also been pervasive. Antitrust considerations have been put aside, certain exports have been vigorously promoted, and certain sectors—for example, steel and shipbuilding—have been intentionally aided by government policymakers.

In contrast, the dominant U.S. view of IP can probably best be characterized as emphasizing the virtues of private capitalism. U.S. policymakers have generally been reluctant to intervene into private industrial matters, at least in a positive manner, and have shown a great disdain for performing planning functions. This has been partly due to the rich theoretical support the laissez-faire doctrine has provided over the past two hundred years. Probably even more important, though, is the fact that in the post-Depression era free enterprise has worked in the U.S. context. At least until the 1970s, it did not lead policymakers to question the vigor of their method of economic growth.

What U.S. Industrial Policy Has Not *Been*

Because of the relatively small role of IP in the United States, perhaps it is best to begin by describing what U.S. IP has *not* been. It has not been, for example, the widespread use of industry-specific policies. While most U.S. policies have, in fact, had sectoral and regional effects, for the most part these have been unintentional and unplanned. U.S. policymakers have been extremely reluctant to favor industries that appear to have great innovation or export potential. More specifically, they have not consciously chosen national champions—that is, industries to promote with special tax policies, special subsidies, or concentrated research-and-development efforts. This is due partially to a strong U.S. ideological belief in the concept of fair play which suggests that politicians should not put one group's interests above those of others. In part it is because of the pervasive noninterventionist spirit of laissez-faire capitalism. Also, it is related to traditional theoretical arguments that specific interventions lead to sectoral distortions, market inefficiencies, and reduced welfare.

IP in the United States has also not been widespread nationalization of core industries like steel, automobiles, coal, and aircraft. In fact, the United States has been extremely reluctant to nationalize even such natural monopolies as telephone service, railroads (in large part), electricity production, and natural-gas service. Recently the United States has even sought to deregulate such industries. There is a deep-seated feeling that private enterprise inherently performs most tasks more efficiently than do public enterprises. The United States has also been hesitant to bail out financially troubled private firms with loan guarantees or other temporary support. While there have been three major bailouts in the past decade, all have occurred following close votes on congressional floors; thus no true policy can be said to exist.

U.S. IP has not taken the form of rationalization, cartelization, or merger promotion, either. In fact, rather than encouraging firms to join together to achieve economies of scale, the United States has generally enforced its antitrust laws, widely held to be the strictest statutes of their type in the world. The recent U.S. suit to break up the IBM Corporation, for instance, stood in sharp contrast to the efforts of many other governments, which actively encourage mergers with the hope that companies like IBM will evolve.

IP in the United States has also not provided comparatively strong government support for exports. While other nations provide heavily subsidized export financing, the United States has historically been committed to market-dictated loan rates and has tried to resist the momentum toward a global subsidization war. The U.S. Eximbank, for example, is virtually the only official export-financing agency in the world that is legally required to be self-sustaining—that is, that does not receive annual budget subsidies. The United States also offers relatively few tax incentives to encourage exports. The DISC Program, for instance, which allows income taxes on 25 percent of foreign profits to be deferred, is nowhere near as extensive as the programs of most other industrial countries, which essentially allow firms to avoid such taxes altogether through various devices.

U.S. Industrial Policy

Perhaps most important of all, U.S. IP has not enforced conscious, coordinated, and well-planned industrialization programs. Generally, U.S. policies have been ad hoc in nature and have represented government responses to specific problems, such as lagging investment, inflation, sagging exports, or an energy crisis. Because positive intent has often been absent from U.S. decision making, and because a certain dimension of intent is inherently implied in standard definitions of IP, it can be concluded that the United States has actually bordered on not even having any *traditional* IPs.

What U.S. Industrial Policy Has Been

It is fair to say that U.S. IP has been to maintain a basically favorable climate for business, given the social, environmental, and safety constraints imposed on a modern society. Tempering business cycles, fostering an investment climate conducive to capital formation, and maintaining political stability have been the primary stated goals of U.S. policy. More accurately, rather than *an* IP, the United States has really had a series of policies that have affected industries. The distinction is made because of the ad hoc nature of most policies and the general lack of coordination and intention. For these reasons, the latter sections of this chapter, which look at U.S. IPs in more detail, take a functional approach. That is, they focus on specific functions of the U.S. government and assess how these policies affect industry.

Perhaps the most notable feature of many U.S. policies that affect industry is the extent to which they result from necessary government actions—for example, satisfying defense and social obligations. In the area of government procurement, for example, huge U.S. purchases of military hardware, aircraft, and space-program equipment obviously have strong sectoral effects, but there is no real indication that such policy has had intentional industrial objectives. The same is true about government research and development outlays that have flowed in the same directions. Examples of policies to meet social obligations that have inadvertent industry effects are even more common. Functional regulation, like the imposition of environmental standards, is probably the classic example. Another is the regulation of specific industries for social reasons (for example, preventing abuses of economic power).

On the other hand, the U.S. government has undertaken some intentional positive IPs. While for the most part these types of policies have been used only infrequently, there have been notable exceptions. Along sector-specific lines for example, the United States has had an agricultural-policy program over the years to direct production (through programs like Set-

Aside), manage demand (through government buying programs like P.L. 480), and promote technological and scientific innovation (often through agricultural-research centers). Along more industry-specific lines, the United States is currently in the process of promoting the synthetic-fuels industry through an $88 billion program of loans, loan guarantees, and guaranteed markets. In addition, policymakers are currently discussing the wisdom of selectively reducing environmental and safety restrictions to favor certain industries (such as steel and automobiles) that are suffering from falling profitability and heavy unemployment. Selective accelerated depreciation allowances have also been discussed and have been implemented in a few cases.

The main U.S. industry-specific policies (ISPs) have perhaps been in the area of promoting structural adaptation. Since trade-adjustment assistance became law with the Trade Expansion Act of 1962, the United States has channeled funds—over $100 million in 1979—into industries thought to be declining because of lost comparative advantage and tariff reduction. Industries like textiles, apparel, handbags, and footwear have been the main beneficiaries. Generally, these programs have not only promoted technical innovation and the installation of new capital equipment but have also encouraged producers to shift to new lines of manufacturing. Related programs have attempted to promote labor adaptation by helping workers retrain or relocate for alternative employment.

More common in the U.S. context than sector or ISPs, however, have been activity-specific (ASPs) and nonselective policies (GIPs). A series of policies, beginning with the approval of accelerated depreciation allowances for business in 1954, have attempted to stimulate capital formation across all industries, for example. In fact, the adoption of shorter asset life guidelines and the investment-tax credit in 1962, and the massive 1981 depreciation advantages—both for the expressed purpose of stimulating economy-wide investment and promoting technological adaptation—were among the most planned and conscious activity-specific industrial policies the U.S. government has ever undertaken.

Other ASPs have attempted to positively influence U.S. exports. In addition to the DISC Program, government export financing, (some of it at subsidized rates) is administered through agencies like the Eximbank. The United States also has the Webb-Pomerene Act of 1918, which reduces antitrust worries for corporations wanting to jointly promote exports, and it subsidizes some U.S. shipping. One point should be underscored, however. As mentioned before, these policies are not well-coordinated or well-planned. This is illustrated by events like the September 1980 congressional recess that left Eximbank appropriations unintentionally cut off. The fact that such an oversight could occur emphasizes the general lack of consistency of U.S. policy in this area.

Finally, the U.S. government has undertaken some programs to consciously encourage technological change and innovation. Much of the knowledge gained in the areas of defense and space research and development, for example, is transferred to the civilian sector through government technology-dispersing centers, usually established with university links. Much government-funded research—over $1 billion in 1979—is also performed in basic sciences that contribute to the nation's technology base. Of course, government support of public education, higher education, and university research might also be considered components of such a technology policy.

Review of U.S. Thinking

Although there has been a historical U.S. bias against the use of IPs, some literature on the subject does exist. In fact, there are records from colonial days suggesting that IPs were in use even before the United States became a nation. According to Bishop (1868), in 1643 the government of Massachusetts granted a new smelting-and-iron company an exemption from taxation and the exclusive privilege of producing iron for twenty-one years to encourage the industry, while in 1772 Rhode Island gave prizes and bounties to stimulate the production of sailcloth. Bounties, premiums, free land, and subsidized loans were not infrequently granted to individuals willing to establish industries throughout the colonial period.

Theoretical arguments for IPs were first made in the independent United States by Alexander Hamilton in 1791. In his *Report on Manufactures,* Hamilton departed radically from the classical laissez-faire philosophy of Adam Smith and advocated strong government involvement in the development of new industries through a system of high protection tariffs, bounties, and premiums. Protection was necessary, he argued, to help infant industries get established, to acquire the skills of manufacturing, and, not coincidentally, to ensure a home supply of commodities needed for defense. Bounties and premiums were proper, according to Hamilton (1791, p. 42) because other nations used them to develop their industries, and because:

> Capital is wayward and timid in lending itself to new undertakings, and the State ought to excite the confidence of capitalists, who are ever cautious and sagacious, by aiding them to overcome the obstacles that lie in the way of all experiments.

Following other theoretical justifications for infant-industry tariffs by Mill, List, and others, the United States did construct high protectionist walls in the second half of the nineteenth century. Republicans from Morrill (Morrill Tariff Act of 1861) to McKinley (McKinley Tariff Act of 1890) expounded the virtues of protection on economic grounds but, even more importantly, on political or ideological grounds. The United States had experienced rapid industrial growth over the period and employment had been protected, but arguments like preserving U.S. markets for U.S. producers or McKinley's 1888 comparison of outside competition to foreign military interference, seemed to be the ideas that actually motivated this IP. It is perhaps fair to say that most U.S. IPs ever since have also relied more on security and social justifications than economic justifications.

It was during the 1930s that a heightened discussion of IP first developed in the United States. The Depression led many to question the ability of unfettered capitalism to achieve steady economic growth and many observers advocated an expanded federal role. Some saw more government planning as the solution. Ezekiel (1941), in one of the Temporary National Economic Committee (TNEC) Monographs, for example, advocated an Industrial Expansion Plan that called for a commission to set output, prices, wages and profits in all major industries, along with a Production Insurance Corporation that would purchase surplus output (providing a type of government guaranteed market) as the way to revitalize the economy. In fact, similar ideas had temporarily taken form with the National Industrial Recovery Act of 1933 in which industry-by-industry codes were established. Although promoting much debate, however, the main concepts were generally denounced, according to Himmelberg (1976), for relying too heavily on the omniscience of government planners and for leading to the socialization of industry.

Interestingly, the TNEC (1941) also came out strongly for government policies to foster and encourage private enterprise. Although it expressed traditional U.S. fear of authoritarian government, it clearly defined a positive role for government within a market framework. Among the IPs advocated by the TNEC were lowering taxes to encourage business investment, establishing an agency to perform business and economic research, easing patent laws to hasten the dissemination of new technology, eliminating the basing-point system to encourage competition, and creating better product standards to help producers establish national markets and concentrate on the manufacturing of fewer products.

The Reconstruction Finance Corporation (RFC) was one policy response to these kinds of attitudes in the 1930s and 1940s. A lending agency that directly disbursed over $40 billion in loans and investments over its two-and-a-half-decade life, the RFC made loans to enterprises thought likely to develop new technological processes as well as those in such potentially rewarding industries as synthetic rubber, tin, refining, mining, and prefabricated housing. A slightly different response was the creation of the

Tennessee Valley Authority (TVA). Rather than being designed mainly for industrial objectives, however, the TVA, according to Martin (1956), was mainly viewed as an instrument of social policy (to alleviate rural poverty and control flooding) and of defense policy (to develop nitrates for munitions). The important point, though, is that in the 1930s attitudes in favor of government intervention developed that gave rise to some rather advanced IPs. IP has probably not captured as much U.S. attention in either mind or action in all the years since.

In the postwar era, the main trend in U.S. economic thinking has, of course, been toward a synthesis of Keynesian ideas. Government's theoretical role has been to manage the macroeconomy through aggregate demand policy and monetary policy with the goal of providing a stable economic environment for free enterprise. Theoretical support for the laissez-faire view that an economy is basically self-functioning has also remained fairly strong. However, with the exception of policies to stimulate exports or investment to increase aggregate demand, or of policies to correct market failures, neither theory has allowed much of a role for IP. This is true also of traditional growth theory, which has focused mainly on rates of saving and investment and not on the dynamics of leading sectors or leading industries. Not surprisingly, most modern contributions to economic literature have followed these traditional theoretical channels and offered arguments against government interventions for the following reasons: (1) because they disrupt the workings of the market and lead to distortions and inefficiencies; (2) because they offer only second-best solutions; (3) because competition would theoretically work better than specific-industry regulation; and so forth. (See chapter 2 of this book.)

There has been some recent thinking though, that has broken from the mainstream and advocated the use of IPs. Along theoretical lines, the literature is very small and has focused mainly on the benefits of aggregate supply-stimulating policies. Bilson (1979), for example, has argued that policies like an expanded investment-tax-credit program, employment subsidies, and an easing of antipollution standards, can, under certain circumstances, lead to real increases in output, negative inflationary pressure, a stronger current account, and a stronger exchange rate. Reagan administration supply siders have advocated massive tax cuts to stimulate aggregate supply. Although their transmission mechanism is very unclear, and despite their general opposition to active government intervention, they can be said to implicitly promote a very general type of IP—an ASP directed toward saving and investment.

Most thinking has generally been more practical in nature and has focused on certain functional areas of government activity. For the most part debate has not viewed IP in terms of a comprehensive, coordinated, overall plan to strengthen the nation's industrial base. An OECD (1970) study, (*United States Industrial Policies*), for example, basically describes various U.S. policies that have affected industry without trying to synthesize an overriding rationale or to impute industrial intentions. In comparison to its studies of other advanced countries, the OECD's U.S. study is not comprehensive, presumably because U.S. IP is relatively unsophisticated.

We cannot deny however, that within functional areas of the U.S. government, some activities have signaled an awareness of the importance of IPs. In the areas of taxation, as already mentioned, the 1962 and 1981 accelerated-depreciation guidelines were mandated by the U.S. Congress to stimulate capital formation and encourage technological adaptation. In tariff policy, the United States has come to realize that steady tariff reductions have led to the decline of certain industries and necessitated certain adjustment-assistance programs to promote structural adaptation. In the related area of export policy it is interesting that a subcommittee to the Joint Economic Committee (1978b), lamenting the lack of U.S. export-promotion effort but crucially aware of the importance of such effort, entitled a series of hearings on the subject, "Exports: Time For a National Policy." It appears that changes have also been taking place in the area of antitrust enforcement. In fact, a shift in thinking has occurred, even among traditionally liberal editorial sources. Many observers felt, for example, that the recent IBM antitrust suit was perhaps not in the country's best interest when viewed from an IP standpoint.

There has been an extremely small literature that has attempted to view U.S. IP in a more comprehensive manner. Pinder, et al. (1979), in a Trilateral Commission report, for instance, argue that in the areas of steel and energy the United States has been closer to IP than it perhaps realizes. One of the study's most insightful observations, though, is that many interventions or policies undertaken by the U.S. government that would be called IP in foreign countries are not labeled so in the United States. Even so, the study's main conclusion—that there has been no general IP in the United States and, perhaps even more telling, that there has been almost no real understanding of the expression until recently—cannot be overlooked.

This view is basically shared by McKie (1979) in his analysis of U.S. government interventions, especially when he claims that U.S. policy has no apparent long-run goals other than to remedy specific failures in the private system. Even so, he points out that, although not bound together by any grand philosophical design, many seemingly small U.S. policy decisions have a fairly strong aggregate impact and have pushed the economy away from laissez-faire capitalism and closer to socialism. He describes three main types of policy: (1) those to correct market failures (antitrust, regulation); (2) those to support, promote, or operate industry; and (3) those to foster and control the defense, space, and energy industries (procurement policy, research-and-development policy, and so on). Perhaps his most interesting conclusion though is that if all policies were divided into two categories—those fostering equity and those fostering efficiency—it is the equity policies that have been on the ascent whereas the efficiency promoting policies have been on the decline.

New U.S. Attitudes

There is no question that U.S. awareness of the importance of IP has been growing recently. While some of this heightened awareness is perhaps due to recessionary and inflationary forces, most is probably related to underlying and pervasive economic trends like lagging U.S. productivity and slipping export performance. Some interest in IP has undoubtedly been prompted by foreign involvement as well—the retaliation motive. The new view that is emerging in academic, business, and governmental circles focuses on many issues. The need to increase government research-and-development funding, and especially support for basic science that has declined in a relative sense over the past fifteen years, is a typical issue. Another perspective is the contention that environmental and safety regulations may represent fundamental barriers to future U.S. industrial growth and may need revising.

There are myriad issues. Some believe the United States needs to promote industry through, say, fewer political restriction on exports or perhaps less-stringent enforcement of antitrust statutes. A related issue is the need to promote more capital formation through an expanded investment-tax-credit program or a shift to replacement-cost depreciation. Going one step further, some economists believe the United States should move to more ISPs to assist in the development of winner industries or those in which the United States might have a strong international comparative advantage. Some also feel the U.S. government should play a bigger role in certain crucial industries, like synthetic fuels, where government ownership or operation might be justified on grounds of national security.

In the past, the U.S. attitude was that it did not need an IP. IP was viewed as something necessary only for developing countries or those trying to rebuild economies destroyed by war. This view is changing, primarily because of the realization that an industrial base will not always take care of itself automatically. If anything, there is growing agreement on one issue—the need for more planning and better coordination of policies that affect industry.

U.S. Policies Affecting Industry: An Introduction

The interrelationships between the U.S. federal government and U.S. industry are numerous and complex. The government stabilizes the economy through macropolicy: it taxes business net income and regulates competition, environmental impacts, or safety of products in virtually every industry. In addition, it subsidizes some types of business, promotes research and development, imposes tariffs, encourages exports, and purchases many private goods and services. It even enters into joint or mixed ventures, engages in joint management of public utilities, and occasionally owns and operates productive capacity outright.

The following sections have three primary objectives. First, they seek to describe the main U.S. policies that affect industry, providing historical and institutional information where appropriate. Second, they attempt to examine how U.S. IPs have been used and analyze their impacts on important industrial variables like the rate of technical innovation, exports, and capital formation. Third, they compare, where possible, U.S. policies to those of other advanced industrial economies to provide a frame of reference.

We take a functional approach. Rather than looking at the possible goals or objectives of IP and asking which policies were employed to achieve these goals, these sections focus on specific policy areas and study the effects of these policies on industry. This type of approach suits an analysis of the United States because it has not really had a single IP but rather a series of policies. To break the analysis down into active or passive policies or to try to describe sophisticated policy programs for rationalization or to promote national champions might be appropriate in the European context. In the case of the United States, it would imply a degree of policy coordination and planning that simply has not and does not exist.

Direct Government Intervention

Direct government intervention into the affairs of private business has become an important instrument of IP in recent years. Generally speaking, it is possible to identify three primary justifications for such intervention. The first is the traditional economic argument for regulation on the grounds that a natural monopoly exists. Where economies of scale are overwhelming, specific-industry regulation allows monopolies to exist for underlying efficiency reasons while protecting consumers from possible abuses of such power. A second justification is to force the internalization of economic externalities. Functional regulation, as it is called, tries to make private firms legally responsible for certain social costs, like the protection of the environment, that might otherwise be ignored. Third, governments some-

U.S. Industrial Policy

times intervene for political reasons or to achieve certain social objectives. A government might promote a new industry for, say, national-security reasons, or it might want to prevent massive sectoral unemployment.[1] The first two justifications can be thought of as addressing market failures. The third is basically a response to national-planning objectives.

With 8.8 percent of U.S. gross national product (GNP) under price and market entry (that is, specific-industry) regulation in 1975 and 11.9 percent directly affected by health-and-safety regulation, it is apparent that regulation has become a major institutional force affecting economic performance at both the general and sectoral levels. The unique aspects from an IP perspective, however, concern the third type of justification for intervention. In sharp contrast to some of its European trading partners, the United States has remained philosophically committed to private capitalism as the form of economic organization to best maximize industrial output and, implicitly, national welfare. Indeed, the degree of U.S. intervention has been relatively low when compared to the levels in most advanced industrial economies abroad. Not only has the United States avoided Europe's steady march toward increased government ownership of basic industries (like steel and automobiles); if anything, there is a trend toward even less government intervention in the United States today.

Specific-Industry Regulation

U.S. specific-industry regulation began with the Act to Regulate Commerce in 1887. Designed to establish federal jurisdiction over interstate railroad rates and service, it essentially set the precedent of detailed price-and-entry regulation that has prevailed in similar industries to the present. Since that time the scope of regulation has increased somewhat to include control over service standards, financial structure, and even choice of accounting methods. It is still applied to the same kinds of industries, however—those where market self-regulation has failed because of ever-declining costs. Regulation of interstate transportation (trucking, railroad, and airline), communications (telephone and broadcasting), and electricity production had become widespread by the 1930s. Natural-gas and pipeline transportation were added to the list in the 1950s.

It is difficult to generalize about the economic effects of specific-industry regulation on the six or seven industries just listed. While some economists, like MacAvoy (1979), claim that it has had great negative effects and led industries from healthy growth to reduced profitability, under investment, and severe reductions in service, others support the opposite view. The truth probably lies somewhere in between. In the 1950s and early 1960s most of these industries enjoyed healthy profits as unit-production costs declined because of technological breakthroughs and the existence of increasing economies of scale. Regulators generally supported prices in the hope of encouraging an expansion of services. During the later 1960s and early 1970s, however, the generally positive attitude of the regulators was offset by an end to decreasing costs and a regulatory lag problem aggravated by inflation. With lags averaging five quarters during this period, rates of profit generally fell below industrial averages and in response investment levels dipped also with a lag. By the mid-1970s, however, there was evidence to suggest that the situation had turned around. In the period from 1974 to 1977, for instance, six out of these seven regulated industries had rates of return that exceeded the market rate of return and most were significantly higher. Overall, the effects of regulation have been mixed, depending on the industry and time span. It may be fair to say, though, that while certain industries (like natural gas) may have been hurt, others (like the trucking industry) have almost certainly benefited.

There has been a new shift in U.S. regulatory policy toward deregulation over the past five years or so. Beginning with the deregulation of the airline, trucking, railroad, gas (and oil), and communications industries, the new policy will presumably spread to the other oligopoly-type regulated industries. Generally, the new U.S. policy is to set broad operating guidelines while revoking minimum-price standards. Most regulation is being phased in over a number of years (for example, five years for the airline industry), and includes temporary restrictions on price increases (no more than 5 percent-above the rate of inflation a year without a formal rate review for the airline industry).

This trend is very interesting from a philosophical point of view. The return of previously regulated industries to at least oligopolistic-type competition signals a major IP shift in the United States toward increasing reliance on competition, and concomitantly, a position of less government intervention into the affairs of these industries. Actually, it was economists who initiated this drive toward systematically weakening regulatory controls in the 1970s. Phillips's (1975) series of industry studies, for example, suggests that airlines, surface transportation, electric power, communications, and other industries would perform better unfettered in the marketplace than with government regulation. They could adapt more quickly to changes and would not render economically inefficient services. Phillips outlines the main theoretical arguments: Regulation is a second-best solution and therefore cannot lead to allocative efficiency (except by fluke); fair rate of return rate making for a decreasing average-cost industry can never lead to the socially optimal price; and fair return rate making imparts a managerial bias toward greater capital intensity than is economically efficient (the so-called Averch-Johnson Effect). The crucial point though is that while Europe turns toward ever-greater government intervention and regulation, the United States is moving in the opposite direction.

The effects of specific-industry regulation on innovation and technological progress are just beginning to be studied. While Phillips (1975) suggests a heavily negative influence, some economists, like Mansfield (1976), have contended that, for example, regulation of the airline industry in the 1960s encouraged *too rapid* a rate of technical growth in the aircraft industry. Capron's (1971) studies suggest that such regulation has had mixed effects. He argues, for instance, that the rate of technological progress in the railroad and trucking industries has been slowed because the Interstate Commerce Commission (ICC) has been too interested in protecting the interests of its regulatees. The studies suggest that the impact of regulation on the pace and pattern of innovation in communications has probably been positive, mainly because of the Averch-Johnson Effect and that the impact on the airline industry and electric utilities has been marginally positive. Capron concludes, though, that the flow of federal research and development money has been a much more significant factor, with industries like aircraft and communications receiving a lot of aid and others, like railroads, receiving very little.

Functional Regulation

One of the most powerful ways that government can influence the activities of private industry is through functional regulation. The main areas of functional regulation are well known: consumer products, discrimination in employment, traffic safety, consumer finance, job safety, and environment and resources. This regulatory movement in the United States basically coincided with the movement of growing social awareness in the 1960s and grew in the 1970s. Key pieces of legislation were such acts as the Air Pollution Act of 1962, the Water Control Act of 1965, the Equal Pay Act of 1963, the Food and Drug Amendment of 1962, and the Occupational Safety and Health Act of 1970.

Aggregate Effects on Industry. While it is impossible to measure accurately the total effects of functional regulation, there are many estimates. Weidenbaum (1978), for example, claims that in fiscal year 1979 the total cost to the U.S. economy of functional regulation was $102.7 billion—$4.8 billion in direct government outlays to maintain forty-one regulatory agencies and $97.9 billion in private compliance costs. Kreps (U.S. Congress, Joint Economic Committee, 1978*a*) states that national pollution abatement alone cost the private and public sectors together a cumulative $135 billion over the period from 1972 to 1976. These expenditures were equal to 2 percent of GNP in 1975 and 1976.

Regulations of this scale obviously have impacts on a nation's industries. One effect is on labor productivity. Denison (1978) reports that functional regulation was responsible for a 0.5-percent decline in the growth of labor productivity in 1975. He also claims that output per unit of input was 1.4 percent smaller than it would have been had 1967 regulatory statutes been in effect. Functional regulation also affects research and development and innovation. It has at least slowed the pace of new-product introduction, and is generally felt to have dampened the innovation process as well. Peltzman (1973) contends, for instance, that functional regulation of the pharmaceutical drug industry has delayed the introduction of effective new drugs by four years, led to higher drug prices, and seriously hurt U.S. drug-export potential. Friedlander (1971) has estimated that just the functional regulation of railroads has retarded railroad innovation greatly, resulting in a loss to the industry of somewhere between $12 million and $41 million per year.

Because it is so hard to estimate the costs of functional regulation, even in one industry, it is nearly impossible to compare broad programs internationally. It is worth noting, though, that while most other advanced industrial economies do have roughly similar types of regulations, they are often more lenient in allowing new products to enter the market (especially new drugs), seem somewhat more reluctant to shut firms down for environmental reasons (especially when many jobs are at stake), and rely more on voluntary guidelines that producers are expected to meet if at all possible. It is also hard to compare government subsidies and tax expenditures to assist compliance with regulations. In the United States, for example, qualified pollution-control equipment is eligible for special five-year amortization (along with the investment-tax credit). In fiscal year 1980, this program represented a tax expenditure of $15 million.

Industry Effects. Naturally, these regulations hit some industries much harder than others. MacAvoy (1979) claims, for instance, that while industry in general spent $6.6 billion for pollution-related investment in 1975, five industries—chemicals, nonferrous metals, paper, electric utilities, and petroleum refining—accounted for 70 percent of these outlays. MacAvoy says over 10 percent of the total net investment undertaken by each of these five industries, and also by the steel and construction-materials industries, were devoted to pollution control. MacAvoy further states that Occupational Safety and Health Administration (OSHA) regulations, while requiring industry in general to lay out about $4 billion to increase the safety of U.S. work places in 1975, also hit certain industries harder than others. The automobile, paper, chemical, metals, and wood industries were among the most affected. In addition, he claims that National Highway and Transportation Safety Administration safety requirements forced the automobile industry to increase its investment spending by an estimated $0.5 billion in the same year.

From a theoretical viewpoint, increased regulation-related expenditures for industries most affected by regulation could be expected to increase their operating costs and lead to higher prices, lower output, and a lower growth of productive capacity, other factors being equal. MacAvoy (1979) presents quantitative evidence to suggest that these effects have in fact occurred. Between 1973 and 1977, the seven industries most heavily affected did in fact raise prices faster than the manufacturing sector as a whole, and with the exception of the chemical industry, all seven saw production actually decrease while it increased for the less-regulated industries. Of course, from an IP viewpoint, the impact on profitability is perhaps most important. Over the first part of the 1970s, the mining, construction, paper, and chemical industries had greater than average rates of return, while the stone, clay, and glass, primary metals, and automobile industries were significantly below average. This suggests that some of these industries have had trouble pushing the burden of social regulation onto consumers. More dramatically, in the nuclear-power-equipment industry, regulation has not only contributed to lower profits but may contribute to the closing down of the whole industry in the United States.

Recent Trends. Substantial support has recently emerged for easing the functional regulatory burden on business in general and on specific industries in particular. On a theoretical level, the movement is extremely interesting for it provides a focal point for new U.S. attitudes toward the proper role of government intervention and, more fundamentally, changing U.S. attitudes toward the concept of IP. In the past in the United States, the underlying economic question went largely unasked in the construction of regulation policy; that is, the economic effects of policy were often ignored. It was implicitly assumed that the country could afford anything it wanted—whether it was a cleaner environment or whatever—and that industry would just adapt by passing the costs along to consumers in the form of higher prices, and that there would be no other effects.

Other effects have become manifest, however. Higher production costs have hurt U.S. exports of products like steel and coal. Billions of dollars invested in pollution-abatement equipment, although probably wisely spent, have not been available for research programs for increasing worker productivity or for the development of new technologically advanced products. Inflationary and recessionary forces have compounded these problems. The result has been a major reassessment of U.S. regulatory policies. The Reagan administration has established a cabinet-level Task Force on Regulatory Relief, for example, in an attempt to make regulators satisfy a meaningful and objective cost-benefit test before imposing major regulatory standards. Reagan's administration has also been pressing for a general lowering of the regulatory burden on U.S. industry—mainly in the hope of encouraging more investment and bolstering productivity.

The recent postponing of certain environmental and safety regulations for the steel and automobile industries signals an even more fundamental shift in policy. It perhaps constitutes the beginning of a U.S. ISP. The criteria for special government attention are still not clear, although high unemployment and negative profits seem to be factors. To date, the relaxations have been largely ad hoc but the fact that they have been announced in conjunction with other policies to help the industries suggests a degree of planning and coordination that has never before existed.

Public Ownership

Outright public ownership and operation of an industry unquestionably represents the highest form of government intervention. Pryor (1974) gives some idea of the extent of public ownership (all types) in the United States. In 1970, he claims, publicly owned enterprises accounted for 2 percent of the employment in the mining and manufacturing sectors; 21 percent in the transportation and communication sectors; 32 percent in electric, gas, water, and sanitation utilities; 2 percent in commerce and finance; and 3 percent in the agricultural, forestry, and fishing sector.

Perhaps the most interesting observation about public ownership in the United States is the infrequency with which the option has been chosen, at least in comparison to most other industrial countries. In the United Kingdom, France, Italy, and West Germany, airlines, railroads, telephone service, electricity, natural gas, and waterways are all 100-percent publicly owned. In the United States, airlines, gas, and telephone service are virtually 100-percent private. Electricity is 75-percent private; railroads are also largely private. There are big differences concerning public ownership of core industries, as well. Even in the early 1950s, the United Kingdom had such national companies as the Anglo-Iranian Oil Company and British Petroleum, France had the Compagnie Francaise des Petroles and Francolor, Italy had the Ente Nazionale Idrocarburi, and West Germany had the Volkswagen Company.[2] Examples like the British Steel Corporation, Renault, and the British Leyland Motor Corporation would represent only the beginning of any European list today. In contrast, the U.S. government has not been directly involved in industries like steel, automobiles, aircraft, computers, and the extraction of coal, oil, and other minerals as most European countries have.

There are many reasons for these differences. Wilcox and Shepherd (1975) contend that the biggest factor is philosophical and based on cultural preferences. In the United States there has traditionally been a pervasive fear of government encroachment into the industrial sector. This notion is sustained by the strong U.S. feeling that the private sector inherently performs more efficiently. There is another, more practical, reason for reluctance to undertake more public ownership. U.S. citizens have seen Europeans (and especially the British) nationalize one industry after another with the result being ever-lagging productivity, falling output, and the need for constant infusions of government money to cover persistent operating deficits. As Vernon (1974) contends, U.S. citizens have seen the results of nationalization that has not had systematic economic origins, that has not been carefully preplanned, and that has mainly attempted to bail out declining industries, not dynamic sectors with growth potential. As a result, people in the United States have generalized their observations into a widespread condemnation of the whole process.

While it has not generally been U.S. government policy to own or operate productive capacity, there have been several exceptions and it is possible to draw a few generalizations from this small sample. In virtually all U.S. cases, pragmatic social needs or national-security needs have prompted government intervention. Nationalization has not occurred primarily to meet industrial objectives (for example, to increase productivity or expand exports) or out of a feeling that perhaps the government could run the industry more efficiently. In fact, even basic economic problems like unemployment have rarely (except for some of the 1930s programs) been a primary justification for government takeover; this has frequently been a key factor in European nationalization projects.

Consider the TVA Project. The primary objectives of the government were to construct dams to provide flood control and navigation and to develop a nitrate industry at Muscle Shoals, Alabama (mainly to produce munitions). These comprised basically social needs or national-security needs.[3] Flood control and irrigation, not industrial promotion, were the main justifications for the government building the Hoover Dam on the Colorado River in the 1930s, as well.

The nationalization of certain mainly Eastern railroads in the early 1970s by the government corporations AMTRAK and CONRAIL provide more recent examples. Rather than let passenger and freight-rail service in the most densely populated parts of the country disappear completely, the government stepped in. The desire to be a consistent supporter of mass transit and of efficient freight shipping to reduce dependence on foreign oil figured heavily in the government's decision. The takeover was mainly undertaken for social, not industrial, reasons and was a last step after attempts to cure railroad industry problems by allowing easy mergers had failed. The Communications Satellite Corporation (COMSAT) is another example. Originally conceived as a wholly public corporation to operate international satellites, COMSAT did not get off the ground in the early 1960s because of congressional reluctance. It came into being in 1962 only after joint private-public ownership had been arranged.

The largest and most recent public corporation in the United States is the new Synthetic Fuels Corporation. Authorized to allocate up to $88 billion in loans and loan guarantees over the next ten years to promote coal gasification and liquification, the project is uncharacteristic for the United States in some ways. Although it does fit into the mold by being justified mainly on national-security grounds, it does represent a departure in terms of scope, magnitude, coordination, and overall planning. It marks one of the first thrusts by U.S. policymakers into an industrial sector.

Government Bailouts: Rescue-the-Loser Policies

Another form of direct government intervention into the affairs of private industries is the government bailout. Since the Depression years there has been no formal U.S. government bailout apparatus. Generally, bailouts have been rare and when they have occurred, they have been very ad hoc in nature. The cases have generally been debated in the Congress on the basis of the specific facts involved. Government support of the railroad industry aside, there have been three major U.S. government bailouts over the past few years: a $250 million loan guarantee to Lockheed Aircraft in 1971, a $730 million loan guarantee to General Dynamics, Quincy, Massachusetts, shipyard operations in 1977, and a $1.5 billion loan guarantee to the Chrysler Corporation in 1979–1980. Exactly what factors swayed the Congress to support the bailouts are unclear. In the first two cases, the defense orientation of the firms was considered a factor. The desire to maintain competition was mentioned in all three cases, as were the possible unemployment effects. Because of the closeness of the congressional votes it seems appropriate to conclude that the word *response* is probably more accurate than the word *policy* as far as U.S. bailouts are concerned.

Government Support of Research and Development

Another interesting aspect of IP is government support of research and development. Along with private funding and infrastructure characteristics, like a nation's system of universities and laboratories, this support helps determine a country's level of technology. This subject is particularly important for the United States, whose primary comparative advantage is often assumed to be in high technology.

There are basically two standard justifications for government support of research and development. The first is because of market failures or externalities. Private firms will not spend as much money on research and development as they should, for instance, because basic scientific information has powerful externalities associated with it. Even with patents, companies might not be able to internalize all benefits. A related aspect is the high risk of failure associated with research-and-development spending, especially with large projects. It is argued, for instance, that underinvestment would systematically occur in areas like fusion technology because of such risks. The second reason for government involvement is to provide new or improved technology for public-sector functions like space exploration and defense. Since the government is the sole purchaser and primary producer of such goods, some argue that it must bear responsibility for the promotion of technological change in these areas.

A few general observations about U.S. research-and-development policy are appropriate at the start. First, U.S. efforts in this area are similar to U.S. policies toward industry in general. For the most part they are unplanned, ad hoc, and not based on economic reasoning. Mansfield (1976) claims that U.S. research-and-development programs in support of civilian technology are ad hoc and complains that it is hard to understand why we have allocated support in the directions we have. While there has been an historical U.S. commitment to research and development in principle, the goals of such policy have been unclear beyond some vague notion that it would help the United States retain its technological edge.

A related observation is that while selective research-and-development support is generally thought to be the most effective way to improve a nation's technology, political rather than economic forces have tended to influence the directions of government support. Mansfield (1976) claims that there is no good economic reason why the U.S. government has spent so much money on civilian aviation technology and so little on railroad technology or why so much has been spent for agricultural technology and so little for construction technology. He says that while the bulk has gone to high-technology industries, the highest marginal rates of return for federal research-and-development funds might be in textiles or machine tools. The point is that very little theoretical and empirical economic research have gone into U.S. decisions of how much research and development support to provide and how to allocate that support.

Dimensions of U.S. Support of Research and Development

In aggregate terms, the U.S. federal government spent roughly $28 billion for research and development in fiscal year 1979. In addition, the Treasury Department granted business a $1.5 billion tax expenditure during the year due to the tax provision allowing research-and-development costs to be written off quickly. Direct government research-and-development support represented about 5.7 percent of all U.S. government budget outlays in fiscal year 1979 and about 1.2 percent of GNP. Table 6-1 shows these same two percentages for each year from 1960 to 1979, and an interesting trend emerges. Throughout the 1960s there was a remarkable buildup of federal support for research and development that peaked in 1964, with 10.7 percent of total budget outlays and 2.2 percent of GNP going for this purpose. Both of these percentages have fallen in virtually every succeeding year. By 1979, the proportions of government support for research and development were only a little above half of their 1964 level.

As far as the allocation of this money is concerned, a little less than half of the direct funding—43 percent in fiscal year 1979—was for national defense-related research. The second-largest portion by function—17 percent—was spent by the Department of Energy. Funding for space-program

Table 6-1
U.S. Government Support of Research and Development

Year	As Percent of Total Budget Outlays	As Percent of GNP
1960	7.33	1.45
1961	8.13	1.68
1962	8.40	1.75
1963	9.26	1.92
1964	10.69	2.18
1965	10.08	2.02
1966	9.55	2.00
1967	8.92	2.02
1968	8.18	1.89
1969	7.45	1.68
1970	6.99	1.57
1971	6.64	1.47
1972	6.45	1.42
1973	6.08	1.30
1974	5.64	1.25
1975	5.82	1.24
1976	5.66	1.22
1977	5.94	1.26
1978	5.86	1.24
1979	5.66	1.18

Source: National Science Foundation and the Economic Report of the President, 1980. *An Analysis of Federal R&D Funding by Budget Function, 1960-1972, and 1969-1979.*

research and development was 15 percent of the total; health programs, 12 percent; and National Science Foundation programs, 3 percent. Government support of basic research had generally fallen off in a proportional sense over the 1970s, but this funding rose 40 percent over the period from fiscal year 1978 to fiscal year 1981 and was equal to $5.1 billion in the latter year. The Reagan administration, however, appears committed to reversing this recent trend and has generally pledged that declining funds will be available for basic research over the next few years.

There are a number of U.S. policies, in addition to direct and indirect funding, that also affect research and development. The patent system, the tax system, and programs to disseminate technical knowledge are all examples. The patent system, which offers seventeen-year protection for inventors, has probably had mixed effects. While it probably does encourage some innovative effort, there is much evidence to suggest that inventors invent primarily for the human joy of inventing or to make a social contribution, not for any pecuniary reward. The U.S. government also has policies to transfer some of its research-and-development findings to the private sector. Through programs like NASA's Technology Utilization Program and the National Technical Information Service, highly technical information is channeled to private industry through links to university centers and institutes. Several U.S. tax-code provisions are also designed to stimulate innovation. In addition to the 1981 25-percent tax credit on research-and-development outlays, the Internal Revenue Service (IRS) code allows the sale of patents to be taxed at capital-gains rates rather than at regular rates. This provides at least a marginal incentive to sell patents and spread new technology.

Recently, some new trends have emerged in U.S. government policy toward research and development. Several new technology-enhancement programs have been instituted—for example, the National Research and Development Assessment Program, Technical Assistance to Import Injured Industries (under the Trade Act of 1974), and the Experimental Technology Incentives Program.[4] The government has also begun to undertake some cooperative research-and-development ventures with private industry. Recently, for example, the National Science Foundation and the Department of Transportation agreed to fund 50 percent of a joint project with the automobile industry to research ways of increasing the energy efficiency of the nation's automobile fleet. The government money is supposed to come from the Windfall Profits Tax on the oil industry. Government and industry are also equally sharing the costs of a ten-year $700 million program to explore the oil potential of the continental shelf, using the government-owned ship, the Glomar Explorer. Such joint ventures are frequently undertaken in foreign countries.

Specific Industry Effects

The U.S. government supported roughly 36 percent of all industrial research and development that took place in 1977. As table 6-2 vividly illustrates, however, there were widely different impacts of this federal funding across various industrial sectors. Roughly 70 percent of all research and development in the aircraft-and-parts industry group was funded by the government, for example. The fabricated-metals and communications industries were also high, with 53 percent and 49 percent of outlays federally funded, respectively, while electrical equipment and scientific instruments were both near 25 percent. At the bottom of the list, industries like food, textiles, paper, and stone, clay, and glass products had about 1 percent of their total research and development paid for by the U.S. govern-

Table 6-2
U.S. Industrial Research-and-Development Expenditures in 1977

Industry Group	Total Funding (millions of $)	Percentage Government Supported
Guided missiles and spacecraft	$3,035	90
Ordinance and accessories	288	80
Aircraft and parts	3,125	69
Transportation equipment other than motor vehicles	201	55
Fabricated metal products	1,157	53
Communications equipment and electronic components	5,038	49
Electrical equipment, except communications	905	26
Scientific instruments	1,260	22
Motor vehicles	2,611	8
Nonelectrical machinery	3,572	7
Petroleum refining and extraction	473	4
Chemicals, except drugs	2,024	2
Primary metals	327	2
Drugs and medicines	959	small
Stone, clay, and glass products	191	small
Rubber and miscellaneous plastics	378	small
Food and kindred products	350	small
Textile-mill products	96	small
All industries	$28,997[a]	36

Source: National Science Board. (1979). *Science Indicators, 1978.*
[a] Does not total because list is incomplete sampling.

ment. These figures clearly show that federal money has tended to favor highly technical and defense-related industries.

From an IP perspective the interesting aspect is that the four or five industries with the highest proportions of their research underwritten by the government have all become winner industries by almost any definition: aircraft and missiles, electrical and communications equipment, and instruments. Obviously, some type of cause-and-effect relationship is suggested. What is probably not suggested, however, is positive IP intent on the part of policymakers. Perceived defense exigencies have generally directed government-research-support flows, not industrial objectives.

Comparison of U.S. to Foreign Support of Research and Development

In absolute terms, U.S. research-and-development outlays are much larger than those of other nations. In fact, they are greater than those of all other OECD countries combined. There are different trends and widely varying patterns of allocation among countries, however. Table 6-3, which shows national research-and-development outlays as a proportion of GNP in the United States, Canada, France, West Germany, the United Kingdom, Japan, and the USSR, illustrates perhaps the most important trend. Over the decade from 1963 to 1973, only the United States and the United Kingdom saw this proportion fall—by over one-fifth in each case. In contrast, the proportion rose sharply in West Germany, Japan, and the USSR: up 58 percent in Japan and up 71 percent in West Germany. Clearly, these trends

Table 6-3
Total Research and Development as a Percent of GNP in 1963, 1973, and 1978

Country	1963	1973	1978
United States	2.9%	2.4%	2.2%
Canada	0.9%	0.9%	NA
France	1.5%	1.7%	1.8%[a]
West Germany	1.4%	2.4%	2.3%
United Kingdom	2.3%	1.9%	NA
Japan	1.2%	1.9%	1.9%[a]
USSR	2.2%	3.1%	3.5%[b]

Source: National Science Board. (1979). *Science Indicators, 1978.*
[a]1976.
[b]1977.

underscore different government attitudes in promoting technological innovation, even though most of these trends moderated in the 1973-to-1978 period.

While perhaps official government *attitudes* toward research and development as suggested by the trends already noted are very important, the actual money spent does not seem to be as crucial. Japan, acclaimed as having made the most impressive strides in productivity and industrialization since World War II, has actually budgeted very little money for direct research-and-development programs. As table 6-3 illustrates, the Japanese ratio of total (that is, both private and public) research-and-development funding to GNP has been among the lowest of all advanced industrial economies. Japan has apparently proven that close government-industry relations can encourage a great deal of innovative activity without substantial official government financial support.

There are great differences in the internal allocation of research and development funds among countries, too. Japan and Germany, both successful in building advanced technological bases and applying new technology to industrial exports, have spent much less for defense and big science research than the United States. Instead, they have targeted more of their funds toward general university research and development. As table 6-4 illustrates, the United States has historically channeled a large proportion of its funding into military research. In 1976-1977, for instance, the United States put 51 percent of its money into defense-related projects, while Japan

Table 6-4
Percent of Government Research and Development Allocated to National Defense

Country	1961-1962	1971-1972	1976-1977
United States	71	53	51
United Kingdom	65	44[a]	46[f]
France	44[b]	28[c]	30
West Germany	22[b]	15[d]	12
Japan	4	2[e]	2[g]

Source: National Science Board. (1979). *Science Indicators, 1978.*
[a]1972-1973.
[b]1961.
[c]1972.
[d]1971.
[e]1970-1971.
[f]1975-1976.
[g]1974-1975.

allocated only 2 percent for such purposes. The United States has also channeled substantial research-and-development money into areas like environmental protection and occupational safety, where advances are virtually impossible to evaluate in economic terms.

Perhaps the main nonmonetary difference between foreign and U.S. programs is that most other countries are more willing to undertake joint government-private industry projects where industrial objectives, significant externalities, or significant risks are involved. Again, Japanese programs are worth singling out. Most of their research projects are chosen on the basis of their potential importance to the economy, their riskiness, and the possibility that market failures might have hindered private development. Above all, as Peck (1974) puts it, the Japanese seem to view research and development as a natural part of the innovation process, to be considered along with investment, labor, market development, and so on. Emphasizing the importance of an industrial philosophy, Peck says, their government apparently takes a longer-run view of the process.

Issues in Government Support of Research and Development

How Much Does Government Money Help? While this question is crucial to this entire section, there are really two questions implied. The first is whether research and development in general terms (for example, private effort) seems to lead to innovation and technological advancement. The second question is how *government* funding of research affects innovation.

To answer the first question, Mansfield (1976) and others resort to consumers' surplus-type analysis to obtain crude estimates for the social rate of return from particular innovations. The results of such studies depend critically on what social factors are taken into account (for example, how to define related research that was perhaps unproductive) and are therefore subject to some limitations. However, it is interesting that virtually dozens of independent studies, performed using widely different types of data, have concluded that research and development has extremely high payoffs.[5] In fact, studies in agricultural and industrial innovation suggest a marginal social rate of return in the neighborhood of 30 to 50 percent for research-and-development expenditures. Griliches (1975) and others have suggested that the *private* rate of return on such expenditures is at least in the range of 20 percent. These studies suggest that the United States has been investing far less in research and development than is socially optimal and, perhaps surprisingly, less than is privately optimal as well.

The second question deals with how government policies affect innovation. While it might be assumed that federal research-and-development funding would efficiently help stimulate innovation, several recent studies have questioned this conclusion. A study by the Center for Policy Alternatives at MIT (1976) looked at industry-specific and country-specific factors that influence the process of technological advancement. The researchers' main conclusion was that when all forms of government involvement in the development of new technology are taken into account, industrial managers usually perceive the government involvement to be a *negative* influence on project performance rather than a positive one. Perhaps the strongest conclusion that can be reached in this regard is that the effects of government support of research and development are still largely unknown. Further studies, especially to distinguish between government support of basic research and applied research, would prove very useful.

Griliches (1975) has found that the returns from research and development tend to be lower in those fields where much of it is supported by the U.S. government—for example, in the electrical-equipment and aircraft industries. This suggests that the government has not allocated its funds to equalize the marginal returns from research and development in all uses to maximize benefits. This in turn, supports the generalization suggested by Mansfield at the beginning of this section. It also suggests that the United States has implicitly, if perhaps unknowingly, engaged in industry-specific policies in this area.

Market as Guide. Conventional wisdom suggests that technology research should be joined to the market. In particular, government should probably not get involved in the latter stages of development where private firms have generally been much more efficient. Mansfield (1976) and others have claimed, for instance, that the main reason so many U.K. projects have failed is because the government assumed an entrepreneurial role and became too involved in commercial-development activities. Evidence suggests that a government's more-legitimate role is in the area of basic science. Japanese and German efforts have been channeled in this direction, and their results appear to have been quite successful. Starting in 1978, the United States began to allocate proportionally more money in this direction as well; as previously mentioned, the current administration is reversing this trend.

Effects of Defense-Related and Space-Related Research and Development. Earlier discussion implied that the high proportion of U.S. research-and-development funding for defense and space projects was somehow disadvantageous. Critics would counter that such projects have led to significant improvements in civilian and commercial technology. It is important to realize, however, that had the same effort been applied solely on the civilian front, the contribution toward such technology would probably have been

U.S. Industrial Policy

greater. Brooks (1973) has argued that U.S. concentration of research and development in defense and space diverts innovative effort and talent as well as venture capital away from civilian industries. He further states that even taking the spin-off benefits from such research-and-development programs into account, their overall effect on the economy has been a *negative* one.[6] While this statement is rather bold, it is clear that significant substitution and crowding out effects have occurred in the United States because of these programs.

Antitrust Policy and Research-and-Development Efforts. There is, of course, a link between government competition policy and the innovation process. If it could be demonstrated that small, competitive firms were responsible for more than their fair share of innovations, then the argument could be made that antitrust efforts are beneficial. The opposite argument would prevail if it could be shown that a certain level of industrial concentration were needed to encourage rapid technological change.

Unfortunately, numerous studies have not been able to provide strong economic underpinnings for either premise. Mansfield (1976), Jewkes, Sawers, and Stillerman (1970), and Hamberg (1963) have found some evidence to suggest that small firms play a large, and possibly disproportionate, role in conceiving new ideas and making significant innovations. This has been particularly true in the drug, steel, petrochemical, and coal industries, according to Mansfield (1968). The most notable conclusion, however, is that there appears to be a threshold effect. Firms need certain size, (Mansfield claims about five thousand employees) to be able to set up and support separate research-and-development divisions. As firms get bigger than this, they produce only proportionally more innovations. Scherer (1980) confirms this, claiming that increases in industry concentration beyond a very moderate level do not seem to be related to faster rates of innovation.

The thing that does seem to stimulate innovation is the entry of new firms. To the extent that antitrust policy and regulation can reduce oligopoly and monopoly attempts to resist such entry, it will probably advance the pace of innovation. As Mansfield (1976) concludes, probably the ideal market structure to encourage the fastest technological change would be one with a good mixture of various-sized firms and very few unnecessary barriers to entry.

Two Types of Research-and-Development Focus. As Pavitt (1974) points out, there are really two functions toward which national technological capability can be focused: (1) the creation of new technology, and (2) the adaptation and diffusion of existing technology. In the 1950s and 1960s the major European countries and Japan focused on the latter target: the importation and development of U.S. breakthroughs. The United States supported this policy, both for economic and strategic reasons. By the 1970s, though, the omnipotent technological force that makes new technology much easier to imitate than create started to catch up with the United States. Recently, foreigners have been shouldering more and more of the burden of making original contributions. In steel and electronics, for example, many U.S. firms have recently licensed Japanese technology because it is simply more advanced than U.S. technology. The empirical evidence supports this premise. Between 1960 and 1975, the fraction of U.S. patents granted to foreigners doubled to 35 percent, with Germany and Japan receiving the largest numbers. This trend, of course, has profound implications for the United States. In the future the U.S. economy will be spared some of the burden of creating the vast bulk of the world's new technology. On the other hand, some of the comparative advantage the United States has enjoyed in high-technology innovations will tend to be diminished as well.

Fiscal Policies

The federal government's most significant impact on U.S. industry is probably delivered through its fiscal policies. Its spending decisions greatly influence the level of macroeconomic activity and affect the level of capacity utilization and the economy's rate of growth, while its taxation policies profoundly influence the rate of capital formation. Both aspects of fiscal policy are interesting, but this section will focus on taxation policy. Suffice it to say that the major goals of U.S. spending policy have been the promotion of a stable economic environment, the tempering of business cycles, and the fostering of a high level of aggregate economic activity. These are the goals broadly laid out by the Employment Act of 1946.

At the outset, there are a few generalizations that can be made about U.S. tax policy. The first is that U.S. tax laws have usually been nonspecific in nature, at least in intention. This is consistent with the prevalent U.S. attitude that relying on the market mechanism is the most efficient way to promote economic growth. There have been exceptions, though; railroads, airlines, utilities, and other industries have occasionally been singled out for differential tax treatment. Perhaps more important to understand, however, are the sectoral and regional effects of tax policies initially thought to be neutral and distortion-free.

A second generalization is that U.S. tax policy nonetheless has frequently had IP aims. While many tax policies seem to be formulated without a lot of advanced planning and coordination and seem to be ad hoc responses to specific problems (like inflation), some have consciously tried, for example, to increase the rate of capital formation through structural changes. The institution of faster depreciation guidelines and the investment-tax credit in 1962, known as the Kennedy tax cuts, is one example of such an activity-specific IP. Another is the 1981 supply-side tax cut—also intended to spur investment—that significantly accelerated depreciation write-offs and provided leasing arrangements especially generous to less profitable corporations.

This section first looks at these activity-specific goals of U.S. taxation policy, focusing on its effects on capital formation. Second, the discussion mainly examines the industry-specific effects of these taxation IPs. Both intentional and unintentional effects are explored.

Effects of Taxation Policy on Capital Formation

By far, the most common activity-specific task for taxation policy has been the encouragement of capital formation. There are essentially three aspects of tax policy that are important to understand theoretically and describe in practice in this context. They are: (1) depreciation laws, (2) special investment-tax credits, and (3) the overall tax structure.[7] The main issues in depreciation policy are centered around the speed with which industry is allowed to depreciate its capital assets. The sooner a depreciation allowance can be taken, the higher the present value of the tax deduction. The 1981 tax package instituted the Accelerated Cost Recovery System, which lists four basic categories of assets: three-year, five-year, ten-year, and fifteen-year. This system is very generous by historical standards. Most estimates predict that it will save businesses roughly $10 billion in fiscal year 1982 alone, compared to the previous Accelerated Depreciation Range system.

We should emphasize that the United States has historically used original-cost depreciation. In times of high inflation, this practice can lead to large discrepancies between accumulated depreciation allowances and the cost of replacing capital equipment. This in turn has led to overstating business profits, the consequent overtaxing of such profits, and the possibility of a bias against capital formation. The 1981 tax package, by dramatically shortening most tax lives, was an attempt to provide a one-time offset to this effect.

The investment-tax credit is a provision of the U.S. tax code that allows industries a credit against tax liability for 10 percent of the cost of qualified investment (6 percent for three-year assets). The program currently applies to investment in machinery and equipment but not generally to such capital assets as buildings and structures. Generally speaking, the credit has been used as a nonspecific IP, although in its early years it purposefully discriminated against electric utilities. The value of the credit to industry as measured by the so-called tax expenditure has mushroomed in recent years. In fiscal year 1976, the subsidy amounted to $5.37 billion. By fiscal year 1980, the value of the credit had nearly quadrupled to $19.09 billion.

Theoretically, both accelerated-depreciation allowances and the investment-tax credit are supposed to stimulate capital formation by increasing cash flow and subsidizing the cost of capital purchases. This tends to encourage the substitution of capital for labor, which may be allocatively inefficient. The underlying issue is, of course, whether a bias against capital formation already exists in the tax system that makes an investment-tax credit and accelerated depreciation desirable.

An investigation of IPs should also examine the many facets of a country's general tax structure. In the United States, the corporate-income-tax rate is 46 percent, but other aspects of the tax code—like the tax treatment of dividends, leasing provisions, or the option to expense certain items like research-and-development outlays—are also significant. It is interesting to note that the U.S. tax structure is markedly different from the tax structure of most other advanced countries in one particular respect. Most other countries somehow reduce or avoid the so-called double taxation of dividends, usually by rebating taxes on distributed income or simply by taxing that portion at a lower rate. Most other OECD-type countries also had somewhat shorter tax life guidelines than the United States, that is, until the 1981 changes were instituted.[8]

Brief Review of U.S. Tax Policy. Modern U.S. tax law is based, in many ways, on the Internal Revenue Code of 1954, which, for the first time, authorized the use of accelerated-depreciation techniques. Even so, it is generally agreed that some of the most significant changes in U.S. tax policy were instituted in 1962, when asset-life guidelines were shortened by 30 percent to 40 percent and a 7 percent investment-tax credit became law with the Revenue Act of 1962. The justification for the two new policies, according to Treasury Secretary Dillon (1962), was that depreciation practices based on past-replacement costs did not adequately reflect the rapid rate of economic and technological change and had left U.S. business disadvantaged compared to foreign competitors, who enjoyed more favorable tax treatment. The investment-tax credit was originally intended to be a permanent subsidy for capital expenditures. However, its use for counter-cyclical purposes throughout the late 1960s suggested an official view that while capital formation did sometimes need encouraging, it could basically take care of itself without extra incentives.

In 1971 the Treasury Department implemented the Asset Depreciation Range (ADR) System that provided new useful life guidelines and allowed businesses to shorten their tax lives by up to 20 percent. The Treasury claimed that the ADR system was basically an attempt to compensate industry for obsolescence factors due to technological change, the new pollution requirements, inflation, and for foreign competition. Subsequent tax acts in the 1970s generally extended the provisions of the 1971 act.

The 1981 tax package represented a radical policy shift that was similar in scope, perhaps, to the 1962 policies. Based on supply-side economic theory, these policies were designed to offset the effects of the inflation-historic-cost depreciation bias against investment and lead to a strong net increase in the rate of capital formation. The massive size of the incentives was this tax cut's main distinguishing feature. Unlike most other tax cuts, this one also had a second activity-specific goal. It also sought to increase research and development activity by a 25-percent incremental-tax credit on such expenditures.

Empirical Studies of Tax Impacts on Capital Formation. There is no question that these tax-policy changes have affected the U.S. capital-formation process. Perhaps the question that is most important to address in this regard is whether U.S. tax policy has been biased against saving, investment, and capital formation. Over the past fifteen years, several econometric studies have tried to shed light on this issue. Hall and Jorgenson (1971), for example, estimated that the 1954 tax law that allowed accelerated accounting methods and the 1962 investment tax credit had strong impacts on investment, accounting for 17.5-percent and 28.4-percent increases, respectively, in net investment in manufacturing equipment. Klein and Taubman (1971) criticized Hall and Jorgenson's use of a partial equilibrium model and showed completely different results using a complete macroeconomic model. They claimed that the investment-tax credit and accelerated-depreciation techniques together accounted for only 0.9 percent of net investment in the mid-1960s. Between these two extremes, Bischoff (1971) found that the policies stimulated about 5 percent more investment, while Coen (1971) concluded that the figure was closer to 3.5 percent. Eisner and Lawler (1975) used survey data and confirmed the general findings of the latter three studies—that throughout the 1960s, U.S. government policy did not play a major role in encouraging capital formation.

Studies conducted during the 1970s have produced basically similar results. Grazer (1975) claims that the fact that the ratio of investment to GNP remained roughly steady at 15 percent over the entire period from 1960 to 1975 proves that tax policies have been quite ineffective in stimulating capital formation.[9] Brimmer and Sinai (1976) and Tannenwald and Farb (1975), using the Data Resources, Inc., Model, have come to basically the same conclusion, finding very small positive effects. Only Caton, Eckstein, and Sinai (1977) have found fairly strong impacts, suggesting that investment-tax credits and more generous depreciation guidelines have significantly encouraged capital formation.

Interestingly, virtually all of the works cited (except the last study) have shown that a dollar of the lost Treasury tax revenue due to the standard policies like an increased investment-tax credit or faster depreciation allowances stimulates less than a dollar in new investment. However, Tannenwald and Farb (1975) have found that an 18-percent *incremental* investment-tax credit would give a very large ($2.30) investment payoff per dollar of tax revenue lost. This suggests that not only have U.S. tax policies designed to stimulate capital formation been very inefficient in practice, but that with slightly better planning and policy analysis, markedly better results might have been attained.

These quantitative studies lead to the obvious question of how billions of dollars of effective tax cuts can fail to stimulate capital formation. Inflation is the answer. If, after a period of inflation, the aggregate depreciation allowances for an exhausted capital asset are inadequate to replace it, then clearly true expenses have been understated and a bias has been imparted against investment.[10] Indeed, most programs to liberalize capital cost recovery over the past few decades have either explicitly or implicitly been designed to offset the effects of inflation, and most in turn have had their effects nullified by inflation.[11]

The magnitude of the actual inflation distortion depends on many factors, including the rate of inflation, the inventory-accounting methods used, the durability of capital, and the debt-equity structure of the country's industries. Kopcke and Syron (1978) have concluded that even with the faster write-offs Congress granted business in 1954, 1962, and 1971, corporate depreciation allowances fell at least $15 billion below actual capital consumption expenses in 1977, mainly because of inflation. Feldstein (1978) has suggested that historic cost depreciation caused actual corporate-depreciation deductions to be understated by more than $25 billion in the same year. Of course, as inflation reduces the real value of depreciation, it tends to make business profits exaggerated and therefore overtaxed. Feldstein (1978) says corporations paid 20-percent-higher taxes ($12 billion more) in 1977 than they would have had depreciation expenses been accurately represented.

Some studies examine the extent to which various provisions of the tax code offset the effects of inflation. In a study using present-value analysis, Wittenbach (1973) demonstrated that with reasonable assumptions, the use of accelerated-depreciation methods and the ADR system was sufficient to offset 7.5-percent annual inflation. Parker and Zieha (1976) concluded that with the 10-percent investment-tax credit taken into account, the total tax system was sufficient to offset an inflation rate of approximately 11 or 12 percent. Other analyses in the late 1970s tended to confirm the view that even with the investment-tax credit seen solely as an inflation offset (and not as a tool to encourage investment in a net sense), the U.S. tax system was biased against capital formation with inflation rates above the 6-to-8-percent range.[12]

These kinds of studies suggest that over the late 1970s and 1980, when inflation was running in the 10-to-12-percent range, the U.S. tax system probably was somewhat biased against capital formation (even considering that the deductability of interest expenses mitigated this effect).[13] This was true even though the general policy aim was to provide a slight encouragement to investment. The massive 1981 business tax cuts, however, almost certainly wiped out any such bias, at least temporarily. In fact, the shorter tax life spans for capital goods and generous leasing provisions have been so sweeping that they may entirely wipe out tax liability for many U.S. corporations in the near future. The fact that investment has not yet responded to these provisions is somewhat interesting. It shows that all tax policies must be studied in a macroeconomic context. That is, businesspeople cannot be expected to undertake major capital expansion in the face of chronic excess capacity, even if their capital is outmoded, inefficient, and in need of technological updating. In a sense, this obviously brings into question the basic premise of supply-side economics.

Industry-Specific Effects of U.S. Taxation Policy

Although U.S. tax policies have generally been nonspecific in intention, there have been numerous exceptions. The 1981 tax-cut package, for example, gave special write-off privileges for oil drillers and truckers, worth an estimated $11.8 billion and $356 million, respectively, between 1981 and 1986. One depreciation rule on telecommunications equipment is estimated to be worth up to $14 billion to AT&T alone over the same period. Railroads and airlines have periodically been granted special investment-tax credits whereas public utilities have historically been discriminated against by the credit.

More important in the U.S. context however, are the differential sectoral impacts of policies either (1) designed to assist certain industries although made to appear nonspecific for political purposes, or (2) designed to be truly nonspecific but having unintentional sectoral or regional effects. Many contend, for example, that the $27-billion leasing provision (over the 1981–1986 period) that was part of the 1981 tax package was actually designed to aid the depressed automobile and steel industries and is an example of the first type of policy. These industries have been losing money and therefore have been paying essentially no taxes. Thus, faster depreciation and the investment-tax credit were of limited value to them, even given the carry-back and carry-forward possibilities. Because a refundable investment-tax credit was probably deemed politically unappealing, it is possible that these leasing provisions were actually designed as a way to provide backdoor support for these specific industries.[14]

There are virtually dozens of examples of how tax policies designed to be truly nonspecific or neutral have had sectoral or regional effects. Take the investment-tax credit, for example. Because it applies to capital but not to labor, it tends to favor capital-intensive industries at the expense of those less capital-intensive. Also, since the full 10-percent credit applies only for investment goods in the five-year and longer ACRS categories, it implicitly discriminates against those industries relatively dependent on shorter-lived capital equipment. The investment-tax credit is not neutral in a geographical sense, either. Because it does not extend to most buildings and structures, it encourages firms to stay where they are already located and could, for example, inefficiently impede the movement of some industries from the Northeast to the Sunbelt.

By comparing the ratios of investment-tax credits to total investment undertaken for various sectors and industries, it is possible to observe some of these differential impacts. In 1975, for example, 6.08 percent of all investment in the manufacturing sector was paid for by the government through the investment-tax-credit program. The ratio for the less capital-intensive agriculture, fishing, and forestry sector was less, at 5.28 percent. Within the manufacturing sector there was significant variation among industries, with the ratio ranging from 3.46 percent for primary metals to 7.32 percent for leather and leather products. Also low, at 4.78 percent, was the motor-vehicles-and-equipment industry. Among the highest industries were chemicals and allied products, at 7.21 percent; fabricated metal products, at 7.18 percent; and rubber products, at 6.74 percent.

Impact on Research and Development. Tax policy affects research-and-development spending as well as capital-formation levels. As mentioned, firms in the United States are allowed to expense certain research-and-development costs. This provision led to an estimated tax expenditure of $1.78 billion in fiscal year 1980. In addition, the 1981 tax package contained a novel 25-percent tax credit for incremental research-and-development expenditures: those direct labor-and-equipment outlays in the physical and biological sciences that are above a certain base level (usually the average of the three preceding years). Because of the credit's incremental nature it appears that new, small, high-technology industries and firms will benefit most from this policy. This is because they typically channel a high percentage of sales revenue into research and development and also because they probably have low base levels because of their youth. One semiconductor expert predicts, for example, that the provision will be worth $150 million to $200 million to the semiconductor industry in 1982.[15] This compares with

$600 million in total research-and-development expenditures in 1981. In contrast, General Electric, the large, established electrical producer, has estimated that the credit will encourage it to undertake only about 2 percent more research and development in 1982.

It is difficult to compare research-and-development taxation policies internationally. Most OECD-type countries also allow for the rapid tax write-off of capital investment that is for research-related purposes. Some are seemingly even more generous. West Germany, for instance, allows research-and-development venture companies to depreciate up to three times the value of an initial investment before subjecting business income to the corporate income tax.

Impact on Export Promotion. Tax policy also has international ramifications. It significantly affects U.S. exports and international capital flows, for instance. The Domestic International Sales Corporation (DISC) Program is the most obvious U.S. instrument of tax policy designed to stimulate exports. Established with the Revenue Act of 1971, it offers exporters deferred taxes on 25 percent of export income. The program resulted in a tax expenditure of $1.14 billion in fiscal year 1979 and $1.71 billion in fiscal year 1980.

The relevant question, of course, is how this program compares to programs of other advanced countries. Generally speaking, most similar countries have tax policies that allow for the remission of indirect taxes to stimulate exports. In addition, many allow domestic corporations to establish sales subsidiaries overseas and avoid nearly all taxation on sales channeled through them. As table 6-5 illustrates, most countries also have special tax incentives indirectly benefiting exports, partial or total exemption on foreign-source dividends, direct export-tax incentives, and nonenforcement of intercompany pricing rules. Clearly, the U.S. DISC Program is much less extensive.

There is also substantial criticism that the DISC Program is extremely inefficient in terms of exports promoted per dollar of lost Treasury revenue. Among other critics, Gravelle and Wescott (1978) claim that DISC's benefits mainly accrue to large corporations that have already established themselves in foreign markets and who make use of the provisions to save on taxes without really trying to expand their exports. Administratively, the program is also criticized as being biased against small- to medium-sized firms because of its complex provisions. For these reasons and others the DISC program was scaled down in the mid-1970s and may soon be phased out completely. Its ineffectiveness seems to underscore the confusion and lack of cohesion that surrounds U.S. tax policies designed to stimulate exports.

Table 6-5
Tax Incentives for Exports

	Belgium	France	Germany	Italy	Luxembourg	Netherlands	U.K.	Ireland	Denmark
Partial or total exemption on foreign branch income	X	X	X		X	X			X
Taxation of foreign subsidiaries			X						
Foreign losses deductible	X		X	X	NA	X	X	X	X
Partial or total exemption on foreign source dividends	X	X			X	X			X
Special deferrals of domestic income			X	NA				NA	
Export tax incentives		X				X	X	X	
Non-enforcement of intercompany pricing rules	X	X	X	NA	NA	X	X	NA	NA
Border tax adjustments	X	X	X	X	X	X	X	X	X
Tax incentives indirectly benefiting exports	X	X	X	X	NA	X	X	X	X

U.S. Industrial Policy

	Norway	Sweden	Switzerland	Austria	Portugal	Australia	New Zealand	Japan	Canada	U.S.
Partial or total exemption on foreign branch income	X		X		X	X				
Taxation of foreign subsidiaries									X	X
Foreign losses deductible	NA	X		NA	NA	X	NA	X	X	X
Partial or total exemption on foreign source dividends			X	X	X	X	X	X	X	
Special deferrals of domestic income	X	NA				NA		X		X
Export tax incentives	X	X		X		X	X	X		
Non-enforcement of intercompany pricing rules	NA	X	NA	NA	NA	NA	NA	X		
Border tax adjustments	X			X	X					
Tax incentives indirectly benefiting exports	X	X		X	X		NA		X	

Source: U.S. Congress, Joint Economic Committee. (1978). "Exports' Time for a National Policy." Hearings before the Subcommittee on International Economics, August 30 and September 29.

Role of Government Purchasing Policy

Because of the enormity of the U.S. government, and especially the vastness of its military sector, U.S. procurement policies have great impacts on industry. From an industrial viewpoint, the obvious questions in this regard are: What are the dimensions of this involvement? What impacts do these policies have on the speed and direction of U.S. industrial growth? And perhaps most importantly, what are the sectoral impacts of these policies?

Certain general observations are worth making at the outset. The first concerns the intent of policymakers who have spent billions of dollars and helped create the nation's massive military-industrial complex. For the most part, it is fair to say that these policymakers have not put economic or industrial objectives above security concerns as they have promoted the development of this highly technical sector. Winner industries have been created, but this has resulted primarily from perceived defense exigencies, not from a coordinated economic masterplan.

Another observation deals with the relative lack of U.S. concern over the magnitude and power of the military-industrial complex that government procurement has in large part created. Rather than talk of regulating the sector or perhaps even nationalizing it as Galbraith (1973) has suggested, U.S. policymakers have informally adopted the attitude that what is good for large defense contractors is good for U.S. industry. This illustrates strong U.S. philosophical distaste for public corporations and joint ventures that Europeans have developed and fostered for years. It underscores the strong U.S. ideological dependence on the free-enterprise system, even when the government itself seriously distorts that system.

Dimensions of U.S. Government Procurement

The U.S. government spent more than $67 billion for privately supplied goods and services in fiscal year 1978. The vast bulk of this spending was for military and space-program procurement. Historically, the U.S. government's purchase of goods and material made an awesome leap with the beginning of World War II and its procurement spending has remained high ever since. While much of the government's appetite has traditionally been for defense-related products, it has gradually moved into such fields as space exploration, energy development, interstate highway construction, and railroad operation. Overall, government purchases from the private sector have equaled roughly one-quarter of total government expenditures in recent years.

Generally, federal procurement policy requires U.S. buyers to look at price and quality as the main determinants in awarding procurement contracts. Overall cost efficiencies—*not* industrial objectives—are the main concern. There have been some Buy American policies though, which of course represent exceptions to this rule. Also, procurement is sometimes used to meet social objectives. Various set-aside programs, for example, have tried to ensure that certain portions of business are reserved for small firms, minority firms, women-headed firms, and firms in certain regions. Roughly one-third of government purchases have traditionally been highly technical products and, in these cases, the technological capability of the contractors is an important consideration. The other purchases have been more standard commercial products, with price being the predominant factor.

It is the procurement of the highly technical products that is interesting to examine from an IP perspective. Because the buyer in effect influences both demand for and supply of such products, traditional market economics do not apply. Four differences are notable. First, the government participates closely in the definition and development of many products. In many cases, a product does not even exist until the government spends vast amounts of research-and-development money to come up with a suitable design and perhaps a prototype. Second, much of the seller's risk is effectively underwritten by the buyer (that is, the government). Third, major indivisibilities are present. Having a design chosen and being named primary contractor is a big boon, even for a very large company. Finally, there is a difference that is particularly interesting from an IP viewpoint. It concerns the power of defense-related firms to sometimes conceive of certain products on their own and then create a demand for them through lobbying efforts. While it is hard to assess quantitatively the impact of these factors on U.S. industrial development, a consensus is that they have had a strong positive effect, especially in the development of highly sophisticated technical products.

Effects of Government Purchases on Industry in General

One interesting aspect of government purchases is their effect on the degree of industrial concentration. Given the defense orientation of U.S. government spending where large-weapons systems are involved, it would be expected that such purchases would tend to favor larger firms. The available empirical evidence seems to support this hypothesis. Scherer (1980) has reported that the fifty largest firms on *Fortune's* list of the five hundred largest industrial corporations accounted for 25.8 percent of all 1973 manufacturing sales but 36.5 percent of the dollar value of defense prime contracts. This suggests that government military-related procurement has tended to encourage aggregate concentration. In addition, Scherer has found evidence to suggest that there may be an historical trend toward increasing concentration resulting from government procurement.

There are also indirect impacts of government procurement on industrial development. Firms that develop new concepts and equipment while working on U.S. government contracts, especially in high-technology fields like space, electronics, and communications, could build up a comparative advantage in such knowledge over other firms. Usually, the government's policy is to distribute its orders so that several firms gain such knowledge. Scherer (1980) mentions the example of the jet-airliner industry. Boeing's preeminence in the industry was partially based on its work on the B-47 bomber program, but the U.S. Air Force aided the commercial positions of Lockheed and McDonald-Douglas by forcing Boeing to share some of its B-47 work load with them. The government has not always been successful in promoting competition with its purchasing policies, however. For example, Scherer cites IBM's nurturing by huge SAGE air-defense contracts as a major reason for its dominance in the computer industry today.

There is no question that government procurement money has assisted the development of many technologically advanced products in the United States. The space program, nuclear-energy, and defense programs by their very nature involve sophisticated technologies, and many of these have been directly and indirectly useful in the civilian economy. Satellites for military communications are easily adapted for civilian use, as are military aircraft-guidance systems. The same is true about some of the strong, lightweight materials developed by NASA, which have proven very useful in aircraft-making and in building and construction.

However, it is important to remember the relative argument made previously. Although government expenditures have led to great technological breakthroughs that have been transferred from the military and space sectors to civilian sectors, the benefits to civilian technology might have been greater had the money been channeled directly into such technology. For example, the substitution and crowding-out arguments presented suggested that military and space programs have drawn scientists, engineers, and capital away from civilian-technology development, where their efforts would perhaps have been more economically rewarding. Of course, on the other hand, there are critical mass arguments suggesting that only with massive, concerted, government-backed efforts could certain products or processes (perhaps communications satellites or nuclear fission) have been developed when they were. Unfortunately, it is difficult to draw any strong conclusions about the government's impact in this area.

A related issue is the effect of government procurement on U.S. exports. Because U.S. expenditures have favored technological development in areas like military weapons, aircraft, nuclear energy, and computers, U.S. exports of these kinds of products have certainly been assisted.

Economies of scale, higher levels of investment, and lower average fixed costs have all been promoted by U.S. involvement. Again, it is not clear that the military emphasis of U.S. expenditures has stimulated *relatively* more exports than a more civilian emphasis might have. In fact, the experience of Japan and Germany would tend to refute the notion.

Sectoral Effects of Government Purchases

Government expenditures quite naturally do not fall proportionally across all industrial sectors. In fact, several U.S. industries find their direction, growth, investment decisions, and future productive capacity profoundly influenced by government purchases. Stern (1975) has sought to examine these types of interrelationships using an input-output type analysis, and his results are not surprising. Expectedly, Stern found about 91 percent of the ordnance manufacturing industry output to be either directly or indirectly dependent on government purchases. But among other industries, Stern estimated that 80.3 percent of the aircraft-industry's output, 52.2 percent of the radio-, television-, and communications-industry's output, 42.2 percent of the electronic-component-industry's output, and 41.9 percent of the machine-shop-products industry's output were either directly or indirectly dependent on government purchases. Other industries, like farm machinery and equipment, the leather industry, the outerwear industry, and the textile industry were shown to be virtually isolated from the government-procurement process. About 0.5 percent of the textile-industry's output was due to direct government purchases, according to Stern, for example. Clearly, technologically advanced and sophisticated industries are promoted by the U.S. procurement process. Less technical industries like agriculture and textiles are basically unaffected.

The fact that certain industries and firms are heavily dependent on government purchases is emphasized by looking at leading U.S. defense contractors and their average annual new prime-defense contracts as a percentage of their average annual sales. In the period from 1971 and 1973, the largest recipient of defense contracts was Lockheed Aircraft, and 85 percent of its business was accounted for by the federal goverment. Among other leaders, the numbers were also very high—66 percent for Boeing, 75 percent for General Dynamics, 69 percent for McDonnell-Douglas, and so on. These figures illustrate a strong symbiosis between prime defense contractors and the U.S. government. Implicitly, they demonstrate that although there have been exceptions, U.S. spending policy has tended to favor winner industries and even winner firms; of course, the government has also played a large role in making them winners.

Legal Environment

A country's legal environment exerts a subtle yet powerful force on its industrial base. By laying a foundation of laws on which industry is expected to organize, government in effect determines the design of an economy's industrial structure. Legal environment is interesting from an IP viewpoint because it varies greatly from country to country. It is particularly important in this study because the United States is generally credited with having the stiffest antitrust laws in the world. This section focuses on U.S. antitrust laws and merger laws and their effects on industrial structure, exports, research and development, and the innovation process. In addition, the laws are compared and contrasted to those of other advanced countries to lend some perspective to the analysis.

Perhaps the best way to provide an overview of U.S. antitrust philosophy is to refer to the recent suit the U.S. government brought against the IBM Corporation. For twelve years the government, following its traditional pattern of enforcing the nation's strict antitrust laws, tried to break IBM up into several smaller companies. By 1980, the effort had cost the Antitrust Division of the Justice Department $14 million and IBM a reported $50 million to $100 million in legal-defense fees. Even though the case was recently dropped, it clearly illustrates strong U.S. philosophical belief in the virtues of competition and of strict antitrust enforcement.

Recently, however, new thinking has begun to emerge in the United States that questions the wisdom of such philosophy and suggests that industrial objectives be taken into account. In sharp contrast to traditional thinking, this new view holds that exactly what the U.S. economy needs is more companies like IBM—companies that are progressive, innovative, efficient, and well-managed. This view claims that rather than trying to break such companies up and making them divert time and money from, say, research and development to legal defense, the United States should be encouraging more companies to become like IBM. Whether this new thinking will form the basis for future U.S. policymaking is unclear, but the recent decision to drop the IBM suit appears significant. Certainly, foreign acceptance of a basically noninterventionist-type philosophy has contributed some pressure to change.

Comparison to Foreign-Competition Policies

The U.S. legal-industrial relationship is essentially based on three legal pillars: The Sherman Act of 1890, the Clayton Act of 1914, and the Federal Trade Commission Act of 1914. Together, these laws provide harsh penalties for attempts to fix prices, monopolize, or enter into any contract, combination, or conspiracy in restraint of trade. Enforcement is provided by two governmental legal bodies: the Antitrust Division of the Justice Department and the Federal Trade Commission. To give some idea of the scope of enforcement efforts, these two groups had 1978 budget allotments of $31 million and $29 million, respectively, for antitrust activities.

In order to put U.S. antitrust laws into a broader perspective, it is useful to compare U.S. laws and policies with those of other economically advanced countries. To begin, it is interesting to note that in the early twentieth century, while antitrust laws in the United States were becoming evermore stringent, most European countries had no antitrust laws at all. For the most part, price fixing and cartels flourished. Only after World War II did most other developed countries adopt some type of antitrust legislation. Even today, virtually none are as strict as those of the United States. Most, for example, tolerate price fixing as long as it promotes certain national industrial objectives.

In comparing the antitrust policies of the United States with those in other advanced countries, it is convenient to distinguish between the per se illegality of explicit restraints and the rule-of-reason approach. An extended series of court decisions in the United States has interpreted the Sherman Act as making illegal per se all agreements among competing companies to fix prices, set quotas, restrict output, or lessen in any other manner the force of competition. Under a per se rule, the Justice Department need only demonstrate that certain conduct occurred and was so anticompetitive that it should be prohibited per se. In this case, no detailed inquiry into the economic thinking of the companies involved or into the industrial consequences of the antitrust action takes place. Even today, the United States is the only major nation that takes such a strict approach to antitrust law.

Far more common among the other developed countries of the world is the so-called rule-of-reason approach. Using this approach, foreign courts look at each antitrust case separately to determine if extenuating economic circumstances exist that might justify the anticompetitive action. National industrial objectives often provide such justification. Clearly, such an approach is far different from the per se approach.

A review of other advanced countries' antitrust policies can thus be reduced, according to Scherer (1980), to a discussion of what factors or justifications their courts will take into account in determining whether a certain anticompetitive action has been reasonable or not. In the United Kingdom, for instance, firms charged with an anticompetitive action may convince the Restrictive Practices Court that their action provides more positive benefits than harm by one or more of eight gateways. The gateways include such economic defenses as the following: The action is necessary to negotiate fair prices with a powerful supplier; it is needed to maintain a certain level of export earnings; or the agreement's nullification would have severe and adverse effects on local unemployment. West Germany has also used a rule of reason approach that has allowed exceptions to ease the adjustment problems of declining industries, to promote exports, to reduce costs through joint marketing, research and development, or production arrangements, and to cope with exceptional economic circumstances. By 1973, amendments had exempted most anticompetitive actions that promoted efficiency in small- to medium-sized firms (those with a combined market share no greater than 15 percent).

Even less strict are the antitrust laws of Japan and France. In Japan, for instance, Caves and Uekusa (1976) claim exemptions are so liberal that in 1972 there were 9 authorized depression cartels, 10 rationalization cartels, 175 export cartels, and 604 small-business cartels in operation. They say that usually the Japanese Fair Trade Commission, which has enforcement duties for antitrust matters, works closely with the Ministry of International Trade and Industry (MITI) and does not object to the programs it puts together. French firms are exempted from antitrust laws if they can prove that their actions will promote technological progress or lead to improvements in efficiency. According to Clement (1974), because so little effort has been put into antitrust enforcement, even these exemptions have not been very important. In fact, France at times has actively encouraged corporate mergers, laying anticompetitive considerations wholly aside in attempts to develop certain industries (for example, its computer and steel industries) and favor specific regions. In any case, it is clear that virtually all of the U.S.'s major trading partners take industrial objectives importantly into account in determining antitrust policy, while it does not.

It is also noteworthy that most other advanced countries' merger laws have not had the strong rechanneling effects, from horizontal and vertical mergers to pure conglomeration, that U.S. laws like the Cellar-Kefauver Act have had. Most of their mergers continue to be horizontal in nature. In fact, many foreign governments have promoted mergers as a tool of IP. In the late 1960s for example, the U.K.'s Industrial Reorganization Corporation encouraged and even helped finance mergers it hoped would bolster industries subject to stiff foreign competition. The most notable of these mergers was probably the joining of Britain's two largest domestic automakers. France, as mentioned, has periodically encouraged mergers, too. Also in Japan, after approving a 1969 merger between two of the country's largest steel firms, each with nearly 20 percent of the market, the Fair Trade Commission has not challenged another merger since, despite the fact that nearly one thousand a year have regularly been reported.

It is possible to sum up the attitudes of foreign governments toward mergers by saying that they are generally concerned only with preventing abusive conduct. They have often been willing to promote mergers that they believe would improve their international competitiveness in certain industries. These policies stand in sharp contrast to strict U.S. policies against horizontal and vertical mergers, no matter what the justification.

Other Issues in Antitrust Policy

There are few subtle factors that should be mentioned when trying to appraise U.S. antitrust policies. The large size of the U.S. market is one such factor. As the argument is sometimes made, even if U.S. antitrust laws have prevented a certain degree of concentration in various industries, they have not prevented these industries from realizing efficiencies from the use of very large plants because of the huge U.S. market. Proponents would argue, for example, that even if a firm could not capture the entire national market, a regional U.S. market could easily be larger than most domestic European markets and would allow the firm to enjoy substantial economic efficiencies.

There is also the important question of substitutes to explicit price-fixing arrangements and monopoly power. That is, even though the United States has strong anti-price-fixing and market-dividing laws, do subtle forms of collusion, where the law is more permissive make them only academic? The substitutes would include the standard oligopolistic practices of price leadership, open price reporting, and so forth, and might allow an industry to earn higher profits and, therefore, engage in more research and development. Unfortunately, it is extremely difficult to assess the power of this substitution effect in the United States and virtually impossible to make such comparisons internationally.

A third issue concerns attempts to measure the perceived effects of U.S. strict antitrust policy using an indirect approach. Consider the idea of comparing the effects of switching from the current per se illegality of anticompetitive behavior to a rule-of-reason approach. Many experts, including Scherer (1980), contend that the social gains to be realized from relaxing the antitrust laws on a selective basis to look more at industrial issues, for example, would probably be fairly small. As he claims, economic performance does not seem to have been hurt by sharp price competition. He further states that vigorous competition can induce the kind of production specialization that rationalization might achieve.

Impact of Legal Environment on Other Industrial Factors

Exports. The U.S. legal environment affects other aspects of industry. A very interesting exception to the antitrust laws, especially as far as industrial policy is concerned, involves the promotion of exports. The Webb-

Pomerene Act of 1918 exempts from antitrust, price-fixing, and other limitations, those agreements pertaining solely to export sales. Under the act, U.S. firms are permitted to form and operate associations that restrain export trade or set export prices as long as such actions do not affect the U.S. market. In actual practice, however, the act has not had a very great impact. In 1979, for example, there were only twenty-eight Webb-Pomerene Associations, and they were collectively responsible for only 3 percent of all U.S. exports by value that year.

The act has often been criticized by U.S. businesspeople as being so vaguely worded that it has not been exactly clear what is legal. Strict judicial interpretations have further discouraged the formation of associations. Interestingly, the Carter administration, as part of its reindustrialization program, issued statements clarifying the legal use of the Webb-Pomerene Act. Still, overall U.S. antitrust policy is markedly stricter than most other nations' policies affecting exports. Many countries, like Japan and South Korea, have granted various industries the right to form huge trading companies to conduct marketing operations on a global basis. European countries have tended to favor bidding consortia instead.

Reseach and Development and Technological Advancement. As far as innovation is concerned, Mansfield (1976) presents evidence to suggest that smaller firms may tend to be responsible for a somewhat disproportionate share of new inventions. This is particularly true in such high-technology fields as computers, telecommunications, and electronics—the fields in which the United States is often said to have its best comparative advantage. If U.S. antitrust policy were truly effective, it could possibly encourage innovation. There is yet another aspect to the innovation issue. To the extent that cooperative research effort among competing firms in the same industry is prohibited by U.S. law, innovation may be discouraged. This force becomes stronger the larger, more expensive, and more complex the technological innovation becomes. Some economists argue, for example, that U.S. automakers might have been able to convert to the production of small fuel-efficient cars faster and at a lower overall cost had they been able to cooperate, say, in designing new four-cylinder engines. More cooperation would also, of course, lead to less fear of exploitable externalities, which might further encourage innovation.

International Policies

In many ways, the two main U.S. international IPs—tariff policy and export policy—belong to two different eras. In other ways, they are surprisingly closely linked. Tariff policy was really the first industrial policy the

United States ever had, beginning with the Tariff of 1789. Throughout most of the country's early development policymakers implemented and maintained extremely high protective tariffs. Export policy, in contrast, only became important in the middle of the twentieth century. Major industries that had grown rapidly from the days of the industrial revolution began to mature and, having saturated the domestic market with products, began to seek out others. During this time U.S. policymakers came to realize that tariff policy and export promotion policy were inextricably bound together. The only way the United States could get trading partners to lower their protective tariffs to help U.S. exports was through offering reciprocity. This basic reality has dominated all U.S. international IPs for the past fifty years.

Tariff Policy

Brief Review of U.S. International Policies. In the years immediately following World War II, political and strategic considerations rather than economic concerns really dictated U.S. international economic policy. The United States supported, for example, the creation of such organizations as the European Payments Union (EPU) and the European Coal and Steel Community, even though they liberalized intra-European trade, helped reconstruct European industry, and hurt the U.S. export potential to the region. As the EEC emerged as a formidable economic power in the early 1960s, however, the United States began to feel its protectionist impact and shifted its attention more to economic factors, according the Kreinin (1967). In a way, the Trade Expansion Act of 1962 was a manifestation of this new U.S. concern for its export potential. The principal feature of the act was its grant of executive authority to negotiate hefty reciprocal tariff reductions— up to 50 percent. Clearly, the hope was that foreign markets, and especially the European market for agricultural products, would be opened up for U.S. exporters.

There is a fundamental economic inconsistency between trying to lower world tariffs to encourage specialization and increase trade on the one hand, and trying to protect domestic import-competing industries on the other, however. This problem surfaced in earnest during this period. Tariffs, which had been extremely high throughout most U.S. history, had been reduced through successive bargaining rounds to the point where particular industries (especially highly protected labor-intensive industries) were endangered with displacement if tariffs were reduced further. According to Dobson (1976), U.S. policymakers decided to follow the welfare-improvement argument that the nation as a whole would be better off if the winners could compensate the losers and still be better off. With a few exceptions, they continued to reduce tariffs while at the same time providing aid for industries that suffered as a result of negotiated tariff concessions. This concept, known as trade-adjustment assistance, took official form with the 1962 act. Among other things, the government granted affected firms tax allowances and federal assistance to shift production to new types of output. It also provided for extra unemployment compensation and retraining programs for workers.

The attitude that the U.S. economy had developed, had no real infant industries, and could enjoy relatively more advantages from increased exports than from continued protection prevailed in the late 1960s and 1970s. The Trade Act of 1974, for example, granted the president the authority to negotiate another major round of world-tariff reductions within the GATT framework (the Tokyo Round). To give an idea of the magnitude of the tariff reductions over this general period, the ratio of duties collected to free and dutiable imports fell from an average 7.4 percent in the late 1960s to 3.5 percent in 1979. The Trade Act of 1974 also provided for easier import-injury assistance. Firms seeking assistance no longer had to prove that they suffered *primarily* because of negotiated tariff concessions, but only that they were a factor.

In the late 1970s and early 1980s, protectionist sentiment in the United States began to increase. U.S. frustration over high foreign (and especially Japanese) nontariff barriers, concern about foreign-export dumping, and fear about direct and indirect foreign-export subsidies contributed to this attitude. The competitive decline of such traditionally powerful U.S. industries as steel and automobiles was another factor. It is not clear, however, that the United States really intends to take a more protectionist stance in the 1980s. Perhaps it is fair to say that it is still in the process of defining new rules of the game in the new world of low tariffs.

Some Generalizations. There are a few generalizations about U.S. tariff policy that can be made. The first is that tariff policy has been one of the main avenues through which U.S. policymakers have directly intervened into the market and made decisions that have had industry-specific effects. In contrast to virtually all other U.S. IPs that have been nonselective in intention, different tariff rates for different sectors lead to profoundly different price levels, competition, and excess profit characteristics across industries, with some obviously benefiting more than others.

A second generalization concerns U.S. willingness to protect certain domestic industries that appear to have lost their comparative advantage. While it has generally been U.S. policy to press for lower world tariffs (mainly through the GATT process), the country has been reluctant to write off any industry. In a representative democracy, well-organized single-issue groups have often been able to influence political decisions and there is strong evidence that certain U.S. industrial sectors have been particularly successful in influencing tariff legislation. Industries like the textile industry and the shoe industry have historically received relatively high levels of tariff protection, for example. In a sense, these tariffs could perhaps be considered support-the-loser policies. There have also been the adjustment-assistance programs which, while not particularly well coordinated and planned, have attempted to rechannel productive capability. Clearly, both types of IP run counter to the main U.S. ideological current of laissez-faire capitalism.

Effects of Tariffs on Industry. It is extremely difficult to assess the impact of the U.S. tariff system on industry in general and on specific sectors in particular. While it is theoretically known that a tariff will probably allow an industry to earn extraordinary profits in the short run, there is no strong evidence to suggest that a high tariff will help in the long run. Heavily protected industries are often slow to innovate and adopt new technology and may actually decline because of protection. Vaccara (1960) has shown, for instance, that employment in heavily protected, import-competing industries not only fell significantly over the period 1947 to 1954 but fell more rapidly than employment in import-competing industries that were less heavily protected. Of course, it is not exactly clear which way the cause and effect runs in this case.

Table 6-6 shows the current ad valorem tariff rates for imports into the United States. While the average tariff for all industrial products is 4.2 percent, the rates vary widely illustrating a significant policy role. Aerospace equipment can be imported duty-free, for instance, while textiles and apparels face a 17.5-percent tariff. Other relatively highly protected industries include the leather industry, at 8.5 percent; the hand-tools, cutlery, and tableware industry, at 6.7 percent; and the scientific and controlling-instruments industry, at 6.1 percent. In contrast, paper and wood products, nonferrous metals, and construction, mining, agricultural, and oil-field machinery and equipment can all be imported for a tariff of less than 1 percent.

Complete sectoral analyses of the impacts of tariff policy are beyond the scope of this chapter. However, the specific-industry studies performed as part of this research project generally examine the effects of applicable tariffs.

Export Policy

There are virtually dozens of U.S. government policies that affect U.S. exports in one way or another. Some policies, like direct export promotion

Table 6-6
U.S. Tariff Rates, 1979

	Actual Average Final Tariff
Textiles and apparel	17.5
Lumber and wood products	1.8
Paper and products	0.2
Industrial chemicals and fertilizers	1.6
Drugs, soaps, cleaners, and miscellaneous chemical products	2.3
Paints, gum and wood chemicals, and miscellaneous chemical products	1.6
Rubber and plastics material	4.3
Leather and products	8.5
Stone, clay, and glass products	4.0
Ferrous metals and products	3.4
Nonferrous metals and products	0.9
Hand tools, cutlery, and tableware	6.7
Other fabricated metal products	4.2
Construction, mining, agricultural, and oil field machinery and equipment	0.7
Office and computing equipment	3.0
Machine tools, other metalworking equipment, and other nonelectrical machinery	3.8
Electrical machinery, power boilers, nuclear reactors, and engines and turbines	3.8
Consumer electronic products and household appliances	4.1
Scientific and controlling instruments	6.1
Photographic equipment and supplies	3.6
Communication equipment and non-consumer electronic equipment	5.0
Railroad equipment and miscellaneous transportation equipment	4.0
Aerospace equipment	0.0
Automotive equipment	2.6
Miscellaneous manufactures, toys, musical instruments, furniture, etc.	3.7
All industrial products	4.2

Source: 24th Annual Report of the President of the U.S. on the Trade Agreements Program, 1979.

schemes or special tax incentives try to stimulate exports in a straightforward manner. Others, like the export-financing and insurance programs offered by the U.S. Export-Import Bank (the Eximbank), provide institutional support or offer services that indirectly benefit international sales. Finally, there are policies that may actually hinder the export of U.S. products. Consider, for example, the contracts lost to U.S. industry because of U.S. stands on human rights or the Nuclear Nonproliferation Treaty.

Unfortunately, it is not always easy to classify U.S. policy instruments

U.S. Industrial Policy

by this taxonomy. One reason has been the lack of a consistent, coherent, and planned export policy in the United States. As with other aspects of IP in the United States, there has not been a single U.S. export policy, but rather a series of policies that have affected exports. A principal finding of a Joint Evaluation by the Departments of State and Commerce for the House Committee on Government Operations (1977) was that the United States had no real understanding of the purposes of official export promotion or of the extent of need for such policies. Bergsten (U.S. Congress, Joint Economic Committee 1978*b*) concurred, claiming the United States had ignored exports, both in the private sector and in the U.S. government, mainly because of the traditional focus on the huge domestic market. Current policy signals are mixed as well. While on one hand, the Reagan administration is moving to eliminate government hindrances to exports by relaxing foreign corrupt-practices laws, certain antitrust and banking laws, and tax burdens for U.S. citizens working abroad, it has also moved to slash Eximbank financing.

Direct Promotion of Exports. The U.S. government has a number of programs, mainly in the Departments of State and Commerce, that attempt to directly promote U.S. exports. The Commerce Department has the Trade Opportunities Program (TOP), for example, that attempts to identify export opportunities for U.S. businesspeople. In addition there are the World Traders Data Report, which reveals the credit worthiness of foreign firms; the Foreign Service's periodic market research, which assesses sales potential in various countries for different products; U.S. commercial libraries maintained in certain foreign cities; and various U.S.-sponsored trade fairs and exhibitions where domestic industries can display their products. There are also numerous government publications that explain how to set up export markets, including descriptions of the laws involved, applicable tax incentives, and so forth.[16]

In fiscal year 1976, the U.S. government channeled about $64 million into direct export-promotion programs—approximately $32 million through the Commerce Department, $19 million through the Foreign Agricultural Service, and $14 million through the State Department. To put these numbers into perspective, table 6-8 compares the export-promotion spending in 1976 of most of the economically developed countries.[17] The amount of government spending varied from a high of $2.08 per $1,000 of exports for the United Kingdom, down to a low of $0.12 for Switzerland. The United States, which spent $0.56 per $1,000 of exports, laid out more than Switzerland, West Germany, Canada, and the Netherlands, but less than the United Kingdom, Italy, France, and Japan. In other words, the United States spent the median amount of nine advanced countries, suggesting an average intensity of direct promotion effort.

Table 6-7
Export-Promotion Intensity, Major Industrial Countries

	Total Value, 1976 Exports ($ = U.S. millions)	Government Promotion Spending, 1976* ($ = U.S. millions)	Relative Promotional Intensity (spending per $1,000 of exports)
United Kingdom	$46,042	$95.7	$2.08
Italy	36,170	59.8	1.63
France	56,607	80.7	1.43
Japan	67,710	60.7	.90
United States	114,887	64.4	.56
Netherlands	40,592	18.7	.46
Canada	39,028	14.5	.37
West Germany	103,560	15.5	.15
Switzerland	14,938	1.8	.12

Source: "Export Stimulation Programs in the Major Industrial Countries." A study prepared by the Congressional Research Service for the U.S. Congress, House, Committee on International Relations, October 6, 1978.

Other facts suggest a less-positive U.S. effort. The one-hundredth of 1 percent of the federal budget that the United States allocated to export promotion in 1976 was only about one sixth of the average fraction the other eight countries allocated.[18] Further, official outlays for export promotion fell 14 percent in real terms from 1971 to 1978. Finally, it is noteworthy that the United States is the only major trading nation that does not have a single ministry/cabinet-level agency with authority and responsibility to advance exports. While the Japanese MITI is the most famous example, virtually all other nations have a single ministry that bargains with foreign governments to guarantee market access, coordinate export bidding, investigate international markets, and arrange subsidized financing, shipping, and insurance.

Perhaps the most interesting observation to make about direct promotion efforts in general is the widespread sentiment that such efforts are very inefficient. U.S. exporters claim, for instance, that they get markedly better results by attending private trade fairs and appear willing to pay for them. Also, most large exporters rely mainly on private-sector sources of foreign-business information. In addition, small exporters often charge that big exporters merely substitute government programs for efforts they would undertake anyway. These feelings suggest that extra money spent for direct promotion purposes has only a very marginal effect on exports. Indeed, the fact that the United Kingdom spends almost fourteen times more money to promote the same value of exports as the successful exporter, West Germany, suggests that such efforts are inefficient. Underlying comparative-cost advantages and national specialization and expertise seem to be much more important factors influencing the exportability of products than direct government-promotion policies.

Export Financing. Trade financing has perhaps become the most important form of support a government can offer its exporters. Most advanced countries have developed fairly extensive export-financing programs and, in many cases, the availability of such credit or the degree of loan subsidization has determined export flows. The primary official institution designed to provide financing for U.S. exporters is the Eximbank. The Eximbank's main program is direct lending, although it also handles discount loans, loan guarantees, and insurance. It seeks to supplement private export financing that may not be adequate because of the length of the loan needed (five years or more) or the massive size of the contract. Approximately 20 percent of U.S. manufacturing exports benefited from Eximbank credit-and-insurance programs in 1980—up from less than 10 percent in 1976. Direct long-term credits at near-market rates were offered for an average of 42 percent of the contract value of large capital-equipment exports in 1976. The Eximbank also guarantees up to 80 percent of medium-term loans that private banks make and works with the Foreign Credit Insurance Association (FCIA), a consortium of private insurance companies, to offer export insurance against commercial and political risks.

The Eximbank's total lending authority—the amount of loans, guarantees and insurance that it can have outstanding at any particular time—is set by law at $40 billion. Against this, up to $25 billion in guarantees and insurance may be charged at 25 percent of face value. The bank's direct lending authority grew significantly from fiscal year 1977 to fiscal year 1981 from under $2 billion to $5.9 billion. The Reagan administration, however, slashed this authority to under $4 billion by fiscal year 1982 and plans even bigger cuts over time as part of its budget cutting drive. Any loan proposal over $100 million in value must be submitted for congressional approval: In the past, such approval has been essentially automatic, but there are signs that this may be changing.

From an IP viewpont, it is interesting to study which industries have tended to benefit most from these programs. Since about 1977, it is fair to say that the Eximbank has increasingly aided large U.S. aircraft, telecommunications, and power-generating-equipment manufacturers. Of the total dollar value of the bank's fifteen largest loans in 1980, 44 percent was for aircraft, 31 percent for power-generating equipment, 13 percent for telecommunications equipment, and 9 percent for energy-development projects. Seven of the bank's thirteen biggest loans were to support aircraft sales—mainly for just two companies, Boeing and McDonnell-Douglas.

Westinghouse, Western Electric, Hughes Communications, Combustion Engineering, and Lockheed have been other principal beneficiaries.

One obvious question that emerges is whether such a pattern of support implies a favor-the-winner approach. The answer is probably a qualified yes. In fact, as far as aircraft is concerned, U.S. comparative advantage may be so strong that no subsidized financing is economically justified. On the other hand, in areas like nuclear technology or communications, support is perhaps justified in order to offset attractive packages put together by, say, French and German authorities.

Philosophically, the Eximbank has operated much like a private business. Most of its loans, guarantees, and other services have historically been offered at market-prevailing rates. The United States has historically attempted through negotiations to impose this kind of philosophy on the export credit agencies of other countries and has sought to prevent a world-export-financing war with ever-accelerating subsidy programs. In June 1976, the major industrial countries signed the Unilateral Declarations (a one-year consensus agreement) setting minimum standards to bring official financing closer to market norms. Efforts to restrain international financing competition have recently been more unfruitful. Negotiations to reinforce the Agreement on Guidelines for Officially Supported Export Credits broke down in 1978. Foreign governments simply displayed an unwillingness to go along with U.S. proposals to impose stricter limits on export financing. In response, the United States has recently softened many of its own lending-and-guarantee programs.

It is useful to compare the U.S. Eximbank's programs to those of other advanced economies' banks. A study prepared for the Subcommittee on International Economics of the Joint Economic Committee (1978*b*) found that while the U.S. Eximbank compared favorably with the support programs available to exporters and commercial banks in Canada and Italy, it was not comparable especially in interest rates and degree of credit participation in large transactions, with France, the United Kingdom, West Germany, and Japan. Perhaps the main difference is that, unlike other export credit agencies, the U.S. Eximbank receives no annual appropriations and is legally required to be self-sufficient in its operations. From 1976 to 1977, for example, the bank turned a $137 million net profit that flowed into the U.S. Treasury. This stands in sharp contrast to the $450 million appropriation the United Kingdom's export bank, the ECGD, received for interest rate subsidies over the same period. The United States is also the only major country that legislates an annual budget ceiling on its Eximbank disbursements. Most other countries also offer broader insurance programs. West Germany, France, Italy, and Japan offer insurance against exchange-rate fluctuations; France and the United Kingdom offer inflation-indemnity insurance; and several countries, like Japan and the United Kingdom, offer performance bond insurance to assist in the export of complete manufacturing plants. The U.S. Eximbank offers none of these.

There is one other area in which U.S. Eximbank policy is very different from the policies of other advanced countries. The U.S. bank faces political restrictions and is prohibited from making loans for exports to most Communist nations and to countries accused of violating human rights. Only those Eastern-bloc nations that meet the stringent freedom-of-emigration guidelines laid out in the Jackson—Vanik Amendment to the Trade Act of 1974 are eligible for credit. Also, loans to countries with poor human-rights records are often delayed or canceled by the U.S. Department of State. For example, the Eximbank can only extend credit to South African firms that the secretary of state certifies observe the antidiscrimination practices known as the Sullivan Principles. From 1977 to 1978, Eximbank officially denied or delayed $515 million in export financing on foreign-policy grounds.

Because of these political restrictions, the requirement that the bank be self-sufficient, its limited insurance programs, its legislated budget ceiling, and perhaps most of all, its philosophical aversion to subsidizing a significant portion of its loans (until recently, at least) it seems fair to conclude that the U.S. Eximbank probably has placed U.S. exporters at a competitive disadvantage vis-à-vis their foreign rivals. Administration plans to significantly reduce its lending authority would, of course, accentuate the situation.

The United States has other official export-financing programs. Most are directly concerned with providing credit for agricultural sales. The Department of Agriculture offered about $621 million in credit to foreign purchasers at near-market rates through its Commodity Credit Corporation (CCC) in 1976, for example. It also provided approximately $650 million in low-cost food aid to developing countries in 1976 through the Public Law 480 Title I program.[19] Together these two programs financed about 5.6 percent of U.S. agricultural exports during the year, which was over 1 percent of total U.S. exports. Interestingly, there has been congressional testimony suggesting that reducing the political restrictions on such programs would significantly increase farm exports. By one 1978 estimate, for instance, corn exports would have increased by 53 percent by 1981 if Eastern European economies had been made eligible for CCC financing.[20]

In addition, the United States has attempted to encourage private-sector financing of exports through the Edge Act of 1919. Until very recently, Edge Act corporations played a very minor role in the financing of U.S. exports because a series of regulatory and statutory restrictions had limited their effectiveness. The International Banking Act of 1978 contained a series of amendments to the Edge Act, however, that removed many of these restrictions. Edge corporation financing of exports is expected to increase because of these changes.

Agricultural-Export Policies. In addition to agricultural-export *financing* programs, the U.S. government has other official farm-export policies. Most of these have been developed out of a recognition that agricultural exports account for approximately 20 percent of total U.S. exports annually and are crucial to U.S. balance of payments. Agricultural exports, of course, help the domestic economy too, and are responsibile for 1.2 million farm-sector jobs by one estimate.[21] The Department of Agriculture's main export-promotion functions are performed by its Foreign Agriculture Service (FAS).

Even though U.S. farmers are probably the world's most efficient producers of farm products, they face several major challenges. The first is ever-increasing foreign competition, which is often fueled by strong government support. However, since the United States itself has had many programs, it is difficult to compare such policies. An accurate international index of agricultural subsidization is needed. Another problem is that foreign grain exporters have often been organized into official national cartels or monopolies, at least for marketing purposes. The wheat boards of Canada and Australia, for example, are able to enter into long-term supply arrangements with soft pricing and subsidized financing programs for buyers. Foreign grain boards often receive subsidized transportation, too. In Canada, for example, grains moving to export ports receive advantageous railroad rates, while in Australia, the wheat board charters its own bulk carriers and is thereby able to reduce shipping expenses. Historically, there have been no comparable official U.S. policies although changes are now taking place.

Probably the biggest obstacle to increased U.S. farm exports are tough foreign tariff and nontariff barriers. In general, foreign agricultural protection is considered to be much higher than U.S. protection, mainly because of the prevelant use of nontariff barriers by many foreign governments. Cline (U.S. Congress, Senate 1979) has claimed that if foreigners would cut nontariff barriers on agricultural products by the tariff equivalent of 40 percent, U.S. farm exports would increase by about $500 million a year. To date, U.S. negotiators have had a very difficult time winning such concessions.

The Agricultural Export Trade Expansion Act of 1978 is the most recent U.S. attempt to stimulate farm exports. In addition to expanding CCC credit to ten-year terms for certain purposes, the act also made short-term credit available for agricultural exports to the People's Republic of China for the first time. In addition, it expanded the budget for the FAS and provided that its overseas representation be improved. It seems fair to conclude that the huge successes of U.S. agricultural exports have been due at least in part to these kinds of U.S. policies. Natural comparative advantage has, of course, been the predominant factor.

Other Policies. There are other U.S. policies designed to affect exports. Legal policies like the Webb-Pomerene Act are important but have been discussed elsewhere. The same is true for tax policies like the DISC program. It is worth mentioning, however, that according to a Treasury Department estimate, the DISC program increased U.S. exports by more than $8 billion at a revenue cost of about $1.3 billion in fiscal year 1976. The Treasury also estimated that about 300,000 jobs were associated with those DISC-inspired exports.

Exchange-rate policy is theoretically important; however, in actual practice it has not been terribly significant in the U.S. context. The main reason is that the United States has allowed its currency to float rather cleanly. The dollar steadily depreciated against most major currencies during the 1970s and its could be argued that although the United States did not engineer the decline, it is a policy that aided exports. This is not a very reasonable premise, however, because the depreciation of the dollar has mainly been a response to inflation-rate differentials.

U.S. policies on human rights and other political matters need to be reemphasized. Not only are there political limitations on the lending powers of U.S. export-financing agencies, but many contracts and deals have been directly prohibited by the U.S. government. The United States undoubtedly uses such policies more than any other economically advanced nation. The United States usually forbids the sale of nuclear technology to countries that have not signed the Nuclear Nonproliferation Treaty, especially when bellicose or unstable governments like those in Iraq, Brazil, and Argentina are involved. Foreign competitors, like France and Germany, are usually quick to fill the U.S. vacuum. These policies probably help explain the decline of U.S. nuclear exports from 60 percent of total world export megawatt capacity in 1974 to 14 percent in 1976 and zero percent in 1977.

The United States also opposes deals for strictly political reasons. The Commerce Department has speculated that about $2 billion dollars in exports have probably been lost annually because of such restrictions.[22] Embargoes on the export of grain and high-technology goods to the Soviet Union because of its invasion of Afghanistan and its policies on Poland are but two recent examples. Two U.S. firms, Armco and Alcoa, each lost $300 million-plus already-won contracts with the Soviet Union to French and German firms in late 1980 because of the former embargo, for instance.

Another U.S. export-related policy subsidizes ships built for export-import trade. The subsidies, which can offset up to 50 percent of the total cost of construction, have ranged from $100 million to $275 million in recent years. Foreign governments, like Japan, often subsidize even more, however. The U.S. government also grants certain companies that operate U.S. flag vessels an indefinite tax deferral on their net income that is derived from shipping. The amount of this tax expenditure was $70 million in fiscal year 1980. These programs have not been very successful, however. Shipping rates for U.S. exports are 32 percent higher than they are for U.S. imports and 300 percent higher than the Japanese rates. In a world where products are becoming ever more standardized and international, small differences in shipping rates, as in financing rates, will affect sales much more critically in the future.

Concluding Observations

From the preceding discussion, we can summarize the role of IP in the United States. The first observation, made repeatedly throughout this chapter, is that in terms of intention, coordination, and planning, the United States has actually developed and used very little IP, at least in the European sense of the phrase. U.S. policymakers have consistently expounded the virtues of the laissez-faire doctrine and have hesitated to directly subvert the market mechanism, at least to achieve industrial objectives. Those policies that have been designed to affect industry have generally been nonspecific in terms of *intention,* anyway. Taxation policy, for example, has periodically been used to spur on capital formation, but devices like the investment-tax credit have not usually or consciously been designed to favor certain industries. The same is essentially true about most U.S. export-promotion programs like direct promotion efforts and the DISC program.

There have been exceptions to this philosophical stand against ISPs. The agricultural sector has historically been singled out for special treatment and has been aided through a variety of production-control, demand-management, and technology-enhancement programs. Other ISPs have bordered on being rescue-the-loser policies. Industries like textiles, apparel, and shoes, which have probably lost any historical comparative advantage, have been favored through U.S. tariff policy which has always explicitly discriminated among industries. Since 1962, trade-adjustment-assistance programs have also attempted to aid these same kinds of industries, often with infusions of money for new capital equipment. Recently, there has even been some suggestion that environmental standards be selectively relaxed and that special accelerated depreciation allowances be targeted to aid certain depressed industries like steel and automobiles. The United States has also occasionally resorted to the government bailout. In the past few years there have been three major industrial bailouts (Lockheed, General Dynamics, and Chrysler). Concerns about defense needs and sectoral and regional unemployment seem to have been important general considerations behind most of these U.S. policies.

A second observation is that although positive *intent* to influence or promote industrial development has not generally been present, many U.S. policies have had powerful *unintentional* economy-wide, sectoral, and industry-specific effects. U.S. defense policies for example, have unconsciously created several true winner industries. Government support of research and development, for instance, has heavily favored highly technical defense-related sectors. Roughly 70 percent of all research and development undertaken by the aircraft industry in 1977 was funded by the government. Electrical and communications equipment and instruments have also been heavily supported. The obvious effect of such policy has been the encouragement of technological innovation in these important sectors and the strengthening of their comparative industrial positions in a competitive world economy.

Government-procurement spending has also had a strong high-technology bias and has helped create winner industries as well. Over 80 percent of the aircraft industry's output, over 50 percent of the telecommunications-industry's output, and over 40 percent of the electronic-component and machine-shop-products industries' output have either directly or indirectly been dependent on government purchases. Although such procurement has had mainly military rather than industrial objectives, it has fostered high levels of sectoral investment. It has also promoted exports because of the economies of scale or lower average fixed costs that result from effectively guaranteed government markets. Such policies have sometimes even had apparent firm-specific impacts. IBM's prominence in the computer industry can be traced to its nurturing by huge SAGE air-defense contracts, for example.

A final generalization is that the United States has undertaken many policies for political, legal, social, military, moral, and environmental reasons that have knowingly hurt industrial development. Perhaps more than any other industrialized Western country, the United States has been willing to make industrial sacrifices for perceived noneconomic increases in national welfare. The justification has often been that the nation was wealthy enough to afford such sacrifices. The United States, for example, has embargoed exports of certain products, like nuclear-power plants, to countries unwilling to sign the Nuclear Nonproliferation Treaty. It has also forbidden exports to certain countries for strictly political reasons, like the USSR's invasion of Afghanistan.

The United States has persistently enforced its antitrust laws, which are widely described as the strictest laws of their type in the world. Ignoring virtually all efficiency and industrial considerations, U.S. antitrust enforcers invoked legal, social, and moral justifications as they attempted to break the IBM Corporation up into several smaller companies, for instance. Other examples can be found in the area of functional regulation. The United States has imposed a regulatory burden of $100 billion annually (by some estimates) on U.S. industry to make, among other things, work places safer and the environment cleaner. Investments undertaken for these purposes obviously drain funds from other, more economically (although not necessarily socially) productive uses.

These kinds of noneconomic objectives have led to policies with conflicting impacts on industry. The result has been a series of apparent policy paradoxes. Exports of highly technical products have been encouraged by government research support and Eximbank financing, for example, but have then been banned to certain countries for purely political reasons. IBM's development has been greatly enhanced through U.S. military contracts, but then because of outgrowths of its success, the government attempted to split the company apart. Although some policy contradictions could be expected from any modern government with complex and multidimensional political, social, and economic concerns, the problems seem to be particularly manifest in the United States. The lack of any single authoritative U.S. governmental body to coordinate and plan an industrial strategy as policies are developed in various centers is likely involved with this tendency. This in turn reflects historical U.S. distaste for economic or industrial planning.

Perhaps in the area of these noneconomic IPs U.S. thinking has recently been changing the most. In a nation philosophically dedicated to unfettered capitalism, the natural first step toward a general IP would be the selective lessening of disincentives to growth and development. Following this, more positive IPs might gradually be phased in.

Notes

1. Consider, for example, national efforts to develop a synthetic-fuels industry to reduce dependence on foreign imports.

2. Germany was and remains ideologically different, though. It is basically opposed to public ownership. Throughout most of the postwar period, not even the socialist-oriented German political parties have called for public ownership.

3. This does not deny the fact that industrial production may have increased significantly because of these types of government projects. It is intent, though, that is being analyzed.

4. For a brief description of these programs, see Rachel McCulloch (1978).

5. For a good survey of such studies, see Mansfield (1976), pp. 95–99.

6. The basic idea is that because, say, NASA has bid the salaries of scientists up so high, research and development has become so expensive that less of it is done.

7. For a background discussion, see Gravelle and Wescott (1978).

8. See, for example, the Deloitte Haskins and Sells' "International Tax and Business Service" tax surveys of West Germany, Japan, the United Kingdom, Canada, and France.

9. Of course, this argument is simplistic because it ignores the impact of inflation or any other underlying time trend.

10. This theoretical argument assumes no demand, relative price, or technological changes.

11. As always, it is difficult to interpret Congress's actual intent. Both reasons—to spur investment and to offset inflation—are usually mentioned in justifying such tax cuts.

12. See, for example, William D. Nordhaus (1974), pp. 169-208.

13. For a good discussion of the impact of inflation on business profits, see Tideman and Tucker (1976), pp. 36-80.

14. In practice, however, it is beginning to appear as though more profitable industries, the leasors, are also capturing large benefits from the plan.

15. See *Industry Week,* September 21, 1981, p. 34.

16. See, for example, the U.S. State Department (1978).

17. Government export promotion spending includes expenditures and subsidies to encourage exports and outlays through foreign ministries to gather export intelligence. It does not include foreign-economic, military, or food assistance nor official export-financing programs.

18. See U.S. Congress, Senate (1979), p. 10.

19. Historically, P.L. 480 has played a much bigger role. In the mid-1950s, over one-third of *all* U.S. agricultural exports were financed by P.L.480. By 1973, it financed only 13 percent of all agricultural exports. From 1954-1970, the program cost $26.5 billion.

20. See U.S. Congress, Senate (1978), pp. 24-25.

21. See U.S. Congress, Senate (1978), p. 14.

22. See Cook (1978).

References

Bilson, John. "The 'Vicious Circle' Hypothesis." *International Monetary Fund Staff Papers* 26, No. 1 (March 1979):1-37.

Bischoff, Charles. "The Effect of Alternative Lag Distributions," in G. Fromm, ed., *Tax Incentives and Capital Spending.* Washington, D.C.: Brookings Institution, 1971.

Bishop, C. *A History of American Manufactures, Vol. 1,* Philadelphia, 1868.

Brimmer, Andres, and Allen Sinai. "The Effects of Tax Policy on Capital

Formation, Corporate Liquidity, and the Availability of Investible Funds." *Journal of Finance* 31, No. 2 (May 1976):287-308.

Brooks, Harvey. "Have the Circumstances that Placed the U.S. in the Lead in Science and Technology Changed?" in D.W. Ewing, ed., *Science Policy and Business.* Cambridge, Mass.: Harvard University Press, 1973. pp. 14-15.

Capron, William, ed. *Technological Change in Regulated Industries.* Washington, D.C.: Brookings Institution, 1971.

Caton, Christopher, Otto Eckstein, and Allen Sinai. "Tax Reform Studies." The Data Resources Review of the U.S. Economy, August 1977.

Caves, Richard and Masu Uekusa. *Industrial Organization in Japan.* Washington, D.C.: Brookings Institution, 1976.

Center for Policy Alternatives. *National Support for Science and Technology: An Evaluation of Foreign Experiences.* Cambridge, Mass.: MIT University Press, 1976.

Clement B. "An Appraisal of French Antitrust Policy. *Antitrust Bulletin* 19, No. 3 (Fall 1974):587-603.

Coen, Robert. "The Effects of Cash Flow on the Speed of Adjustment," in G. Fromm, ed., *Tax Incentives and Capital Spending.* Washington, D.C.: Brookings Institution, 1971.

Cook, D. "How Carter's Nuclear Policy Backfired Abroad." *Fortune* 98 (October 23, 1978):124-126.

Deloitt, Haskins, and Sells'. "International Tax and Business Service," tax surveys of West Germany, Japan, United Kingdom, Canada, and France. Various years.

Denison, Edward. "Effects of Selected Changes in the Institutional Human Environment Upon Output Per Unit of Input." *Survey of Current Business* 58, No. 1 (January 1978):21-44.

Dobson, John. *Two Centuries of Tariffs.* Washington, D.C.: U.S. International Trade Commission, December 1976.

Eisner, Robert, and Patrick Lawler. "Tax Policy and Investment: An Analysis of Survey Responses." *American Economic Review* 65, No. 1, (March 1975):206-212.

Ezekiel, Mordecai. "Statement to the U.S. Senate Temporary National Economic Committee," included in T.N.E.C. (1941), pp. 417-428.

Feldstein, Martin. "The Impact of Inflation on Capital Formation." Testimony given to the U.S. Congress Joint Economic Committee, July, 1978.

Friedlander, Ann. "The Social Costs of Regulating the Railroads." *American Economic Review* 61, No. 2 (May 1971):226-234.

Galbraith, John K. *Economics and the Public Purpose.* Boston: Houghton Mifflin, 1973.

Gravelle, Jane, and Robert Wescott. "Tax Provisions Affecting Business

Investment." A Congressional Research Service Study. Washington, D.C.: Library of Congress, 1978.
Grazer, Harvey. "Encouraging Capital Formation Through the Tax Code." Seminar before the Task Force on Tax Policy, U.S. Congress Senate Committee on the Budget, September 18-19, 1975.
Griliches, Z. "Returns to Research and Development in the Private Sector." Unpublished, 1975.
Hall, Robert, and Dale Jorgenson. "Application of the Theory of Optimal Capital Accumulation," in G. Fromm, ed., *Tax Incentive and Capital Spending.* Washington, D.C.: Brookings Institution, 1971.
Hamberg, D. "Invention in the Industrial Research Laboratory." *Journal of Political Economy* 71, No. 2 (April 1963):95-115.
Hamilton, Alexander. *Report on Manufactures.* Report of the Secretary of the Treasury to the U.S. Congress, reprinted in part in Ratner (1972), 1791.
Himmelberg, Robert. *The Origins of the National Recovery Administration.* New York: Fordham University Press, 1976.
Industry Week, September 21, 1981, p. 34.
Jewkes, J., D. Sawers, and R. Stillerman. *The Sources of Innovation.* Revd. ed.. New York.: W.W. Norton, 1970.
Klein, Lawrence, and Paul Taubman. "Estimating Effects Within a Complete Econometric Model," in G. Fromm, ed., *Tax Incentives and Capital Spending.* Washington, D.C.: Brookings Institution, 1971.
Kopcke, Richard, and Richard Syron. "Tax Incentives: Their Impact on the Economy and Their Cost to the Treasury." *New England Economic Review* (January/February) pp. 19-32.
Kreinin, Mordechai. *Alternative Commercial Policies: Their Effect on the American Economy.* East Lansing, Mich.: Michigan State Press, 1967.
MacAvoy, Paul. *The Regulated Industries and the Economy.* New York: W.W. Norton, 1979.
McCulloch, Rachel. *Research and Development as a Determinant of U.S. International Competitiveness.* Washington, D.C.: National Planning Association, October 1978.
McKie, James. "Government Intervention in the Economy of the U.S.," in Peter Maunder, ed., *Government Intervention in the Developed Economy.* London: Croom, Helm, 1979.
Mansfield, Edwin. *Industrial Research and Technological Change.* New Haven: Cowles Foundation for Research in Economics, Yale University, 1968.
———. "Federal Support of R and D Activities in the Private Sector," in *Priorities and Efficiency in Federal Research and Development.* A Compendium of Papers submitted to the Joint Economic Committee of the U.S. Congress, October 29, 1976, pp. 85-115.
Martin, Roscoe, ed. *TVA: The First Twenty Years, A Staff Report.* Knox-

ville: University of Tennessee Press, 1956.

Nordhaus, William D. "The Falling Share of Profits," in *The Brookings Papers on Ecoomic Activity, 1974:1.* Washington, D.C.: The Brookings Institution, 1974.

OECD. *United States Industrial Policies.* Observations presented by the U.S. Delegation. Paris, 1970.

Parker, James, and Eugene Zieha. "Inflation, Income Taxes and the Incentive for Capital Investment." *National Tax Journal* 29, No. 2 (June 1976):179-189.

Pavitt, Keith. "International Technology and the U.S. Economy: Is There a Problem? in *The Effect of International Technology Transfers on the U.S. Economy.* Washington, D.C.: National Science Board, July 1974.

Peck, M. "Infusion of Technology and the Mysteries of the Catch-Up." Unpublished, 1974.

Peltzman, S. "An Evaluation of Consumer Protection Legislation: The 1962 Drug Amendments." *Journal of Political Economy* 81, No. 5 (September 1973):1049-1091.

Phillips, Almarin, ed. *Promoting Competition in Regulated Markets.* Washington, D.C.: Brookings Institution, 1975.

Pinder, John, Takashi Hosomi, and William Diebold. *Industrial Policy and the International Economy.* New York: The Trilateral Commission, 1979.

Pryor, Frederick. "Public Ownership: Some Quantitative Dimensions," in W.G. Shepard, ed., *Public Enterprise: Economic Analysis of Theory and Practice.* Lexington, Mass.: D.C. Heath and Company, 1974.

Ratner, Sidney. *The Tariff in American History.* New York: Van Nostrand, 1972.

Scherer, F.M. *Industrial Market Structure and Economic Performance.* 2d ed. Chicago: Rand McNally, 1980.

Stern, Irving. "Industry Effects of Government Expenditures: An Input-Output Analysis." *Survey of Current Business* 55, No. 5 (May 1975): 9-23.

Tannenwald, Robert, and Warren Farb. "Comparative Cost-Effectiveness of Alternative Investment Tax Incentives." A Congressional Research Service Study. Washington, D.C.: Library of Congress, 1975.

Temporary National Economic Committee. *Final Report to the Executive Secretary.* Washington, D.C.: Government Printing Office, 1941.

Tideman, T. Nicolas, And Donald P. Tucker. "The Tax Treatment of Business Profits Under Inflationary Conditions," in Henry J. Aaron, ed., *Inflation and the Income Tax.* Washington, D.C.: Brookings Institution, 1976.

U.S. Congress, House, Committee on Government Operations. "Effectiveness of the Export Promotion Policies and Programs of the Departments of Commerce and State." August 5, 1977.

U.S. Congress, House, Committee on International Relations. "Export Stimulation Programs in the Major Industrial Countries: The U.S. and Eight Major Competitors." A study prepared by the Congressional Research Service. Washington, D.C.: Library of Congress, 1978.

U.S. Congress, House, Joint Economic Committee. "The Cost of Government Regulation." Hearings before the Subcommittee on Economic Growth and Stabilization, April 11 and 13, 1978*a*.

———. (1978*b*), "Exports: Time for a National Policy," Hearings before the Subcommittee on International Economics, Aug. 30 and Sept. 29.

U.S. Congress, House, Senate, Special Committee on U.S. Exports. Part 5 of Export Policy hearings. Washington, D.C.: Government Printing Office, 1978.

U.S. Congress, House, Senate, Committee on Banking, Housing, and Urban Affairs. "U.S. Export Policy." A Report by the Subcommittee on International Finance, February 1979.

U.S. Department of Treasury. Statement by Secretary Dillon, July 11, 1962, on new depreciation rules. Reproduced in the 1962 Annual Report of the Secretary of the Treasury, 1962.

U.S. President. *Twenty-Fourth Annual Report of the President on the Trade Agreements Program,* 1979.

U.S. State Department. "Government and Business: Joint Venture in International Trade." A State Department Monograph. Washington, D.C., 1978.

Vaccara, Beatrice. *Employment and Output in Protected Manufacturing Industries.* Washington, D.C.: Brookings Institution, 1960.

Vernon, Raymond, ed. *Big Business and the State.* Cambridge, Mass.: Harvard University Press, 1974.

Weidenbaum, Murray. *Business, Government, and the Public.* Englewood Cliffs, N.J.: Prentice-Hall, 1978.

Wilcox, Clair, and William Shepherd. *Public Policies Toward Business.* Homewood, Ill.: Richard D. Irwin, 1975.

Wittenbach, James. "Using Present Value Analysis to Explain Inflation Offset Provided by Accelerated Depreciation." *Taxes* 51(October 1973):610–612.

7
Developing-Country Perspective on Industrial Policy

Jere R. Behrman

As a group the developing countries have more experience recently with IPs than do most developed countries. The apparent (and often stated) reasons for the greater use of IPs in the developing countries include perceptions that the developing economies and their economic objectives tend to differ from the developed countries in a number of specific respects. Increasing returns to scale and externalities are more important because of the generally smaller sizes of domestic markets and less-adequate infrastructure. Domestic markets are more fragmented. Private industrial entrepreneurs are less available. Asymmetries in power dealing with large multinational corporations and with trading partners are greater. Development is a more important objective and requires structural changes and quantum leaps, not marginal adjustments. National control over the economic destiny is a more important objective, particularly in light of colonial and neoimperial experiences and the possible spread of underdevelopment in the Gunder-Frank (1966) sense. Income-distribution objectives, both domestic and international, are more important. Basic industries essential for development or symbolic of development are more lacking. There is greater need to impress international organizations and funding agencies with the seriousness of economic interests, and adoption of IPs is one way to do so. Of course, these and other claims have figured predominantly in more general debates about policy strategies in developing nations concerning, for example, specific versus more general policies, inward versus outward orientations, price versus nonprice interventions, nonmarket versus market policies (for example, Meier 1976).

To the extent that such characteristics distinguish developing from developed countries, the experience of developing economies with IPs is not necessarily insightful for developed economies. However, the rapid growth of some developing countries in the past two decades, accompanied by even more rapid sustained growth rates in manufactures and in exports, raises the question of whether the policies of these countries might not offer useful insights for those in the developed countries who are concerned with the relative economic stagnation therein.

Either on a cross-country or historical comparative basis, recent performance of some of the developing countries has been impressive. Table 7–1 summarizes the overall growth and manufacturing and export experience of the high-growth developing countries in 1960–1978 (with an average annual per-capita real growth rate of 4.0 percent or higher used as the criterion for high growth). For comparison, the same statistics are also given for the high-growth industrialized countries and means for five country groups: thirty-eight low-income countries, fifty-two middle-income countries, eighteen industrialized countries, five capital-surplus oil exporters, and twelve centrally planned countries (all by the World Bank, 1980, definitions).

The high-growth developing countries in these two decades (with average annual per-capita GNP growth rates for 1960-1978 in parentheses) were: Singapore (7.4 percent), the Republic of Korea (6.9 percent), Taiwan (6.6 percent), Hong Kong (6.5 percent), Greece (6.0 percent), Portugal and Lesotho (5.9 percent), Yugoslavia (5.4 percent), Togo and Spain (5.0 percent), Brazil (4.9 percent), Tunisia (4.8 percent), Thailand (4.6 percent), Ecuador (4.3 percent), Israel (4.2 percent), Indonesia (4.1 percent), and Turkey (4.0 percent). At the top are the four Asian super exporters, followed by a number of Mediterranean and Southern European countries, two sub-Saharan African countries (Lesotho and Togo), Brazil, Thailand, and two new oil exporters (Ecuador and Indonesia).[1] These are high sustained rates in comparison to 2.4 percent for the United States and 3.7 percent for all sixteen of the industrialized countries (although Japan's 7.6 percent is even higher).

For these high-growth developing countries, manufacturing, exports, and the share of manufacturers in exports almost without exception have grown even more rapidly than gross domestic product (GDP).[2] We note a few of the most prominent cases. The percentage shares of manufacturing in GDP grew between 1960 and 1978 from 12 to 26 percent in Singapore, 12 to 24 percent in Korea, and 22 to 38 percent in Taiwan. Between the same two years exports as a percentage of GDP increased from 3 to 34 percent in Korea, 11 to 59 percent in Taiwan, 14 to 44 percent in Israel, 79 to 98 percent in Hong Kong, 9 to 17 percent in Greece, and 10 to 16 percent in Spain. Between 1960 and 1977, the percentage shares of merchandise exports accounted for by manufacturers rose from 14 to 85 percent for Korea, 10 to 60 percent for Greece, 27 to 71 percent for Spain, 37 to 69 percent for Yugoslavia, 3 to 26 percent for Brazil, 3 to 25 percent for Turkey, 2 to 19 percent for Thailand, and 26 to 44 percent for Singapore. Such rapid expansions in manufacturing, merchandise exports, and manufactured exports are striking in comparison with the experience of most of the industrialized countries and particularly with that of the United States (see table 7-1). The question naturally arises to what extent the greater general use of IPs in the developing countries is associated with these apparent recent growth-and-structural-transformation successes in many oil-importing developing countries.

In pursuit of at least a partial answer to this question, this chapter surveys the experience of the developing countries with IPs. The first section considers conditions under which IPs might be desirable in developing countries. The second section reviews the implications for IPs of several im-

Table 7-1
Growth and Structural Change in GNP, Manufacturing, and Exports in High-Growth Developing Countries and Industrialized Countries, 1960–1978

Country Groups and Countries	GNP per Capita		Growth in Manufacturing (Average Annual Percent Growth Rate)		Manufacturing as Percent of GDP		Growth in Exports (Average Annual Percent Growth Rate)		Percentage Share of Exports				Exports as Percent of GDP	
									Manufactures		Textiles and Clothing			
	Dollars 1978	Average Annual Percent Growth 1960–1978	1960–1970	1970–1978	1960	1978	1960–1970	1970–1978	1960	1977	1960	1977	1960	1978
	(1)	(2)	(3)	(4)	(5)	(6)	(7)	(8)	(9)	(10)	(11)	(12)	(13)	(14)
Developing Countries														
Thirty-eight low-income countries	200	1.6	6.6[a]	4.2[a]	11	13	5.0[a]	−0.8[a]	17	19	12	7	10	12
Lesotho	280	5.9	na	8.7[b]	na	2[c]	na	na	na	na	na	na	12	22[c]
Togo	320	5.0	na	na	8	9	10.5	0.3	4	6	0	3	19	34
Indonesia	360	4.1	3.3	12.4	8	9	3.5	7.2	0	2	0	0	13	21
Fifty-two middle-income countries	1,250	3.7	7.6[a]	6.8[a]	22	25	5.5[a]	5.2[a]	14	37	4	10	15	21
Thailand	490	4.6	11.0	11.5	17[d]	20[c]	5.2	12.2	2	19	0	8	17	21
Equador	880	4.3	na	10.0	14	17	3.7	9.5	1	2	0	1	17[d]	24
Tunisia	950	4.8	7.6	11.0	8[a]	12	4.1	21.1	10	34	1	19	20[d]	31
Korea (Republic of)	1,160	6.9	17.2	18.3	12	24	35.2	28.8	14	85	8	32	3	34

Table 7–1 continued

Country Groups and Countries	GNP per Capita		Growth in Manufacturing (Average Annual Percent Growth Rate)		Manufacturing as Percent of GDP		Growth in Exports (Average Annual Percent Growth Rate)		Percentage Share of Exports				Exports as Percent of GDP	
	Dollars 1978	Average Annual Percent Growth 1960–1978	1960–1970	1970–1978	1960	1978	1960–1970	1970–1978	Manufactures		Textiles and Clothing			
									1960	1977	1960	1977	1960	1978
	(1)	(2)	(3)	(4)	(5)	(6)	(7)	(8)	(9)	(10)	(11)	(12)	(13)	(14)
Turkey	1,200	4.0	10.9	8.7	13	18	1.6	2.5	3	25	0	18	3	6
Taiwan	1,400	6.6	17.3	13.2	22	38	23.7	9.3	na	49	na	23	11	59
Brazil	1,370	4.9	na	9.5	26	28	5.0	6.0	3	26	0	4	5	7
Portugal	1,990	5.9	8.9	4.6	29	36	9.6	-5.9	55	70	18	26	17	20
Yugoslavia	2,380	5.4	5.7	9.3[b]	36	na	7.8	4.8	37	69	4	8	14	17[c]
Hong Kong	3,040	6.5	na	5.6[b]	25	25[c]	12.7	4.8	80	96	45	46	79	98
Greece	3,250	6.0	10.2	6.6	16	19	10.7	13.1	10	60	1	18	9	17
Singapore	3,290	7.4	13.0	9.2	12	26	4.2	9.8	26	44	5	5	163	164
Spain	3,470	5.0	9.7	7.8	27	30[c]	11.6	11.0	22	71	7	6	10	16
Israel	3,500	4.2	na	6.1	23	26[c]	10.9	10.6	61	80	8	7	14	44

Developing-Country Perspective on IP

Eighteen industrialized countries	8,070	3.7	6.2[a]	3.3[a]	30	27	8.7[a]	5.7[a]	66	76	7	5	12	18
Finland	6,820	4.1	6.2	2.8	24	25	6.7	3.0	47	74	1	6	23	31
Austria	7,030	4.2	4.8	3.6	38	29	9.6	6.8	52	84	10	10	24	35
Japan	7,280	7.6	11.0	6.2	34	29	17.5	9.7	79	97	28	5	11	11
France	8,260	4.0	6.6	3.9	29	27	8.3	7.3	73	77	10	6	15	21
Belgium	9,090	4.1	6.2	3.3	30	26	10.8	5.7	76	77	12	8	33	51
Norway	9,510	4.0	5.3	1.9	21	17	9.1	6.3	44	53	2	1	41	42
United States	9,590	2.4	5.3	2.9	29	24	6.0	6.5	63	70	3	2	5	8
Five capital surplus oil exporters	3,340	7.1	na	16.1[a]	na	8	9.5[a]	−1.2[a]	1	1	0	0	na	48
Twelve centrally planned economies	1,190	4.0	na	na	na	na	na	na	na	60	na	4	na	na

Source: Calculated from World Bank (1980, Tables 1, 2, 5, 8, 9). Low-income developing countries have GNP per capita in 1978 of 360 U.S. $ or less. High-Growth is defined to be an average annual per capita increase in real GNP of 4.0 percent or more in 1960–1978. The countries are listed within the major country groups in order of increasing 1978 GNPs per capita.

[a] Median.
[b] 1970–1978.
[c] 1977.
[d] 1961.

portant recent studies in foreign sector policies in the developing countries. The third section considers the developing country experience with state enterprises.

Bases for Industrial Policy in Developing Countries

This section elaborates on the reasons why IPs might be better for developing than developed economies.[3]

A consideration of such reasons implicitly, if not explicitly, begins with a *social-welfare function*. This is defined generally over the dynamic growth paths of income and its distribution over time, as well as other goals.

Many international organizations (for example, the World Bank) and development specialists seem to suggest that the widespread existence of absolute poverty and relatively great distributional inequality in the developing world means that the developing countries should place much more relative weight on distributional concerns that do more developed nations. Although some developing countries (for example, Sri Lanka, Taiwan, Tanzania) may agree, it is not clear that this value judgment is generally shared. In fact, as previously noted, some observers claim instead that the developing countries should weight relatively heavily long-run development as such because of their relatively low overall incomes.

Among the other goals might be the development and/or national ownership of particular industries (that is, the commanding heights of the economy in Choksi's, 1979, terminology), a degree of national economic independence (particularly in immediate postindependence eras), and the exportation of systems of beliefs or of institutions. For these examples, most developing countries probably tend to place greater relative weight on the first two and less on the third than do many developed countries. Such differentials are largely reflections of differential current and historical positions in the international distributions of political and economic power. There is nothing wrong with such objectives, assuming that the welfare function is appropriately defined.[4] For efficiency in pursuing overall social welfare, however, it is desirable to know what the trade-offs are among such goals as well as the traditional income and distribution goals and to assure that the marginal trade-offs are commensurate with the marginal relative benefits.

Given welfare functions that probably differ somewhat between developing countries and more developed countries (or, equivalently, in which the weights for different arguments are partially related to the level of development), the reasons for instituting IPs may also differ. Before turning to specific possible reasons, it is useful to mention briefly the argument of *the second best* and Corden's (1974) related notion of a *policy hierarchy* referred to in chapter 3. Such a discussion is useful because it can add insight into whether or not IPs (or more or less specific forms thereof) are likely to make sense because of a particular situation common to many developing countries.

The basic Corden policy hierarchy notion is as follows. If a distortion exists in the economy, a first-best package of corrective policies removes the distortion in the marginal incentives directly at the source, which minimizes negative by-product distortions. However, first-best policies such as lump-sum transfers may not be possible, so alternatives must be considered. Generally, there is a hierarchy of policies: first best, second best, and nth best. As one moves down this hierarchy, additional welfare-costing by-product distortions are introduced.[5]

To illustrate, Corden discusses the policy hierarchy if the marginal private cost of labor to the manufacturing sector in a developing country exceeds the social cost of this labor, a phenomenon considered common due to minimum wages, union power, and a Lewis (1954) "unlimited supply of labor" from the traditional sector proportional to the average (not the marginal) income level therein. Corden's hierarchy of corrective policies is given in figure 3–5 in chapter 3. First-best policy is the sector-specific policy (SSP) of subsidizing labor in manufacturing (or equivalently, taxing labor in nonmanufacturing) which has no by-product distortion. Second-best policy is the SSP of subsidizing manufacturing production, but this has the by-product distortion of encouraging too much use of the nonlabor factors (for example, scarce capital and foreign exchange). Third-best policy is the SSP of imposing a tariff on manufactured imports in combination with an export subsidy at the identical rate on manufactured exports, but this has the by-product distortion of encouraging too much use of nonlabor factors in manufacturing and an additional by-product consumption distortion. Fourth-best policy is the SSP imposition of a tariff on manufactured exports alone, which has the added by-product distortion of a home-market bias for manufactured products. Still lower in this policy hierarchy are ISPs, and project-specific (PSPs) or firm-specific (FSPs) policies.

The basic point is that IPs, at least the more specific versions, might be used to attempt to address myriad problems in efforts to improve social welfare in developing countries. But in many cases they are fairly low on the policy hierarchies with many by-product distortions and probably are dominated by policies that are higher in the hierarchies. Nevertheless, there may be some situations in which IPs may be fairly high in policy hierarchies in the developing countries and therefore be desirable.

We now turn to the specific reasons why IPs might be more appropriate for developing than for developed countries. Subsequently, we shall discuss some of the important assumptions that underlie this discussion.

1. *Externalities* may be broadly defined as effects of an industry's activities on the preference or production functions of others that are not transmitted through the product and factor prices of the industry and thus are not considered in the profit-maximizing decision of firms in the industry.[6,7] These may be positive or negative, and short- or long-run in dura-

tion. If such externalities are tied with the overall activity of an industry, the case is strong for specific IPs. The first-best policy in such a case would be internalize such externalities by adjusting prices to reflect the full social costs and benefits.

Externalities often emphasized include the production of pollution and of congestion. Pollution and congestion reduction, however, seem to be income-elastic or luxury goods of much more relevance in the objective functions of more developed countries than in those for the developing countries. Therefore the bases for IPs to control pollution and congestion is likely to be less strong in developing countries than in more developed countries.

Nevertheless, the development literature emphasizes the importance of positive externalities. However, well-based illustrations of those that seem to warrant IPs are not common.

For example, a frequently cited supposed exernality in developing countries is the training of workers on the job, whether by specific programs or by learning by doing. But it is not clear that such training necessarily involves an externality at all, and it is even less certain that it involves an externality that calls for IPs of a specific nature. Clearly no externality is involved if the training is specific to the firm. If the training is general and if capital markets were perfect and wages were flexible, no externality would be involved since workers could borrow on the capital market for current consumption and finance their training to the optimal level by accepting lower wages and then reap the returns from this investment in the form of subsequent higher wages (from the training firm or from other employers). Given real-world imperfections in the relevant-factor markets, such worker-financed human-capital investment is likely to be suboptimal. In developing countries there may be more possibilities for general training than in developed countries because workers all tend to be less schooled and less accustomed to time constraints and so forth necessary for many modern production techniques.

But higher than IPs in the policy hierarchy are likely to be improvements in factor markets or SSPs such as subsidizing labor in manufacturing or the other examples given earlier. IPs are likely to be high in the policy hierarchy only if particular industries have an unusual amount of *general* on-the-job training and factor markets are imperfect. While such cases are conceptually possible, important examples of such industries in the developing world are not obvious.

2. *Increasing returns to scale,* which are large relative to market size, may call for specific IPs to ensure pricing equal to marginal social-resource costs. Important examples of increasing returns to scale may be found in many infrastructure activities (for example, transportation, communications, and irrigation systems), research activities, and public goods like

defense.⁸ In such cases average-cost curves may be above the marginal-cost curves over the whole relevant range and production may not be tradeable, so marginal cost pricing is possible only with subsidies to cover differences between average and marginal costs. The resulting more-efficient resource allocation has benefits in the form of increased user (consumer or producer) surplus due to the lower price than otherwise would be charged (sometimes referred to as pecuniary externalities). The relative importance of such economies of scale in nontradeables probably is greater in developing than in more developed economies because of the relatively smaller size of developing economies. If these returns to scale are associated with particular industries, specific IPs may be high in the policy hierarchy.⁹ But note that if the returns to scale are related to a specific activity like research, then more general activity—specific policies directed toward that activity—are higher in the policy hierarchy than are specific IPs.

There also may be substantial increasing returns to scale in internationally tradeables with the minimum average-cost point at a scale of production that is large relative to domestic markets. Because of the relatively small size of national markets in developing as compared to more developed countries, such a phenomenon may be more frequent for the former than for the latter, *ceteris paribus*.¹⁰ Once again, pricing above marginal costs is inefficient and may cause undesired income-distribution effects. The first-best remedy in this case is not specific IPs, but to expand the market by integration with the international market. As Corden (1974) emphasizes, the same policy implication holds if there are two (or more) industries that reciprocally increase the returns of each other above what the individual returns would be were the other at small scale through pecuniary externalities.¹¹

Up to this point, We have been discussing true economies of scale, not so-called dynamic returns to scale or the pseudo-infant-industry case in which a firm's average costs decline over time because of learning by doing. Such cases, in which firms' cost curves might be expected to decline significantly with experience, probably are relatively more common in developing than in more developed economies because of the relatively small industrial base and limited industrial experience. However, such a possibility does not justify specific IPs. If market prices reflect true social-opportunity costs,¹² the critical question is whether or not the firm's private present discounted value of (expected) profits is negative or positive. If it is positive, then the firm should proceed but needs no specific IPs to induce it. If it is negative, the firm should not go ahead and IPs should not be offered to induce it since the social cost is negative also.

This argument may appear to be missing something critical. If there are dynamic returns to scale, will not users gain surpluses over time due to declining costs (prices) and does not the private calculation of return miss this dimension? This question, although legitimate, seems of much more relevance for the developed than for the developing countries because the former are much more likely to be on the leading edge of new innovations than are the latter. In the case of developing countries (and quite often for developed countries) there is often already a world market in such tradeables. If so, a first-best policy is to allow imports of the tradeable at the constant (given a small-country assumption) world price while the firm is learning by doing. In this case there is no gain in user surplus as the firm moves down its dynamic cost curve until it can produce at or below the world price (c.i.f.). At that point, such a gain is possible, but will not occur if the firm is permitted to sell at the world price to cover its initial large set-up costs. It seems unlikely that such a developing country firm can produce at much below the c.i.f. price, so that the loss in user surplus at this point is not likely to be large. Of course if the firm can produce at a significant scale below the world price there is a strong inducement for it to move actively into exports until its marginal costs are equated to the world price.

3. *Fragmented markets* probably are much more common in developing than in developed economics. In fact, some analyses of development make such fragmentation the essential feature of developing countries (for example, dualism and pluralism models inspired by the seminal work of Lewis 1954). The existence of such market fragmentation means that different entities face different incentives for product-and-factor use and that spatial monopolies as described by Chamberlain (1956) may prevail, with negative effects on static and dynamic efficiencies and perhaps on distribution.

Specific IPs could be used to offset such fragmentation. Once again, they are not likely to be very high in the policy hierarchy. If particular factor prices do not reflect true social costs due to such pluralism, for example, policies to compensate for this distortion for all users of the factors (not just those in a particular industry, firm or project) are higher in the policy hierarchy. Only if a single industry or a small group of industries are subject to such distortions are specific IPs likely to be desirable. In the longer run, in any case, the appropriate policies probably should be directed toward integration of markets.

4. *Private industrial entrepreneurs* probably are less common in most developing countries than in the developed world (although developed-country competitors with East Asian exporters may not be certain). Thus specific IPs could be used to increase rewards for entrepreneurship or to direct private or public resources to desired industries to which they otherwise would not flow because of the paucity of private entrepreneurship. But the successful implementation of such policies presupposes that policymakers have enough information to be able to identify entrepreneurial opportunities. If so, this provision of general information would be higher in the

Developing-Country Perspective on IP

policy hierarchy than specific IPs. If such information is made generally available and other distortions are removed, entrepreneurship may be induced by its high rewards in a Hirschman (1959) fashion.

5. *Multinational corporations and trading partner countries* probably tend to be more powerful relative to entities in developing countries than relative to entities in developed economies, although in some areas (for example, mineral and fuel resources) recent shifts may have been toward increased relative power in the hands of the developing countries. If such international relations are actually or potentially concentrated in a few industries, specific IPs may be used to attempt to assure a relatively favorable outcome for the developing countries from duopoly bargaining. Usually more general policies (for example, related to activities like the terms of foreign investment, tax treatment, capital repatriation, worker training) are likely to be as high in the policy hierarchy.

6. Some *nonefficiency objectives,* as noted earlier, tend to be more important in the developing than in the developed nations. Examples include control over the national economy or at least of some basic components of it such as natural resource-based activities and other basic industries and perhaps distribution goals. Specific IPs are likely to be very high in the policy hierarchy for pursuing the subset of such objectives that are tied specifically to a particular industry. If national control of mineral resources or development of a steel industry is weighted heavily in the social-welfare function, IPs related to mineral resources or to the steel industry may be the best way to pursue such objectives. But in cases in which there is not a direct tie between such objectives and specific industries, specific IPs are likely to be fairly low in the policy hierarchy. For example, for distributional goals, general-employment, human-capital, transfer, taxes, and food-provision policies are likely to be much higher in the hierarchy.

7. *Planning* tends to be advocated more broadly in the developing countries than in the industrialized West. It may be advocated for some of the previously mentioned considerations (for example, because of externalities or increasing returns to scale or nonefficiency objectives). Still other reasons sometimes emphasized in favor of planning in the developing economies include the desire to avoid market fluctuations, to assure bilateral and multilateral lending and aid agencies that there is a serious commitment to development and perhaps distribution goals, and to avoid reliance on a market system that may be identified negatively with former imperial or current neoimperial powers.

Planning, unless it is the purest indicative type, almost always involves specific IPs. Whether this is sensible or not, once again, depends on how high these IPs are in the policy hierarchy. Examples have been given of some cases in which they are likely to be quite high, and also of a number of cases in which they might be relatively low.

8. *Infrastructure development* has been mentioned as an example of increasing returns to scale that may call for specific IPs for efficiency. But it has been emphasized so much as a special or critical factor in the development literature that it is useful to identify it as a separate reason for IPs.

Many basic services that are taken as a matter of course in the developed industrial world often are deficient or absent in developing economies. This contributes to the fragmentation of markets noted earlier, with the attendant distortions. Examples of infrastructure include electrical-power, irrigation, water-and-sewage, transportation-and-ports, and communication systems, all of which may be critical in the general-development effort.

Because of the large increasing returns to scale and possible externalities, private entities are unlikely to supply adequate quantities of such infrastructure without special policy incentives. Therefore the case often is quite strong for IPs. Moreover, the required policies are likely to be very specific—PSPs that take the form of construction of a particular road or port, for example. Furthermore, in most cases the service provided by the infrastructure cannot be imported (although the inputs used in the construction of necessary capital often are) so the world market cannot be used to encourage efficiency as easily as for many other goods and services.

The lack of such a check from the world market means that the risk often is higher for infrastructure projects than for other activities that particular political objectives such as prestige play more important roles in decisions about related resource allocations. Such a tendency may be reinforced by the development of government organizations with a strong private vested interest in expanding such infrastructure, even beyond socially optimal levels (for example, the U.S. Army Corp of Engineers and its dam construction provides a well-known example from the industrialized countries).

Again, political or nonefficiency objectives are not wrong; every society must have them. But it is desirable to pursue them as efficiently as possible, with awareness of the nature of the trade-offs. Are the prestige and efficiency gains of a new modern international airport worth the opportunity costs in terms of resources diverted from agricultural research, preventive medical measures, and other uses? Such questions should be raised, and procedures for making resource allocations to infrastructure should embody mechanisms to assure that they are. The frequently large increasing returns to scale and the lack of imported substitutes for infrastructure services make it difficult. But the effort must be made through the political process and through mechanisms such as widespread bidding for intrastructure projects (perhaps including international contractors, such as the Koreans, who apparently have low-cost construction capabilities), or the losses can be very high.

Finally, note that many developing-country planners and policymakers have attempted to extend the definition of infrastructure to include basic construction materials like steel and cement or basic consumption goods like food staples. Such goods indeed may have special characteristics because the cost of supply disruptions may be very high. However, such goods generally can be imported and do not have such strong increasing returns to scale as do most infrastructure elements of the types already discussed. Therefore, to lump them with the standard infrastructure case may be misleading in regard to analysis and policy design.

Additional Considerations

Much of the discussion to this point has been based on standard assumptions of profit maximization, fixed independent preferences, perfect information and costless policies. Now we discuss some of the implications of relaxing these assumptions for the use of IPs in developing countries.

Dropping the assumption of profit maximization allows for the existence of "X-inefficiency" (Leibenstein 1966) or "satisfising behavior" (Simon 1961). In a world of complete information, this would not greatly affect the case for IPs in developing countries. In the real world of imperfect information, however, it probably tends to argue against more specific IPs because of their tendencies to create privileged positions for pioneering or existing firms and to encourage X-inefficiency.[13] If there is legitimacy to the characterization of those in developing countries being less oriented toward economic goals than those in developed countries, the resulting losses are likely to be relatively greater in developing countries.

A counter case might be made that IPs could be used by a developing country to help create a general atmosphere that is propitious to the attainment of society's objectives and that reduces X-inefficiencies. The government might mobilize greater private efforts by demonstrating its interest and concern in the social objectives through implementing IPs. But this signaling or catalytic possibility does not seem inherently to favor IPs over other policies. To the contrary, for this purpose IPs probably are dominated in the policy hierarchy because of their added negative by-products.

If the assumption of exogenous tastes is dropped, welfare analysis becomes even more difficult (perhaps impossibly so). But for developing countries, a case often has been made for specific IPs to avoid changes in tastes due to the international demonstration effect which might alter consumption preferences in ways detrimental to attainment of the original social-welfare function. As a result ISPs have been advocated and adopted to preclude importation and/or production of certain luxury items.[14] If such luxury items are fairly specific in nature, then such IPs probably are more appropriate in these cases than more general policies would be. But the appropriateness of any such policies may be strictly indeterminate because of the hypothesized possible underlying change in preferences.[15]

If information is imperfect, policymakers with the best of intentions may err in either direction. That is, they may introduce IPs in cases in which the net social returns are negative (type I errors), and they may not do so in cases in which net social payoffs would be positive (type II errors). Even if the brightest and the best enter government service (which is not always the case), policymakers often may not be well informed about the relevant grubby details for making decisions regarding ISPs and PSPs and, as a result, be overdependent for information on interested parties who stand to gain from the IPs. There probably is thus a bias toward type I errors. And once PSPs are introduced, whether or not they originally are appropriate, a strongly focused lobby usually makes it hard to disband them if subsequently the (generalized) losses outweigh the more narrowly focused gains. Thus the initial bias toward encouraging X-inefficiency (Leibenstein 1966) and rent-seeking (Krueger 1974*b* and Tullock 1967) tends to become stronger over time. This may become a greater problem in developing than in developed countries because government-industry ties often are stronger and general consumer lobbies are relatively less common and less effective. Such activities not only are inefficient but lead to more regressive income distribution, a further loss given any egalitarian concerns in the social-welfare function.

With imperfect information, moreover, there are likely to be further drawbacks to specific IPs in developing countries. For example, the motives of policymakers and overseers may not always be coincident with the public interest. ISPs or PSPs because of the complications and the need to interact closely with specialized-interest groups, lend themselves much more than do general policies to situations in which policymakers and overseers can pursue their own power or income aims, despite conflicts with social goals. If information is imperfect, such private pursuits may be followed for considerable periods of time at substantial social cost. Information is likely more imperfect, lines between social and private ends are less clearly drawn, and there is less of a tradition of such questions being raised by an independent press or consumer group in many developing countries than in most developed countries. If so, imperfect information may cause PSPs to be relatively more costly for this reason as well as others.

As a final example, imperfect information means that monitoring costs of ongoing IPs might be considerable. Such monitoring costs are probably higher for specific IPs than for general policies per unit of effective policy[16] because of the relatively specific and detailed nature of the policies and because of possible negative by-products. Whether these costs are likely to be greater or lesser in developing countries than in developed countries is difficult to determine. For the same monitoring tasks, the costs are likely to be greater in the developing countries because of the greater opportunity costs of skilled persons and the lesser availability of information from other sources (for example, tax records). However, the tasks that need to be monitored might be less complicated due to the use of less-sophisticated technology.

Finally, policy design, implementation, and monitoring are all costly; in the developing countries this often is in terms of scarce highly skilled individuals. Such costs should not be ignored, and they probably tend to be higher for detailed IPs than for broader policies.

Summary

There are reasons why IPs may be more desirable in developing than in developed economies: Externalities, increasing returns to scale, fragmented markets, entrepreneurial shortages, asymmetries in dealing with multinational corporations and trading partners, certain nonefficiency objectives, and a planning orientation all tend to be greater. In some cases, such conditions imply that ISPs or PSPs are quite high in the relevant policy hierarchy. For example, there may be increasing returns to scale, nonefficiency objectives, and, perhaps, international transactions for which quite specific IPs are desirable.

Generally, these special conditions in developing countries imply that nonspecific IPs or SSPs or activity-related policies are much higher in the relevant policy hierarchies than are the more ISPs or PSPs. The latter simply usually have too many negative by-product distortions even under the most favorable of assumptions. The negative by-products or specific IPs are likely to increase relatively once possibilities like X-inefficiency, imperfect, rent-seeking, and resource costs of policies are incorporated into the analysis. Thus specific IPs in particular should be scrutinized before adoption by the developing countries.

Experience of Developing Countries with Foreign-Sector Industrial Policies

Foreign-sector policies tend to be more important in the developing countries than in developed countries like the United States. This is so because the smaller size of the developing economies makes them (as well as smaller developed countries) more trade-dependent for the following reasons: (1) their domestic economies cannot support as wide a range of industries (particularly those with large increasing returns to scale); (2) their foreign-trade institutions permit policy control more easily relative to domestic institutions within fragmented markets in developing countries; (3) in many cases, control of foreign entities is an independent concern in the social-welfare function; (4) most developed countries are in the early debt phase of the development life cycle for nations and thus are dependent on foreign savings at the margin; and (5) foreign sources may provide relatively cheap innovations for latecomers. An additional reason that foreign-sector policies are critical for many developing countries is that historical import-substitution and domestic-currency-overvaluation policy choices have left them very vulnerable to slight drops in the availability of foreign exchange.

Because of the importance of foreign-sector policies in developing countries, an examination of them tells a great deal about developing-country experience with IPs. Prior to 1970 there had been little systematic analysis of the details of the foreign-sector policies of the developing countries. Fortunately, in the 1970s individual studies and the results of at least four major projects that have been concerned with characterizing foreign-sector policies (usually broadly defined) and their implications for economic-goal attainment in the developing world became available: (1) the OECD project on industry and trade in six developing countries under the directorship of Little, Scitovsky, and Scott (1970);[17] (2) the NBER project on foreign-trade regimes and economic development in ten developing countries under the directorship of Bhagwati (1978) and Krueger (1978);[18] (3) the IBRD project on the structure of protection in six developing countries under the directorship of Balassa (1971);[19] and (4) the Kiel Institute of World Economics project on the industrialization policies of fifteen semiindustrialized countries under the directorship of Donges (1976a).[20] The purposes and the scopes of these studies differ, but taken together they provide important empirical documentation of the general relations between foreign-sector policies and economic outcomes in developing countries and some insight into the particular role of IPs. The eighteen developing countries covered include a range of sizes and natural-resource bases and many of the more interesting high-growth and/or large-exporter cases.[21] These voluminous results are summarized first with respect to their general implications for patterns of foreign trade and development-goal attainment and then with regard to the nature of specific IPs as reflected in differential policies across industries.

General Patterns

There is considerable variation among countries, yet there seem to be some patterns.

When these developing countries began to pursue substantial industrialization actively (the Latin American and European ones in the Great Depression of the 1930s, if not earlier; the Asian ones in the late 1940s and 1950s), they generally selected import-substitution strategies in which domestic industries were protected so that they could replace previous manufactured imports in domestic markets.[22] Generally, import substitution first focused on consumer goods and then moved toward intermediate and sometimes capital goods. In most cases, levels of tariff protection were quite high in comparison to recent developed-country experience, with nominal protection escalating with the stage of processing so that effective protection rates on value added were even higher. Nominal tariffs often were reinforced by deposit requirements, quantitative restrictions, and myriad fiscal and credit incentives. Exchange rates tended to be overvalued with a bias against traditional and new exports. Frequently, foreign exchange become an increasingly severe constraint because of enlarged demands for imported inputs for the import substitution industries and reduced relative supplies from discouraged exports. Overall economic growth generally was high in comparison with historical standards or with many other countries, manufacturing grew even more quickly, and imports as a proportion all total domestic absorption declined strikingly, particularly for consumer goods.[23] Usually labor absorption by the import-substitution industries grew much less rapidly than did real value added, and overall income distribution frequently became more unequal. Cyclical fluctuations and inflation problems, often exacerbated by increased vulnerability to foreign-sector fluctuations (because of little fat left in imports and low reserves) were not uncommon, particularly in a number of Latin American countries.

Beginning in the late 1950s a growing number of countries became increasing skeptical about the further benefits that could be expected from ongoing import-substitution possibilities since import-to-total-supply ratios had been reduced to such low levels, particularly for consumer goods. In part, this reflected a growing perception of a number of inadequacies of past inward-looking policies: limited labor absorption, inefficiencies and underutilization of capacities because of protection from external competition, distortions in cost structures to favor use of scarce capital relative to abundant labor, increased vulnerability to foreign-sector constraints due to enlarged dependence on imports of raw materials and intermediate inputs, unintended distributional consequences due to local monopolies, and too little exploitation of economies of scale because of the small size of domestic markets. Such views were not universal, but they became more common and were held increasingly by international experts, some of whom were in influential positions regarding the availability of foreign loans and grants.

In the next decade or so, most of these countries responded by adopting more outward-oriented policies and moving relatively toward export promotion. Generally, the smaller and the East Asian countries took the lead, perhaps because the limitations of the sizes of the domestic markets became evident earlier. Not all of the moves toward outward orientation were monotonic. Often there were fits and starts because of the adjustment difficulties and competing interests. Not all of the countries pursued such changes with the same intensity, but generally the pendulum shifted from inward to outward orientation (Turkey may be a notable exception).

In many cases, the first major policy step of the new orientation was a major currency devaluation, usually accompanied by the unification of any multiple-exchange-rate systems. In a number of cases (not always successful), efforts were made to avoid subsequent currency overvaluation by adopting floating rates (for example, Korea in 1965) or sliding-peg exchange rates (for example, Brazil, Chile, and Colombia). At times, comprehensive monetary- and fiscal-austerity programs were undertaken (for example, Brazil in 1964-1967, Chile in 1974, Spain in 1959, and Turkey in 1958). Korea and Taiwan tried to reform their capital markets by increasing substantially interest rates for savings and loans. All of these countries eased existing industrial-licensing requirements, encouraged more direct foreign investment, and tried (with considerable success) to abolish restrictive export provisions in licensing contracts with foreign enterprises. Most countries at the margin reduced the use of quantitative restrictions and tariffs which favored import substitution (although the exchange-rate movements were partially compensating on the average in a number of cases) and increased general and specific export-promotion policies (for example, through remission of or exemption from custom duties paid on imported intermediate inputs used in exports and/or partial or total exemption from direct taxes on exports).[24] Generally, policy biases toward exports were reduced significantly, although rarely eliminated entirely. In some of the more notable growth-success cases, however, such as Korea after the mid-1960s and Brazil after 1967, according to Krueger (1978) there was an export bias, and Hong Kong and Singapore have basically neutral regimes in this dimension.

The shift to more outward policies has been remarkably successful in a number of dimensions. Real GNP has grown at high rates compared with past performance of these or of most other countries. Table 7-1 above provides a number of illustrations. Relatively high growth rates were maintained, particularly by the more outward-oriented developing countries, in the 1970s despite the international shocks the countries experienced due to OPEC oil-price increases and recessions in the industrial countries. This outcome reflects their ability to exploit new comparative advantages at times of duress, their relatively great credit worthiness and access to international financial capital, and their lesser vulnerability to marginal curtailment of imports. Real value added in manufacturing generally grew more quickly. In a few cases (for example, Israel, Korea, and Taiwan) the expanding manufacturing sector absorbed more than half of the increment in the total labor force, although generally labor absorption was less dramatic. Perhaps what is most striking is the general export expansion marked by an unprecedented increase in manufactures exports in most of these countries (Donges 1976*b*). The responses of both traditional and non-traditional exports to reduction in bias against exports of policy regimes has revealed much higher elasticities than generally had been presumed previously. (See table 7-1.)

As noted earlier, the outward-oriented policies often were imposed at the margin on a somewhat reformed mosaic of inward-looking policies. Not surprisingly, such a process, particularly in a world of imperfect information and adjustment problems, hardly has led to anything like first-best policies in the sense discussed earlier. Donges (1967*a*), for example, refers to several instances from a number of countries (for example, Brazil, Colombia, Egypt, India, Israel, and Spain) in which manufactured exports were overpromoted in the sense that the domestic-resource costs of earning foreign exchange through exporting manufacturers exceeded the value of the foreign exchange. As mentioned previously, in most developing countries, the foreign-sector policy regimes remained biased (usually toward imports, but less so than earlier) instead of neutral and generally employment absorption has been less than desired.

But, conditional on there being a reasonable expansion of the world economy,[25] a more outward policy approach has certain advantages. First, more outward-oriented policies are much less likely to encounter the severe balance-of-payments constraints that are almost inevitable with the inward-oriented policies. Therefore the restraining effects of other bottlenecks, such as slow traditional agricultural-sector growth, can be mitigated. Second, economic factors such as returns to scale and the impact of competition on X-inefficiency[26] probably are more effective under outward- than under inward-oriented policies. Third, outward-oriented strategies tend to place certain constraints on policy choices and implementation, which limit the severity and longevity of policy errors, limit inducements to divert scarce skills to rent-seeking (Krueger 1974*b* and Tullock 1967), and generally require price rather than quantitative interventions (and avoid the frequently capricious impact of the latter).[27] Fourth, the dynamic evolution over time seems to favor outward-looking policies since there appear to be significant increasing returns to locating foreign buyers, penetrating foreign markets, establishing national good will, and meeting foreign labeling, quality, and other critical nonprice specifications. In contrast, inward-oriented strategies inevitably eventually become increasingly more costly to pursue because of the limits on the size of the domestic market and the related need to move to production of items in which a country has less and less true comparative advantage. A fairly broad consensus on this view, at least for the middle-income developing countries, seems to have emerged.[28]

IPs have been very important in both more inward and more outward policy regimes. The projects under review provide considerable empirical evidence about the patterns of specific IPs across industries in the form of estimates of effective protection rates. Subject to standard qualifications (related to quality differentials, prohibitive quantitative restrictions, monopoly rents, and changing premia for fixed quantitative restrictions as supply-and-demand conditions vary), the effective protection rates loosely represent the differential nature of incentives across industries due to specific IPs regarding tariffs, quantitative restrictions, and domestic credit and fiscal policies.[29]

The patterns of available effective protection rates for developing economies have six general characteristics.

First, manufacturing has generally been favored relative to the primary sectors, which may underlie some of the relative stagnation in the latter. Furthermore, in many cases this sector-specific distortion has contributed significantly to a balance-of-payments crisis by discouraging price-responsive traditional exports and by discouraging domestic provision of foodstuffs and industrial raw materials. Another negative by-product is increased incentives for rural-urban migration despite limitations on modern urban-sector labor absorption.

Second, the pattern across industries has considerable dispersion and unpredictability (with much of the latter originating in varying import premia associated with quantitative restrictions). Frequent changes of regulations or in the administration of regulations may make the industry-specific incentives appear quite capricious from the point of view of potential entrepreneurs.

Third, the dispersion in effective protection rates is associated with considerable dispersion in domestic-resource costs across industries, thus indicating a fair amount of inefficiency. Not uncommonly, the association between the two is not negative nor even nonzero, but positive (for example, Behrman 1976, gives a value of .79 for Chile in 1961) so that the specific IPs are generating greater incentives in the more resource-costly industries.

Fourth, the greatest incentives for domestic protection paradoxically often have been given to industries that produce goods that have been characterized as nonessentials. This outcome frequently has been the result of severe limitations by high tariffs and/or quantitative restrictions on using scarce foreign exchange for such items but not restrictions on domestic production (the Korean practice of also proscribing domestic production, noted earlier in regard to possible taste changes, is an exception). The resulting incentive for domestic production (sometimes at an inefficiently small scale, as automobiles) has been great.

Fifth, government officials have not been notably successful in encouraging industries with social benefits above private ones. A number of individual studies in the projects cite frequent examples in which avowed objectives relating to regional distribution and the utilization of abundant unskilled labor have not been accomplished well by specific IPs.

Sixth, with a shift from inward- to more outward-oriented policies, the dispersion in the differential incentives offered different industries has tended to decline and greater rationalization has occurred. The reasons for such changes are the same as those for the greater general success of more outward looking strategies discussed earlier.[30]

The implication is not a very positive one for ISPs. But one can go further and ask whether or not there is evidence of any significant empirical association between the cross-industry pattern of effective protection rates induced by specific IPs and any variables that might be associated with goal attainment in the developing countries.

Bhagwati and Srinivasan (1978) review several empirical correlations between the effective protection rates and growth-related variables across industries in developing countries. They conclude that the results are fairly mixed. They also note that the theoretical rationale for such an association is weak because effective protection rates are not unique (in the sense that a given effective protection rate can result from different combinations of nominal tariffs on inputs and outputs and hence with different effects on production and consumption of the product of interest), differential Engel curves and other effects are not controlled for in such simple correlations, and the general-equilibrium implications for price changes on output changes require a full general-equilibrium scheme.

But within-country cross-section studies, in any case, are not revealing about the effect of specific IPs on growth or other goal attainment, as opposed to the effect on resource allocation. Comparisons are required between different specific IP regimes over time within a country or across countries. The sixth general characteristic of IPs in developing countries noted earlier depends on a comparison within a country over time, but no such comparisons have been subject to statistical testing.

We now turn to the results of a crude test of the hypothesis that the variation in effective protection rates across industries within a country is inversely associated with real growth in GNP, in total exports, and in manufactured exports. In this test, quinquennial growth rates are regressed on a measure of the variation in available effective protection rates at the center of the five-year period and other variables to control for shifts in the terms of trade, the general export-import bias, and the degree of overvaluation.

There are at least three qualifications, in addition to those noted by Bhagwati and Srinivasan, in regard to this test. First, the estimates of effective protection rates and the definitions of industries are not all consistent, but it would be far beyond the scope of the present project to develop consistent estimates. Second, although these regressions control for some variables that might affect growth in the developing countries, there are many others that are important and for which they do not control, which causes omitted variable bias if these variables are correlated with the measure of dispersion of the effective protection rates. Third, other variables are measured for the five-year period centering on the year of the effective protection rates under the assumption that the effective protection rates have an impact throughout that quinquennium. But the actual protection rates may have changed considerably within that five-year period, even if the overall international-trade regime did not vary substantially.

Despite these limitations, such a test is suggestive about the general impact of specific IPs on the important growth goal of developing countries. Table 7-2 summarizes the resulting estimates, which suggest that there is a significant positive association between foreign-exchange reserves (relative to exports) and growth rates in both GDP and exports. There is also a significantly negative relation (at the 10 percent level) between foreign-exchange-market disequilibrium (as measured by the ratio of the black market to the official exchange rates) and growth in GDP. Thus there is some evidence of an association between the foreign-sector position and growth. But at the standard significance levels, there is no evidence of a significant effect of foreign-sector-specific IPs (as represented by the variance in effective protection rates) on growth. Therefore these estimates neither support the hypothesis that such IPs increased attainment of the growth goal nor that they hindered such attainment.

Developing-Country Experience with Industry Policy in the Form of State Enterprises

Another perspective from which the data are available to characterize somewhat broadly the developing-country experience with specific IPs is in regard to their experience with state enterprises. In many developing countries this experience has been broader than in the developed countries for reasons mentioned earlier. Choksi (1979) has surveyed this experience. This section summarizes his work with emphasis on the concerns of this chapter and refers interested readers to it for a much more extensive discussion.

Promoting and operating selected public-sector enterprises, of course, can be viewed as a form of specific IPs. In the extreme, such enterprises are subject to direct policy controls. Frequently, however, they are subject to many policies similar to private enterprises, despite the ownership differences. As such, they may be subject to only very general policies, but typically they are affected by a number of specific policies. The analytical basis for having or not having such specific IPs is the same whether an

Table 7-2
Multivariate Regression Estimates of Impact of Variance in Effective Protection Rates on Quinquennial Developing-Country Growth Rates

	Dependent Variables	
Right-Hand-Side Variables	GDP Growth	Export Growth
Variance in effective protection rates	.03 (0.2)	.3 (0.6)
Terms of trade	−.005 (0.1)	−.034 (0.3)
Foreign-exchange reserves relative to exports	4.5 (2.6)	22.3 (3.6)
Black-market exchange rate relative to official exchange rate	−2.6 (1.6)	−5.8 (1.0)
Constant	8.5 (2.0)	11.8 (0.8)
$\bar{R}^2$	.48	.55

Note: The variances in effective protection rates were calculated from the estimates available in the studies discussed earlier in this section after aggregation of such estimates to comparable sectoral levels. The effective protection rates refer to a particular year. All of the other variables are five-year averages centered on that year under the assumption that the effective protection rate of that year characterized the situation for at least the quinquennium centered on that year. Under the point estimates are the absolute values of the t statistics. The nineteen observations are for Spain in 1966, Pakistan in 1963, Brazil in 1966, Chile in 1961 and 1967, Mexico in 1960, Malaysia in 1965, Colombia in 1969, Egypt in 1966, Ghana in 1969, India in 1968, Israel in 1958 and 1967, Korea in 1968, Yugoslavia in 1970, Costa Rica in 1966 and 1971/1972, Tanzania in 1966, and the Phillipines in 1965. In addition, six incomplete observations were used for some additional regressions: Norway in 1954, Egypt in 1954, Taiwan in 1966, Turkey in 1954 and 1964, and Kenya in 1963. The effective protection rates are mostly from the studies that are reviewed in the text. The black-market exchange rates are from various issues of Pick's *Currency Yearbook*. The other data are from standard United Nations, World Bank, and International Monetary Fund sources.

enterprise is state- or private-owned and operated. (See Bases for Industrial Policy in Developing Countries.)

Available studies of the performance of public enterprises in developing countries are incomplete. Generally, the evidence focuses on financial profitability as the primary indicator of performance. On this basis, state-owned enterprises appear to be suffering, as they face large and continuing financial losses (Choksi 1979).

For example, Gantt and Dutto (1968) studied the aggregate financial performance over an average period of seven years of sixty-four government-owned corporations operating in railways, other transport systems, petroleum, electricity, communications, and other industries in twenty-six countries in Africa, Asia, Europe, and Latin America. The average operating deficit of this sample was −16 percent of the value of current activity (with variations across industries ranging from 13 percent for petroleum to −40.5 percent for railways). If investment requirements are included, on the average 66 percent of the required funds had to be provided from external sources (generally about half from government transfers, with the rest from government loans or from national and international private sources). Some corporations generated surpluses in some years, but these were exceptions. Thus according to Gantt and Dutto (1968), state-owned enterprises have not only failed in their mission to collect resources for their own investment, but they have become a financial burden for the parent government.

Country-specific reviews of public enterprises in Turkey, India, Ghana, and Nigeria lead to the same conclusion: Ongoing and substantial financial deficits have been experienced, often despite specific IPs substantially favoring the terms on which such enterprises are relieved from tax obligations, receive credit, and so on. In contrast, studies for Korea and for pre-Amin Uganda indicate financial surpluses on the average. Choksi suggests that these differences are due to great incentives for growth (and sanctions for failure) and a highly skilled and energetic labor force in Korea and to the emphasis on profitability and autonomy in Uganda.

Of course, financial profitability may not be a very good indicator of success. If any of the conditions discussed earlier are relevant (for example, externalities, large increasing returns to scale, nonefficiency objectives, and so on), financial losses *may* be consistent with social success. The question naturally arises: What do the available studies tell us when such possibilities are considered?

The answer, unfortunately, is less clear than if financial profitability alone is considered. The reasons are twofold. First, the other factors are more difficult to measure given standard data-generating procedures. Second, most studies tend to focus on the financial question, perhaps in part because of the measurement problem.

Nevertheless, some generalizations can be made. Quite often, state enterprises have *not* been very successful even once these special possibilities are incorporated into the analysis because (1) the objectives have been very muddled in the eyes of the managers, (2) the appropriate shadow pricing for the nonefficiency objectives has not been indicated, (3) arbitrary ad hoc and often inconsistent policy interventions have been made by different government bureaucracies, and/or (4) specific IPs have permitted X-inefficient and allocative inefficient operations which divert scarce resources from the nonefficiency objectives.

Based on his reveiw of the often unsuccessful experience of state enterprises, Choksi suggests that desirable policy strategies do the following:

1. Encourage X-efficiency and allocative efficiency, if possible, by allowing private enterprises and imports in the same industry (as Mexico has done for steel) rather than excluding them by fiat as, say, India did in its early experience.
2. Allow managers of state enterprises autonomy and instruct them to pursue a net revenue-maximizing objective.
3. Introduce explicit subsidies that are tied to specific externalities or nonefficiency objectives.

Essentially, these suggestions are designed to clarify the social-resource costs of pursuing various objectives and to induce an optimal pursuit of the multiple objectives, including the nonefficiency ones. Of course, following these suggestions is not always simple and to do so does not always lead to the most satisfactory outcomes.

The first suggestion, for example, is feasible only if operations are not mutually exclusive and if minimum-average-cost points are at a scale small enough to permit more than one enterprise or if transportation costs are low enough to permit imports. Moreover, while such a suggestion probably would encourage allocative and X-efficiency, private-enterprise production would not guarantee pricing at social-marginal costs if there is private-market power from increasing returns to scale or if there are externalities or nonefficiency objectives.

The third suggestion, for another example, requires a difficult evaluation of hard-to-measure externalities and nonefficiency benefits. Some such judgments are required, at least implicitly, to deal with the possibility of externalities and the other objectives. Choksi's suggested explicit recognition of their social evaluation is noteworthy. The setting of explicit subsidies probably provides information for public discourse on their true value and induces the collection of better information on which to make the necessary decisions.

What does the experience of developing countries with state enterprises suggest for the more general formulation of specific IPs? First, it points to the need to be clear about the nature and the magnitude of the industry-specific increasing returns to scale, externalities, and nonefficiency objectives that legitimately might underlie the adoption of specific IPs. A wave of the hands with reference to externalities, and so on is not sufficient. Second, it emphasizes the need to devise policies that encourage allocative and X-efficiency as defined from the point of view of the overall social-welfare function. Even if many of these aims are nonefficient in a narrow or private sense, it is important that resources be used efficiently in the broader sense to maximize overall goal attainment. Opening up markets more broadly probably encourages the X-efficiency dimension and (particularly if international trade is possible) the allocative efficiency dimension as well. Third, empirical experience reinforces the second-best considerations regarding the desirability of choosing policies from the policy hierarchy that relate as directly as is possible to the distortion being remedied. It also reinforces the policy-hierarchy notion in that policies low in the hierarchy often have many unintended negative by-products.

Concluding Remarks

This review of the general developing country experience with IPs and the case studies in the appendixes lead to several important conclusions.

First, there are plausible reasons why IPs might tend to be more appropriate for developing than for more-developed economies: externalities, returns to scale, fragmented markets, entrepreneurial shortages, asymmetries in dealing with multinational enterprises and with other trading partners, and weights on certain nonefficiency objectives, all tend to be greater. Moreover, among developing countries, these factors are likely to be more important in low-income than in the middle-income cases because the process of development tends to lessen their relative importance.

Second, if these effects are fairly industry- (or firm- or project-) specific, as they may be (at least for increasing returns-to-scale and nonefficiency objectives such as establishing national control over basic industries), then specific IPs may be appropriate. But more specific IPs probably have greater risks than do more general policies of causing high social costs due to allocative and X-inefficiency, rent seeking, and resource costs of policy analysis, implementation, and monitoring. Often in the developing-country experience, these costs apparently have been considerable. In other words, many of the special conditions in the developing countries do not imply very high positions in the relevant policy hierarchies for specific IPs, particularly in a world with partial information and rent seeking. Policymakers in the developing world have not demonstrated particular success in picking winners. Therefore policy strategy should probably tilt, if anything, toward being too general rather than too specific.

Third, a related point is that policies should be aimed as directly as possible toward the supposed distortion between private and social costs or benefits. This lessens other negative by-products of the policies in the Corden (1974) sense, encourages the collection of information about the nature of such divergencies, and facilitates a more general evaluation by the body politic of their true value. The Choksi (1979) suggestion that managers of state enterprises be told to maximize net revenues with explicit subsidies received for specific distortions between private and social costs is an example of such a strategy. As noted earlier, there are some cases in which such a procedure implies narrow IPs. But specific IPs should not be used if the distortions are of a more general activity-related (for example, research) or sectoral (for example, the private cost of unskilled labor in manufacturing exceeds the social costs) nature.

Fourth, in an uncertain world with rent-seeking and X-inefficiency possibilities, competition should be allowed to encourage efficiencies and to limit excesses due to mistakes in IP choices and implementation. The most effective way to do this for tradeable goods is through a general open- and outward-oriented strategy. The East Asian general (not specific) export promotion is a noteworthy example of such a successful strategy. For nontradeables the problem is more difficult, but the development of a multiplicity of autonomous entities (whether public, private, or mixed) and allowing competition in input provision (from the foreign sector if possible) in many cases may increase the probability of IPs leading to desired objectives.

Notes

1. Among the capital-surplus oil exporters, Saudi Arabia averaged 9.7 percent, Iran 7.9 percent, Libya 6.2 percent, and Iraq 4.1 percent.

2. Among the countries for which data are available, Hong Kong is the only exception to this statement. For Hong Kong, manufacturing has grown at the same rate (not faster) than GDP, so its share in GDP has remained constant at 25 percent. For the poorest countries (Lesotho, Togo, and Indonesia) the growth in manufacturing share of GDP has been least.

3. See chapter 3 for a more extensive discussion of the general theoretical bases for IPs. Corden (1974) and Grubel (1966) discuss the infant-industry subset of these arguments.

4. I do not pursue here the difficult question of how such a function is determined nor whether different national social-welfare goals are consistent.

5. Corden's discussion proceeds as if there is only one distortion at a time in the economy, but it could be restated more realistically in terms of probabilities and expected values given distortions elsewhere.

6. Because of the focus here on IPs, externalities are characterized here with regard to activities of an industry; but more generally, activities of other entities also could generate externalities.

7. Note that the focus here is on technological externalities, *not* on pecuniary externalities that work through prices (see the discussion on increasing returns to scale that follows).

8. For public goods the marginal costs of additional users is zero, which can be viewed as high increasing returns to scale. This classification

is somewhat arbitrary and others may prefer some alternative, but the essential points remain the same.

9. As Corden (1974), Grubel (1966), and others point out, increasing returns to scale are not an appropriate argument for infant-industry protection. However, here we are considering IPs in general, not only the subset of infant-industry arguments. If average costs are above marginal costs, IPs to enable marginal-cost pricing may be warranted on efficiency grounds.

10. However, large returns to scale may be more common in high-technology or capital-intensive industries which are more suited for factor proportions in developed economies than for those in developing countries, which would work in the opposite direction.

11. That is, assume that industries A and B both use the other's output as one of their inputs. Suppose in a closed economy the real return to each is 2 percent if the other is at small scale, but 15 percent if the other is at large scale. In such a case the first-best remedy is not balanced growth so that both can reap the higher returns but opening the economy to international trade so both can do so if the opportunity cost in terms of resources is not greater than that available internationally.

12. If market prices do not reflect true opportunity costs, then policies should be adopted to offset this distortion for all firms, not just those in a particular industry.

13. In principle, specific IPs can allow completely for entry and not cause this distortion. In practice, however, they often seem to result in some restriction or relative disincentive for new entrants, at least temporarily.

14. In many cases, only importation has been precluded, with the result that scarce domestic resources have been drawn into domestic production and the demonstration effect is not avoided, but domestic demand is satisfied at a higher social cost. Westphal (1978) claims that Korea, in contrast, had IP preclusions on both imports and production, in part for this reason.

15. There is no analytical problem if changes in the preferences of individuals do not cause changes in the social-welfare function, as might be the case in an autocratic society.

16. An IP that affects few firms probably costs less to monitor than a sector-wide GIP such as a research subsidy, but the former probably has a much smaller impact. Therefore, the vague term *per unit of effective policy* is included because some such normalization is required.

17. Individual country volumes in this project include Bergsman (1970) on Brazil; Bhagwati and Desai (1970) on India; Hsing, Power, and Sicat (1970) on the Philippines and Taiwan; King (1970) on Mexico; and Lewis (1970) on Pakistan.

18. Individual country volumes in this project include Baldwin (1975) on the Philippines; Behrman (1976) on Chile; Bhagwati and Srinivasan (1975) on India; Diaz-Alejandro (1976) on Columbia; Frank, Kim, and

Westphal (1975) on Korea; Hansen and Nashashibi (1975) on Egypt; Krueger (1974a) on Turkey; Leith (1975) on Ghana; and Michaely (1974) on Israel. Bhagwati and Krueger (1973) summarize many earlier results and Bhagwati (1978), Krueger (1978) and Bhagwati and Srinivasan (1978) give later summaries.

19. Balassa and Associates' (1971) book includes country studies for Brazil, Chile, Malaysia, Mexico, Pakistan, and the Philippines.

20. The countries are: Brazil, Colombia, Egypt, Hong Kong, India, Israel, Malaysia, Mexico, Pakistan, Singapore, South Korea, Spain, Taiwan, Turkey, and Yugoslavia.

21. The projects involve a certain amount of overlap in country selection, with Brazil most examined and India, Mexico, and Pakistan next. Nine of the fourteen high growth middle-income developing countries in table 7-1 are included in at least one of these projects. The eighteen countries included in at least one of these projects in 1978 accounted for 78 percent of GNP, 56 percent of exports in all developing countries, and 56 percent of the population (*not* counting Indonesia nor Bangladesh among the eighteen). The more interesting and/or prominent cases not included are the oil exporters—Argentina, Bangladesh, China, Cuba, Indonesia, and most of Africa, but particularly Nigeria, and Thailand. In a more recent project on the relation between trade policies and employment in developing countries under the directorship of Krueger (1980), a few of these countries are covered. Keesing (1979b) reports that in yet another more recent effort at the IBRD under the directorship of Balassa several West African countries are being studied.

22. Hong Kong, Singapore, possibly Yugoslavia, and Malaysia are the major exceptions (the first two because of the very small domestic markets and poor national-resource bases and the third because early bilateral barter-trade agreements required some manufactured exports in addition to widespread import substitution).

23. During the 1950s the share of manufacturing in real value added increased in all of these countries, with some of the most impressive changes in Brazil (from 14.8 to 21.6 percent), Korea (4.7 to 12.1 percent), Pakistan (4 to 12.1 percent), and Spain (15.4 to 27 percent). By the end of the 1950s or early 1960s the ratio of imports to total domestic supply was 2 percent for consumer goods and 8 percent for producer goods in Brazil (1964); 5 and 2 percent in India (1961); 13 and 42 percent in Korea (1959); 3 and 23 percent in Mexico (1960); and 6 and 22 percent in Spain (1958). Source: Donges (1976a).

24. Ranis (1980) contrasts the general export promotion of the East Asian super exporters with the specific export promotion strategy of Latin America.

25. This condition is not trivial, as experience demonstrates from the

past and as some pessimists fear for the near future. Some of the most inward-looking of the developing countries in the first two postwar decades, for example, had been among the most outward-directed economies before the Great Depression wrecked havoc on their open economies. Chile, in particular, had a change in exports to less than a sixth of previous levels and a cut in national income of one-half. Chile responded by moving from a very open economy to a very closed one. (See Behrman, 1976, for further details.)

26. Bergsman (1974) presents estimates that suggest that the combination of X-inefficiency and monopoly rents (and, he hypothesizes, each of these individually) due to import prohibition were much higher than misallocation costs in Brazil, Mexico, Pakistan, and the Philippines.

27. Generally, Krueger (1978) argues, the political pressures from competing economic interests are more balanced, the greater visibility of mistakes (for example, high export subsidies with overvaluation of the exchange rate) is likely to reduce their duration, and there is less likelihood of major decisions in a crisis atmosphere. For further discussion of all of these points, see Krueger (1978). Donges (1976a) also emphasizes the lessened likelihood of balance-of-payments crises.

28. For example, see Keesing's (1979a) recent survey on trade policy for developing countries. For more qualifications see Diaz-Alejandro's (1975) survey.

29. Bhagwati and Srinivasan (1978) elaborate on the necessary qualifications and provide references to the relevant theoretical literature.

30. Bhagwati and Srinivasan (1978) and Bhagwati (1978) discuss the first three of these. Donges (1976b) emphasizes the last three. Krueger (1978) discusses them all and emphasizes the last two. Individual studies in the projects provide the empirical basis for these summary characteristics.

References

Balassa, Bela. "Industrial Policies in Taiwan and Korea." *Weltwirtshaftliches Archiv*. 106 (1971):55-77.

Balassa, Bela, and associates. *The Structure of Protection in Developing Countries*. Baltimore and London: Johns Hopkins University Press, 1971.

Baldwin, Robert E. *Foreign Trade Regimes and Economic Development: The Philippines*. New York: Columbia University Press for N.B.E.R., 1975.

Behrman, Jere R. *Foreign Trade Regimes and Economic Development: Chile*. New York: Columbia University Press for N.B.E.R., 1976.

———. *Macroeconomic Policy in a Developing Country: The Case of Chile*. Amsterdam: North-Holland Publishing Co., 1977.

Bergsman, Joel. *Brazil: Industrialization and Trade Policies.* London: Oxford University Press for O.E.C.D., 1970.

———. "Commercial Policy, Allocative Efficiency and X-Efficiency." *Quarterly Journal of Economics* 87 (1974):409–433.

Bhagwati, Jagdish. *Foreign Trade Regimes and Economic Development: Anatomy and Consequences of Exchange Control Regimes.* Cambridge, Mass.: Ballinger for National Bureau of Economic Research, 1978.

Bhagwati, Jagdish, and Padma Desai. *India: Planning for Industrialization.* London: Oxford University Press of O.E.C.D., 1970.

Bhagwati, Jagdish, and Anne O. Krueger. "Exchange Control, Liberalization and Economic Development." *American Economic Review* (1973):419–427.

Bhagwati, Jagdish, and T.N. Srinivasan. *Foreign Trade Regimes and Economic Development: India.* New York: Columbia University Press for N.B.E.R., 1975.

———. "Trade Policy and Development," in Rudiger Dornbusch and Jacob A. Frenkel, eds., *International Economic Policy: Theory and Evidence.* Baltimore: Johns Hopkins University Press, 1978.

Chamberlain, E. *The Theory of Monopolistic Competition.* Cambridge, Mass.: Harvard University Press, 1956.

Choksi, Armeane M. "State Intervention in the Industrialization of Developing Countries: Selected Issues." Mimeographed. Washington, D.C.: World Bank Staff Work Paper No. 341, 1979.

Corden, W.M. *Trade Policy and Economic Welfare.* Oxford: Clarendon Press, 1974.

Diaz-Alejandro, Carlos F. *Exchange Devaluation in a Semi-Industrialized Country: The Experience of Argentina 1955–1961.* Mass, and London: MIT Press, 1965.

———. "Trade Policies and Economic Development," in P. Kenen, ed., *International Trade and Finance: Frontiers for Research.* Cambridge: Cambridge University Press, 1975. Pp. 93–150.

———. *Foreign Trade Regimes and Economic Development: Colombia.* New York: Columbia University Press for N.B.E.R., 1976.

Donges, Juergen B. "A Comparative Survey on Industrialization Policies in Fifteen Semi-Industrial Countries." *Weltwirtschaftliches Archiv.* 112 (1976*a*):626–659.

———. *La Industrializacion en Espana.* Barcelona: Oikos-Tau, 1976*b*.

Donges, Juergen B., and James Riedel. "The Expansion of Manufactured Exports in Developing Countries: An Empirical Assessment of Supply and Demand Issues." *Weltwirtschaftliches Archiv.* 113, No. 1 (1976): 58–87.

Frank, Charles R., Jr., Kwang Suk Kim, and Larry E. Westphal. *Foreign Trade Regimes and Economic Development: South Korea.* New York: National Bureau of Economic Research, 1975.

Gantt, A., and G. Dutto. "Financial Performance of Government-Owned Corporations in Less Developed Countries." *International Monetary Fund Staff Papers* 25 (1968):102–142.

Grubel, Herbert G. "The Anatomy of Classical and Modern Infant Industry Arguments." *Weltwirtschaftliches Archiv.* 97 (1966):325–344.

Gunder-Frank, Andre. "The Development of Underdevelopment." *Monthly Review,* September, 1966.

Hansen, Bent, and Karim Nashashibi. *Foreign Trade Regimes and Economic Development: Egypt.* New York: Columbia University Press for N.B.E.R., 1975.

Hirschman, Albert O. *The Strategy of Economic Development.* New Haven: Yale University Press, 1959.

Hsing, Mo-Huan, John Power, and Gerard Sicat. *Taiwan and the Philippines: Industrialization and Trade Policies.* London: Oxford University Press, 1970.

Keesing, Donald B. "Trade Policy for Developing Countries." Mimeographed. Washington, D.C.: World Bank Staff Working Paper No. 353, 1979*a*.

———. "World Trade and Output of Manufactures: Structural Trends and Developing Countries' Exports." Washington, D.C.: World Bank Working Paper No. 316, January 1979*b*.

King, Timothy. *Mexico: Industrialization and Trade Policies Since 1940.* London: Oxford University Press for O.E.C.D., 1970.

Krueger, Anne O. "Some Economic Costs of Exchange Control: The Turkish Case." *Journal of Political Economy* 74 (1966):466–480.

———. *Foreign Trade Regimes and Development: Turkey.* New York and London: Columbia University Press for N.B.E.R., 1974*a*.

———. "The Political Economy of the Rent-Seeking Society." *American Economic Review* 64 (1974*b*): 291–303.

———. *Foreign Trade Regimes and Economic Development: Liberalization Attempts and Consequences.* Cambridge, Mass.: Ballinger for N.B.E.R., 1978.

Krueger, Anne O., Hal B. Lary, Terry Monson, and Narongchai Akrasanee. *Trade and Employment in Developing Countries, 1: Individual Studies.* Chicago: University of Chicago Press for National Bureau of Economic Research, 1981.

Leibenstein, Harvey. "Allocative Efficiency vs. 'X-Efficiency'." *American Economic Review* 56 (1966):392–415.

Leith, J.C. *Foreign Trade Regimes and Economic Development: Ghana.* New York: Columbia University Press, 1975.

Lewis, Stephen R., Jr. *Pakistan: Industrialization and Trade Policies.* London: Oxford University Press for O.E.C.D., 1970.

Lewis, W. Arthur. "Economic Development with Unlimited Supplies of Labor." *Manchester School* 22 (May 1954):139-191.

Little, I.M.D., T. Scitovsky, and M. Scott. *Industry and Trade in Some Developing Countries: A Comparative Study.* London: Oxford University Press, 1970.

Meier, Gerald M., ed. *Leading Issues in Economic Development.* New York: Oxford University Press, 1976.

Michaely, Michael. *Foreign Trade Regimes and Economic Development: Israel,* New York: Columbia University Press for N.B.E.R., 1974.

Ranis, Gustav. "Challenges and Opportunities Posed by Asia's Super-Exporters: Implications for Manufactured Exports from Latin America." Mimeographed. New Haven: Yale University, 1980.

Simon, Herbert A. *Administrative Behavior.* 2d ed. New York: John Wiley and Sons, 1961.

Tullock, Gordon "The Welfare Costs of Tariffs, Monoploy and Theft." *Western Economic Journal* 5 (June 1967):224-232.

Tyler, William G. *Manufactured Export Expansion and Industrialization in Brazil.* Kieler Studien. 134. Tubinger: J.C.B. Mohr, 1976.

Westphal, Larry E. "The Republic of Korea's Experience with Export-Led Industrial Development." *World Development* 6 (March 1978): 347-382.

World Bank. *World Development Report, 1980.* Washington, D.C., 1980.

Part II:
Country Studies

8
Recent Approaches to Industrial Policy in Australia

Peter Urban

Typically, as growth occurs in a developed economy, the relative sizes of the agricultural and manufacturing sectors decline while the tertiary sector expands. This pattern of growth is displayed by the Australian economy as by many others. The share of GNP contributed by manufacturing and agricultural industries has declined; the proportion of the labor force employed by these sectors has also declined. However, in the case of the Australian economy, the rapid expansion of the mineral-export industries has been an important factor in the structural changes occurring in the economy. The rate of growth of mineral exports has averaged over 15 percent per annum over the period 1953–1954 to 1976–1977, and minerals are likely to be the leading sector in Australia for some decades to come.

These rapid changes have exerted significant pressures on the competitiveness of many industries with slower productivity and demand growth. Manufacturing industries in particular have faced severe problems and there have been repeated calls from many industries, including automobiles and textiles, for government measures to reduce these pressures. In this chapter, we survey the main Australian thinking on IP. We separate the discussion into two broad groupings: (1) government-based studies; and (2) academic contributions.

Within these groupings, IP discussion has also been separated into tariff policy and other policy measures. This emphasis on tariff policy derived from the balance-of-payments problems of the 1950s and early 1960s and the use of import-replacement policies. The expansion of mineral exports since the mid-1960s stimulated a reevaluation of these earlier policies. At the same time, the resultant upward pressure on the exchange rate following the mining boom increased the demands for protection from imports; hence, tariff policy remains an important aspect of IP in Australia.

Next we review the three major government elements of IP—namely, the *White Paper on Manufacturing Industry,* the *Crawford Study Group Report,* and Industry Assistance Commission studies. Subsequently the nongovernment material is surveyed. Finally we draw conclusions on the Australian approach to IP.

Government Studies

The government set out in the *White Paper on Manufacturing Industry* (1977) the general, though potentially conflicting, policy goals of full employment, rising hiring standards, equality of opportunity, and freedom of choice.

For IP, these goals were specialized to the following:

1. generating a wider and fuller understanding of the significance of the changing environment for Australian manufacturing
2. ensuring that, in times of economic downturn, manufacturing has adequate support so as to alleviate economic and social disruption and minimize the erosion of employment opportunities
3. in the longer term, encouraging future development in activities that have the best prospect for expansion without the need for excessive support from consumers or taxpayers
4. providing a basis on which businesses can plan for the future

In outlining the proposed approach to IP, the *White Paper* indicated that policies would be oriented to developing a more efficient, specialized manufacturing industry which requires minimum levels of government support.

This commitment to a simpler and more stable tariff structure is mitigated by the need to avoid disruption and aggravation of short-term economic problems. Thus it summarizes its approach in this regard as seeking the following goals:

1. a more specialized and stronger manufacturing industry in Australia
2. concentration of effort in the areas where industry has the best market opportunities
3. major adjustments at a pace that does not cause undue economic or social disruption
4. new investment and job opportunities to permit adjustment to occur with beneficial results

While emphasizing greater specialization, the White Paper specifically rejects picking the winners:

> The Government has been repeatedly asked to nominate "key" industries or "desirable" industries or "growth" industries in which it believes further investment should be made, or to indicate the future role of a particular industry or sector in the Australian economy. . . .

This White Paper does not nominate "desirable" industries. The Government believes that international competitiveness in Australia manufacturing is possible not only in mineral and rural processing industries, but also in a wide range of activities where greater specialization and the use of management skills and innovation are of key importance. But the competitive pattern is subject to constant change and must be assessed in detail by enterprises. The Government cannot accurately predict—let alone govern—changes in the Australian industrial structure, and wrong predictions by it could seriously hinder the adjustment process and retard the competitive position of Australian industry.

The *White Paper* also noted the contribution of research and development and management and employee training to productivity. Thus it supported the following:

1. provision of industrial research-and-development incentives
2. assistance to inventors
3. operation of interfirm comparison studies
4. provision of research, design, testing, and advisory services in materials handling and packaging
5. undertaking of research, provision of advisory services, and dissemination of information relating to human relations in the work environment
6. provision of research and advisory services and the active encouragement of improved standards in the physical working environment

In addition, the government proposed to continue to encourage industry-based and associated bodies concerned with the development of industrial and product standards, industrial design, quality control, and to support many others concerned with improving technological and management capability.

Thus it appears that the policy approach to be followed in Australia conforms to the general principles outlined in chapter 3—namely, that policies should avoid being activity-specific and instead be designed to reduce distortions (such as underinvestment in research and development, economies of scale, and so on) common in a number of industries. In detailing the approach to avoiding disruption associated with tariff reductions and short-term economic downturns, however, the *White Paper* outlines a framework that reduces the likelihood of any significant tariff reform. The Industries Assistance Commission (IAC), charged with advising on industry assistance, is required to report explicitly on:

1. the method and level of tariff and other assistance necessary adequately to protect the industry against import competition

2. whether the industry could be more efficient, the basis for judging efficiency, the possible improvement in efficiency, and the level of tariff or assistance then required
3. whether the industry should be restructured and, if so, how this should be done and the likely consequences thereof
4. whether the industry is less efficient than it could be due to fragmentation, insufficient specialization, or some other restriction
5. the probable consequences—economic, social, and otherwise—of changing existing levels of tariffs or assistance

In certain cases the commission must:

1. report on the employment effect of its recommendations, including their effects on employment in decentralized locations
2. relate any recommendations for change to the capacity of the economy to absorb the changes involved
3. report on the assistance required to maintain the present level of activity and employment in the production of the goods under reference and, if a lower level of assistance is recommended by the commission, give the reasons why it does not recommend the assistance required to maintain the present level of activity and employment

These requirements are likely to mean that tariffs will be reduced only in unusual cases. Importantly, the slow growth characterizing much of the recent period could be construed as limiting the capacity of the economy to absorb any further changes and, hence, would preclude substantial tariff reform.

In fact, the emphasis on short-term economic problems and the support for temporary assistance given by the *White Paper* supports the view that policy in the near future is likely to rely more heavily on tariffs and quotas than in the past. This contradiction of the *general* principles to be followed extends to picking the winners.

The policy approach to be adopted is likely, as in the past, to give greater emphasis to political pragmatism and expediency than to any notions of economic efficiency. This view is reinforced when the emphasis on employment, not welfare, is noted in the earlier quotations. In terms of economic welfare, employment is not in itself an objective but is at least an intermediate target. In political terms, however, it may indeed be a target.

Crawford Study Group Report

The Study Group on Structural Adjustment was formed in 1978 to advise on policies needed by manufacturing industry (particularly the highly pro-

Australian Industrial Policy 193

tected industries). The group's report (hereafter referred to as the *Crawford Report*) identified two basic tasks in meeting this request: (1) to study the nature and extent of adjustment problems of Australian industry; and (2) to advise on the essential elements of a long-term strategy to deal with these problems.

The group's discussion of the first task reads like a litany of problems of mature economy in that it identified the need for a strategy as arising out of technological change, movements in relative wages, demographic shifts, increasing competition from exports from developing countries, the mining boom, and changes arising out of shifts in domestic consumption. The report also cites impediments to the economy's capacity to absorb changes—wage and price inflexibility, labor immobility, and constraints on the capital market.

In addressing the second task, the group saw the creation of employment opportunities as the primary objective of any successful adjustment policy (a similar emphasis as the earlier *White Paper*). Just as the White Paper endorsed the need for a long-term rationalization of the Australian tariff and quota structure, so did the *Crawford Report*.

The emphasis on employment also led the group to view high unemployment as a constraint on the ability to implement this longer-term policy. While the report covered a broad spectrum of alternative policies, including manpower policies, capital-market reform, and information provision, the most important recommendation centered on the group's proposals for export promotion.

Noting that, Australian industries needed to take advantage of export markets to achieve the internationally competitive scale economies that were precluded if they restricted themselves to the small domestic market and that the existing tariff structure acted as a tax on exporters, the group recommended an increase in the existing Export Expansion Grants Scheme.

Often, these export grants have similar general-equilibrium effects on the noncovered export industries as an increase in the tariff and, for the import-competing industries, as a reduction in the tariff. In a review of the *Crawford Report,* Stoeckel and Urban (1979) compared the effects of export grants with those of tariff reductions. The export grants may result in more industries being adversely affected although the import-competing industries bear the burden of the tariff cuts and, hence, would be expected to prefer the export grants.

Another study of the quantitative impact of technological change, export grants, and reduced barriers to world trade (Stoeckel, Paterson, and Urban 1979) found that the net employment effects of export grants may be negative. This occurs because industries that would benefit from the grants are capital-intensive whereas the industries that are adversely affected are relatively labor-intensive.

Overall, we can see that the *Crawford Report* subscribes to the same long-term philosophies as the *White Paper* and gives the same emphasis to short-term economic problems as a constraint on IP. However, whereas the *White Paper* supports the use of tariffs and quotas as temporary measures, the *Crawford Report* proposes the use of generally available export grants. Although such an approach is within the framework outlined in chapter 3, provided significant increasing returns to scale exist in the industries eligible for the grants, the evidence referred to suggests that these economies are either *small* or are associated with more complex considerations such as research and development, infrastructure, and so on.

Industries Assistance Commission Reports

Through its various reports, the IAC unfortunately may be viewed as commenting on IP only in a negative sense: The government passes to the IAC requests by industry for assistance to meet developing problems or requests to review existing assistance measures. Nevertheless, the almost-total reliance on industry-assistance measures in the form of tariffs and quotas in IP has meant that the IAC has developed considerable experience in the benefits and costs of such IP measures. Further, the commission has contributed to the growing public awareness of the need to rely on a wider range of IP instruments.

The IAC discussion of IP may be considered in regard to: (1) pairing of instruments and goals; and (2) measures. In the case of pairing, the IAC recommended separate measures for pursuing separate policy objectives. For example, goals of equity in the distribution of income and wealth may be best pursued through taxation policies and social-welfare programs, whereas economic-efficiency goals would be best pursued through IPs.

Thus the IAC (like Corden 1974) emphasizes the need to match target and instrument in a first-best sense. This emphasis is common in theoretical writings on economic policy; its importance in the case of the IAC is related to the commission's legislated-policy advisory role.

The IAC believes that IPs should be restricted to maintaining full employment and a properly functioning market when, for a variety of reasons, markets fail to reflect the true costs and benefits of production and consumption opportunities. Examples of such IPs include the Trade Practices Commission, which serves to regulate market behavior and government provision of information through its own preparation of reports or through its support of research elsewhere on such issues as: market prospects, alternative-employment opportunities, and alternative-investment opportunities.

This apparent disavowal of a more-activist role for IP (for example, through subsidies to industries with potential increasing returns to scale) seems based on both its experience with this argument as a basis for tariff assistance and the belief that these industries would be encouraged by decreasing high levels of assistance rather than by increasing low levels of assistance or providing assistance to industries that currently have none.

We see that all three elements accept the importance of long-run reform of the existing tariff structure. The *White Paper* tempered this support by arguing the need for short-term assistance to industries in order to maintain employment. The *Crawford Report* proposed the alternative of export grants. The IAC believes that continuous reform is necessary. It proposes another element of IP, however—namely, the corrective forms of intervention in structural adjustment presently available such as unemployment benefits and retraining schemes. Such measures may remedy or ameliorate the adverse consequences of change and provide solutions to problems such as redundant skills, obsolete plants and equipment, and adverse regional effects.

Conflicts in the elements of government discussion of IP are likely to mean that no single element will dominate until a public concensus emerges. Thus nongovernment debate could indicate the final form of IP.

Nongovernment Contributions

The Australian nongovernment literature on IP is extensive and many of the contributions (for example, Corden's) have been important to the international discussion of commercial policy. This richness has in many ways resulted from attempts by economists to improve public understanding of the limitations of existing policies and to suggest alternative policies. A second feature of the Australian literature comprises the significant contributions of agricultural economists; this derives from: (1) the importance of agriculture in the economy; and (2) the fact that there have been substantial shifts in the economic conditions facing many rural industries. These shifts have generated demands for government intervention. Responses to these demands have exhibited many of the features of policies recommended for manufacturing industry and, hence, experience with agricultural policy should cast light on general IP.

In this section, we discuss the approaches to IP in three areas: (1) general contributions on commercial policy; (2) the agricultural-policy experience; and (3) other relevant issues.

General Contributions

As apparent from the earlier discussion, much of the Australian writings on IP have merely discussed tariff policy. Given the emphasis on tariffs in actual policy, this is not surprising. However, among those who argue for tariff reform (Lloyd, 1975), for example, there is the presumption that the existing tariff structure imposes substantial costs on the community.

Early attempts at measurement of this cost included Corden (1957) and Evans (1972); these studies found gains from tariff reform to be small. However, in a simple three-commodity model that allowed for possible increasing returns in two of the industries, Dixon (1977) found that the gains may be as high as 20 percent of GNP and he concluded that the small gains produced in earlier models resulted from the restrictive assumptions inherent in the models.

Beyond indicating the potential benefits of tariff reform, the Dixon study indicated the likely importance of increasing returns as an argument for IP. In addition, issues such as defense and externalities have been discounted in the Australian context (Lloyd 1978). Even the employment argument has less clear-cut support; for example, the Scott, et al. study (1975), which centered on the employment issue, was strongly criticized by Lloyd (1978) on practical grounds.

In relation to policies to mitigate distortions arising from increasing returns, Pursell and Snape (1973) show that export subsidies (not tariffs) are the appropriate policy response. Thus there is support for the Crawford Report's recommendation. This proposal even encompasses the idea of export-promotion through the negotiation of bilateral trading agreements.

Under this proposal, Australia would link tariff preference for particular countries (such as the LDCs, whose exports are subject to punitive tariffs) to the negotiation of long-term contracts for certain Australian manufacturing exports. This would stimulate expansion of industries subject to increasing returns and would allow reform of the existing tariff structure, thus avoiding the major criticisms of the Crawford Report proposal. The unanswered question is whether Australia and foreign governments are ready to enter into such negotiations.

The most detailed criticisms of the tariff reform proposal have been made by Gunnerson (1973) and Norman (1975). These criticisms are not aimed at tariff reform as such, but rather at the procedure by which reform would take place. Most advocates of tariff reform have advocated that tariffs be decreased through a percentage reduction in the level of effective protection. Both Gunnerson and Norman point out the problems associated with measurement of effective protection and conclude that reform based on these measurements may in fact lead to increases in inefficient resource allocation.

A separate line of criticism of the tariff-reform policy has been developed by Gruen (1971), Harris (1975), and A.G. Lloyd (1977). In their view, removal of tariffs will not be possible because of, for example, political considerations. They thus propose increasing the level of assistance to industries now receiving low levels. Both Lloyd (1975) and Warr (1977) point out that this second-best argument relies heavily on the fixity of the existing tariff structure, and they question the capacity of policymakers to determine the appropriate level of assistance for particular industries.

Overall, the nongovernment debate suggests that the final IP approach will be a combination of tariff reform with selective promotion of individual industries, with the extent of tariff reform determined by the capacity of the economy to absorb the changes. In relation to the question of the capacity to adjust, the experience in agriculture is relevant.

Agricultural Policy

Just as balance-of-payments problems in the 1950s and early 1960s were an important stimulus for tariff policy, they generated a corresponding complex set of home-price schemes, tax concessions, subsidies for export promotion, and government involvement in agricultural research-and-extension services that attempted to encourage rural exports and offset the effects of the tariff on costs. However, this balance-of-payments pessimism (Edwards and Watson 1978) disappeared in the mid-1960s with the growth in mineral exports.

The disappearance of the underlying rationale for these policies was combined with growing public acceptance of criticisms of many of these policies by agricultural economists—for example, Lewis (1961), Longworth (1966, 1967), Watson and Duloy (1968), and A.G. Lloyd (1971). Where policy attempted to promote the development of new industries such as cotton growing on the Ord Scheme, the adverse comments of Davidson (1965), among others, provided an important brake.

Agricultural policymaking entered the 1970s without the bias toward fragmented policies that encouraged substantial misallocation of resources in the manufacturing industries. At the same time, policy was not oriented to handling problems arising out of the fall in the terms of trade of the major rural industries that began in the late 1960s. This situation gradually changed with Australian agricultural economists being especially influenced by the arguments of Schultz (1961). In this view, resource immobility in agriculture as a result of lack of training, inadequate information, and asset-fixity problems warranted government intervention.

Policy reflected these views and a variety of rural-reconstruction schemes developed. The major instrument of these programs was the provision of long-term loans at below-market rates. The IAC (1976), reporting on rural reconstruction, endorsed the general principles of the measures but recommended greater provisions be made for farmers to leave agriculture and removal of the subsidy implicit in the low-interest rate applying to the loans provided.

The general availability of adjustment assistance has reduced pressures for ad hoc temporary policies that may lead to substantial inefficiencies in resource allocation. The conclusion supports the IAC approach to IP.

Other Relevant Policies

The discussion so far has emphasized the tariff within the context of IP in Australia. However, other forms of government policy have influenced IP. The measures may be divided into: (1) wage policy; (2) competition; (3) financial regulation; and (4) ownership and control.

Wage Policy. A distinguishing feature of the Australian economy is the centralization of wage setting under a number of statutory authorities, the most important being the Federal Conciliation and Arbitration Commission (CAC) whose decisions influence the various state tribunals. This centralization of wage setting would appear to provide the Australian government with a mechanism for operating an incomes policy as part of an overall IP.

In practice, this has not been the case for three reasons:

1. The authorities have influence over only *wages* and not over the incomes of many professional groups.
2. They take into account considerations beyond economic efficiency when setting wages.
3. They are not directly responsible to the government and, hence, cannot be used as an instrument of policy.

The latter two points are particularly important. If wages are to be used as an instrument of IP, then they need to be varied in accord with industry circumstances. However, real wages in Australia have been held up in the presence of substantial unemployment. The role of the CAC in this maintenance of real wages stems from its rejection of economic considerations in determining wages.

Competition. The small size of the Australian market place means that government policy toward monopoly and oligopoly is simultaneously more critical and needs to be more realistic than in larger countries. The Trade Practices Act (1974 and 1977) prohibits both monopolization and anticompetitive mergers. Monopoly as such is not prohibited, however; rather, the use of monopoly power to *damage* a competitor is prohibited.

Unfortunately, increasing returns to scale in many industries would be expected to result in such damage. The 1977 act recognized this paradox and placed greater emphasis on *net* public benefit.

Overall, the current policy position on competition is neutral. It limits the scope for restricted trade practices (for example, collusion) but does not discourage innovative efficiency-improving changes in industrial organization (Allan, Nieuwenhuysen, and Norman 1979).

Financial Regulation. The importance for IP of intervention in the financial market derives from its role in determining the cost (and, hence, allocation) of capital. In Australia, the Reserve Bank regulates banks with reserve requirements and regulation of their portfolio structure.

This has resulted in the development of nonbank financial intermediaries. The Financial Corporations Act of 1974 was enacted to broaden financial regulation beyond the banking sector. Implementation of this legislation has been slow, however, and currently the banks remain the only intermediaries subject to reserve requirements. The major change in financial regulation has been through the establishment of government-backed institutions such as the Commonwealth Development Bank (CDB) in 1960, the Australian Resources Development Bank (ARDB) in 1969, and the Australian Industry Development Corporation (AIDC) in 1970. The role of both the CDB and AIDC is to provide short-, medium-, and long-term loans to small firms perceived to be disadvantaged relative to large firms. The ARDB's role was to facilitate consortium lending for large projects requiring long-term capital.

There are a number of lesser government-owned institutions. Each aims at filling a perceived gap in the private financial market. In practice, they all aim at providing government assistance to particular industries or groups and, hence, must be viewed as instruments of IP.

Government policy toward overseas capital flows has also had a significant influence on financial markets, given the substantial influence of such funds on domestic financial markets. The rationale for policies such as deposit requirements has been twofold: (1) to reduce the destabilizing effects of such flows on the balance of payments and the money supply; and (2) to limit foreign ownership and control of Australian assets, particularly in natural resources.

The overall trend in financial regulation has been away from regulation of specific institutions toward more general controls and greater use of open-market operations to achieve macroeconomic targets. Where financial regulation has had specific IP targets, this has usually been achieved through lending from government-backed institutions.

Ownership and Control. The extent of foreign control of Australian companies has generated unfavorable public opinion and calls for government restrictions on foreign investment. The government response has included exerting controls on capital inflows, passing the Foreign Takeovers Act in 1975, and establishing the Foreign Investment Review Board. These measures were aimed at four main areas of investment:

1. inhibiting future foreign investment in real estate or property except for immediate residential purposes
2. screening all foreign investment in nonbank financial intermediaries and insurance companies, including large existing business where the growth rate of assets was in excess of 15 percent per annum
3. examining all new-business proposals where the foreign investment totaled $1 million or more
4. requiring minimum Australian participation levels in mining ventures within Australia

Although the application of these measures diverges from the aggressive attitude of the mid-1970s in that foreign investment is now encouraged, each project is evaluated on its own merits and some are subject to modification. For example, in its report in November 1977, the FIRB stated that it rejected only 7 applications out of a total of 1,043 in the fifteen months to June 1977. It approved another 449, subject to modification, however.

The key IP implication of these measures is the fact that the government is, on occasion, prepared to place less priority on industry-development objectives than on overall objectives of Australian ownership. This is less true in the case of manufacturing industries than in the case of ownership of natural resources.

Conclusions

The foregoing review identified three prominant elements in the discussion of alternative approaches to IP in Australia:

1. the use of ad hoc temporary-assistance measures on an industry-by-industry basis (*White Paper*)
2. broad export promotion (*Crawford Report*)
3. avoidance of positive IPs in favor of adjustment-assistance measures (IAC)

We argued that the first approach was a product of political expediency and, as such, would be influenced by shifts in public opinion. The other two policy approaches were based on economic considerations.

The *Crawford Report* argued for export expansion on two grounds: (1) The costs of rationalization of the existing tariff structure, given the current economic circumstances, were high; and (2) increasing returns existed in many industries. Subsidies to these industries would stimulate their expansion and result in a smoother transfer of resources away from the inefficient tariff-assisted industries.

The IAC, while noting the basis of this view, argued that past experience indicated that the outcome of this approach was not certain. Instead, it opted for a passive approach to IP through measures aimed at removing impediments to resource reallocation: retraining schemes, unemployment benefits, improved information on employment, and investment opportunities, and so on.

We see experience with agricultural policy as providing some support for the IAC view. In this sector, policy has opted for an increasingly passive approach to IP rather than promotion of specific industries or provision of ad hoc measures although such measures are still common. We may note that agriculture has, in recent years, experienced significant increases in real incomes; partly results from improvements in commodity prices. Nevertheless, the shift of resources into the broad-acre industries, which benefited most from this improvement, may be seen as an indication of the trend to a passive approach.

A number of other policies are important, including wages, ownership and control, competition, and financial regulation. In Australia, there are potential conflicts between wages, competition and ownership, and control policies and industry-development objectives.

With regard to wage policy, the centralization provides, prima facie, an important mechanism for coordinating wage policy with IP. In reality the existing institutional arrangements result in substantial conflicts, with wages being determined irregardless of economic circumstances.

Overall, the Australian approach to IP must be viewed as a series of shifts. The emphasis in the 1950s and 1960s was on ad hoc measures. The 1970s brought a realization of the need for policy rationalization. This need is likely to be emphasized in the 1980s as the mineral-export industries again attract substantial foreign investment and as new projects begin production, swelling exports.

Both developments can be expected to result in upward pressure on the exchange rate and, hence, reduce the competitiveness of traditional export- and import-competing industries; this will, in turn, lead to pressure for assistance from the affected industries. Which approach the government will take to these demands is unclear. It is inevitable, however, that the debate will continue to be polarized.

References

Allan, R.H., J.P. Nieuwenhuysen, and N.R. Norman. "Government Intervention in the Economy of Australia," in *Government Intervention in the Developed Economy,* P. Maunder, ed. London: Croom Helm, 1979.

Corden, W.M. *The Theory of Protection*. Oxford: Clarendon Press, 1971.
———. *Trade Policy and Economic Welfare*. Oxford: Clarendon Press, 1974.
Crawford, Sir John, et al. *Study Group on Structural Adjustment*. Canberra: Australian Government Printing Service, 1979.
Davidson, B.R. *The Northern Myth*. Melbourne: Melbourne University Press, 1965.
Dixon, P.J. "The Costs of Protection: The Old and New Arguments." *Australian Economic Paper*, 1977.
Edwards, G.W., and A.S. Watson. "Agricultural Policy" in *Surveys of Australian Economics*, F.H. Gruen, ed. Sydney: George Allen & Unwin, 1978.
Evans, H.D. *A General Equilibrium Analysis of Protection*. Amsterdam: North-Holland, 1972.
Gruen, F.H. "Stabilization and All-Round Protection in Australian Agriculture," in D. Douglas, ed., *National Rural Policy*. Sydney: Sydney University Extension Board, 1971.
Gunnerson, T.H. *The Effective Rate of Protection and the Tariff Board*. Melbourne: AIDA Special Bulletin, 1973.
Harris, S.F. "Tariff Compensation: Sufficient Justification for Assistance for Australian Agriculture." *Australian Journal of Agricultural Economics* (1975).
Industries Assistance Commission. *Some Issues in Structural Adjustment*. Canberra: Australian Government Printing Service, 1977.
———. *Annual Report*. Canberra: Australian Government Printing Service, 1974.
———. *Rural Reconstruction*. Canberra: Australian Government Printing Service, 1976.
Lewis, J.N. "Organized Marketing of Agricultural Products in Australia." *Australian Journal of Agricultural Economics* (1961).
Lloyd, A.G. "Quotas: Some General Issues, with Particular Reference to the Dairy Industry." Paper presented at the 15th Annual Conference of the Australian Agricultural Economics Society, Adelaide, 1971.
———. "Farm Income Stabilization: Some Options." Paper presented at the 21st Conference of the Australian Agricultural Economics Society, Brisbane, 1977.
———. "Tariff Compensation: An Undesirable Policy." *Australian Journal of Agricultural Economics* (1975).
———. "Protection Policy," in *Surveys of Australian Economics*, F.H. Gruen, ed., Sydney: George Allen & Unwin, 1978.
Longworth, J.W. "The Australian Wheat Industry Stabilization Scheme: An Analytical Model." *Economic Record* (1966).
———. "The Stabilization and Distribution Effects of the Australian

Wheat Industry Stabilization Scheme. *Australian Journal of Agricultural Economics* (1967).

Norman, N.R. "The Effective Rate of Protection." Canberra: AIDE, 1975.

Pursell, G., and R.H. Snape. "Economies of Scale, Price Discrimination and Exporting." *Journal of International Economics* (1973).

Schultz, T.W. "A Policy to Redistribute Losses from Economic Progress." *Journal of Farm Economics* (1961).

Scott, W.D., and Co. "A Study of Resource Allocation Strategy in Australia." A.C.M.A., Sydney, 1975.

Stoeckel, A.B., P. Paterson, and P.J. Urban. "Some General Equilibrium Effects of Three Aspects of Structural Change in Agriculture," in *The Economics of Structural Change and Adjustment,* C.J. Aislabie and C.A. Tisdell, eds., Institute of Economics, University of Newcastle; Newcastle, 1975.

Stoeckel, A.B., and P.J. Urban. "Study Group on Structural Adjustment—A Summary Appraisal." Mimeographed. Canberra, 1979.

Urban, P.J. "Industrial Policy: Some Theoretical Considerations." Philadelphia: Industry Policy Study, University of Pennsylvania, 1981.

Warr, P.G. "Tariff Compensation Via Input Subsidies." *Economic Record,* 1977.

Watson, A.S., and J.H. Duloy. "Wheat Stabilization Policy—A Supply Study." Armidale: New England Marketing Studies No. 2, N.S.W., 1968.

White Paper on Manufacturing Industry. Canberra: Australian Government Printing Service, 1977.

9 Industrial Policy in Canada: A Survey

William J. Milne

In Canada, international developments and the slowdown in productivity growth in the developed economies have focused attention on the need for a more positive role by government in forming policy to deal with industrial structure and performance. Both federal and provincial governments in Canada have long been concerned with promoting industrial and regional development. This interest has become more prominent over the last decade as Canadian manufacturing industries have exhibited slower productivity growth and deteriorating export performance in conjunction with a weakening Canadian dollar. This chapter explores IP followed by Canadian governments.

We must note that IP in Canada varies considerably from that of other countries. As Rea and McLeod (1976) point out:

> The story of business and government in Canada is a complex one, reflecting the distinctive Canadian environment, but it does not reflect nineteenth century British norms of laissez-faire or American norms of the relative separation of the state and commerce. In Canada, the history of the state and economic life are inextricably interwoven and inseparable. (p. 11)

Policy has grown out of concern about regional economic disparities, a rapidly growing labor force, and proximity to the large U.S. economy. With the world economy experiencing a shift from reactive to more active and aggressive IPs (due to the establishment of cartels, strategic pricing, the existence of trading blocs, and the emergence of the Third World in the industrial world) an even closer partnership between government and business in the area of IP is needed.

In the next section, we consider the rationale for IP in Canada. We then examine the Canadian experience, considering the use of direct government intervention through public ownership, the promotion of research and development, international policies to promote industrial development, the promotion of regional economic development, government-procurement policies and, finally, the role of taxation in an IP package. We conclude with a summary and identify issues for the 1980s.

Basis for an Industrial Strategy in Canada

In Canada, industrial strategies are viewed as attempts to reduce the difference between the actual output of a sector and the socially optimal level. Typically, these strategies are conceived of for only the industrial sector (and, in particular, the manufacturing industries), but clearly a policy that affects the industrial sector will also affect other sectors of the economy.

Chapter 3 identified reasons why the actual output level may not coincide with the socially optimal level: These include externalities, risk, evidence of monopoly, past government intervention, and nationalism.[1] In fact, what makes government pursue a particular IP is some complex combination of these justifications.

In the Canadian setting, we have seen IP enacted for many reasons. Specifically, industrial assistance has taken many forms, including cash grants, loan guarantees, tax subsidies and rebates, direct government intervention through ownership, regulation and restriction, technical aid for research and development, manpower retraining programs, and procurement policies.

An often-cited reason to justify government assistance to Canadian industry is the economies-of-scale argument. That is, observers suggest that the lower average output per person in the manufacturing industries in Canada compared to the United States is due to inefficiencies in the production process which, to some extent, can be traced to the size of the market, the size of the firm, and the length of the production run. This point is made by Daly and associates (1968) and more directly by Wonnacott (1975), who claims that there are "unexploited economies of scale in the small Canadian market" (p. 537-538).

This general philosophy of aiding manufacturing has steered many of the assistance programs in Canada. There is a general finding that protection must be given to the manufacturing sector through tariff barriers, tax incentives, and so on, in an effort to overcome the scale inefficiencies and to foster East-West trade in Canada. Next we will identify the instruments that have been used to achieve this goal.

The Canadian Experience

Canadian government assistance to business is a time-honoured tradition, dating back more than three centuries to May 2, 1670 when King Charles II granted a charter to the "Company of Adventurers of England trading into Hudson's Bay," usually known as the Hudson's Bay Company. This charter gave the company much of what is now Canada and assured a monopoly on trade.

In 1879, Canada became a high-tariff country through the development of the National Policy. This legislation represented a decision to promote industrialization in terms of a Canadian rather than a North American market. The protectionist policy fostered manufacturing development in Ontario and Quebec. In addition to this, Macdonald (then prime minister) gave the Canadian Pacific Railway $100 million in subsidies and land grants to complete the intercontinental railway—a PSP effort to encourage East-West trade and promote industrial growth.[2]

Reliance on high tariffs to encourage industrial development continued until the late 1940s, when there was strong support in Canada for a reduction in world trade barriers. This led to Canada's participation in the General Agreement on Tariffs and Trade (GATT) negotiated in 1947. This tariff policy, while encouraging the development of the manufacturing sector, also led to costs such as inefficiency in production, lower productivity, and substantial foreign ownership and control (an important issue in the Canadian context).

The issue of foreign ownership has been debated in Canada over the last two decades since many economists felt Canada was becoming a branch-plant economy, following all the direct investment from the United States. There is substantial foreign ownership of Canada's manufacturing industry. Canada's dependence on U.S. direct investment in 1970 was ten times higher than the average of a group of thirteen of the most industrialized OECD countries. This concern about foreign ownership led to the establishment of the Foreign Investment Review Agency (FIRA)—an agency that screens new investment proposals by foreigners—in 1973.

Since the mid-1970s, there has been considerable debate about Canadian IP. In answer to different policy proposals suggested by different groups,[3] in early 1978 the federal government set up twenty-three sectoral task forces to evaluate government-business interaction. The reports of these task forces were reviewed by a government committee whose mandate was to make recommendations about factors and policies that cut across sectoral lines. Themes stressed in these overview committee reports focus on measures to increase industrial competitiveness, the support of regional economic-development goals, and the improvement of government, business, and labor cooperation.

The remainder of this section deals with government policy toward business—in particular, direct government intervention, governmental role in research and development, international policies, with regard to both tariffs and bilateral agreements, IPs in the regional framework, government-procurement policy, and government tax policy toward business.

Government's Direct Role in Industrial Policy

Governments sometimes opt for direct involvement in industry through public ownership. In North America, public ownership is generally considered exceptional. In Canada, however, public enterprises are becoming more numerous. In terms of an overall IP there are a number of rationales for this:

1. to spur regional economic development
2. to operate where private enterprise is unable or unwilling to go
3. to measure and promote economic performance in the private sector
4. to function as part of a national economic policy

There are a number of important federal-government enterprises (crown corporations)[4] and an even larger number chartered by the provinces. In Canada, the government historically found itself the owner and operator of infrastructure (for example, canals) and the heavy subsidizer of privately owned railways in an effort to combine the rapidly growing but sparsely populated economy. In the 1930s and 1940s the effects of the Depression and the war years inspired public ownership.

In the present Canadian industrial sector, public enterprise is not massive but is growing. Three industry groups stand out: (1) steel, (2) pulp and paper, and (3) petroleum exploration and production. Two of the publicly owned steel firms, Sidbec and Sysco, can be traced to financial difficulties of the Dominion Steel and Coal Co. Sidbec was created in the late 1960s by the Quebec government in an effort to aid industrial development. A third steel firm, Interprovincial Steel and Pipe Corporation (IPSCO) is a joint public-private venture, the public portion being shared by Alberta and Saskatchewan. Provincially owned pulp-and-paper firms can be found in Newfoundland, Manitoba, Saskatchewan, and British Columbia. These represent a mixture of economic-development schemes and employment maintenance.

The predominant sector receiving public enterprise in the 1970s was petroleum and natural gas. Crown corporations engaged in exploration and development and production of hydrocarbons have been established at the federal level (PetroCanada) and in the provinces of Quebec, Ontario, Saskatchewan, Alberta, and British Columbia. These endeavors are largely in response to the oil crisis of the early 1970s and the desire for greater Canadian control of an industry dominated by foreign-owned firms. PetroCanada, created in 1975, is the most visible of these corporations. Recent government announcements suggest an even-more-important role for crown corporations in the area of research and development and as an information source.[5]

Through development corporations, provinces have often attempted to attract industry with discouraging results. Mathias (1971) discusses five cases of this forced growth. Sometimes, direct intervention by government was undertaken jointly with a foreign-owned firm.

The federal government established the Canada Development Corporation (CDC) in 1971 as a crown corporation. It was designed as a vehicle through which (1) Canadian investment in resident companies could be increased; (2) Canadian businesses could be created or developed; and (3) venture capital could be supplied to a variety of enterprises at reduced risk. Initial capitalization of the CDC came from the federal government, but the ultimate goal is for 90 percent equity ownership by the investing public. The CDC chooses enterprises based on: (1) whether they have high profit-growth potential; and (2) whether they belong to the petroleum-and-natural-gas, petrochemicals, mining, pipelines, or health-care sectors. This corporation has been generally successful.

Government Support of Research and Development

Compared with other industrialized countries, Canada currently ranks near the bottom in research-and-development spending. While Canada spent approximately 0.9 percent of its GNP on research and development in 1977, the United States spent 2.4 percent, West Germany spent 2.0 percent, France expended 1.8 percent, and Japan directed 1.7 percent of GNP to research and development.[6] Furthermore, the ratio of research-and-development expenditures to GNP has exhibited a downward trend since 1967. The Canadian government aims to increase expenditures on research and development to 1.5 percent of GNP by 1983, reflecting the government's recognition of the importance of developing a viable research-and-development sector in Canada.[7]

Industrial intramural research-and-development expenditures vary significantly across industries. Recently, approximately 70 percent of the expenditures are funded by the reporting company whereas the federal government provides slightly more than 10 percent of the funds. Most of the federal funding comes in the aircraft and electronics industry and is primarily related to defense.

Research-and-development incentive programs in Canada are either income-tax related or take the form of specific government grants or loan guarantees. They are all designed to increase the productivity of Canadian industry and to assist in the creation of new technology by encouraging business to undertake or increase the level of research-and-development activities.

Federal assistance falls into three main categories: (1) information and services; (2) support for industrial research, innovation, and product development; and (3) government research and technology transfer.

Information and Services. The federal government provides information on new inventions and developments, operates government testing-and-laboratory facilities, and administers the patents program. The National Research Council (NRC) assists with technological or scientific problems.

Innovation and Product Development. Assistance in meeting professional and technical-staff costs of research projects is provided through several federal programs. The Industrial Research and Assistance Program (IRAP) was established in 1962 to encourage and assist Canadian industry in setting up private research-and-development teams. In 1973, the program was altered to increase the commercial capabilities of companies by providing financial support to research workers engaged in projects with prospects of high return and plans for success. In recent years, the IRAP has supported two hundred and fifty projects each year, with grants totaling nearly $20 million annually.

The Scientific and Technical Employment Program (STEP) was introduced in April 1978 as an experiment designed to increase the opportunity for permanent employment in the private sector for scientific or technically skilled persons who are currently unemployed. A related program, STEPEX, provides subsidies for unemployed research staff hired by universities or research institutes to carry out projects requested by private-sector firms. These two programs had a budget of $5.9 million for fiscal year 1979–1980.[8]

The Industry Energy and Development Program (IERD), an energy-conservation program, introduced in 1978, is designed to provide funds for research-and-development projects that may result in significant energy savings and for which the developed technology would be widely applicable in Canada. The program budget for fiscal year 1979–1980 was $1.5 million, and the costs are shared on a fifty-fifty basis.

Under the Enterprise Development Program (EDP), up to $60 million a year is now provided to small- and medium-sized manufacturing and processing companies for high-risk innovative projects. The EDP was started in April 1977 and combined several assistance programs.[9] This is one of the major programs sponsored by the Industry, Trade and Commerce Department of the federal government. Innovative assistance comes in the form of shared costs and there are eight classifications of innovation projects: proposal preparation, identification of new projects, product development and design, project exploitation, productivity enhancement, special assistance for specified industries,[10] protective contributions, and pollution abatement.

There is also support provided to specific industries to aid research and development.

The Defense Industry Productivity Program (DIP) supports Canadian international defense cooperation on research and development and production. It originated in 1959 when the Canada/U.S. Defense Production Sharing Agreement was met. This allows Canada to benefit from advanced technology by the development of defense and defense-related products for the international market. Over $40 million per year of assistance is provided to aid firms in sustaining and developing their technological capability for defense-export sales or associated civil-export sales, primarily to the aerospace and electronics industries.[11] Grants of up to 50 percent of eligible costs are available.

The programs outlined are, in general, shared-cost programs; that is, government attempts to assist private industry by offering assistance in business-research programs rather than undertaking research and development itself. Second, these policies were designed to overcome particular problems—for example, to reduce high risk or to take advantage of externalities.

In addition to grants and cost-sharing agreements, the federal government supports research-and-development expenditures through various tax incentives. For example, there are full tax write-offs for expenditures on scientific research; there is a special deduction of 50 percent for research-and-development-expenditure increases over the previous three-year average; and, there are investment-tax credits, depending on the region in which the research is carried out.

Government Research and Technology Transfer. The federal government now contracts out as much as possible of the science and technology requirements to the private sector. Consequently, numerous Canadian companies receive research-and-development-project contracts from the federal government.

The provincial governments are also concerned with research-and-development expenditures. As recently as January 27, 1981, the Ontario government announced a major program of IP. Part of this program is to ensure international competitiveness and achieve economic growth by promoting research and development and aiding high-technology industries.[12] This policy brings a new organization—the Innovation Development for Employment Advancement (IDEA). Its mandate is to promote the development of new technologies, to increase the supply of skilled manpower, and to facilitate the application of the latest technology to industry.

As is clear from the many existing programs to aid research and development, the various levels of government are concerned with the historical record in Canada. The problem largely stems from the structure of Canadian industry, with its high proportion of foreign ownership resulting in the business-enterprise sector's doing only a small proportion of research compared with the government sector. This has resulted in less-successful research-and-development programs in Canada than in many other countries.[13]

International Policies

Canada followed a protectionist policy until the original GATT negotiations in 1947 and thereafter headed toward free trade. There are basically two sets of programs involved in dealing with international policies: (1) those dealing with promoting exports and limiting imports and (2) those setting up bilateral agreements.

Bilateral Agreements. Perhaps the most widely known of the bilateral agreements is the Canadian-American Auto Pact of 1965. Before the agreement there were 17.5 percent-tariff barriers, which resulted in the domination of the Canadian auto industry by U.S. companies which operated subsidiaries in Canada. Furthermore, exports to the United States were very low due to a 6.5-8.5 percent tariff enacted by the United States. This resulted in short production runs, inefficiency, and substantially higher unit-production costs in Canada. The agreement was designed to increase the assembly of vehicles and manufacture of parts in Canada by eliminating tariffs at the manufacturing level on automotive vehicles and parts.

Undeniably, this agreement worked to Canada's advantage through the middle 1970s. The trade balance on motor vehicles and parts improved substantially through the early 1970s; in addition, production of cars in Canada increased by 135 percent between 1964 and 1973. Indeed, through 1973, Canada's share of North American production increased from 7 to 11 percent; wage rates in the Canadian industry rose to U.S. levels. However, there was no change in the pattern of foreign ownership or in the research-and-development location. Also of concern to Canada was the deterioration of the trade balance through the 1970s. In addition, a commission set up by the Canadian government found that more of the parts manufacture was done in-house by the large car manufacturers while independent parts manufacturers were failing (see Reisman 1978). This led the Ontario government (1981) to establish an Automotive Parts Technology Center to provide adequate testing facilities and skilled tradespeople in an effort to offset this trend.

Another important agreement with the United States was the Canada-U.S. Defense Production Sharing Program signed in 1959. This program was developed during the 1950s in response to the realization that Canada could not efficiently develop or produce its own major weapons systems. Under the terms of the bilateral agreement, Canadian defense goods are excluded from the provisions of the Buy American Act and from U.S. customs duties. A balance-of-payments clause was added in 1963, stipulating that Canadian imports from the United States must roughly balance Canadian exports. This program has protected and promoted the defense industry in Canada and has emphasized the high-technology sectors of aerospace and electronics.[14]

Policies to Promote Exports and Limit Imports. The government has established a considerable number of programs to assist Canadian export-trade companies. Government assistance is provided through promotional events and cost-sharing programs for companies that show a need to share the financial risk of developing or adjusting to a foreign market.

The federal government also operates a crown corporation, the Export Development Corporation (EDC), which provides insurance, loan guarantees, and other programs necessary for exporters to compete in international markets. In view of other countries' more aggressive policies in this regard (for example, Japan and the Western European countries), there is considerable sentiment in Canada to upgrade these programs.

The Machinery Program was introduced in 1968 to increase the efficiency of Canadian industry by enabling machinery users to acquire advanced capital equipment at the lowest cost while affording Canadian machinery producers tariff protection on their products. This program emerged from changes in the Canadian tariff structure arising from the Kennedy round of tariff negotiations. The duty otherwise payable on machinery accessories, attachments, control equipment, tools, and components may be remitted if it is in the public interest and if the goods imported are not available in Canada. The program covers general-purpose machinery, metalworking and woodworking machinery, construction and materials handling equipment, and various special types of industry machinery. The tariff imposed on these activities allows the Canadian industry to develop unhindered.

Four sets of tariff rates make up the Canadian tariff: British Preferential (BP), most-favored nation (MFN), general, and general preferential. BP tariffs are applied to imported commodities from the Commonwealth countries whereas the MFN rates, which are usually higher than the BP rates, are applied to countries with whom Canada has a trade agreement. These are regulated through GATT. In general, the tariff schedule favors manufacture of products that are at a relatively finished or nearly finished stage. In addition, Canada has an Anti-Dumping Act (enacted in 1968) which provides, in simplest terms, that where goods are dumped on the Canadian market (export price less than the normal value) an antidumping duty can be imposed.

A number of authors—for example, Daly and Globerman (1976)—have pointed to tariff protection as the cause of the poor competitive structure of Canadian industry. They argue that tariff protection provides a shelter for inefficient firms and has allowed technologically obsolescent industries to survive. Also, as discussed earlier, high tariffs encourage foreign ownership and consequently reduce research-and-development expenditures.

Regional Assistance Programs

In 1969, the federal government created the Department of Regional Economic Expansion (DREE) to coordinate its efforts to reduce geographical income disparities across Canada and in 1970, through the Regional Development Incentives Act (RDIA) DREE was given the power and financial capability of subsidizing firms that invest in certain designated areas. The strategy of DREE, in these programs, comprises three elements: (1) industrial incentive, designed to generate productive employment by making investment more attractive in slow-growth regions; (2) infrastructure assistance to facilitate economic expansion; and (3) social and rural development to provide greater access of labor in rural areas. RDIA gives discretionary cash grants or loan guarantees. These programs are of particular interest since they have the potential of altering the geographical allocation of resources and can affect the way capital and labor are combined in production.

Several issues have been involved with these grants:[15]

1. New investment associated with DREE grants may displace investment that would otherwise have been undertaken since established firms in a designated area may not expand if a competing firm is attracted to the area through a grant.
2. Some grants may go to firms that would have undertaken investment anyway.
3. There has been a substantial increase, not decrease, in unemployment in some designated areas.
4. Investments requiring subsidies are likely to be those with a lower rate of return. This means that national income may fall whereas income in the region increase.

Perhaps the best-known Canadian regional-assistance case is that of the French Michelin Tire Company. Michelin received cash payments, tax credits, and loans from various levels of government to establish two tire-manufacturing plants in the Maritimes to stimulate regional economic growth and development. This was one of the more-successful endeavors under RDIA.

Government-Procurement Policy

Purchase policy of government is a flexible instrument of government policy that can easily adapt to new goals without significant legislative or administrative delay. The mere number and variety of goods and services purchased by the government indicate this policy's importance for industry.

On a federal level, the Department of Supply and Services is responsible for giving preference to Canadian industries and workers. In general no more than a 10-percent premium should be paid for Canadian content. A recent study has shown, moreover, that substantial benefits—both economic and social—accrue to Canadians from this unofficial buy-Canadian policy which outweigh the short-term costs to the taxpayer.[16] In fact, government regulations prohibit offshore purchases of shoes, textiles, food, motor vehicles, ships, appliances, fine paper, and wood furniture by the government. Governmental policy with regard to procurement can be considered a nontariff barrier to trade as Stegemann (1973) indicates.

Tax Programs

During the 1960s, the federal government instituted a number of measures to aid investment in the manufacturing industries. These included a two year write-off on machinery and equipment by Canadian-owned manufacturing firms in 1963 through the end of 1966. In addition, there was a special deduction instituted to fund scientific research. Some of these policies also had a regional dimension; that is, areas with high unemployment were allowed even larger tax write-offs. Through the 1960s there were broad-based tax incentives to the manufacturing and processing industries.[17]

In 1972, the finance minister announced a new industrial strategy aimed to develop manufacturing industries that are dynamic, vigorous, and resourceful; that develop new and better products; and that aggressively seek to expand their markets in Canada and abroad. This new policy was implemented through reductions in corporation income taxes and accelerated capital-cost allowances introduced for the processing and manufacturing industries. In addition, in 1975, the government added an investment-tax credit of 5 percent. Throughout the 1970s, there have been various tax measures to encourage investment. Most of these program objectives are similar to the philosophy given in the following quotation from the 1978 budget of the federal government:

> The budget proposes major tax incentives for private investment that will lead to improvements in productivity and help contain cost increases. They will encourage modernization in important sectors of the economy and act to promote more balanced growth patterns of development across Canadian regions.

Note the role given to productivity increases and to regional development.

To aid production for resource-based industries, the federal government instituted other tax-incentive programs. In the National Energy Program of 1980, a petroleum-incentives program (dependent on Canadian ownership) gives payments for approved costs in the production process. In addition, there have been several depletion-allowance programs.

On the provincial level, sales-tax rebates to aid particular industries have been used extensively. Good examples of this are found in Ontario, where the sales tax was removed on furniture and trucks; the philosophy of this program was to aid industries affected by particular economic conditions. For instance, for the furniture industry the aim was to aid adjustment in the face of high interest rates and, consequently, lower housing starts.

Summary

The various Canadian industrial-assistance programs outlined in the foregoing discussion, while not large, are nonetheless impressive. These programs have not been formulated with a consistent or precise national strategy in mind. Federal- and provincial-government programs have evolved in piecemeal fashion as industrial needs have emerged, reflecting a national view of development goals for the Canadian manufacturing sector. These goals include support of research and development, maintenance of employment in specific industries, and facilitation of the domestic-industry adjustment to the effects of liberalized trade barriers.

Issues for the 1980s: Summary

In recent years, significant controversy has emerged regarding the effectiveness and philosophy behind Canadian IP. For example, some argue for a more nationalistic policy whereas others stress the need for free trade. Furthermore, some studies of the effectiveness of particular programs indicate only partial success. For instance, May (1980) finds that "the evidence from econometric studies shows that the investment incentive measures were not that successful in meeting the stated policy objectives" (p. 21).

Usually in arguments concerning a more-nationalistic IP, emphasis is placed on the development of the high-technology manufacturing sector in Canada (1) to aid in productivity growth; (2) to limit foreign investment in order to avoid export restrictions that may be imposed on the subsidiary firm by the parent company; and (3) to maintain tariff protection for weaker industries.[18]

Those in favor of free trade emphasize Canada's moving toward eliminating tariffs. They claim this should not cause major problems and that the adjustment should be facilitated by the presence of multinational firms.[19]

These are important concerns in the Canadian economy in the 1980s. The evolution of the industrial structure through government intervention or a movement toward free trade will be a source of continuing debate. A reduction in tariffs could warrant substantial industry- or worker-adjustment policies by the government in an effort to ease the burden of displacement.

In summary, this chapter has outlined the mechanics and philosophy of IP in Canada. Policies have been motivated not only by the desire to build a stronger and broader national industrial base but also by the great diversities between Canada's provinces and by the desire to establish a Canadian-owned industrial presence. IP in Canada has affected many sectors, including manufacturing, transportation, agriculture, and, particularly, the resource-based sector. A broad range of policy initiatives, including trade policies, support for research and development and other GIPs, and public corporations representing FSPs and PSPs, have been seen. Results have been mixed. Through the 1980s IPs surely will remain important as Canada adjusts to the changing international economic environment.

Notes

1. These are problems for which economic theory can suggest some solutions. For example, the externality issue can be solved by appropriate use of taxes and subsidies; risk can be shared through government loan guarantees; monopoly, if it is perceived to be a problem, can be dealt with through anticombines legislation. Often, past government intervention can cause problems in policy due to second-best arguments (see Lipsey and Lancaster 1956–1957).

2. For further information on the National Policy, the first IP of Canada, see Mackintosh (1964).

3. The Economic Council of Canada (1975) has proposed a free-trade solution to eliminate inefficient firms from operating in the manufacturing sector. The Science Council of Canada (1979) argues that technological advance is the important issue in promoting industrial structure. Shepherd (1980) suggests an IP of a stronger market economy, a more active role for government, and protection for some industries. For its part, the Ministry of Industry, Trade and Commerce is seeking debate as shown by the title of their report from the overview committee: *Action for Industrial Growth: Continuing the Dialogue.*

4. Many of these crown corporations are concerned with transportation—for example, the national airline, Air Canada, and rail line, Canadian

National. These were established to guarantee access to places where private industry was unwilling to provide service. More recently, the federal government has been involved in energy crown corporations.

5. For example, the National Energy Program announced in October 1980 suggested that the government may buy a foreign-owned oil company currently engaged in exploration in Canada. PetroCanada's purchase of Petrofina subsequently took place in March 1981.

6. See Canada, Statistics Canada (1979) for the source of these numbers.

7. See Canada, Budget Speech, 1979.

8. These policies may be called worker-adjustment policies.

9. The assistance programs combined to form EDP included: PAIT, program for advancement of industrial technology; IDAP, industrial-design assistance program; PEP, program to improve productivity; GAAP, general-adjustment assistance program; AAA, automotive-adjustment assistance program; FTIAP, footwear-and-tanning-industry adjustment program; and PIDA, pharmaceutical industry-development assistance program. These programs were started throughout the 1960s.

10. Under the EDP program, special support is provided for: (1) shipbuilding through subsidies to Canadian firms to maintain and improve competitiveness in bidding for new orders; and (2) footwear, clothing, and textiles through import quotas to allow modernization of production facilities.

11. For example, the EDP program guaranteed private-sector funding of $128 million to Canadair for the development of the Challenger business jet which was successfully flown in November 1978.

12. See Ontario Government Board of Industrial Leadership and Development (1981), p. 26.

13. For a more complete discussion of the pros and cons of promoting research and development, see Kotowitz (1979).

14. Some argue that this has resulted in the elimination of the link from the resource-based sector to the manufacturing sector. (See Shepherd 1980, p. 12).

15. There has been some evaluation of the RDIA programs. See Usher (1975) and Woodward (1975).

16. See, Canada, Bureau of Management Consulting (1978).

17. A more complete discussion of historical tax incentives for investment can be found in Bird (1980).

18. A supporter of this view is the Science Council of Canada (1971, 1979).

19. Supporters of this view include the Economic Council of Canada (1975), Wonnacott (1975), and Biggs (1980).

References

Biggs, M.A. *The Challenge: Adjust or Protect?* Ottawa: The North-South Institute, 1980.

Bird, R.M. *Tax Incentives for Investment: The State of the Art.* Toronto: Canadian Tax Foundation, 1980.

Breton, A. *A Conceptual Basis for an Industrial Strategy.* Economic Council of Canada Report. Ottawa: Information Canada, 1964.

Canada, Budget Speech, Department of Finance, 1972.

―――. 1978.

―――. 1979.

Canada, Bureau of Management Consulting. *Economic Justification for Payment of a Procurement Premium.* Vol. 1. Ottawa: Supply and Services, June 1978.

Canada, Department of Regional Economic Expansion. *Annual Report.* Selected issues.

Canada, Energy, Mines and Resources. *The National Energy Program,* 1980.

Canada, Ministry of Industry, Trade and Commerce. *Annual Report.* Selected issues.

―――. *Action for Industrial Growth: Continuing the Dialogue,* February 1979.

Canada, Ministry of State for Economic Development. *Assistance to Business in Canada.* Ottawa: Supply and Services, 1979.

Canada, Statistics Canada. *Annual Review of Science Statistics, 1979.* (Cat. 13-212) Ottawa: Supply and Services, 1980.

Daly, D.J., B.A. Keys, and E.J. Spence. *Scale and Specialization in Canadian Manufacturing.* Staff Study No. 21, Economic Council of Canada, March 1968.

Easterbrook, W.T., and H.G.J. Aitken. *Canadian Economic History.* Toronto: Macmillan, 1956.

Economic Council of Canada. *Looking Outward: A New Trade Strategy for Canada.* Ottawa: Information Canada, 1975.

Gordon, M.J. "A World Scale National Corporate Industrial Strategy." *Canadian Public Policy* (Winter 1978).

Graham, M.R. *Canada Development Corporation.* Study No. 4. Ottawa: Royal Commission on Corporate Concentration, 1977.

Green, C. *Canadian Industrial Organization and Policy.* Toronto: McGraw-Hill Ryerson, 1980.

Kirton, J.J. "The Consequences of Integration: The Case of the Defense Production Sharing Agreement," in A. Axline et al., ed., *Continental Community? Interdependence and Integration in North America.*

Toronto: McClelland and Stewart, 1974.

Kotowitz, Y. "Industrial Structure, Regulation and Innovation: Perspective on Canadian Science Policy." Mimeographed. 1979.

Lipsey, R.G., and K. Lancaster. "The General Theory of Second Best." *Review of Economic Studies* 24 (1956–1957).

Mackintosh, W.A. *The Economic Background of Dominion-Provincial Relations.* Toronto: McClelland and Stewart, 1964.

Mathias, P. *Forced Growth.* Toronto: Lewis and Samuel, 1971.

May, J.D. "Investment Incentives and Industrial Strategy." *Canadian Public Policy* (Winter 1979).

Ontario Government, Board of Industrial Leadership and Development. *Building Ontario in the 1980s.* January 27, 1981.

Rea, K.J. and J.T. McLeod. *Business and Government in Canada.* Toronto, Methuen, 1976.

Reisman, S. *The Canadian Automotive Industry: Performance and Proposals for Progress.* Ottawa: Supply and Services, 1978.

Science Council of Canada. *Forging the Links: A Technology Policy for Canada.* Ottawa: Supply and Services, 1979.

Science Council of Canada. *Innovation in a Cold Climate: The Dilemma of Canadian Manufacturing.* Report No. 15. Ottawa: Information Canada, 1971.

Shepherd, J.J. *The Transition to Reality: Directions for Canadian Industrial Strategy.* Ottawa: Canadian Institute for Economic Policy, 1980.

Stegemann, K. *Canadian Non-tariff Barriers to Trade.* Montreal: C.D. Howe Research Institute, 1973.

Usher, D. "Some Questions About the Regional Development Incentives Act." *Canadian Public Policy* (Autumn 1975) pp. 557–575.

Volpe, J. *Industrial Incentive Policies and Programs in the Canadian American Context.* Montreal: C.D. Howe Research Institute, 1976.

Voyer, R. "The Case for an Industrial Strategy." *Options* (September 1980) pp. 51–54.

Williams, J.R. *The Canadian–United States Tariff and Canadian Industry.* Toronto: University of Toronto Press, 1978.

Wonnacott, R.J. "Industrial Strategy: A Canadian Substitute for Trade Liberalization." *Canadian Journal of Economics* (1975).

Woodside, K. "Tax Incentives versus Subsidies." *Canadian Public Policy* (Spring 1979).

Woodward, R.S. "The Effectiveness of DREE's New Location Subsidies." *Canadian Public Policy* (Spring 1975).

10 French Industrial Policy from 1945-1981: An Assessment

Francois DeWitt

As economist Alain Cotta has remarked, the development of France's productive capacity has been led, since the first industrial revolution, by decisions that involved connivance or at least complicity between administrative authorities and entrepreneurs, both private and public. In fact, no major business decision (a merger, an investment abroad, a new field of research) is (or, to a certain extent, can be) made in France without policymakers at least informing government officials.[1]

Thus government is naturally involved in the process of industrial development. To a large extent, top managers and high civil servants share the same educational background (Ecole polytechnique, Ecole nationale d'administration)[2] and therefore tend to develop similar attitudes toward business goals and guidelines. One can say that over the years, culturally speaking, the civil servant, operating in the general interest of the population, free from market constraints (namely, profit generating) has been the dominant figure of French society.

In a politically centralized country like France, where government intervention is a deeply embedded tradition, high civil servants' (and government officials') concern about industrial development is widely accepted. Government has therefore been given credit, even by businesspeople, for conceiving and implementing IPs.

Economist and advisor to the minister of industry Christian Stoffaes has remarked that the concept of *administrative guidance*, of informal discussion and persuasion, is one of the main features of French IP. The important role of technically highly qualified civil servants is a characteristic of the French IP model, which compares only to that of Japan.

Obviously, brilliant civil servants, of which France has always boasted, have ideas as to what should be done. These ideas have long amounted to cliches, each one leading to a specific policy line. For example, the adage, "French industry is too concentrated in certain regions," translates to a policy to encourage plant relocation.[3]

Examples such as this show that government has tended to think that national policies had an overpowering effect on industrial development and that industrial policymakers were inclined to pursue conflicting policies at the same time and to lay the burden of such policies on industry. The agricultural sector remained highly protected and the service sector was considered necessary but not a priority.

It is difficult for the observer to draw the line between industrial and labor, regional or price policies. Each affects the others, and it is difficult to determine if the global effect of such a mixed-bag of policies has been profitable to French industry.

The purpose of this chapter is threefold: (1) to describe the various IPs issued since 1945; (2) to describe certain successes and failures of ISPs; and (3) to appraise the positive and negative effects of industrial policymaking in France.

Industrial-Development Policies: Historical Trends

Broadly speaking, France's industrial-development policy throughout the last thirty-five years has had three different phases: (1) From 1945 to 1958, the main goal was *rebuilding;* (2) from 1958 to 1976, the objective was *sovereignty;* and (3) from 1976 to 1981, the accent was on *adjustment.*

During these years, IPs were selective as well as *horizontal.* In the first case (ISP), government officials select specific sectors, projects or companies which they stimulate (or assist) in various ways; horizontal measures, on the other hand, are GIPs aimed at encouraging general industrial growth.

1945-1958: Rebuilding

At the end of World War II, France was badly damaged. The major aim of the government was to make optimal use of funds (the Marshall Plan grants, for instance) by channeling them into activities and firms whose growth would have a catalytic effect on industrial development. This was the purpose of the First Development Plan, called *Modernisation a Decadence,* which was released in 1947.

This plan's special feature appears to be that, although its goals were generally *indicative,* six basic programs, concerning coal, electricity, steel, cement, agricultural machinery, and inland transportation (and in 1951, also fertilizers and oil) were *programmatic.* In these sectors, the capacity objectives were to be met during the time span of the plan. As Jean Monnet, the author of the plan, saw it: These activities are destined to open the way for all the others. Since the rest of the economy depends on the resources they produce, their development is an absolute and permanent necessity.

One might add that this development was favored by the fact that railways (SNCF) were nationalized in 1936, followed by electricity (EDF) and coal (CDF) in 1945. Psychologically, the plan's impact was overwhelming. The Modernization Committees included government, trade-union, and business representatives. The plan's implementation was led by the Commissariat General du Plan, the unquestioned wielder of IP.

The Second Plan (1954–1957) marks a deep change in methods. At first, its goals were merely indicative and have remained so; second, the selectiveness disappeared. The plan covered all of manufacturing industry. As John McArthur and Bruce Scott stated in their book, *Industrial Planning in France,* (1969) "the branches and sectors not included in the First Plan exerted pressure on the government and the Commissariat du Plan to be included in the Second." Third, quality and efficiency of production were included in the objectives.

During this period, various *horizontal measures* were taken in favor of investment, the major initiatives being the introduction of VAT to encourage spending on plant and equipment and to favor exports, and the start in 1955 of the Fonds de Developpement Economique et Social (FDES), an administrative board devoted to financing industrial projects.[4]

The general economic policy was, in many ways, favorable to industrial growth. Trade barriers kept out imports while frequent devaluations of the franc encouraged exports. Investment funding was easily carried out through a booming stock market and low interest rates. A regular increase in purchasing power stimulated demand. Growth was more sought after than was efficiency.

Certain governmental measures—price controls, for instance—were clearly detrimental to industry. Furthermore, old-age-pension schemes which were beneficial to executives (in 1947) and to all workers (in 1957) and were two-thirds financed by employers, significantly increased labor costs. Minimum wages were introduced in 1952. During this period two basic elements of infrastructural equipment—telecommunications and roadways—were entirely neglected. On the other hand, instability hampered structural policies.

1958–1976: Sovereignty

The 1957 Rome Treaty, clearly advantageous for French agriculture, was considered an obvious threat to the rather vulnerable, inefficient, and self-centered industry in France.

However, at least until 1973 and the first oil shock, industry was the driving force of a rapid and remarkably steady growth rate of close to 6 percent per annum. This growth was supported by a very high savings rate (15 to 18 percent of disposable income) and a loose monetary policy favoring long- and short-term borrowing. Due to an exceptional investment effort, from 1960 to 1967, productivity rose at the average annual rate of 5.5 percent and of 7 percent during the following five years of the Pompidou regime.

Christian Stoffaes (1978) has remarked that by signing the Rome Treaty and by opening the country to European competition, the French government played a decisive part in the industrialization process. All the same, its role consisted more in accompanying than in guiding the sustained growth and reshaping of industry. Its main intervention concerned price controls and fiscal measures in favor of investment.

Planning, although stressed by de Gaulle as an *ardente obligation,* tended to decline, inasmuch as its goal remained indicative and thus little respected, even by publicly owned corporations. From the private point of view, businesspeople realized that the state did not respect the plan's objectives[5] and that the sectoral projections were theoretical (most often surpassed) and useless as guidelines for their corporate strategy.

Planning did, however, stimulate the effective creation of large broad-based industrial corporations. It is in the wake of the fifth and sixth plans (and with the help of fiscal advantages voted in 1965) that groups such as Rhône-Poulenc (chemicals); Saint-Gobain-Pont-à-Mousson (glass and steel productions); Pechiney-Ugine-Kuhlmann (metals and chemicals); Thomson-Brandt (electronics); Agache-Willot (textiles); and Compagnie Générale d'electricité were formed. The public sector was also restructured, and vast groups such as Elf-Erap (oil), SNIAS (aeronautics), Banque Nationale de Paris, and Berliet-Saviem (trucks) appeared.

Size was then considered the key to efficiency and productivity—the economies-of-scale effect. To assure rapid external growth of leader corporations (one or, if possible, two in each branch, in order to stimulate competition), control of foreign investment was tight. The official policy was to favor foreign investment (particularly in the 1969–1973 Pompidou era) but this primarily pertained to new plants, especially when they were set up in regions with labor problems.

On the contrary, when a foreign group wished to take over a French company, its request was submitted to the foreign-investment committee who, in most cases, got in touch with potential French purchasers to try to find a French solution with (or, ideally, without) the help of government funds. This defensive attitude concerned the whole of industry and not only officially strategic industries like armaments, energy, and high-technology electronics—the basic philosophy being that in a time of world competition and emerging multinational corporations, France must not relinquish its industrial potential to foreign interests. Such a nationalistic policy was greatly influenced by Jean-Jacques Servan-Schreiber's *American Challenge* (1967) as well as by the fact that in 1964, the government had failed to find a

French solution to the sale of Compagnie des Machines Bull, a potential competitor of IBM.

ISPs were focused at the time either on ailing industries (like shipbuilding or steel) or on prestige projects whose objectives were not so much aimed at international competitiveness as at avoiding dependence on foreign technology and showing the world the capabilities of French research (see tables 10-1 and 10-2).[6] Many of these projects have a military background: For example, jet-fighter research led to the Concorde project of 1962; the atomic bomb led to nuclear-power-plant development. Lyndon Johnson's refusal in 1965 to deliver a high-performance computer for military use led to the Plan Calcul—that is, the starting point of a national data-processing industry. But, as Stoffaes points out, often selective policy definitely lacked strategic insight.

Besides investment incentives, *horizontal policies* were mainly aimed at *regional development* (particularly in areas like Britanny where the agricultural population was still large), *research,* and *exports* (particularly of

Table 10-1
Examples of Industrial Priorities Given To or Determined by the Ministry of Industry

1947 (first plan)	Coal, electricity, steel, cement, farm machinery
1951 (first plan)	Oil, fertilizers[a]
1955	Nuclear-energy production
1965 (fifth plan)	Machine tools,[a] data processing, oil
1966	Mechanical engineering,[a] steel
1967	Machine tools,[a] electromechanical equipment,[a] shoes, textiles,[a] public-works equipment[a]
1969	Nuclear energy
1970 (sixth plan)	Mechanical engineering,[a] chemicals,[a] electronics,[a] data processing
1973	Nuclear energy
1975 (seventh plan)	Machine tools,[a] auto parts,[a] computer terminals,[a] instruments,[a] wood and paper,[a] electronic components, fine chemicals,[a] printing,[a] watch making
1976	Space-related industries
1978	Trucks
1979	Robots, household electronics, offshore activities, office automation, biochemicals, energy-saving equipment, innovative textiles, wood and paper, space-related industries

Notes: A considerable number of priorities never reached the implementation phase; industries of the future have only appeared very recently, which makes government forecasting somewhat questionable; industries in which France enjoys a reasonably good international position (like automobiles, apparel, engineering, household appliances, glass, or aluminum) have never been industrial priorities.
[a]Did not lead to any specific policy or plan.

Table 10-2
Industrial Sectors Most Heavily Supported by Government

Sector	Form of support
Aeronautics (civil and military)	Loans, subsidies, refundable aids, government orders
Shipbuilding	Subsidies, regulations, public orders, export aids
Steel	Nonrefunded loans, interest rebates, EEC protection
Professional electronics and telecommunications	Subsidies, refundable aids, research contacts, government orders, export aids
Machinery (electrical and mechanical)	Subsidies, guarantees or loans, government orders
Data-processing, electronic components	Subsidies, government orders
Food industry	Subsidies to cooperatives, tariff barriers (EEC)
Railway equipment	Government orders
Industrial vehicles (trucks)	Preferential interest rates to Renault, trade barriers (EEC)
Wood, paper	Loans
Textiles	Trade protection (EEC, MFA), assistance to ailing business, parafiscal tax
Leather, shoes	Trade barriers (EEC), assistance to ailing business

Source: Stoffaes (1978).

machinery and equipment). Concerning the first point, the government feared that the powerful attraction of Paris would, in the long run, turn the French countryside into a wilderness and therefore the government not only discouraged new plant development near the capital but gave grants to companies willing to build factories in formerly agricultural regions and near the location of the declining coal industry. The Delegation à l'Aménagement du Territoire (Datar) became a very active administrative board in the sixties.

Exports were considered a fundamental means for stimulating new industrial capacity and thus creating jobs, as well as the only way to counterbalance the trade deficits with which the French economy was plagued since the rebuilding period. Loan guarantees, interest subsidies, and insurance plans helped spur a new attitude of French business toward foreign trade.[7] Between 1959 and 1978, the share of exports in GNP grew from 9 to 21 percent.

During the 1958–1973 period, and for several years after, *general economic policy* was based on the quest for full employment. (This goal was achieved in that unemployment was, until the last few years, significantly lower than in other developed countries.) To meet this target, the government aimed at stimulating internal demand (external demand was encouraged by the rapid growth of international trade) through rapid increases in wages (particularly under Pompidou) and social benefits on one hand and through encouraging investment, both public and private, on the other. Industrial-capacity growth was at the core of this strategy because industry exports, invests, creates jobs, and introduces technological change.

However, at the end of the period, analysts began to realize that growth does not necessarily mean efficiency. Rapidly increasing labor costs and debts strongly affected competitiveness, which the 1969 devaluation and the 1973 floating franc were unable to improve. The 1973–1974 oil crisis then threw industry out of balance.

Curiously, no major change in French IP appeared in the aftermath of the first oil crisis. In 1974–1975, the Chirac government still thought that France could avoid the depressive effects of quadrupled oil prices. Loose monetary policy, comparatively low interest rates, and strong pressures on wage increases remained guidelines of general economic policy.

The high inflation of 1974 (although prices remain controlled), the growing budget deficit, and the staggering growth of the money supply led to restrictive policies (Fourcade Plan, June 1974) that reduced industrial production 12 percent in six months and doubled unemployment. Slightly more than a year later, a classic Keynesian recovery plan was launched (public works, investment grants, and so on) with a resultant fantastic trade deficit in the early months of 1976 and a weaker franc and renewal of inflationary pressures. Obviously, the government had not yet realized the enduring depressive effect of the new oil prices. At this point (August 1976) Raymond Barre came into power.

During the 1974–1976 period, ISP mainly consisted of pursuing assistance policies for shipbuilding, steel, paper and pulp, as well as leading positive policies in four directions: aerospace (after the Concorde project became unrealistic, the Airbus was developed); data processing (the French company CII, unable to compete on a worldwide basis, merged in 1975 with Honeywell's data-processing division after an attempt to reach a European solution); telephone-switching equipment; and nuclear power (through EDF as a purchaser and the state-owned Commissariat a l'energie atomique).[8]

Another feature of ISP during this period was assistance to companies—*whatever their activity*—who needed to reduce costs through layoffs. Due to rising unemployment (and to pressure by local authorities at a time when the socialist-communist *programme commun* was gaining ground) the key words were no layoffs. A government body—the Comité interministériel d'aménagement des structures industrielles (*Ciasi*)—was set up at the end of 1974 to prevent bankruptcies of medium-sized firms with strong local bases and, if possible, without spending too much taxpayer money. According to official figures, it was hoped that Ciasi would secure 270,000 jobs. But to what effect and for how long?

As to major corporations, political pressure offered no alternative but to keep idle workers on the job. A prominent French businessman commented that to arouse the interest of industrial policymakers, one had better lose a lot of money (a situation one finds elsewhere—in Italy, Britian, Germany, or even, in the United States today).

The GSPs of the Chirac government consisted mainly in encouraging exports, particularly in oil-producing countries with which the French government has developed rather close ties.

1976-1981: Adjustment

Raymond Barre's arrival triggered a radical change in economic policy. Pressure was put on wage settlement: money supply became tight, interest rates rose, the French franc was vigorously defended. In the fall of 1978, industrial prices were decontrolled for the first time since the late 1940s, but the positive effect of this measure on profits was undermined by the fact that growth was slow (1 to 2 percent per annum) and social charges, if not wages, were increasing rapidly. The Barre government also adopted a more comprehensive view on the effect of excess labor on productivity. Layoffs were more freely accepted, and thus there was a rather sharp decrease in the industry work force.

ISPs saw some major changes. The Chirac lines were pursued and even reinforced, with the addition of three new instruments. First of all, selected *companies* with growth potential were assisted (both by subsidies and preferential interest rates) within the framework of development contract (started in 1975). The rule of the game was that the subsidies were to be paid back in case of failure to meet the goals. Currently, one hundred companies have signed such contracts.

The second initiative concerns equity funding to promising companies whose debt-equity ratio was too high. Through the "Comite interministerial pour le développement des investissements et de l'emploi" (*Cidise*) created in July 1979 these companies were to receive participative loans—that is, a new type of loan, similar to equity capital and at a low interest rate accompanied by a dividend bonus. In one year, the Cidise helped over three hundred projects.

The third mechanism was the "Comité interministériel pour le developpement des industries stratégiques" (*Codis*) launched at the end of 1979. Its purpose was to support (through grants and preferential loans) projects

French Industrial Policy

in growth industries drawn up by the ministry of industry and currently includes off-shore activities, consumer electronics, robots, office-automation equipment, energy-saving devices, biochemicals, and innovative textiles.

The Codis, a multiministerial body, is apparently the first attempt in thirty-five years at selecting the growth sectors that can induce development of a competitive French industry. These various initiatives has two unique features with respect to the former ISPs. First, the focus is not just on broad sectors, like steel or shipbuilding, but rather on individual companies seen as reasonable bets by the state (FSP). To a certain extent, the ministry of industry acts like a banker. Second, there is a relationship between grants and results; prior to that, government subsidies or loans were somewhat automatic. If the company had a certain size or exported to a certain country, it was eligible for certain forms of government assistance.

Certain broad ISPs were nonetheless pursued from a defensive rather than positive point of view. In order to contain import pressure, protected sectors tended to develop. Shoes and steel benefited from safeguard clauses while textiles, although assisted by the Multi-fibre Agreement, were covered by specific import restrictions that protect the inefficient and hamper profitably run companies.[9] The automobile industry, for another, is protected by a limitation on imports of Japanese cars to a level of 3 percent of the home market.

As to GSPs, the main initiatives concerned equity funding through the July 1978 Monory law to encourage savings invested in business activity. Companies that raise capital as well as individuals who buy stocks have been granted tax advantages over a seven-year period for the former (no taxes on dividends related to new shares) and a four-year period for the latter (annual deduction of 5,000 francs of purchased shares from taxable income).

Another GSP has made funds (grants and preferential loans) available through a specific government entity (le Fonds spécial d'adaptation industrielle) to companies who agree to set up new plant capacity in distressed areas (namely, in the steel region of Lorraine and in the shipbuilding areas—Dunkerque, Marseille, and Nantes). In 1979–1980, subsidies amounting to Fr 1 billion—twice the normal amount devoted to regional development—were thus distributed in a rather desperate effort to prevent social and political upheaval.

Finally, the government has been concerned since 1978 by the slowdown in private fixed investment. A typical U.S.-type tax credit (10 percent of pretax profits) was thus granted to firms for new investment over the 1981–1985 period.

More freedom (concerning price and labor policies); more funds available (to ailing industries, for innovation, job creation, and new small business or exports); and a greater selectiveness concerning specific projects have been the main features of recent IP. Simultaneously, for the first time in over twenty years a prominent figure in the business world, André Giraud, former chairman of state-owned Atomic Energy Corporation (CES), was appointed as minister of industry in 1978.

Three remarks must be made, however:

1. Although industrial development has been officially considered a priority, figures show that industry was far from receiving priority treatment as compared to agriculture, housing, or the public sector. In fact, only 10 to 12 percent of total public aid to the economy went to industry.
2. Efforts to increase competitiveness of industrial products (through grants, government orders, fiscal incentives, and so on) may prove fruitless because of the effects of general economic policy. For instance, the strong-franc policy led by Barre to a certain extent offset exports—noncompetitive exports in any case—which was precisely one of the goals of such a policy, while the considerable increase in social costs since 1974 bore down on profits, tight money on growth, and high interest rates on balance sheets.
3. A feature in the Barre-administration policy has been called Albert's theorem, named for its author, Michel Albert, the Commissaire du Plan: Employment comes from growth, growth comes from exports. Exports come from industrial adaptation. What Barre changed was an attitude toward industry and toward business in general. He considered enterprises, and no longer the state, the main agent responsible for economic adaptation. Bruce Scott argued recently that contrary to the former dirigisme, which had made use of price controls and low interest rates to make corporations sensitive to government pressure, Barre's objective had been to develop resources and autonomy of firms in hopes that they would spontaneously invest and modernize to compete with foreign industry.

However, for social and political reasons—the threat of a socialist regime remained—Barre was forced to take various measures such as bailing out steel, imposing import controls (on textiles and cars), or supporting job funding (the FSAI), which appear contradictory to the general lines of his policy. The reshaping of French industry, a key notion since the first oil shock, led to more government assistance than ever before. Such was not M. Barre's initial goal. But then, is it possible to lead a consistent, forceful IP in a nonconsensual democracy?

Successes and Failures of French Industry: Specific Policies

The question, What is the measure of success of industry policy? is relevant to this discussion. One might see it as the building up of an internationally competitive, profitable industrial base—one that would not have been developed without public assistance. Until recently, however, profitability has not been the main criterion of ISPs. It is thus very difficult to use profitability as a measure of success. Moreover, certain apparent successes in this field relate to publicly owned companies whose strategy was not focused on profitability and whose accounts are very difficult to evaluate.

Contrary to general assumptions, ISPs have played only a minor role in French IP. For instance, as far as private business is concerned, the funds available *excluding research grants* represented only Fr 4.4 billion in 1978, approximately the same amount that is devoted to horizontal measures. Furthermore, the total of horizontal *and* industry-specific measures amounted to only 2 percent of industrial added value.

Aid to industry—*both private and nationalized*—was highly concentrated on: (1) high-technology industries; (2) declining industries (70 to 80 percent of these sums are granted to *nine* major companies.[10] Throughout the years, countless sectoral plans have been announced, discussed, and tentatively launched. In fact, the list of activities which government officials have noted if not funded is impressive. But the plans have suffered typical Gallic drawbacks:

1. Because the plans often stemmed from circumstance more than from strategic research, they were dropped either as soon as business looked brighter or when political pressure relaxed (after elections) or the day a new minister of industry took office.[11]
2. In some cases, policymakers could not agree on the limits of the focal sector; such was the case of chemicals in the early 1970s.[12]
3. Sectoral plans never seem to work when applied to industries that comprise a large number of companies. What company and what product is to be favored, and on which financial basis?[13] The adverse effects of selective measures—arbitrariness in the choice of priorities, economic distortions, and slowdown in the decision-making process—were well known to the Commissariat du Plan officials.

Various ISPs are rudimentarily classified on the basis of their effectiveness as follows:

Successes	Failures
Oil	Data processing[a]
Aircrafts	Steel
Space industries[a]	Shipbuilding
Nuclear energy[a]	Machine tools
Telecommunications[a]	Paper and pulp
	Food industries
	Trucks[a]
	Matchmaking

[a]This judgment is preliminary.

Experience shows that an industrial strategy works if and when an administration or a government-owned company acts as a major (or unique) supplier to and/or purchaser from the selected market. France's oil policy goes back to 1928 and has been pursued on somewhat the same basis ever since. It is led by the ministry of industry through two state-owned companies—Compagnie francaise de petroles and Elf-Aquitaine—which control half of the French oil-products market and are reasonably profitable by international standards. The nuclear policy, already considered a sure success[14] has been led by Electricite de France (purchaser); by CEA, Commissariat a l'energie atomique (developer of technology); and by Cogema, a recently created government corporation involved in producing and reprocessing fissionable materials.

Privately owned companies affected by the nuclear policy (mining and production of vessels or turbines, for instance) all operate as suppliers of state-owned companies. The same applies to telecommunications, the Direction generale de telecommunications (a department of the Post Office) being the sole purchaser of large-capacity switching units.

Another state-owned body, the Center national d'etudes des telecommunications (CNET), is the inventor of the French digital-switching equipment. Aircraft industries rely heavily on military orders and research programs (the major producer, Societe nationale des industries aerospatiales, is nationalized) whereas space-related industries exist because of the government's commitment to launchers (the Ariane rocket) and to weather and communications satellites.

Such policies owe their success to the following: When one body has control of the market (thus acting as an oligopoly), as is the case of EDF or the Direction generale des telecommunications, its suppliers completely depend on its strategy. If this strategy is based on long-term targets, it has an evident stimulating effect.

But when orders are divided into a large number of government (state or local) bodies, a buy-French policy can be quite inefficient, as has been the case with computers (IBM's position remains as strong as CII-Honeywell Bull's as far as public orders are concerned) or trucks and buses, a branch of which Daimler-Benz or Iveco (Fiat-Deutz) have gained a significant market share of, notwithstanding the government's effort to put state-owned Renault in the leading position.

However, the positive effect of a unique state-owned purchaser on its supplier's profits is not as great as one might expect. In fact, such powerful policymakers tend to consider that, inasmuch as they represent a significant share of their supplier's market, they can exert pressure on prices (and, consequently on profits). To have been granted capacity utilization and research development seems sufficient. A 1979 government report on government aids to industry notes that in Germany the main beneficiary of government research aid, Siemens, in fact, is subject to important indirect aid, insofar as the prices at which public orders are issued (for power-plants and telecommunications) seem 20 percent above the prices that EDF or Direction generale des telecommunications are willing to pay.

On the other hand, for firms operating on a vast, multicustomer market (that is, where government orders represent a low percentage or, if even this percentage is high, like in data processing, where the orders come from a wide range of administrative bodies), ISPs have generally proved inefficient. Two cases will be examined: machine tools and steel.

Machine Tools

A high civil servant commented that since the first Republic, there has probably never been a minister of industry who has not set up a machine-tool plan. This has occurred for two reasons which are quite characteristic of the way the French, regardless of political preference, tend to envisage IP: (1) machine tools are essential to industrial development because they are machines for manufacturing machines, hence France must be able to boast a strong machine-tool industry; (2) France has always been plagued with a huge trade deficit (a 50 percent export/import rate) in such a basic field. French firms suffer several characteristic handicaps: dispersion and insufficient capital, thus insufficient cash generation to develop new capacity (in order to recapture the home market) and to develop new products like digitally-controlled machine-tools.

However small the machine-tool industry might be (25,000 workers, Fr 2.5 billion in sales) there has always been sufficient reason to support it. But how? As economist and now-Minister Lionel Stoleru suggested in 1969, experience has shown that in this field as in others, failure to intervene or reliance on unorganized intervention, was undesirable, either because private initiative was too hesitant or because other governments treated their local industries more favorably.

Since World War II, in fact, nothing happened with respect to machine tools although the first and third plans had both pointed out the necessity of a powerful machine-tool industry. Unfortunately, the first plan recommended concentration and specialization of firms, while the third clearly stated that the number of manufacturers must remain relatively large and each one must be able to produce a wide range of materials. Obviously, government officials had no clear idea of what the industry's strategy should be nor could they reshape it through government orders, which represented a very small portion of the product outlet.

Therefore, in the 1970s the policy was to intervene indirectly by making financing available to investment banks (owned in part by the state), in order to provide dynamic machine-tool manufacturers with equity necessary for development. Also, two state-owned companies—Snias and Renault—were encouraged to purchase companies in order to create driving forces within the industry framework. Concentration and specialization were making a decisive comeback.

This policy has proved unsuccessful. In 1981, fully 50 percent of the machine-tools industry nearly, if not effectively, bankrupt. This leads to two conclusions: (1) It is most difficult to carry on ISP in a multiproduct, multicompany type of industry such as machine tools. Dispersion of efforts and funds leads to inefficiency. (2) It is probably impossible to develop any market-oriented industry without entrepreneurs. Aside from a few specific examples, the French have never had any particular proclivity toward producing machine tools. In that case, intervention, despite its form, is doomed to be ineffectual.

Steel

The steel industry is a unique case in France's industrial history. This industry has no strategic quality (like armaments, energy, or electronics, for instance) and has made few technological breakthroughs since the Austrians invented the basic oxygen process early in this century. In the 1970s, steel has appeared as a commodity, manufactured in a growing number of countries (thus prone to overcapacity), and furthermore, is highly energy consuming.

In spite of all these drawbacks, steel has been France's most supported privately owned industry. The reasons are numerous and are not always directly related to IP:

1. *Historical.* Steel is the backbone of the industrial revolution. An industrial country must have a strong steel industry. (France, furthermore, has iron-ore-production capacity.)
2. *Political.* Steel production is one of the keys to industrial independence. No country, either developed or developing, considers the possibility of discarding its steel industry. Steel means prestige.
3. *Social.* In France, the steel industry has traditionally been located in historically industrialized regions like Lorraine and the north. To close factories in these regions would be an obvious source of social unrest.
4. *Cultural.* The steel makers and the civil servants who supervise their activities have the same educational background: l' Ecole Polytechnique. They think similarly and offer each other mutual support.

In the 1950s steel prices were closely controlled (particularly in 1959 and in 1963, when they should have sharply increased), which prevented the French steel industry from making the necessary profits and investments to reach international competitiveness. At the time, the industry did not request price decontrol. Businesspeople considered themselves operating for the *interêt national;* their sacrifices would be repaid in due time through state support of investment programs.

In 1964, however, the system, which was based more on philosophy than on sound facts, started to collapse. In the past five years, capacity had increased by 34 percent and production grew by 17 percent; prices plummeted. The debt-to-revenues ratio moved to 70 percent (46 percent in 1960) and the cash flow of the industry fell from 12.5 percent (in 1960) to 6 percent. New plant building and cuts in capacity seemed inevitable. But where to find the money, in view of the stock market's having sharply declined since 1962?

Fortunately, the government was totally committed. Lengthy discussions led to a convention signed in 1966, according to which: (1) The government provided several billion francs in low-interest loans, plus state-guarantees for loans floated by the industry; and (2) the industry agreed to merge the five major firms into two new bodies, each creating a major seaboard plant relying on imported iron ore, and to reduce the work force by approximately 20 percent (120,000 versus 150,000) in order to improve productivity.

Protected by the state, the steel industry borrowed, merged companies, and laid off half of the work force as stipulated by the agreement. But it did not reduce capacity, particularly in Lorraine, because after difficult times in the 1960s, the 1970s appeared extremely promising.[15] In fact, because of the new plants in Dunkerque and Fos (Marseille), in 1974 employment remained at the same level as in 1960! The oil shock hit the business very hard: Losses amounted to Fr 4 billion in 1975 and 1976, Fr, 6 billion in 1977, and long- and medium-term debt surpassed sales figures of which interest payments represented 15 percent.

Nevertheless, capacity reductions—and therefore layoffs—were delayed, for political reasons (the 1974–1977 period being touch and go between the Gaullist majority and the socialist-communist forces). The steel industry had no alternative but to obey government measures. It did so all the more willingly since it knew that, in the end, state (or taxpayers') money would bail it out.

This happened in 1978 when the state wrote off Fr 9 billion of state debt, covered Fr 13 billion of private debt, made state-owned bodies majority shareholders in Usinor and Sacilor, and requested a reduction in the work force to 110,000 (and capacity to 27-million tons); obviously, management was changed. The effects of this salvage plan have still to be measured.

Certain lessons can be drawn from the French steel-industry collapse.

1. When a privately owned business considers itself as politically and socially fundamental, it is not inclined to adapt itself to market conditions.
2. When a government *directly* supports one specific industry, it: (a) inevitably puts excess stress on social and political considerations vis-à-vis market conditions; (b) acts a substitute to market forces (banks or equity market) whose responsibility is to finance companies with growth and profit potential; and (c) distributes funds on a broad basis through business associations and therefore does not differentiate between efficient and inefficient companies.

To a certain extent, this last lesson has been learned. Recent ISP have, to a great extent, given up the sector approach and concentrated on assistance to *specific companies,* whatever their activity may be. The general idea is that no activity—such as textiles, leather, ball bearings, or toys, for instance—is totally condemned by Ricardian principles, as long as certain firms have proved they could remain successful and profitable in an open-market environment.

Such firms now have the opportunity to request government assistance on the basis of development contracts. These contracts have two basic advantages: (1) They stimulate growth inasmuch as they are signed only if the company's management decides to go a step further in a certain direction (export position, growth of a certain product line, and so on) and, therefore, they are not expensive; and (2) the money is paid back only in case of failure to meet the target.

However, such a method has two drawbacks. First, civil servants audit private companies to see if and why they may fail to meet their goals. This is not part of government responsibility or competence. Second, such a method is too direct, insofar as it tends to make government officials take the place of the more natural suppliers of capital (that is, the capital and credit markets). The highly successful Japanese IP seems to stem from government initiative—locating the growth sectors—and from private financing of projects with obvious government support.

Purpose of French Industrial Policies

Counteracting market forces is inefficient for it leads to waste of resources and economic distortions. IP consists in counteracting market forces. Therefore IP is inefficient.

Such an obvious syllogism has not prevented industrial policymaking throughout the world. Of course, the paradox is merely superficial since no government relies entirely on the market's invisible hand to correct economic distortions. But all the same, it deters misleading opinions concerning IPs. To what extent has the French economy benefited in the last thirty-five years from industrial policymaking? And what have been the negative aspects of such a policy?

Beneficial Effects

The sustained focus on France's industrial development has been beneficial psychologically, as French businesspeople have gained confidence in their aptitudes. France has become a major exporting country; productivity in industry has significantly increased.

Confidence. Historically, France was a land of agriculture and trade with a medium-size, rather unproductive (and protected) industrial sector. The change in the last thirty-five years has been quite dramatic. The stress put on industry (through research and investment) by politicians and high civil servants has undoubtedly had an anything they can do, we can do better effect.

This attitude started with the first plan developed in the 1960s, when the French minimultinationals were formed and was reinforced in the 1970s, when medium-sized, dynamic companies[16] began to appear on the world market. These companies were not necessarily financially supported by government but at least they were acknowledged and encouraged, officially as well as through the media. While France had become industry-conscious, it was growing profit-conscious. A new generation of entrepreneurs appeared.

Such entrepreneurs were welcome to discuss their plans with government officials. They were often offered the opportunity to purchase companies that wanted to sell out to foreigners and that were highly regarded by banks. Analysts found that their financial records compared favorably to those of their foreign competitors. Furthermore, in the nationalized sector, companies like Elf-Aquitaine, Renault, or Air France proved that they could show reasonable profits without government support.[17]

In recent years, leading politicians (Barre or Monory) have particularly stressed the necessary profitability and competitiveness of industry. Their predecessors (Pompidou or Chaban-Delmas) had used the same terms but had also inspired doubts. Barre has been certainly the first French statesmen to be open-minded and determined on the subject. Even though the polls indicate the opposite, confidence in the feasibility of IP has improved.

Exports. From 1972 to 1977 (that is, during a rather difficult phase of economic growth) French exports increased by 17 percent per annum and exports of machinery by 24 percent. From 1969 to 1970, France was the only country other than Japan to improve its share of the export market. Here is the direct effect of one of the most successful lines in French IP: export assistance. Such assistance has taken multiple forms: political contracts with oil-producing countries; linked aid to developing countries (low interest rates with a buy-French clause); guidance by embassy personnel; low rates for investments based on export drives; and specific insurance contracts (like the guarantee against economic risk).

A guarantee against economic risk may appear questionable. It has proved rather costly (see table 10-3). But it has helped French companies underbid foreign competitors and is, in fact, the main explanation for France's current international position in fields like engineering and general contracting. But macroeconomically speaking, the results of such a policy have been rewarding.

Things are not as bright from the corporate point of view. Garantie du risque economique has enabled French companies to take on orders although their manufacturing costs should have priced them out of the market. Experience has also shown that once a new outlet is secured, exporters do not strive to improve on productivity, in order to stand on their own feet, but continue to rely on government support. The question is: Which major exporting country does not rely on such crutches to improve foreign-market penetration?

Productivity. Measurement of industrial productivity is difficult. It is even more difficult to decipher what is due to market drive, to quality of labor, to business efficiency, and to IP measures and there is no clear explanation for the high increase in French industrial productivity. But, to a certain

Table 10-3
Direct Aid to Industry
(in billion francs)

Type of Aid	1970	1971	1972	1973	1974	1975	1976	1977	1978
Specific sectoral aid	2,446	3,371	3,691	3,509	4,463	5,290	5,997	5,522	4,400
Aeronautics	1,131	1,668	1,865	1,507	1,992	2,294	2,170	1,793	1,591
Shipbuilding	309	465	610	626	784	1,124	1,071	964	1,041
Electronics and data processing	0	283	223	215	329	701	1,228	741	450
Steel	494	534	370	530	760	570	1,260	1,618	507
Food industries	142	142	110	121	153	186	178	174	204
Paper	0	14	15	14	19	20	15	20	27
Equity funding	370	265	498	496	425	395	75	212	580
Nonspecific aid	843	1,171	1,272	1,625	1,949	2,628	4,151	4,042	4,102
Regional development	434	346	299	453	435	256	213	447	518
Research	116	128	150	154	179	417	494	408	604
IP grants	0	0	72	107	109	148	141	106	124
Bonuses for investment	129	189	170	240	283	401	515	864	744
Export guaranties	164	459	550	585	682	1,206	2,223	1,772	1,203
Bonuses for export credits	0	0	0	24	197	128	484	400	800
Miscellaneous	49	49	31	62	64	72	81	45	109
Total	3,289	4,542	4,963	5,134	6,412	7,918	10,148	9,564	8,502

Source: Direction de la Prevision, Direction des relations economiques exterieures.
Note: The calculations in this table do not include public-sector aids.

extent, growth is due to GSPs (VAT in 1954, accelerated depreciation in 1959, and high borrowing at relatively low interest rates) rather favorable to industrial investment. In the 1960s and the early 1970s fixed investment ran at 26 to 29 percent of GNP, a level unequalled outside of Japan.

Today, except in certain declining sectors (textiles, apparel, steel, and shipbuilding) French production costs compare rather favorably to those of other European countries. Such was not the case thirty years ago. This result may be due to purely natural causes; on the other hand, one may be led to believe that, were it not for the government's permanent will to stimulate and develop investment, France might be today in the same situation as is the United Kingdom.

Limitations. It is difficult to evaluate the overall effect of French IP, but there is common agreement that it could have been more efficient. Economists like Lionel Stoleru, Alain Cotta, or Christian Stoffaes have, over the last ten years, pointed out certain limitations such as miscalculation of market response, exaggerated stress on job creation, and technological development, dispersion of effort among too many administrative bodies leading to inefficiency, and lack of logic in selective policies.

Adverse Effects of National Independence Policies

Efforts to develop a 100-percent-French nuclear-power plant through graphite-gas technology proved fruitless and were dropped in the late 1960s. It has proved equally impossible to market computers that were noncompatible with IBM equipment as had been the ambition of the 1967 Plan Calcul.

In an increasingly intertwined world economy, a medium-sized country depending heavily on foreign trade (as is the case of France) will probably find it difficult to develop from-scratch technologies that are marketable on a worldwide basis. European cooperation, quite visible in the successful Airbus and Ariane (satellite-launcher) programs, purchasing of U.S. or Japanese patents, and know-how are obviously necessary.

The 1978-1982 components plan illustrates a major change in the industrial policymakers' attitude. According to this plan, Fr 600 million of public funds were made available to four French firms, three of which have launched joint ventures with U.S. semiconductor manufacturers, in order to develop MOS computer chip technology. In an obviously strategic sector, the French government thus accepted the necessity of copying U.S. technology and opening the French market to U.S. products. Clearly, efficiency and competitiveness now tend to overshadow the quest for national independence.

Exaggerated Stress on Job Creation. French policymakers have consistently considered industrial development as the main source of new jobs, and, as such, the means to overcome unemployment. Government aid (particularly regional grants) has to a large extent been linked to the number of new jobs created on specific recommended sites. This attitude has led to significant distortions. Inefficient companies have been able to start up new plants only insofar as they did not pay market interest rates.

In the late 1960s and early 1970s, the Delegation a l'Amenagement du territoire attempted to redistribute jobs by encouraging new plants in agricultural and remote regions (Central France, Britany, and the Southwest).

In the last few years experience shows that unemployment has grown more rapidly in these sheltered regions than in the traditionally industrialized parts of the country. Having been newly and somewhat artificially industrialized and staffed with underqualified personnel, these regions were the first to be hit by the depressive effect of the oil shocks.

French industrial policymaking has involved too many administrative bodies. Who, for instance, is in charge of IP? The natural answer would be the ministry of industry. However, such a ministry does not, for one, cover industries such as armaments (ministry of defense), aircraft and shipbuilding (ministry of transportation), food (ministry of agriculture), telecommunications equipment (post office), or contracting (ministry of environment). In fact, the ministry of industry covers little over one-third of industrial potential, and even within its own field, it is not necessarily the main policymaker. The 1966 steel plan, for instance, was implemented by the Commissariat general du Plan and the 1967 Plan Calcul was fashioned by an agency that reported directly to the prime minister.

Furthermore, the financial means of the ministry of industry are limited. The ministry of economy and finance (split in 1978 to become the ministry of economy and ministry of budget) has almost complete control over grants, subsidies, and preferential loans. It also supervises, through the budget, government or administrative orders to industry. It can and often has deferred or opposed specific policies initiated by the ministry of industry or by the Commissariat general du Plan. (In fact, there has always been a certain degree of competition and dissent between the high civil servants of the ministry of industry, who usually come from the top-ranks of the Ecole polytechnique, and those of the Finance Ministry, who come from the Ecole nationale d'administration.)

The prime minister's and president's offices also have their specialists on industrial matters who naturally take advantage of their position. Lack of coordination among multiple administrative agencies and conflicting interests lead to delay and to misallocation of resources. A ministry in charge of an industrial project will have to work things out with the ministry of finance (concerning subsidies, but also price-policy and antitrust regulations); the ministry of research (concerning research-and-development contracts); the Delegation a l'Amenagement du Territoire (concerning plant location); the Ministry of Labor (concerning job qualification or eventual layoffs); and the Credit National, a government-managed long-term credit bank (concerning preferential loans). Thus the final project turns out to be very different from what had initially been decided.

Doubtless activity of administrative agencies to handle IP must be reorganized. Steps in this direction have been taken in recent years. New administrative industry oriented bodies like the Ciasi, the Codis, or the Cidise all include representatives of the various ministries and agencies involved and operate on a team basis. Their decisions are therefore more efficient; the idea of creating a French MITI has likewise gained ground.

Inconsistency in Selecting and Pursuing Priorities. Business has never given great consideration to ISP because experience has led to the belief that they were mainly based on particular circumstances: (1) salvaging a declining region or industry (for political and social rather than for economic reasons); (2) building up France's industrial prestige, and so on; (3) or even merely reassuring businesspeople.

In fact, historical trends clearly show that unlike Japan, France has set few priorities (except in 1947) and when plans have been initiated, they have been rapidly dropped. In recent years, the government had tried to be more specific in its choices and more consistent in its efforts. The Comite de developpement des industries strategiques has selected seven industrial priorities that should receive significant government support. Certain grants have already been made in fields like office automation and robot production; others are pending in textiles and offshore activities. But the proper selection of beneficiaries has taken some time.

Selecting and assisting given companies with growth potential—whatever their activity may be—is the other innovative feature of recent industrial policymaking. Since development contracts are granted not on a broad sector basis but to selected profitably run firms, development contracts should lead to less waste in government funding as well as to an even-more aggressive attitude by market-conscious beneficiaries. These contracts also indicate a certain change in mentality: Instead of merely favoring technology, the government encourages efficiency.

However, the concept in itself may appear questionable. How can government officials evaluate the feasibility of projects? This is not their normal task. Furthermore, the development-contract system supposes that penalties are paid by companies who fail to reach their goals. If and when a company has failed, to what extent can it afford to pay back without jeopardizing its future? Also, how can government officials determine if failure is due to unexpected adverse market conditions or to mismanagement?

French Industrial Policy

Prior to the development-contract approach, government subsidized projects (particularly in aircraft and space-related fields) on the basis that grants were refunded if the goals were surpassed. Companies thus tended to *overestimate* their possibilities. Having failed to meet their target, they did not pay back. Now they tend to *underrate* their possibilities for the same reason. Neither method seems completely satisfactory.

Unarguably, IP have become more clear-cut and efficient. Three remaining points deserve noting.

First, industrial development is not, in effect, and by far, the major objective of government policy. This clearly appears in the figures concerning government assistance to the economy. According to these figures, released by the Industry Commission of the eighth Plan, such assistance amounts to 46 percent of the value added of agriculture, 30 percent of the value added of nationalized companies, but only 12 to 20 percent of the value added of housing, and 2 to 3 percent of the value added of other industry.

Even though a major part of assistance to agriculture and nationalized firms goes to old-age-pension coverage, the figures do indicate that however important the government has claimed industry to be, industrial development has not been a priority, at least budget-wise.

In a period of fierce international competition and oil shocks, one might assume that industrial development is entitled to a bigger share of the taxpayer's money. However, experience seems to show that government policies aimed at specific industries (steel and shipbuilding) or at specific objectives (exports or regional development), tend to alleviate market pressure and therefore have negative effects on product competitiveness. In France, at least, ISPs do not necessarily lead to industrial efficiency.

Second, general economic and social policies have been and still remain to a certain extent highly detrimental to industry. Rising social costs (particularly since 1974), antilayoff policies (in the early 1970s), and credit-and-price controls, for instance, have negatively effected industrial development. As a journalist once put it, industrial policy consists in trying to counterbalance the negative effects of previous or current antiindustrial policies.

Excess multidirectional government pressure has probably been placed on the average French industrialist through the last thirty-five years. This leads to the third point: The key to successful IPs, like those led with remarkably different methods by the Germans and the Japanese, seems to be in businesses' willingness to meet new challenges and financiers' willingness to support them. If competitive spirit is lacking as is still the case in a large portion of French industry, IPs tend to amount to that much wasted assistance.

Such pessimism must be corrected. In recent years, the attitude of government and business has changed in the right direction. But it is a rather slow-motion process, which can unfortunately be offset by a change in political strategy.

Political change is the signal for changes in IP as well. While it is too early to evaluate the effect of the Mitterand government on French IP, we can say that a new chapter with different priorities and different perceptions of the relationship between government and business is underway.

Notes

1. Every productive activity in the country is submitted to the guidance (*tutelle*) of a given Ministry. And, quite naturally, tutors tend to consider their pupils as not being of age to see to themselves.
2. Chief executives in private industries are very frequently recruited in the ranks of the administration.
3. This is on the basis that it is easier to bring the factory to the worker than the worker to the factory.
4. Initially, the FDES was under the control of the Commisariat du Plan. In fact, due to the important role it plays as a purveyor of funds, the ministry of finance took it over.
5. The powerful minister of finance, for instance, tended to pursue policies that do not conform with planning indicatives. A typical case was Giscard d'Estaing's stabilization plan released in 1963 midway in the IVth Plan.
6. Various ministers of industry and successive plans do indicate sectoral priorities but aside from the fact that these priorities were often modified, there was very little real implementation.
7. The main clause introduced during the period is the "guarantee against economic risks." According to this guarantee if the customer of a French exporter, of turn-key factories, public works or any form of heavy equipment requiring several years to produce, refuses to accept price increases (due to rise in costs) the government-owned insurance company covers the difference.
8. The CEA eventually replaced Westinghouse as minority share holder in Framatome, the French nuclear vessel producer.
9. A unique clause forbids a textile manufacturer to import more than 10 percent of its sales from abroad.
10. Snias, Dassault, Thomson-CSF, Compagnie generale d'electricite, CII-Honeywell Bull, Charbonnages de France, CEA, Creusot-Loire and Alsthom-Atlantique.
11. Having succeeded Olivier Guichard in 1968, the new Minister of Industry Andre Bettencourt considered that horizontal measures were more effective than the various plans (machine-tools, public works equipment,

and heavy machinery) set up by his predessor. In 20 years, the only plan to be fully—but unsuccessfully—implemented was the 1966 steel plan.

12. The VIth Plan (1971-1975) had put chemicals on the list of priorities but government officials never managed to agree to whether public assistance should concentrate on basic or *fine* chemicals. Hence, no plan was drawn.

13. The 1967 mechanical engineering plan appeared totally impossible to set up and was subsequently dropped.

14. This is primarily because it has created 120,000 jobs, is expected to significantly reduce French dependence on OPEC oil and has obvious export potential, particularly since foreign competition has generally been forced to slow down its pressure due to antinuclear home policies.

15. In 1974, production hit a peak of 27 million tons. But the VIIth Plan (1975-1980) forecast was 31 million to 36 million tons in 1980.

16. Like Moulinex (appliances) Moët-Hennessy, Skis Rossignol, Poclain (excavating), Dumez and Bouygues (contracting), Bidermann (apparel), Essilor (glasses), etc. In a recently released study, the Ministry of Industry found that 200 industrial companies (out of 33,000) had had a growth rate exceeding 15 percent, in real terms, over the 1970-1976 period. Their work force had tripled and they had multiplied by ten their return on investment. Their average cash-flow was three times that of industry in general (but credit cost represented, in 1976, 7.3 percent of their value-added). All such companies were medium-sized.

17. In fact, the Barre administration has tried to deregulate public service prices in order to reestablish management of state-owned companies on a profitable basis.

References

McArthur, John, and Bruce Scott (1969). *Industrial Planning in France.* Cambridge, Mass.: Harvard University, Division of Research, Graduate School of Business Administration.
Servan-Schreiber, Jean-Jacques (1967). *Le Defi Americain.* Paris: Denoel.
Stoffaes, Christian (1978). *La Grande Menace Industrielle.* Paris: Calman-Levy.

11 Industrial Policy in the Federal Republic of Germany: A Survey

Gerhard Wagenhals

This chapter gives a survey on the main elements of literature focused on IP in the Federal Republic of Germany and a general overview of IP in the sixties and seventies.

Although the economic development in the Federal Republic since 1949 is characterized by large structural changes, these changes by and large have been determined by market forces rather than by public policies.

For many markets in West Germany the formation of prices takes place without state intervention. The federal government tries to orient the strategies of IP as far as possible through markets. It regards its role to be mainly a means of fostering economic growth. Thus it rejects those structural policies that aim at preserving the status quo, except in some special cases.

The targets of economic policy in West Germany are laid down in the Law for the Promotion of Stability and Economic Growth[1]: federal and state governments must achieve: (1) price stability; (2) a high level of employment; (3) external equilibrium; and (4) constant as well as adequate economic growth in the framework of a market economy. The stress is on macroeconomic steering of demand; industrial and sectoral intervention is not explicitly mentioned among the aims of economic policy.

The economic setting for IP is fixed in the Principles of the Federal Government's Sectoral and Regional Economic Policy.[2] IP is considered part of the fostering of economic growth, facilitating and furthering structural change. These baselines have been emphasized often and are still valid today.

German postwar development can roughly be divided into two parts. The first period, 1950–1967, is characterized by four business cycles and a slightly decreasing growth trend. The first few years after the currency reform have sometimes been called the years of the economic miracle because real GNP increased by 67 percent and industrial production rose by 110 percent between 1948 and 1952. This development cannot be reduced simply to ISP. It is true that, in spite of the principles of laissez-faire, the heavy industries (especially steel and coal mining) were heavily supported by special tax allowances and, to a small extent, by subsidies. This was, however, only one prerequisite for the fast economic development. Further conditions of Germany's quick revival were a strong fostering of corporate savings, an adequate labor supply supplemented by skilled refugees from the Soviet Zone and foreign help, particularly the American Marshall Plan, which alleviated the balance-of-payment problems of the young state. ISP played a minor role in economic policy and, as such, was purely ad hoc.

The second period of German postwar development began with the recession of 1967. The sectoral change in the last one-and-a-half decades is characterized by slow growth of the industry, in contrast to the first twenty years after the currency reform of 1948, where industry was the moving force behind economic development. In the last few years, many enterprises have been affected by a large increase of wages, by exchange-rates fluctuations, and by an intensification of the international division of labor. Nevertheless, most export-oriented industries were able to increase their world-market shares, but they had to face decreasing profits which weakened their propensity to invest. Therefore, as in many other industrialized countries, problems of industrial adaptation have characterized the last few years in West Germany.

Since the recession in the mid-seventies more and more economists and politicians have pleaded for a medium-run, supply oriented active structural policy to supplement the preponderant policy of a global steering of the market, but most in principle still prefer structural change produced by market forces to a guidance of sectoral-adjustment processes by the state. Until now, however, authorities have been reluctant to intervene in the market beyond the guidelines of 1968 act.[3]

Objectives

The literature about IP[4] in the Federal Republic distinguishes three main goals: (1) structural formation (that is, the development of economic growth and productivity); (2) structural adaptation (that is, the alteration of the speed of adjustment); and (3) structural conservation (that is, the maintenance of old sectors against market dynamics).[5]

Promotion of growth is one of the main targets of structural policy in West Germany. It is necessary to the sectors central to the macroeconomic progress, which may make too little and too slow headway without state assistance.[6] Therefore innovations with considerable macroeconomic significance and promising potential demand on the world markets are particularly fostered.

In line with the spirit prevailing in most European countries, the policy of structural adaptation tries to change the pace of adjustment, to improve factor mobility and the flexibility of entrepreneurial decision making.[7]

Excessively rapid adjustment processes are to be decelerated to reduce their sociopolitical drawbacks and to help industries that could preserve or restore their competitiveness at a slower speed of accommodation. An acceleration of the pace of adjustment would be called for if legal or traditional habits hamper the mobility of production factors and economic growth.[8]

During postwar reconstruction the removal of bottlenecks was an important target of IP, especially in the heavy industries.

IP in the Federal Republic has preponderantly tended to preserve old structures against market forces.[9] The most important targets of this structural preservation policy are: (1) the stabilization and improvement of factor incomes; (2) the security of employment opportunities; and (3) the protection of sales and market shares.

In the last few years, a new argument gained considerable importance in the public discussion: A domestic supply of products for primary needs should be secured and a certain degree of self-sufficiency should be protected.[10]

Methods and Extent of Industrial Policy

The means of IP used in the Federal Republic can be classified according to objectives. Although they differ from branch to branch, some general observations on the methods and on the rationale for the proposed policy initiatives can be made.

Methods To Influence Structural Formation

Sponsoring research and development has been the main method of facilitating and improving structural formation because innovations are considered very important sources of economic growth. Besides, the promotion of mergers has been temporarily favored to adapt the organizational form and the size of an enterprise to the changing competitive situation and to benefit from economies of scale.[11]

Economists regard some industries as the key sectors of technological development with great importance for the future of the German economy (for example, electronic data processing, nuclear energy, and the aeronautics and aerospace industry) because they perceive that there is a positive differential between social and private benefit.[12]

The main reasons for state intervention in favor of structural formation are risk, infant industry, and noneconomic motives.

Two arguments support risktaking by the state. Some argue that risks in the development and application of new technologies tend to lead private enterprises to cover known demand by applying known technologies. The compensation of this deficit, allegedly a characteristic of market economies, the argument goes, should be the task of the state.[13] Therefore research-and-development funds must be directed to particular areas rather than across the board.

Although support of very risky investments for new products or technologies is not contested, many economists believe that demand-oriented enterprises should have free scope in the choice of innovations. The state should bear part of the risk because, in addition to the risk takers, other agents in the economy would benefit from such investments.[14]

Current governmental policy is sometimes criticized as hampering competition because the main part of government resources devoted to promotion of innovations favors large enterprises.[15] Proper evaluation techniques have not been found to assess the impact of this policy.

Though the issue of risk is the main reason for a policy of structural formation, the infant-industry argument has been quoted often. Special problems resulting from the late takeoff after the foundation of the Federal Republic allegedly led to a lag in competition and a technological gap, which West Germany has had to compensate for by protecting key industries in an early stage of development.

Besides these economic reasons, particular nonprofit research projects sometimes have been fostered because of political or even emotional motives. They may be vaguely described by terms such as *national pride* or *national manhood*.

The criteria for selecting target industries suitable for assistance by structural formation methods are not very precisely defined. Target industries are key sectors of economic growth with insufficient means due to disproportionate risks in relation to short-run sales and very high research-and-development expenditures.[16]

The Extent of Growth Policy

The main industries favored by the policy of structural formation are aeronautics, data processing, and nuclear energy.

Accelerated depreciation of the cost of machinery and equipment was abolished in 1974. Since 1970 grants may cover up to 7.5 percent of acquisition costs of a research-and-development project under certain conditions (15 percent since 1978). The loss of tax revenue in this connection was as high as DM 1,1185 million from 1971 to 1975.[17]

Three electronic data-processing programs supported research and development in industries and at universities as well as training for the use of computers. The expenditures amounted to DM 386.6 million in 1967–

1970, DM 2,409.9 million in 1970–1975, and DM 1,574.9 million in 1976–1979.[18]

The creation and development of the aeronautics and nuclear-energy industries is to a significant extent an explicit IP, but nevertheless, the part of the federal budget dedicated to research-and-development assistance for this industry is relatively small.

Table 11–1 shows that the support to research-and-development has been considerably lower in Germany compared to the United States with regard to important growth industries as well as with regard to total industrial research-and-development expenditures.[19]

Table 11–2 shows the absolute amount of research-and-development expenditures given to specific industries.[20]

Methods to Improve Structural Adaptation

In the Federal Republic there are numerous ways to influence the pace of economic adjustment.[21]

Table 11–1
Government Research-and-Development Expenditures as Percent of the Total Sources of Funds for Research-and-Development in the United States and West Germany, 1975

Industry	West Germany	United States
Aerospace	58	79
Data processing and electrical	14	38
Chemicals	1	8
Motor vehicles, shipbuilding, and other transport equipment	1	15
Total industry	18	36

Table 11–2
Federal Research-and-Development Expenditures by Industry
(in millions of DM)

Industry	1974	1975	1976	1977
Coal mining	137.8	247.7	99.7	143.4
Chemicals	125.5	134.6	180.5	158.2
Aeronautics	912.6	857.9	777.4	677.1
Machinery	318.8	253.7	252.3	264.0
Electrical (including computers) industry	692.8	813.2	823.9	870.0

Methods to decelerate the pace of adjustment are the traditional means of protectionism—above all, subsidies, tax allowances, taxation of substitutes, voluntary import quotas, and other trade restrictions.[22] The Law Against Restrictions of Competition (1957)[23] allows cartels in case of a structural crisis provided that a plan for capacity reduction exists. Hitherto, such cartels played no important role in slowing the pace of adjustment.

If a cutback of excess capacity by the market process is intolerable for macroeconomic or sociopolitical reasons, subsidies for capacity restrictions can be used as a last resort.[24] This implies, however, a tendency to reduce the risk of investment, and, therefore, these subsidies would introduce a wedge in the competitive allocation mechanism. The only example of the application of this measure in the Federal Republic is constituted by bounties for shutdowns in the coal-mining industry.

To increase the pace of adjustment, the main policy tool in West Germany is the development of resource mobility.[25]

There are many methods to further labor mobility and to develop workforce skills: Vocational training, on-the-job training, and changes to understaffed occupations are promoted. Geographic mobility is encouraged by means of relocation assistance.[26]

Measures to enlarge capital mobility are aid to rationalization, subsidies, and taxation measures that allow general capital write-offs.

Improving the information about structural-change processes also favors the speeding up of adjustment and leads to better decision making. Thus institutions have been established to promote information and give economic-technical advice.

The selection of industries suited for the policy of structural adaptation is based on the following standards: (1) intensity of raw materials and labor use; (2) maturity of production; and (3) standardization of production.[27]

Extent of Adaptation Policy. From 1971 to 1975 aid to assist structural adaptation totaled almost DM 13 billion[28] or 2 percent of total government expenditure. Two-thirds of this sum comprised expenditures for vocational training and retraining.[29] The rest encouraged geographical and occupational mobility, aided the establishment of businesses, and increased factor mobility in general.

Measures and Extent of Policies To Protect Existing Industries

Measures to decrease the pace of structural adaptation sometimes are merely camouflaged methods of protecting existing industries, especially if they lead to a long delay in adjustment.

Subsidies, including tax allowances,[30] play the crucial role in the policy as a means of protecting existing industries. Besides direct price interventions of the state, various restrictions of competition (for example, limiting market entry, sales quotas, and taxation of competitive goods) have been practiced. These methods have been supplemented by trade policy that protects noninternationally competitive industries (for example, textile and clothing) or which are highly protected by other nations (for example, shipbuilding).

In the last few years the necessity to be sufficiently independent of foreign energy supplies has often been stressed. IP methods are also used to this end.

Precise guidelines of industries eligible for assistance have not been defined. Measures aiming at this target often have been established ad hoc in crisis times and tend to become permanent. Various procedures practiced in coal mining exhibit this feature. The federal government argues for industrial-assistance policy if the international competitiveness is hindered by subsidies, by fixed prices, or by interventions of foreign countries.[31] This is the case in the shipbuilding industry.[32] Cases of potential jeopardy of economic and strategic security are another rationale for this policy. Maintenance subsidies are most important for the shipbuilding and the mining industries.

Policy Issues

Although West German economy by and large works along free-enterprise lines, there is an acceptance of ISP and SSP to alter the intertemporal allocation of resources and to help when markets fail.

Subsidies and tax privileges supporting existing industries have played a critical role in the SSP of the last decade. SSP has been to a large extent protective. The German Council of Economic Advisors even has asserted that the flexibility of fiscal policy is seriously hampered by the size of subsidies.[33] The share of subsidies to industries is relatively small, however.

Although many aids are considered to be only temporary incentives, the industries aided are inclined to consider them permanent. It seems difficult to end these privileges and to refuse new demands for patronage, particularly if they are bound up with the preservation of jobs. An uncontrolled influence of interest groups is often criticized and, indeed, the federal government admits that some groups are confronted with structural change call for interference and exert pressure to prolong the limits of intervention.[34] Some authors go one step further and advocate that government interference itself is, as a rule, the consequence of incorrect interventions.[35]

Besides the already-mentioned problems, observers have often argued that the aims and means of IP are not clearly defined or are insufficiently coordinated: Cost-benefit analysis and a clear assessment of the impacts of government intervention are lacking.[36]

The rationale for policy initiatives that have been proposed is sometimes vague, especially as far as assistance to existing industries is concerned. Methods used to select appropriate target industries are clearer only for growth industries. Therefore, lack of sufficient transparency is another large problem of German IP.

In the last few years the federal government has acknowledged these critiques to a certain extent and has taken measures to improve the information basis of IP.

Reports on subsidies and tax allowances have been published since 1967.[37] In 1978 five independent economic-research institutes were commissioned to analyze the connections between structural and macroeconomic development, to assess the impact of macroeconomic policy on the structure of the West German economy, to improve information about the impact of SSP on the economy as a whole, and to broaden the availability of information to the business community.[38]

The Success of Industry-Specific Policy

ISPs play a relatively smaller role in the Federal Republic, as compared to other European countries. It is important to note, however, that such policies have been carried on to a larger extent than was envisaged by the 1968 law.

Many industries (for example, chemical, machine-tool, and car industries) developed without considerable state interference. Only aeronautics, shipping, and shipbuilding as well as coal mining receive significant subsidies. The support of research and innovations in some industries is also sizable. However, subsidies to most industries amount to less than one percent of their production value.[39]

The following examples show the extent of the success of German IP.

1. Federal assistance helped to increase international competitiveness in aeronautics. The Airbus program, especially, so far appears to be successful in a world market hitherto dominated by Boeing so that the government could claim a dividend on its investments.
2. Industry-specific measures, which focused on shipping and shipbuilding, alleviated the adjustment to the slump in world demand. Assistance to improve the order position of the shipbuilding industry is limited until the end of 1981.
3. The computer industry illustrates that strong government support is not

a necessary condition for business success: The Nixdorf Computer AG has done well in the last few years without considerable state assistance, in sharp contrast to other German computer producers (especially Siemens, Germany's largest subsidized computer company, which reported a loss in its computer operations in 1979).
4. A boost in domestic energy production was the result of supporting the coal-mining industry. This was supplemented by assistance to research and innovation in the energy sector in general. These measures helped to decrease West Germany's dependence on the world energy markets.

Therefore, IP in the Federal Republic helps to improve productivity and modernization in the high-technology industries; sometimes increases international competitiveness; and supports the adjustment to changing world markets. In the next decade technological innovations in electronics and data processing are even more likely to influence industrial productivity to a significant extent. Structural change in the world economy will not stop nor will the necessity to adjust the structure of the economy to changing relative prices in the world markets cease.

IP can and will contribute to economic development in a world of high technology where resource constraints must be overcome. This will happen provided that the chief stress of IP lies not on structural preservation but on the facilitation of economic adjustment and, above all, on the promotion of productivity.

Notes

1. "Gesetz zur Förderung der Stabilität und des Wachstums der Wirtschaft" of June 8, 1968.
2. See Bundesregierung (1968).
3. See Bundesregierung (1968; 1970, p. 7; 1978, p. 16) and for example, Oppenländer (1974, p. 3), Klatt (1975), Sachverstandigenrat (1976), Kommission für Wirtschaftlichen, und Sozialen Wandel (1977).
4. Short surveys on German industrial policy in English are, for example, OECD (1971, 1975, 1978), Kuster (1974), Mueller (1975), Fels (1976), Garner (1976), Carmoy (1978), or Owen-Smith (1979). For more complete descriptions (in German) see for example, Giersch (1964), Dörge (1968), Gäfgen (1970), Peters (1971, 1975, 1977, 1978), Klatt (1975), von Krüchten (1975), Voss (1975, 1977), Hamm (1977), and Finking (1978).
5. The federal government considers only structural formation and adaptation as targets of IP.
6. See Bundesregierung (1970, p. 7).

7. See Clasen (1966), Schlecht (1968, p. 24), and Wissenschaftlicher Beirat beim Bundeswirtschaftsministerium (1979, p. 50).
8. See Bundesregierung (1969; enclosure I, p. 6).
9. See Sachverständigenrat (1976, p. 133; 1979, p. 142).
10. See Wissenschaftlicher Beirat beim Bundesministerium für Wirtschaft (1979, p. 48).
11. See Bundesregierung (1969, pp. 6 and 20), OECD (1971, p. 25).
12. See Bundesregierung (1969, p. 25) and Wissenschaftlicher Beirat beim Bundesministerium für Wirtschaft (1979, p. 46).
13. This argument has been defended by Hauff and Scharpf (1975, p. 48).
14. The federal government stresses that industrial research and development is the task of the enterprises themselves. See Bundesregierung (1969, p. 10).
15. See, for example, Sachverständigenrat (1978, p. 204) and the discussion between Hauff (1980) and Lenzer (1980).
16. Zweites Programm für die mittelfristige Wirtschaftspolitik (1969, p. 33).
17. Calculated from OECD (1978, p. 171).
18. Peacock et al. (1980, pp. 66-85) give a good survey on the economic policy toward the computer industry in West Germany.
19. These are calculations from OECD (1979a).
20. The source is Bundesregierung (1979a, p. 399).
21. Although an alleged growth in the pace of industrial change has been the argument for intensifying IP in the Federal Republic, it is not certain whether structural change has increased in West Germany during the last ten years. For this problem see, for example, Cramer, et al. (1976), Krengel (1977), or Voss (1979).
22. For a survey of the effective protection of industry in West Germany see Donges, Fels, Neu, et al. (1973), Hiemenz, and von Rabenau (1976), and Fels (1976).
23. See Gesetz gegen Wettbewerbsbeschränkungen, 1957, amended in 1965 and 1973.
24. See Tuchtfeldt (1964) and Schlecht (1968, p. 27).
25. The promotion of the mobility of factors sometimes is considered an objective rather than a method of IP. See Bundesregierung (1978, p. 7).
26. See Molitor (1969) for a survey on the policy of labor mobility.
27. See Kommission für wirtschaftlichen und sozialen Wandel (1977, p. 129).
28. These are calculations from OECD (1978, p. 171).
29. These are calculated from OECD (1978, p. 120).
30. The notion of subsidy is somewhat contested in the German economic literature. See for this discussion, for example, Hansmeyer, et al.,

(1963), Andel (1970), and Albrecht and Wesselkock (1971). Zavlaris (1970) and Juttemeier and Lammers (1979) give surveys on the development of subsidies in the Federal Republic since 1951. Albrecht (1978) gives an excellent account of the subsidy reports.

31. See Bundesregierung (1970) and Friderichs (1974).

32. Langer (1974) gives an excellent survey on the objectives and impacts of subsidies in the shipbuilding industry of the Federal Republic.

33. Sachverständigenrat (1979, p. 142).

34. See Bundesregierung (1978, p. 5).

35. This argument can be traced to von Mises (1929). Today this view is promoted, for example, by Hamm (1977) and Hansmeyer (1979).

36. See for example, Peters (1971, p. 179), Hamm (1977, p. 482), or Voss (1977, p. 49).

37. These reports are sometimes criticized because of lack of transparency. See, for example, Dickertmann (1980).

38. See Bundesregierung: Jahreswirtschaftsbericht (1978, p. 17; 1979, p. 19) and Gorzig, and Kirner (1978). Preliminary reports have already been written by HWWA-Institut (1979), Krieger et al. (1979), and Dohrn et al. (1979). Preparatory sectoral disaggregated econometric models have been published by Frerichs and Naujoks (1976), Kubler (1977), and Fronia (1979).

39. See Schwarze (1980, p. 155).

References

Albrecht, D. (1978). "Subventionen: Problematik und Entwicklungen." *Schriftenreihe des Bundesministeriums der Finanzen.* Heft 25. (Bonn, 1978).
Albrecht, D., and Wesselkock, K. (1971). "Subventionen und Subventionspolitik." *Schriftenreihe des Bundesministeriums für Wirtschaft und Finanzen.* Heft 19. (Bonn, 1971).
Andel, N. "Subventionen als Instrument des finanzwirtschaftlichen Interventionismus." Tübingen: J.C.B. Mohr, 1970.
Bundesregierung. "Jahreswirtschaftsbericht." Bonn, annual.
Bundesregierung (1968). "Grundsätze sektoraler und regionaler Strukturpolitik." Bundestagsdrucksache 2469 (Bonn, 1968).
Bundesregierung (1969). "Strukturbericht." BMWI-Texte No. 75. (Bonn, 1969).
Bundesregierung (1970). "Strukturbericht." Bundestagsdrucksache VI/761. (Bonn, 1970).
Bundesregierung (1978). "Sektorale Strukturpolitik." Bundestagsdrucksache 8/1397. (Bonn 1978).

Bundesregierung (1979). "Bundesbericht Forschung VI," Reihe Berichte und Dokumentationen, Band 4. Bundesminister für Forschung und Technologie (ed.). Bonn, 1979.

Carmoy, G. de (1978). "Subsidy Policies in Britain, France and West Germany. An Overview," in *International Trade and Industrial Policies. Government Intervention and an Open World Economy.* London, 1978.

Clasen, S. (1966). "Die Flexibilität der volkswirtschaftlichen Produktionsstruktur." Wirtschaftspolitische Studien 4 aus dem Institut für Europaische Wirtschaftspolitik der Universität Hamburg. Göttingen, 1966.

Corden, W.M., and Fels, G. (1976). "Public Assistance to Industry. Protection and Subsidies in Britain and Germany." Trade Policy Research Centre and the Institut für Weltwirtschaft, Kiel. London, 1976.

Cramer, U., et al. (1976). "Zum Problem der strukturellen Arbeitslosigkeit." *Mitteilungen aus der Arbeitsmarkt- und Berufsforschung* 5 (1976):70–83.

Dickertmann, D. (1980). "Mehr Transparenz im Subventionsbericht." *Wirtschaftsdienst* 3 (1980):143–151.

Dohrn, R. et al. (1979). "Analyse der strukturellen Entwicklung der deutschen Wirtschaft." Zwischenbericht zum Gutachten im Auftrag des Bundesministers fur Wirtschaft, Bonn. Rheinisch-Westfälisches Insittut für Wirtschaftsforschung, Strukturabteilung. Essen 1979.

Donges, J.B., Fels, G., Neu, A. et al. (1973). "Protektion und Branchenstruktur der westdeutschen Wirtschaft." Kieler Studien No. 123. Tübingen, 1973.

Dörge, F.-W. (1968). "Strukturpolitik wohin? Erhalten–Anpassen–Gestalten." Opladen, 1968.

Fels, G. (1976). "Overall Assistance to German Industry," in Corden, W.M., and Fels, G. (1976), pp. 91–119.

———. (1977). "Strukturwandel und Beschaftigung." *Allgemeines Statistisches Archiv.* 61 (1977):1–15.

Fels, G., and Glismann, H.-H. (1975). "Adjustment Policy in the German Manufacturing Sector," in *Adjustment for Trade,* Organisation for Economic Co-operation and Development. Paris: Development Centre, 1975.

Finking, G. (1978). "Grundlagen der sektoralen Wirtschaftspolitik. Eine problemorientierte Einführung mit einem Kompendium wichtiger Begriffe der sektoralen Wirtschaftspolitik." Bund-verlag, (Köln, 1978).

Franzmeyer, F. (1979). "Industrielle Strukturprobleme und sektorale Strukturpolitik in der Europaischen Gemeinschaft." *DIW-Sonderheft* 130 (Berlin, 1979).

Frerichs, W. (1975). "Ein disaggregiertes Prognosesystem für die BRD. 1. Die Staatssektoren." (Meisenheim, 1975).

Frerichs, W., and Naujoks, W. (1976). "Quantitative Struktureffekte der Wirtschafts—und Finanzpolitik. Eine empirische Analyse unter Berucksichtigung der mittelstandischen Wirtschaft." *Schriften zur Mittelstandsforschung* No. 69 (Göttingen, 1976).

Friderichs, H. (1974). "Strukturpolitik heute und morgen." *Ifo-Schnelldienst* 2 (1974).

Fronia, J. (1979). Ein ökonometrisches Modell zur Produktions-und Preiserklärung in der deutschen Industrie." *IAW Schriftenreihe* 33 Tübingen, 1979).

Gäfgen, G. (1970). Strukturpolitik," in *Staatslexikon*, 11. Band 3. Ergänzungsband, 6., vollig neu bearbeitete und erweiterte Auflage. Freiburg, 1970.

Garner, M.R. (1976). "Relationships of Government and Public Enterprises in France, West Germany and Sweden." National Economic Development Office, Background Paper 2. London, 1976.

Giersch, H. (1964). "Aufgaben der Strukturpolitik." *Hamburger Jahrbuch für Wirtschafts—und Gesellschaftspolitik*. (Tübingen, 1964):61–90.

Gorzig, B., and Kirner, W. (1978). "Konzeption einer Strukturberichterstattung für die Bundesrepublik Deutschland. Möglichkeiten und Grenzen der Analyse sektoraler Strukturentwicklungen." Deutsches Institut für Wirtschaftsforschung, Sonderheft 122. Berlin, 1978.

Hamm, W. (1977). "Strukturpolitik, sektorale," in W. Albers et al. (ed.), "Handwörterbuch der Wirtschaftswissenschaft," Vol. 7. 479–491.

Hansmeyer, K.-H. (1979). "Missverständliche Thesen." *Wirtschaftsdienst* (1979) 218–220.

Hansmeyer, K.-H., et al. (1963). "Subventionen in der Bundesrepublik Deutschland." *Finanzwirtschaftliche Forschungsarbeiten N.F.* 25 (Berlin, 1963).

Hartwich, H.-H., and Dörge, F.-W., eds. *Strukturpolitik. Aufgabe der achtziger Jahre. Fachwissenschaftliche Analyse. Didaktische Planung.* Opladen, 1980.

Hauff, V. (1980). "Ein aufgebauschter Grundsatzstreit." *Wirtschaftsdienst* 1980/VI, 267–270.

Hauff, V., and Scharpf, F.W. (1975). *Modernisierung der Volkswirtschaft*. Frankfurt am Main, Koln, 1975.

Hiemenz, U., and von Rabenau, K. (1973). "Effektive Protektion: Theorie und Berechnung für die westdeutsche Industrie." *Kieler Studien* No. 123 (Tübingen, 1973).

———. (1976). "Effective Protection of German Industry," in Corden, W.M., and Fels, G. (1976), pp. 7–45.

Hoppen, H.E. (1979). "Industrieller Strukturwandel. Eine empirische Untersuchung der sektoralen und regionalen Veranderungen im Sekundarbereich der Bundesrepublik Deutschland." Berlin, 1979.

Horn, E.J., Schmidt, K.D., and Zumpfort, W.D. (1977). "Konzeption einer Strukturberichterstattung für die Bundesrepublik Deutschland. Möglichkeiten und Grenzen der Analyse sektoraler Strukturentwicklungen." Kiel, 1977.

HWWA-Institut (1979). "Analyse der strukturellen Entwicklung der deutschen Wirtschaft. Zwischenbericht." HWWA-Institut für Wirtschaftsforschung, Hamburg, Forschungsgruppe Analyse der Sektoralen Wirtschaftsstruktur. Forschungsauftrag des Bundesministers für Wirtschaft. Korrigierte Auflage. Hamburg, 1979.

Jüttemeier, K.H., and Lammers, K. (1979). "Subventionen in der Bundesrepublik Deutschland." *Kieler Diskussionsbeiträge* 63/64. Kiel, 1979.

Kantzenbach, E. (1976). "Industriestrukturpolitik durch verschärfte Konzentrationskontrolle," in Wirtschaft und Wettbewerb. Düsseldorf. 26, 1976. 11/12: Wirtschaft im Wettbewerb, 732–738.

Klatt, S. (1975). "Die Problematik einer Steuerung des Strukturwandels," in *Strukturwandel und makroökonomische Steuerung. Festschrift für Fritz Voigt zur Vollendung des 65. Lebensjahres.* S. Klatt and M. Willens, eds. Berlin, 1975.

Kommission fur wirtschaftlichen und sozialen Wandel (1977). "Wirtschaftlicher und sozialer Wandel in der Bundesrepublik Deutschland." Gutachten. Gottingen, 1977.

Krengel, R. (1977). "Strukturwandel im Bereich der Produktionsfaktoren." *Allgemeines Statistisches Archiv.* 61 (1977):31–42.

Krieger, C., et al. (1979). "Möglichkeiten und Grenzen einer Regionalisierung der sektoralen Strukturberichterstattung." Forschungsauftrag des Bundesministers fur Wirtschaft. Institut für Weltwirtschaft an der Universität Kiel, Abteilung Infrastruktur und Weltwirtschaft. Kiel, 1979.

Kubler, K. (1977). "Ein disaggregiertes Prognosesystem für die Bundesrepublik Deutschland. 2. Die Unternehmenssektoren." Meisenheim am Glan, 1977.

Kuster, G.H. (1974). "Germany," in R. Vernon, ed., *Big Business and the State. Changing Relations in Western Europe."* Cambridge, Mass.: Harvard University Press, 1974. Pp. 64–86.

Langer, J. (1974). "Ziele und Auswirkungen der Subventionierung der Werftindustrie in der Bundesrepublik Deutschland." *Veröffentlichung des HWWA-Instituts.* Hamburg, 1974.

Lenzer, C. (1980). "Zukunftsorientierte Forschungs-und Technologiepolitik." *Wirtschaftsdienst* 1980/VI, 271–274.

Molitor, B. (1969). "Zur Politik der Arbeitsmobilität." *Hamburger Jahrbuch für Wirtschafts-und Gesellschaftspolitik.* 14, 1969.

Mueller, R. (1975). "Some Aspects of the Relations of Government and Industry in the Federal Republic of Germany." *The Business Economist.* (Watford: Society of Business Economists), 7, No. 3 (1975): 106–118.

Niehans, J. (1964). "Strukturwandlungen als Wachstumsprobleme," in *Schriften des Vereins für Socialpolitik, Neue Folge*, Vol. 30/I, Strukturwandlungen einer wachsenden Wirtschaft. Berlin, 1964.

OECD (1971). "Industrial Policies of 14 Member Countries." Organisation for Economic Co-operation and Development. Paris, 1971.

———. (1975). "The Aims and Instruments of Industrial Policy: A Comparative Study." Organisation for Economic Co-operation and Development. Paris, 1975.

———. (1978). "Selected Industrial Policy Instruments. Objectives and Scope." Organisation for Economic Co-operation and Development. Paris, 1978.

———. (1979). "Report on the Role of Industrial Incentives in Regional Development." Organisation for Economic Co-operation and Development. Paris, 1979.

———. (1979*a*). "Trends in Industrial R&D in Selected OECD Member Countries 1967–1975." Organisation for Economic Co-operation and Development. Paris, 1979.

Oppenlander, K.H. (1974). "Ansatzpunkte und Probleme der sektoralen Strukturpolitik in der Bundesrepublik Deutschland." *Ifo-Studien*. 20 (1974):1–18.

Owen-Smith, E. (1979). "Government Intervention in the Economy of the Federal Republic of Germany," in P. Maunder, ed., *Government Intervention in the Developed Economy*. London, 1979.

Peacock, A., et al. (1980). *Structural Economic Policies in West Germany and the United Kingdom*. London, 1980.

Peters, H.-R. (1971). "Grundzüge sektoraler Wirtschaftspolitik." *Beitrage zur Wirtschaftspolitik*. Band 15. Freiburg, 1971.

———. (1975). "Grundzüge sektoraler Wirtschaftspolitik." 2. Auflage. Bern, Stuttgart, 1975.

———. (1977). "Konzeption und Wirklichkeit der sektoralen Strukturpolitik in der Bundesrepublik Deutschland," in *Probleme des Strukturwandels und der Strukturpolitik*. Tübingen, 1977.

———. (1978). "Ordnungspolitische Grenzen sektoraler Strukturpolitik in marktwirtschaftlich orientierten Ordnungen," in *Stabilitat im Wandel. Wirtschaft und Politik unter dem evolutionsbedingten Diktat. Festschrift fur Bruno Gleitze zum 75. Geburtstage*. Berlin, 1978.

Sachverstandigenrat zur Begutachtung der gesamtwirtschaftlichen Entwicklung. *Jahresgutachten*. Mainz, Stuttgart. Annual.

Schlecht, O. (1968). *Strukturpolitik in der Marktwirtschaft*. Forschungsinstitut für Wirftschaftsverfassung und Wettbewerb e. V., Heft 46. Koln etc. 1968.

Schmidt, K.-D. (1978). "Probleme der Strukturpolitik und der Strukturberichterstattung." Gesellschaft zur Förderung des Instituts für Weltwirtschaft. Kiel, 1978.

Schwarze, U. (1980). "Subventionen, spürbare Beeinflussung des Wirtschaftsgefüges? Die sektorale Verteilung der Subventionen in der Bundesrepublik im Zeitraum 1970 bis 1977," in *Rheinisch-Westfalisches Institut für Wirtschaftsforschung. Mitteilungen* 31. 1980, 1. 135-156.

Tuchtfeldt, E. (1964). "Engpässe und Überkapazitaten als Probleme der Strukturpolitik," in H. Ohm, ed., *Methoden und Probleme der Wirtschaftspolitik*. Berlin, 1964.

———. (1970). "Infrastrukturinvestitionen als Mittel der Strukturpolitik," in R. Jochimsen, and U.E. Simonis, eds., *Theorie und Praxis der Infrastrukturpolitik*. Schriften des Vereins für Socialpolitik, Neue Folge, Band 54. 125-151.

von Kruchten, M. (1975). "Sektorale Strukturpolitik" in Konrad, Adenauer, and Stiftung, eds., *Wirtschafts-und Gesellschaftspolitik im freiheitlich-sozialen Rechtsstaat*. Pp. 444-479.

von Mises, L. (1929). *Kritik des Interventionismus*. Jena, 1929.

Voss, G. (1975). "Strukturtrends und Strukturpolitik." Köln, 1975.

———. (1977). "Sektorale Strukturpolitik. Anspruch und Praxis." Beiträge zur Wirtschafts-und Sozialpolitik. Institut der Deutschen Wirtschaft. Köln, 1977.

———. (1979). "Strukturveranderungen im Wirtschaftswachstum." Beiträge zur Wirtschafts-und Sozialpolitik. Institut der Deutschen Wirtschaft. Köln, 1979.

Wissenschaftlicher Beirat beim Bundesministerium für Wirtschaft (1979). "Staatliche Interventionen in der Marktwirtschaft." Göttingen, 1979.

Zavlaris, D. (1970). "Die Subventionen in der Bundesrepublik Deutschland seit 1951. Eine Untersuchung ihres Umfangs, ihrer Struktur und ihrer Stellung in der Finanz-und Volkswirtschaft." Beitrage zur Strukturforschung, Heft 14. Berlin, 1970.

"Zweites Programm für die mittelfristige Wirtsschaftspolitik." Amtsblatt der Europäischen Gemeinschaften 12, No. L129, May 30th, 1969.

12 Industrial Policy in Italy: A Survey

C. Andrea Bollino

The objective of this chapter is to review the main features of the Italian experience with IP during the last three decades. Specifically, this survey attempts to answer the following questions: First, what are the relationships between the characteristics of Italian economic development and the policies pursued by the authorities? Second, what are the relationships between objectives and instruments? In particular, to what extent were the objectives feasible and the instrument choice appropriate? In a broader perspective, some answers have already been provided in the survey of European experiences (chapter 5 of this book). Nonetheless, there are some points that have remained unresolved there and this chapter aims to fill in the gap through a more refined analysis. The next section describes the major decision-making centers that operate in the Italian policy arena and the main philosophic positions that they have adopted through time. The third section reviews the main objectives pursued and the assignment of instruments to objectives in an attempt to clarify what is a very confused collection of administrative and legislative actions. In particular, I shall analyze how bureaucratic difficulties—many acts regulating the same subject—have prevented efficacious application of the instruments. The fourth section attempts to reinterpret the IP experience in the light of structural developments by discussing the relevance of the main philosophies adopted and the effectiveness of the policies. The final section summarizes the major findings.[1]

In many ways, analysis of the Italian case could be considered a most-challenging task given the richness and the extent of state intervention and involvement in the Italian economy. At the same time, it may sometimes be frustrating given the complexity, inconsistency, and ineffectiveness of many policies accumulated over time by numerous short-lived governments.[2]

In some respects, Italy (as a member of the EC) shares common economic characteristics with its northern European neighbors. Its economic development pattern, however, possesses specific features that make Italy different from other European partners. As a consequence of the close interrelationship between economic developments and IP, an analysis of these features is helpful in understanding Italian IP better. The main facts are summarized in the following discussion.

First, the industrialization process occurred more recently in Italy than in northern Europe (for example, Fua 1980) and it was heavily shielded from foreign influence and assisted by state intervention during the interwar period. Second, an historically inherited dualistic regional structure (well known even in non-Italian economic literature—(for example, Lutz 1962 and Rosenstein-Rodan 1955) persists in the disparities between northern and southern Italy. Moreover, a recent stream of thought in Italy has identified an additional regional pattern in the Northeast and along the Adriatic coast—the so-called three Italies pattern (Bagnasco 1977 and Antonelli and Momigliano 1980). Third, there is a dualistic industrial structure that fractures Italian business into a few big enterprises on the one side and a large base of small and medium enterprises on the other side, resulting in productivity differentials. Moreover, the increasing phenomenon of the so-called underground economy tends to exacerbate this dualism. Fourth, state participation in productive activities, which in the past have been crucial in various stages of development and diversification of industrial base, has recently shown an increasing pattern of commitment. In fact, in 1962, public enterprises originated 8 percent of GNP (Posner and Woolf 1967); in 1972 government controlled[3] roughly 7 percent of manufacturing value added and 24 percent of transportation and communication value added. In 1974, these figures rose, respectively, to 9 percent and 26 percent and in 1978 to 14 percent and 28 percent (Grassini 1979). Fifth, as a result of conflicting interests among different forces in the society, the Italian economy has been recently characterized by a high degree of immobility of resources, especially labor.

Decision-Making Process: An Overview

Protagonists of Industrial Policy

The extent of state intervention in the Italian economy could be clarified with a review of the main decision-making centers. Among the protagonists of IP, I shall identify the following centers, in descending order of officiality.

First, there are ministers and so-called Interministerial Committees (IC). In particular, the minister of industry, the minister of state share holdings, and the minister for Mezzogiorno (southern Italy) are in charge of specific policies in their respective spheres of influence beyond the traditional macroeconomic policy range. Moreover, the IC for Credit and Saving (CIRC) is in charge of administrative control over financial intermediation activities[4]; the IC for Economic Policy (CIPE) coordinates the entire public intervention in the economy, while the IC for industrial policy (CIPI) controls specifically public industrial undertakings. Finally, other ICs coordinate administered-prices policy, export-promotion policy, and regional policy in Mezzogiorno.

Second, there are the local governments (established in 1970), which enjoy a limited autonomy in decision-making. They will be discussed only as far as regional aspects of IP are concerned.

Third, there are enterprises under the government's sphere of influence. I shall consider them as decision-making centers rather than just instruments of government policy because in many respects, they have not always acted in accordance with public authorities' directives. In fact, although Posner and Woolf's (1967) definition of the Italian public sector—"a machine without a driver"—may be too severe,[5] it appears that government control over public enterprises is quite fragmented. For instance, ENEL (the result of the 1963 nationalization of electric power generating companies) is controlled by the minister of industry.[6] The state holding institutions—IRI, ENI, EFIM, and EGAM[7]—are controlled by the minister of state holdings, in the sense that their corporate capital comes from central-government budget allocations. Their original function was to administer government properties in basic industries of particular interest although they have expanded over time in other fields (see table 12-1).[8] In addition, under the control of the minister of budget there is GEPI, a special institution that is supposed to engage in rescue operations with private partners with the ultimate aim to turn back control into private hands after successful healing.

Another protagonist of IP is the group of special financial institutions (especially, IMI, Mediocredito, Cassa Mezzogiorno [from now on, CASMEZ]). They provide long-term financing to industrial activities as well as to regional development under the government supervision and recently, also under the government political pressure.

Main Industrial Policy Philosophies

The crucial feature of Italian IP efforts can be summarized as follows: In absence of a political consensus on the direction in which transformation of the society was to be pursued, Italian authorities have generally adopted an ad hoc attitude, merely responding to a sequence of external market shocks. This attitude may be depicted as an ex-post approach—that is, the attempt to salvage the market whenever there is a threat of failure or disruption of the resource-allocation mechanism.[9]

There have been, however, few exceptions, which involve two other types of IP philosophies. These latter are, respectively, the nonselective approach, aimed at establishing favorable conditions for the market, and the

Table 12-1
Public Enterprise, Areas of Intervention, 1980

1. Iron, steel
2. Cement
3. Metalworking, machinery, transportation, equipment
4. Electronics, electrical machinery
5. Shipbuilding
6. Energy sources and electricity (virtual monopoly in electricity since 1962)
7. Chemicals
8. Textiles
9. Telephones and telecommunications (monopoly since 1957)
10. Highways (virtual monopoly)
11. Thermae
12. Cinematography
13. Broadcasting (virtual monopoly until 1978)
14. Food processing
15. Paper and pulp
16. Glass
17. Banking and insurance
18. Transportation (virtual monopoly in Air and Railways)

Source: Guizzetti (1977).

ex-ante approach, aimed at leading the market whenever it is promising, as discussed in an earlier chapter.

As far as the nonselective philosophy is concerned, there have been two interesting examples of this approach to IP in the early history of Italian IP. The first is a report written in 1947, (Saraceno Report quoted in Scognamiglio 1979) which envisaged the government role in IP as one of promotion of aggregate demand through massive public spending. The second, an economic plan proposed by labor unions in 1949, suggested to use public spending and public infrastructures as propelling forces of IP.

The reader expecting to recover from these examples a flavor of laissez-faire philosophy along German lines might be disappointed at this point. It was not until the mid-1970s, indeed, that this stream of thought had come back into fashion from its confinement in the academic environment. This new laissez-faire view, adopted by the employers' union, can be summarized with the expression of the governor of the Bank of Italy (Banca d'Italia 1974): "ridurre i lacci e lacciuoli dell'economia" (literally: to reduce laces and bridles that are tying up the economy).

In addition, in the Triennial Plan for 1979-81 (Italian Government 1978) it is argued that it would be illusory to believe that public investment alone can sustain economic growth; its task is to provide public goods. The government role is to induce autonomous private investments (rather than to crowd it out) through available financial channels and to induce an improvement in economic agents' expectations through a more certain environment.

This new government position should be compared with the one prevailing during the 1960s, when Italian decision makers were arguing that stimulation of private investment during downturn periods was like pushing on a string and that, consequently, public enterprise had to fulfill the role of stabilizer in the national interest.

As far as the ex-ante philosophy is concerned, an important example of this approach could be identified in the steel-industry reorganization plan carried on between 1948 and 1954 by IRI. This plan envisaged a long-run strategy of development of three integrated-cycle technology plants limiting public intervention to basic production and assigning to private enterprises more flexible lines of production—namely, specialties and rods for cement. A second steel plan issued by the government in 1956 called for further expansion of public production with a fourth integrated-cycle plant in Southern Italy. A third government plan in 1970 (bitterly opposed by IRI) envisaged a fifth steel plant in southern Italy, fortunately never built, given the well-known current European crisis of excess capacity plaguing the steel industry.

A second case could be considered the foundation of ENI, which was motivated by the desire for an autonomous national-energy policy. ENI unified the previously uncoordinated activities of state-controlled companies in the fields of exploration of production and distribution of oil and (domestic) natural gas, petrochemicals, fibers, engineering, and nuclear energy. Although ENI's management efforts to gain independence from the major international oil companies failed, there is no doubt that this state holding company has performed an important role in spurring Italian economic development in the early period, for its net output grew between 1957 and 1962 by 141 percent. From 1962 onward, however, ENI attempted to spread into areas hitherto reserved for private capital, acquiring control of a major textile group and expanding into fertilizers (both in Mezzogiorno) in order to vertically integrate its fibers and basic-chemical productions.

Although there are other examples of this approach,[10] those just discussed are sufficient to highlight two important characteristic of Italian IP. First, it is seldom clear whether the state holding company or the public authority has been the originator of the industrial strategy. In fact, in the case of the 1956 steel plan, the government was blamed for merely legitimizing an independent decision already taken by IRI. In the case of ENI's attempt to expand its activities into the new field of petroleum, Posner and Woolf's comment suffices:

> Whereas when one of the major international oil companies needs funds it can raise equity, ENI is barred from so operating. ENI's sorrow is, there-

fore, not just overambition in the past, but the fact that it has been pursuing entrepreneurial policies with a capital structure more appropriate to a municipal gas company.

Second, there appears to be an attitude on the part of the public authorities to transform a winner into a loser in order to pursue social and political objectives. Accordingly, in the case of the steel industry, the government thought that what had been a success in the 1950s, (first IRI steel plan) could be replicated in the 1970s (development of the fifth steel plan). The fact that the political necessity of investments in southern Italy overweighed economic considerations is demonstrated by the pugnacious debate among IRI, CIPE, and the minister of Mezzogiorno, which lasted until 1977 (when the project was finally postponed permanently), long after a steel crisis had become evident throughout Europe. In the case of ENI, the government was unwilling to give up the current structure of its political control over the holding when a different status of autonomy could have been desirable.

In conclusion, two points must be clear. First, the encouragement of investment in the South and control of a state holding company were not mistakes. The mistake was the attempt to force capital-intensive investment in a labor-abundant region in an industry that was already suffering from excess capacity. Second, it has been the intrinsic myopia of the government coupled with an inconsistency in the assignment of instruments to targets from an economic viewpoint that have led to an accumulation of short-run policies, attempting to solve one problem at a time when a long-run and broader perspective (for example, along the French lines) might have been more effective.

Objectives and Instruments of Industrial Policy

Economic Environment and Major Goals

In the Italian economic literature, it is customary to divide the postwar history into five major periods (see, Scognamiglio 1979a, Savona 1979, and Graziani 1975). First, the reconstruction period, 1946-1953, was characterized by the implementation of the Marshall Plan and the reconversion to civilian production. Second, a period of sustained growth 1954-1963, embracing the so-called economic-miracle period from 1958-1963, was characterized by low wages, high exports, and favorable terms of trade—a miraculous combinaton of conditions, indeed, unique in the Italian history (for example, Grilli and Kregel 1980). Third, a period of slower growth, from 1964-1968, was induced by a deflationary policy pursuing balance-of-payment adjustment in 1964 (for example, Onida 1975). Fourth, a period of structural crisis, from 1969-1973, was characterized by sudden increase in unit-labor costs fueled by increasing union demands. During this period massive government assistance to the private sector began. Fifth, the postoil-crisis period, 1974 to present, has been characterized by high inflation, decline of gross fixed-capital formation, and increasing rescuing of ailing industries.

In this framework, many IP goals have been formulated. Using the classification scheme of chapter 2, they can be divided into four groups:

1. *Development of Basic Industries in the 1950s and Early 1960s.* In the first two periods of spontaneous high growth, public authorities pursued the development of those activities that the private-capital market was not willing to bear. In chapter 3, these are characterized by high risk and/or divergence between private and social costs.

From the viewpoint of a market-characteristics objective, concentration efforts have been conducted with direct intervention of public enterprise since the beginning of the 1960s. While in some cases national-monopoly considerations were justifiable, in other instances clear economic rationale could not be found. In addition, a conflict has plagued this policy for public enterprises have used monopolistic rents for self-financing purposes, while government attempted to break those rental positions through administered prices control.

2. *Development of Mezzogiorno since the 1960s.* During the miracle period it became apparent that Mezzogiorno was being left behind (between 1951 and 1960, the per-capita-income ratio between North and South rose from 2.3 to 2.4, and the percentage of investment in the South stagnated at 15.7 percent between 1951 and 1959); public authorities gave priority of the objective of industrialization of this region. The persistent failure of attempts to close the North-South gap has rendered the Mezzogiorno development objective an everlasting feature of Italian IP.[11]

3. *Preservation of Employment in the 1970s.* The structural crisis of 1969 and the subsequent oil crisis of 1973 which slowed down economic growth, shifted the attention of the authorities toward the problem of rescuing troubled industries one at a time and marked the beginning of employment-preservation attempts. As Prodi (1980*b*) puts it, the restructuring difficulties appear when nothing new comes up to replace the old. Government IP, instead of promoting new business, has tried to prevent the disappearance of old ones . . . Since full employment is a primary objective and as new job development in the tertiary sector is limited (by this policy indeed), the deindustrialization process has been delayed through maintenance of industrial employment, mainly in big enterprises. The lack of a comparative analysis of private and social costs versus private and social benefits of this policy is too well known to be discussed further (for example, Savona 1980).

It is not difficult to identify output and capital adaptation as the main objectives of Italian IP in this period. In addition, one may be tempted to call this policy structural labor nonadaptation, for intervention in each ailing industry has discouraged interindustry labor mobility.

4. *Industrial Reconversion and Restructuring since 1977—the New IP Course.* The failure of the previous approach has led to the last group of objectives, which is the first coordinated IP strategy by the government in a general-equilibrium framework. The debate on reconversion and restructuring has involved all the IP protagonists, who have engaged in strenuous lobbying to influence government decisions, especially on the issue of financial restructuring. Although there is skepticism about the viability of this new approach (for example, Castellano 1980, Camagni 1979, and Guerci 1978 among others), the IP course, nonetheless, stimulated an intensive intellectual effort of clarification of the public role in the economy.

This period marks the beginning of an innovation policy in Italy, for research and development promotion has been virtually a nonexistent IP objective until the end of the 1970s. Although de facto some support has been given in this direction since 1968, it has had negligible results (Momigliano 1980). This could be explained by the fact that a cultural dependence on the product life-cycle hypothesis seems to have influenced policy decisions aimed at imitating the example of Italy's northern European neighbors. The failure of this approach became apparent only in the mid-1970s, when it was recognized that the Italian specialization pattern possessed characteristics quite different from a simple textbook product-life-cycle model (Onida 1980 and Onida et al. 1978).

As far as structural adaptation in the new IP course is concerned, it suffices to mention the meaning attributed, respectively, to restructuring and reconversion[12] (Savona 1980). The former is defined as economic activities aimed at achieving optimal input factor combinations in order to enhance productivity. The latter is defined as activities aimed not only at changing factor combinations, but also at changing the product itself. Finally, concerning commercial policies, it should be mentioned that export promotion—one of the critical objectives in the late 1970s (for example, Dell'Oro, et al. 1977)—has been preferred over restrictive import measures (for example, Grilli 1980).[13]

An Overview of Main Instruments

Italian IP is characterized by two broad classes of instruments: national plans and legislative acts.[14] In principle, national plans provide a macroeconomic framework in order to coordinate the design of specific acts. At a practical level, however, national plans have often legitimized ex post a collection of measures envisaged by various acts, typically, some forms of government budgetary outlays.

The Italian planning experience has been characterized by three phases, summarized in table 12-2. In the first phase, the plan (1955-1965) was nonbinding over a ten-year horizon and envisaged broad IP areas of intervention, such as development of public utilities, infrastructures, and some strategic industries (steel and electricity).

The second phase has been characterized by the influence of the French experience with a shorter horizon (five-year plans for 1965-1970 and 1971-1975) and a more dirigiste approach. The unsolved debate between centralized- or decentralized-planning philosophies led to a total failure of the planning experience, abandoned de facto for several years during the surge of the oil crisis. Out of eleven detailed industry plans envisaged by the plan (1971-1975), only a chemical plan has been implemented at the beginning of the 1970s, with quite unsuccessful results.[15]

The last phase of planning has an even shorter horizon (three-year plans for 1979-1981 and 1981-1983) in the attempt to focus on efficient coordination of macroeconomic policies with IP interventions called for by a new set of industry plans.

As far as legislative acts are concerned, Appendix 12A provides a chronological list of principal measures undertaken since 1945. Four interesting considerations can be drawn from the analysis of the list of measures. First, concerning type of instruments, the predominance of preferential loans as the most-used incentive for industrialization purposes is striking, while fiscal tools seem to have played a more-modest role compared to other European countries. The lack of coordination among financial incentives has led to a two-tier regime in the capital market (preferential versus ordinary loans) (Cassese and Graziosi 1980), resulting from the fact that public authorities have extended horizontally privileges from one sector of the economy to another.[16]

Second, as far as the time horizon is concerned, it is interesting to notice the shift from long-run to short-run intervention, for the importance of increases in endowment funds to public enterprises has grown from the end of the 1960s until 1977-1978, when a coordinating effort of long-term structural intervention has been undertaken (Acts 675 or 1977 and 787 of 1978). This is typical of a one-at-a-time problem-solving attitude, for the authorities have tried to replenish operating losses of public enterprises when it was in danger of shutdown until they were forced to modify the bankruptcy law for a massive emergency rescue (for example, Act 602 of 1978).

Third, as far as the selectivity of instruments is concerned, there is a predominance of industry- and firm-specific measures. A deeper analysis, however, suggests that the net effect has been much less selective as com-

Table 12-2
The Italian Planning Experience

Title	Relevant Characteristics
Phase 1	
Piano Importazioni, 1946	Strategic imports to relieve production bottlenecks at the end of the war.
Piano Vanoni 1955-1965	Long-term framework to coordinate industrial growth and development. Targets: 61 percent annual GNP growth; 18 percent annual saving rate; Additional employment (3.2 million new jobs) with a capital/worker-investment requirement of LIT 1.5 million development of public utilities (steel plan).
Nota Aggiuntiva 1962	First official document analyzing three types of structural imbalances in Italian economy: sectoral-social-geographical.
Relazione Previsionale e Programmatica 1964-	Annual report laying down government forecasts and programs for economic activities.
Proposta di Politica dei Redditi 1962	Income policy modeled after British and French examples; never implemented.
Phase 2	
Piano Pieraccini 1966-1970 (Originally 1965-1969 and adopted in 1967)	Economic-policy-coordination plan. Targets: ensure adequate technological dissemination and financial flows for investment; curb public enterprises needs for capital. Roles assigned to public enterprises: to promote high-technology industries; spur competition: lead Mezzogiorno industrialization process.
Progetto 80-Piano Economico 1971-1975	Last nail in the coffin of Italian planning experience. Targets: correction of structural weakness of the economy by the means of horizontal intervention (on technological innovation services for industrial development, rationalization of capital markets); relevent detailed industry plans (only chemical plan has been issued).
Relazione Sullo Stato dell'Industria 1978	Report on economic situation of the industrial sector. Target: to guide public authorities in designing a new IP strategy.
Piani di Settore 1978-1979	Industry plans. These are supposed to be at the same time *industry studies* and *policy proposals* for the following industries: chemicals; steel; food processing; machinery; paper and pulp; fashion made in Italy (textile, clothing, footwear); electronics. These plans are supposed to be also coordinating instruments for: export-promotion policy; energy policy; and environmental policy.

Table 12-2 continued

Title	Relevant Characteristics
Phase 3	
Piano Triennale 1979-1980	Economic-policy-coordination plan. Targets: reduction of government deficit, which implies healing of loss-making industries; expansion of industrial base; additional employment (mostly in the South). Implementation of industry plans.
Piano Triennale 1981-1983	Economic-policy-coordination plan. Targets: curbing of government deficit; additional employment; development of Mezzogiorno; reduction of balance-of-payment deficit; general-equilibrium approach to IP.
Piano Energetico Nazionale 1980-1990	Energy plan (still under discussion). Targets: reduction of oil dependence from 68 percent to 50 percent of total energy consumption; increase nuclear share in electricity production from 1.4 percent to 14 percent; incentives to conservation in residential heating, industrial production, agriculture, and transportation.

pared to the original intentions, for many measures have tended to cancel each other out as privileges granted to one industry have been extended to others. In addition, insofar as state holding companies have expanded their influence across various industries, measures designed for specific industries under the control of PE have lost their selective nature. As a result of the attempt to preserve employment, the intervention has become paradoxically nonselective, insofar as any industry in trouble could apply for government assistance—the so-called barrier-to-exit phenomenon (Momigliano 1979a).

Finally, as far as the regional impact of policies is concerned, a substantial portion of the legislation is directed toward the problem of Mezzogiorno, either South-specific[17] (infrastructural development and requirements for public enterprises to carry a specified proportion of their investments in the South) or selective regionally (more favorable financial and fiscal measures as compared to the rest of Italy).[18]

Although Mezzogiorno develoment strategies appear to have been more coordinated than other parts of Italian IP, they have suffered of at least two main shortcomings. First, there is a contradiction between a balanced-growth approach, which envisages a diffuse territorial development of public infrastructures and incentives to small and medium enterprises (for example, Act 1575 of 1951 and 159 of 1953), and a spatially selective approach, which sees the promotion of development poles in selected urban areas where modern industries could fulfill a propulsive role for Mezzogiorno development (for example Act 634 of 1957 and Act 717 of 1965). The second weakness is the fact that almost all incentives to industrialization have been targeted to the reduction of production costs (capital, labor, and infrastructures), overlooking to a large extent the problem of marketing and commercialization of whatever was supposed to be produced in the South (Graziani 1972).

The new IP course has attempted to go beyond a mere Mezzogiorno policy, coordinating IP at a regional level. Some decision power has been granted to local governments with regard to location policy in not sufficiently developed areas and vocational-training policy. The centralized structure of Italian government, however, casts some doubt on the effectiveness of these regional efforts (Colle 1979, Camagni 1978, and Cappellin 1978).

Assignment of Instruments

A more-detailed analysis of the objectives-instrument relationship is represented by table 12-3. Each cell is filled with the relevant IP measures (acts of Appendix 1 are identified by number and year), providing a clear picture of historical development as well as of differential regional impact (marked with "R") of each policy.

Table 12-3 confirms the predominance of financial instruments assigned to output, new production, capital, and export-promotion objectives throughout the entire postwar period. A long history of preferential loans and capital subsidies reveals that the strategy adopted since the second half of the 1950s—basic industries and industrialization of Mezzogiorno—has gradually given place to a recurrent injection of public money whenever previous funding had dried up.[19] This is the case of frequent increases in funds to public enterprises during the 1970s. It is also the case of increasing engagement in rescuing operation of special financial institutions and the case of extension of financing and tax credits (mainly, social-security-contribution exemption) from the textile to other industries (Acts 1101 of 1971 and 464 of 1972) as well as from small and medium enterprises to big enterprises (Act 91 of 1979). An important exception is constituted by export-financing measures which represent a rare case of long-term coherent strategy, supporting small and medium enterprises specializing in activities constituting traditionally strong Italian exports (for example, clothing, leather, footwear, furniture, and jewelry).

We must take into account, however, the major effort of coordination

Table 12-3
Italian Industrial Policy Matrix

National Plans			
Focus: Market Characteristics			
Instruments	*Competition*	*Antimonopoly*	*Concentration*
Price control		896(47)–494,496 (73)	
Exchange-rate control			
General tax structure	633(72)		
Tax credits			170(65)–134(76)
Subsidies/grants			1643(62)
Loans: special rate and guaranteed loans	1419(47)–623(59) 1470(61)		184(71)–1,101(71)
Export financing and insurance			
Share participation			Telecommunications highways, natural gas
Manpower retraining			
Development contracts			Telecommunications R
Public purchases			
Infrastructure service-type facilities			717(65)
Technical standards and regulations	216(74)		
Tariffs and other barriers			

Table 12-3 continued

National Plans Focus: Innovation Instruments	Research and Development	New Technological Processes	New Production
Price control			
Exchange-rate control			
General tax structure			
Tax credits	1,089(68)		1,598(47)R–1,482(48)R 105(55)R–
Subsidies/grants	933(60)–853(71)	933(60)	853(71)R–38(55)R
Loans: special rate and guaranteed loans	1,089(68)R–558(71) 675(77)	942(52)–703(59) 422,423(67)–471(69)	891(47)–298(53)R–38(55)R– 634(57)R–902(70)R–616(77)R– 675(77)R–
Export financing and insurance			
Share participation	728(63)	136(53)	136(53)
Manpower retraining			
Development contracts			computers, telecommunications, railways, equipment, pharmaceuticals
Public purchases	Public Enterprises Program 81-83 for the South		
Infrastructure service-type facilities			646(50)–616(71)R
Technical standards and regulations			211(46)
Tariffs and other barriers			

Italian Industrial Policy

National Plans			
Focus: Structural Adaptation Instruments	Output	Capital	Labor
Price control			
Exchange-rate control			
General tax structure	741(64)–973(67) 95(79)	936(77)	589(71)R 590(71)
Tax credits	1,598(47)R–1,482(48)R 105(55)R–1,575(71)R 1,101(71)–464(72)–787(78)	1,018(58)R–717(65) 1,329(65)–1,089(68)R 216(74)–904(77)	
Subsidies/grants	605(45)–1,395(47)–123(65)–717(65) 1,072(69)–184(71)–243(73)–253(73) 493(75)–206(76)–675(77)R–279(78)	949(52)–54(56)–717(65)–183(76)–602(78)	1,115(68)–464(72)–493(75)–183(76)–675(77)R–285(77)–501(77)–1,258(77)–502(78)–215(78)–795(78)
Loans: Special rate and guaranteed loans	889(47)–445(50)R–952(51)–159(53)R 942(52)–298(53)R–623(59)–634(57)–657(60)R–1,470(61)–123(65)–184(71)R–1,101(71)–464(72)R–878(73)–573(76)–350(76)–699(76)–902(76)R–675(77)R–1,258(77)–787(78)–602(78)–91(79)	258(50)–949(52)–623(59)–1,470(61) 124(65)–471(69)–184(71)–493(78) 183(76)R–664(77)R–675(77)R–272(78)	
Export financing and insurance			
Share participation	905(37)–605(45)–1,643(62) 184(71)R–350(76)–787(78)		62(76)
Manpower retraining			478(73)–285(77)–501(77)
Development contracts	717(65)R		
Public purchases	1,066(47)R–835(50)R		
Infrastructure service-type facilities	646(50)R–647(50)R 949(52)R–159(53)R 717(65)R–492(75)R 616(77)R		
Tariffs and other barriers		211(46)–54(56) 634(57)R–274(73) 350(76)–902(76)	300(70)–502(78)

Table 12-3 continued

National Plans			
Focus: International Economic Relations			
Instruments	Import Limitation		Export promotion
Price control		Undervaluation of exchange-rate policy	
Exchange-rate control			
General tax structure	VAT on luxury imports		
Tax credits		374(76)	
Subsidies/grants			
Loans: special rate and guaranteed loans	1,470(61)	897(47)	
Export financing and insurance		955(53)–172(54)–1,196(57) 703(59)–635(61)–442(67) 167(69)–842(72)	713(74)–231(75) 374(75)–492(75) 71(76)–227(77)
Share participation			
Manpower retraining			
Development contracts			
Public purchases			
Infrastructure service-type facilities		374(76)–71(76)	
Technical standards and regulations	373(76)		
Tariffs and other barriers	Custom-duties legislation, EEC, GATT treaties		

and rationalization of IP undertaken in 1977-1978 coordinating the restructuring of industry (Act 675 of 1977); the Acts 183 and 902 of 1976 coordinating preferential loans; and the Act 787 of 1978 allowing for intervention of bank consortia for a maximum of five years in order to consolidate corporate debt of businesses in temporary difficulties. Operational delays and duplications among different measures have, however, prompted skeptical reactions in the literature especially in the case of a major chemical group (for example, among others Camagni 1979, Castellano 1980, Ventriglia 1977, Visentini 1979, Ranci 1980*a*, Filippi 1979 and 1980, Baratta 1979, and Scognamiglio 1979*b*).

Three other considerations emerge from table 12-3. First, in accordance with European trends, promotion of competition has been abandoned at the beginning of the 1960s as an objective (substituted de facto by EC treaties) to leave room for explicit promotion of concentration. Act 1101 of 1961 provides preferential loans to enterprises threatened by the new EC competition and may be considered the grandfather of the later rescue philosophy (Scognamiglio 1979*a*). The bulk of concentration was carried on in the mid-1960s with the nationalization of electricity-generating companies and natural-gas-diversification network and tax credits for mergers (Act 170 of 1965) which favored concentration in the chemical industry.

Second, promotion of innovation has been characterized by erratic and intermittent flow of resources. In fact, it has not been until 1976-1977 that an adequate flow of resources has been allocated to this objective (Act 902 of 1976 and Act 675 of 1977). Extensive analysis of public support to research and development in Italy (the lowest in Europe) highlighted the lack of coordination among instruments and inadequacy to promote innovation for policies have been leashed by rigid bureaucratic schemes, even in the new legislation of 1977 (Momigliano 1979*b* and 1980). In fact, this latter envisages at the same time the concept of restructuring, reconversion, and modernizing an industry within the rigid boundaries of the statistical industrial classification, (Filippi 1979, and Guerci 1979). It follows, therefore, that either the innovation falls into the appropriate statistical category or it would not be eligible for support.

Third, the late discovery of labor-adaptation issues, which started explicitly in 1968 (Act 1115), emerges. It is interesting to note that the employment-preserving philosophy has led to legislation creating structural rigidities in the labor market (for example, Acts 464 of 1972, 230 of 1975, and 502 of 1978) leading to a two-tier regime: On the one side are the guaranteed jobs (especially primary-labor-force) and on the other side are jobs constituting the underground economy. In addition, the new IP course, which is supposed to improve overall labor mobility (Act 625 of 1977 and 795 of 1978), as well as employment of the young and women (Acts 285 of 1977 and 493 of 1975) seems to be inadequate, for it attacks the labor-adaptation problem separately within each industry rather than on a geographical basis (Ranci 1980b).

In conclusion, the picture of Italian IP is characterized by extensive, repeated efforts of the authorities to shape, guide, and supplement the free market. We have highlighted the main inconsistencies in the general philosophy adopted as well as in the design of specific measures. The next section will review historically the relevance and the effectiveness of policies in the light of structural developments.

Economic Structure and IP: A Reinterpretation

Performance of the Italian Economy

A reinterpretation of Italian IP should begin with a closer look to the industrialization period during the late 1950s—the so-called economic miracle. In this period Italian industry started to specialize in transformation of raw imported materials, resulting in a pattern of exports with high content of imports. This illuminates the fact that two of the three miraculous conditions in this period (low salaries, high export growth, and favorable terms of trade) were exogenously determined. Between 1958 and 1963, exports grew at an annual rate of 14 percent, while import and export prices showed a divergent pattern, respectively -2 percent and $+3.8$ percent.

These three conditions already mentioned favored a pattern of specialization in activities characterized by low capital intensities and readily available imported technologies (Grilli and Kregel 1980). Therefore, there was no need for detailed investment planning, as reflected in the nonbinding nature of the long-term plan for 1954–1964.

The slowdown in the following periods can be similarly interpreted as a consequence of the disappearance of the previous conditions. Between 1964 and 1969 import prices grew faster than export prices, and real wages grew less than productivity. After 1970, in addition to worsening terms of trade, wages accelerated substantially while investments declined both in absolute terms and as a percentage of GDP (especially investment in machinery and equipment). Finally, we must remember the increasing competition from new industrial countries (NICs) to which Italian exports are particularly vulnerable.

Mezzogiorno Policy 1951–1973

Divergence between efforts and results of the industrialization of the Mezzogiorno has been widely debated, and our attention shall be confined to only some considerations relevant for IP issues.

The pertinent features of authorities' effort to develop the Mezzogiorno are summarized in table 12-4, which shows that the proportion of total investment in Mezzogiorno rose from a level of 15 percent in the 1950s to almost 20 percent and over 40 percent at the beginning of the 1970s. This phenomenon reflects the investment requirement imposed on public enterprise by legislation: The proportion of public enterprise industrial investment in Mezzogiorno as percentage of total industrial investment of public enterprise tripled from 17 percent in 1957 to 60 percent in 1971. It is crucial to recognize the concentration of public-enterprise commitment in Mezzogiorno in steel, machinery, and especially, chemical industries (table 12-5).

As far as IP financial instruments are concerned, table 12-5 shows an increasing relative importance of CASMEZ in financing investment in Mezzogiorno and the shift from infrastructural developments (55 percent of total in 1955) toward industrial incentives (63 percent of total in 1966-1970 and 68 percent in 1971-1975), mainly concentrated in metallurgy, machinery, and chemicals.

The frustration of these policies can be summarized in four disappointing facts: first, a constant proportion of workers employed by PE in Mezzogiorno as percentage of national public-enterprise employment throughout the 1960s; second, a slight reduction in absolute terms in employment in consumer industries; third, a deterioration of net exports as percentage of regional GDP from an already-negative -15 percent in 1951 to -24 percent in 1973; and finally, the persistent per-capita-income gap (South per capita income was 62.6 percent of the national per-capita income in 1951 and 67.4 percent in 1972).

A common explanation of policy failure can be found in the perversity of promoting capital-intensive activities in a labor-abundant region. A more comprehensive explanation (Faini 1981) focuses on the effects of removal of the protection that was enjoyed by Mezzogiorno traditional industry before the massive industrialization effort: high transportation costs and small market size. The policy-induced opening up of Mezzogiorno to external influence can indeed explain the decrease in employment in the traditional sector (mainly, consumer goods) displaced by competition from northern firms. At the same time, it can explain the failure of the propulsive role envisaged for the capital-intensive activities promoted by PE for this modern sector has relied on northern production for necessary inputs, in spite of the legislative constraints that required public enterprise to purchase a specified proportion of their inputs from local enterprises.

This simplified picture of Mezzogiorno problems highlights a crucial feature of IP efforts: It seems that during the 1960s authorities tried to replicate in Mezzogiorno the miracle-type growth of the previous periods without the same conditions. In fact, promotion of basic industries with public enterprise coexisted well with private enterpreneurship during the miracle period because both were benefiting from favorable exogenous conditions

Table 12-4
Intervention in Mezzogiorno

	Industrial Investment in Mezzogiorno as Percentage of Total Industrial Investment	Public Enterprise Industrial Investment in Mezzogiorno as Percentage of Total Public Enterprise Industrial Investment	Industrial Employment in Mezzogiorno as Percentage of Total Industrial Employment	Public Enterprise Employment in Mezzogiorno as Percentage of Total Public Enterprise Employment	Employment in Consumer-Goods Industry in Mezzogiorno (000)	Employment in Other Industries (000)	Mezzogiorno Net Exports as Percentage of Regional GDP
1951	15.7	—	19.7	—	571	214	−15.8
1954	14.3	—	19.3	7.3	584	232	−17.5
1958	15.1	19.4	19.2	7.2	596	259	−16.4
1960	17.6	36.9	18.5	7.2	593	274	−22.2
1963	26.2	50.8	17.4	8.1	595	301	−23.9
1967	24.4	44.0	18.4	8.6	618	346	−17.3
1970	31.2	52.8	17.5	10.2	594	382	−21.9
1973	43.9	58.0	17.9	18.1	552	443	−24.0
1976	—	39.0	—	—	—	—	—

Source: Adapted from Graziani 1979.

Italian Industrial Policy

(export-led growth and favorable terms of trade) coupled with internal conditions (low wages and high investment).

At that time, however, a confusion between causes and effects induced the authorities to believe that low wages combined with high investment rates was sufficient for the miracle. Accordingly, they promoted investment in Mezzogiorno, which enjoyed lower wages (partly due to the *gabbie salariali,* a mechanism establishing wage differentials for the same skill level across different geographical areas, which was abolished in 1969).

The opening up of the Mezzogiorno economy, coupled with infrastructure investment (in a first phase) and industrialization (afterward) did not result in a virtuous cycle of export-led growth, as shown by the worsening of current balance. The lack of export potential is reflected in the critique by Graziani (1979), according to whom authorities completely overlooked the problem of marketing and commercialization of whatever was supposed to be produced in Mezzogiorno as a result of incentive policies. The undesired result has been to promote a modern sector highly integrated with the North at the expense of disastrous contraction of the traditional sector. As Faini (1981) points out, market research has confirmed that both the share of imports from the North in Mezzogiorno (expenditures for food, furniture, and textiles) and share of exports to Mezzogiorno in northern firm production show a marked upsurge after 1960 (Mancinelli 1979, and Colonna 1979).

The official data, however, do not show the recent development of a vital hidden sector. According to D'Antonio (1980), there is scattered evidence that local enterpreneurship is gradually revitalizing those traditional industries once in decline.[20] Although further analysis is necessary, we may conclude, at this stage, that a new Mezzogiorno policy has begun to provide incentives to the new entrepreneurial spirit, abandoning the heavy investment strategy (for example, Faini and Schiantarelli 1982).

Public Enterprises and Reconversion-and-Restructuring Policies

Public enterprises and reconversion-and-restructuring policies have been intertwined since the end of the 1960s. Although we cannot identify a precise date, it was after the structural difficulties of the late 1960s that public enterprises (until then, pursuing chiefly Mezzogiorno development) and reconversion-and-restructuring policies (until then focusing on small- and medium-enterprises assistance) were pooled together in the authorities' minds in order to pursue industrial rescues.[21]

Detailed data on government intervention are available since 1973, distinguished in direct government transfer to enterprises (table 12-6) and

Table 12-5
Investment of Public Enterprises in Mezzogiorno as Percent of Total Public Enterprises Investment in Each Industry

Year	Steel	Machinery	Oil Refining	Chemicals	Textiles
1957	24.1	—	28.9	—	100
1960	26.3	27.1	52.4	30.8	81.3
1963	55.4	30	50.6	47.7	40
1966	54.4	26.3	32.5	72.2	21.5
1969	52.2	49.4	29.2	69.1	40.4
1971	76.3	53.8	20.6	73.5	40.6
1973	75.5	45.1	10.3	85.0	35.9
1976	57.7	46.2	16.8	75.9	40.0

Source: Graziani 1979.

Casmez Tot Financing, 1951-1975
(percentage composition)

Industry	Prefer Loans	Capital Subsidies
Food	7.6	12.3
Textile-clothing leather	4.5	5.7
Metallurgy	12.4	20.3
Machinery	9.4	16.6
Stone, Clay	8.2	10.9
Chemicals	40.4	23.6
Artificial fibers	8.5	1.0
Plastics	1.1	1.9
Other	7.9	7.7
Total industry	100	100
	(6172.6)	(1,104.1) billion LIT

Adapted from Rodgers (1979).

Casmez Intervention

	Casmez Investment as Percentage of Total Investment in Mezzogiorno	Total Financing Percentage Composition		
		Infrastructure	Industrial	Other
1951–1955	17.5	55.5	9.0	35.3
1956–1960	21.2	35.6	35.3	29.1
1961–1965	27.5	23.3	58.8	17.9
1966–1970	25.1	22.7	63.3	14.0
1971–1975	32.0	23.6	68.0	8.4

Note: *Other* column refers to mainly agricultural and services development.

preferential loans by special financial institutions under government control (table 12-7). The total commitment of resources to government intervention rose from .94 percent of Italian GDP in 1974 to 2.17 percent in 1978. This constitutes empirical evidence of the issue discussed in chapter 5 according to which a persistent philosophy of assistance may induce an increasing commitment of resources. This in turn may increase the divergence between market conditions and the specific situation of the (assisted) industry, calling for more assistance.[22]

As far as the relative importance of rescue policies is concerned, endowment funds to public enterprise rose from 60 percent to 72 percent as a percentage of direct government transfers between 1973 and 1977.

This phenomenon stimulated a hot debate in the recent Italian literature focusing on the hypothesis that state has become a hidden banker (Monti and Siracusano 1979 and 1980, and Nardozzi and Onado 1980). In this respect, there was an inverse correlation between loans (based to some extent on economic considerations) and capital subsidies (based to a large extent on political considerations) to public enterprise, suggesting that government has indeed crowded out the banking system in financing public enterprise. (In the 1950s endowment funds represented 11 percent of public-enterprise source of financing versus 55 percent in 1978.)[23]

Research-and-Development and Export-Promotion Policies

As far as research-and-development support is concerned, the proportion of government transfers devoted to this objective stagnated between 1 percent and 2 percent during the 1970s (table 12-6).[24] At the same time, export financing and insurance (envisaged by the series of acts listed in table 12-2, especially the new legislation of 1977) has recently taken a considerable proportion of preferential loans from 29 percent in 1973 to 54 percent in 1978, showing an increase in the ratio of loans to export value.

It is important to understand these two phenomena. Italian postwar industrialization was based on readily available imported technologies and high export growth. As this initial development of the Italian economy proved successful in the 1950s, authorities acted noninnovatively.

At the same time they provided financing to the export-oriented sector of the economy—typically, small and medium enterprises that were not in a position to pay for sales efforts abroad.[25] Therefore, in evaluating the success of export promotion policies, it is perhaps superfluous to mention that the Italian technological balance is negative and that the strength of Italian exports relies to a large extent on traditional goods. This does not obscure

Table 12-6
Government Transfers to Industrial Sector 1973–1977
(current billion LIT)

	Interest Subsidy	Capital Subsidy	Casmez Interest Subsidy	Casmez ENEL	Casmez Capital Subsidy	Mediocredito	Endowment Funds State Holdings	Endowment Funds ENEL	Endowment Funds GEPI	Total	Percentage GDP
1973	57.1	24.6	147.6	9.8	93.2	200	531	100	—	1234.7	1.50
1974	61.1	16.1	158.0	5.1	110.1	100	307	50	30	966.5	.96
1975	89.2	39.9	208.7	3.7	198.7	—	405	50	66	1287.8	1.13
1976	122.9	57.8	200.6	28.1	216.4	204	80	550	180	2040.3	1.43
1977	161.6	41.5	201.5	19.4	268.3	4	803	500	144	2414.5	1.41
1978	162.4	55.0	305.7	14.0	270.0	204	2347	600	324	4796.7	2.17

Percentage Composition by Objectives

	Governmental Capital Subsidies	Casmez	State Holdings	ENEL	GEPI	Mezzogiorno	Exports	SMEs (Acts 623, 949)	Restruc. (Acts 1470, 464, 1101)	Research and Development Funds	Other Funds
1973	2.4	9.1	51.8	9.8	—	7.5	4.5	8.2	—	.6	6.7
1974	1.6	11.3	31.6	5.1	3.1	19.2	8.0	8.9	3.5	2.1	5.6
1975	3.0	14.7	30.1	3.7	4.9	17.2	9.6	8.6	1.2	1.1	5.9
1976	3.0	11.1	4.1	28.1	9.2	7.7	12.3	11.2	3.8	2.2	7.3
1977	1.6	10.4	31.1	19.4	5.6	4.0	13.5	5.9	3.2	1.0	5.2
1978	1.3	6.3	54.7	14.0	7.5	1.4	8.2	1.3	1.5	0.5	3.3

Source: Adapted from Artoni and Termini (1980).

Table 12-7
Preferential Loans Granted by Special Financial Institutions, 1973-1977

Year	Mezzogiorno Approved Ex Ante	Actual	Export	SME (Acts 623, 949)	Restructuring (Acts 464, 1470, 1101)	Other	Total
1973	(968)	398.7	566.2	577.8	24.4	386	1,953
1974	(730)	602.1	502	438.6	104.3	250	1,897
1975	(405)	740.8	677.6	567.6	60	394	2,440
1976	(198)	435.4	1,046.8	926.6	232.8	714	3,355
1977	(484)	323.4	1,553.7	871.2	216	822	3,786
1978	(320)	197.7	1,688.7	256.5	240.3	764	3,147

Percentage Composition

	Mezzogiorno	Export	Loans as Percentage of Total Export Value	SME	Restructuring	Other	Total
1973	20.4	29.0	(4.4)	29.6	1.2	19.8	100
1974	31.7	26.5	(2.6)	23.1	5.5	13.2	100
1975	30.3	27.8	(3.0)	23.3	2.5	16.1	100
1976	13.0	31.2	(3.8)	27.6	6.9	21.3	100
1977	8.5	40.0	(4.4)	23.0	5.7	21.8	100
1978	6.3	53.7	—	8.2	7.6	24.2	100

Source: Adapted from Artoni and Termini (1980).
Note: *Other* column includes shipbuilding, retailing sector, natural catastrophies, craftsmanship assistance, and applied research funding.

other high-technology Italian exports; it simply points out that they do not seem to be explicit results of Italian IP.

Concluding Remarks

The Italian economy—once experiencing a miracle type of growth—has been on a path of stagnation since 1970. In this chapter we have identified a pattern of declining investment, rising labor rigidities and associated unemployment and underground economy, worsening of terms of trade, and persisting regional disparities.

These facts raise a question: Have the authorities tried to reverse this pattern? Or have they favored it through IP? A simple answer cannot be provided. In fact, during the 1960s, the authorities responded to structural problems with increasing intervention both at the central planning level and at the one-at-a-time strategy level. The one-at-a-time level prevailed during the 1970s.

In order to understand why rescuing has become the prevailing approach, it is important to recognize that government intervention led to two drastically different outcomes in the 1950s to early 1960s versus the 1970s (Prodi 1980*a*). In the first case, when manpower released from agriculture was available for rapid industrial growth (both domestic and abroad), ad hoc government intervention followed the trend, promoting certain industries that were lagging and that were considered basic for national economic development. In the 1970s, however, as the phenomenon of declines in industrial employment became apparent throughout Europe—the so-called process of deindustrialization (Blackaby 1979)—Italian authorities attempted to preserve the existing structure.

The objective of preservation of industrial employment has been de facto accomplished through support to unprofitable public enterprises, failure to encourage innovation and research, and rigidities in resource allocation. These policy-induced rigidities, in turn, have worsened structural problems by increasing divergence between the Italian economy and the rest of the world (in the sense of a distortion of comparative advantages) through calling for more government intervention.

The lack of a general equilibrium view has led, however, to a virtually total failure of IP when the problems at stake (labor rigidities and oil crisis) were too big to be attacked with the current piecemeal approach. In fact, according to Scognamiglio (1979*a*), the government's policy has been inspired by the principle of *primum non laedere*—that is, noninterference in those processes the results of which turned out better than expected (in the short run). The government's priorities between short-term successes and long-term failures are obvious.

In conclusion, Italian IP has not been successful in reversing the current pattern except for the new IP course and export-promotion intervention. First, there was a consistent negative rate of return of public enterprises during the 1970s, which shows that despite government subsidies, no improvement has yet occurred. Second, there is inconsistency between restructuring objectives and the decline of investment in public enterprises. Restructuring without investment seems impossible, even in the country of the economic miracle of the 1950s.

This conclusion does not overlook Italian IP's partial merit. From a social point of view, the government has probably prevented massive unemployment for it has acted as a buffer absorbing external shocks, and at the same time it has allowed the growth of a vital hidden economy. The efforts undertaken under the new IP course leave some hope for reversing the situation during the 1980s, although difficulties and delays in implementation still plague Italian economic policy.

Notes

1. A methodological note: Official documents are grouped in sub-alphabetical order in the bibliography under the entry, Italian Government.
2. The average life of an Italian government is roughly one year, based on historical trends in the postwar period.
3. Here, control means that the government has the relative majority in equity capital.
4. For instance, direct corporate debt issues over Lit 2 billion must be approved by CIRC.
5. It must be pointed out, however, that public enterprises without government control do not imply negative results as such. It merely highlights the fact that often public authorities have legitimized ex post as policy objectives the actions of public enterprises, some of which were inconsistent with previous policies, while others were simply filling the gap created by nonexistent government policies.
6. In this survey, I shall not discuss the other nationalized enterprises—namely; Italian Railways, (nationalized since 1905); ANAS (local and national roadways excluding highways); and the Tobacco and Salt State Monopolies (dissolved during the 1970s).
7. I shall not discuss two other minor holdings: EAGAT, which controls thermal baths, hotels, and bottling of spring water, and ENTE-CINEMA, which controls cinematographic distribution and Cinecitta, the Italian Hollywood. In addition, I shall not discuss the radical changes envisaged in a government *White Book on State Holdings* completed in 1981, for it still needs substantial parliamentary debate before being approved.

8. The dust has not yet settled over the debate on the role of public enterprises in the framework of Italian IP (see the survey by Giorgetti 1975). It seems that the controversy can be summarized as follows. On the one side, advocates a strict government control of public enterprises stresses that the function of the latter should merely have been one of instruments in public hands in order to pursue policy objectives, even if these objectives were unrealistic. On the other side, advocates of greater autonomy of public enterprises stressed that they displayed an entrepreneurial spirit that had to be encouraged and unleached from government control. In other words, this so-called additional entrepreneurship expressed by public enterprises management—once freed—could have been a complementary force (to private enterprises) for economic development.

9. For instance, according to P. Saraceno (quoted in Scognamiglio 1979a), the first plan for reconstruction issued in 1946 was already permeated by this philosophy insofar as it was aimed at relieving bottlenecks to industrial production (planning imports of necessary inputs) rather than focusing on potential structural changes.

10. IRI's exploitation of telephone equipment's captive market for electronics is one. *Latu sensu,* export-promotion intervention could be another one, insofar as it has favored specific export-oriented industries.

11. This does not mean that industrialization was the only policy pursued in order to close the historical North-South gap, for there were also social and cultural goals. In this IP survey, however, industrialization is the main one.

12. For a critique of these definitions see Guerci (1979).

13. In fact, import substitution—as an objective of industrial reconstruction in the immediate postwar period—was soon abandoned as an export-led pattern of economic growth became apparent.

14. The distinction is merely functional, for national plans are adopted by the government with official acts as well. The term *Act,* although improper, simplifies the differences existing among parliamentary acts, government acts, decrees of the president of the republic, and ministerial decrees.

15. The reasons for the failure of the chemical plan have to be found (as in the steel case) in the myopia of the authorities, who have encouraged building up of excess capacity and capital-intensive investment in the South for social and political purposes.

16. Some examples are: extension of privileges from Mezzogiorno to small and medium enterprises (Act 135 of 1954); from small and medium enterprises to big enterprises (for example, Acts 853 of 1971 and 91 of 1978); from the private sector to public enterprise (for example, all the acts extending preferential loans originally reserved to private enterprises to state holdings for investment in Mezzogiorno).

17. Acts 646 of 1950, 634 of 1957, 1523 of 1967, and 183 of 1976.

18. For a more-detailed discussion of the relationship between IP and regional policy in Italy, see Faini and Schiantarelli (1982).

19. For a detailed quantitative analysis of policy impact on the price of investment goods, see Marotta and Schiantarelli (1981).

20. For instance, an attempt to measure the importance of the underground economy has been conducted analyzing the electricity-consumption pattern of growth, which has almost doubled in Mezzogiorno as compared to the rest of Italy in the period 1973-1977.

21. During the 1960s, a total of LIT 32 billion have been devoted to reconversion and restructuring (explicitly to SMEs) versus LIT 520 billion in the period 1971-1977. The paradoxical divergence between committed and granted resources in the period 1971-1977 has been explained by the fact that 80 percent of enterprises applying for restructuring funds (under Act 464) were borderline bankrupt and the necessary bureaucratic procedures had not been completed before the actual occurrence of bankruptcy (Pontarollo 1980).

22. The same conclusion could be drawn from the increasing differential between preferential rates and normal rates of long-term financing (from 400 basis points in 1966 to above 800 in 1978) (Marzano 1980).

23. In this respect, some have argued (Grassini 1980) that government assistance to industry has only been assistance to public enterprise.

24. We must point out, however, that often support to research and development in the form of preferential loans is obscured in the group Other in table 12-7.

25. In 1977, 50 percent of Italian exports originated from 217 large enterprises with export sale over 10 billion; 32 percent originated from 2,747 medium enterprises with export sales between 1 and 10 billion; and 16 percent originated from 67,649 small enterprises with export sales less than 1 billion. Onida (1979) points out that the share of small and medium enterprises is increasing over time.

References

Antonelli, C., and F. Momigliano. "Area Economiche, Modelli di Sviluppo Alternativi e Politiche Pubbliche di Intervento in Italia." *L'Industria-REPI,* N.S.I., n. 3, (Lug 1980):395-409.

Aquino, A. "Il Tasso di Cambio Come Strumento di Politica Economica," in Gobbo and Prodi, eds., 1980b.

Artoni, R., and V. Termini. "I Trasferimenti dello Stato All'Industria." *L'Industria-REPI,* N.S.I., n. 1, (1980):7-38.

Bagnasco, A. *Tre Italie: La Problematica Territoriale dello Sviluppo Italiano.* Bologna: Il Mulino, 1977.
Banca, d'Italia. *Relazione All'Assemblea dei Partecipanti.* Rome: Centro Stampa BI, 1974.
Baratta, P. "Sul Risamamento Finanziario delle Imprese," in Cassone, ed., 1979.
Blackaby, F., ed. *Deindustrialization.* London: Heinemann, 1979.
Camagni, R. "Struttura Regionale della Politica Industriale," in *Mondo Economico,* n. 31, 1978.
———. "Per Una Nuova Politica Industriale." *Economia e Politica Industriale,* n. 21, (March 1979):127–146.
Cappellin, R. "Regioni e Politica Industriale," in *Mondo Economico,* n. 30, (1978):46.
Cassese, S., and G. Graziosi. "Quale Futuro Per Il Sistema Degli Incentivi?" *L'Industria-REPI,* N.S.I., n. 3, (1980):333–341.
Cassone, A., ed. *Politica Industriale e Piani di Settore.* Milano: F. Angeli, 1979.
Castellano, C. "Alcune Osservazioni Sulla 675, e il Sistema della Imprese a Partecipazione Statale," in Gobbo and Prodi, 1980b.
Colle, B. "Il Ruolo delle Autonomie Locali a Sostegno delle Attivita' Produttive Industriali," in Cassone, 1979.
Colonna, M. "Il Mezzogiorno Come Mercato di Sbocco Nazionale," in Graziani and Pugliese, 1979.
D'Antonio, M. "La Diffusione delle Attivita' Manifatturiere nel Mezzogiorno." Mimeographed. Convegno CNR-University Bocconi, 1980.
Dell'Oro, A., E. Rodolfi, and C. Roveda. "Le Esportazioni e la Riconversione Industriale." *Rivista di Economia e Politica Industriale* 3, No. 2, (1977):299–323.
Faini, R. "Deindustrialization and Cumulative Processes in an Open Region. The Case of Southern Italy 1951–73." *ESSEX Economics Papers,* No. 167. University of Essex, February 1981.
Faini, R., and F. Schiantarelli. "Regional Implications of Industrial Policy: The Italian Case." E.C.R.P. Workshop on Industrial Policies in OECD Countries. Aarhus, Denmark, March 1982.
Filippi, E. "I Problemi dei Piani di Settore," in Cassone, 1979.
———. "Ristrutturazione Industriale e Risanamento Finanziario delle Impresse," in Gobbo and Prodi, 1980b.
Fua', G. "Problems of Lagged Development in OECD Europe: A Study of Six Countries." Mimeographed. 1980.
Giorgetti, G. "Le Partecipazioni Statali Come Strumento di Politica Industriale." *Economia e Politica Industriale* No. 10. 1975.

Giorgetti, G., and G. Lizzeri. "Politica Industriale e Piani di Settore." *Economia e Politica Industriale* No. 15 (November 1976):3-34.

Gnes, P. "Ristrutturazione Industriale e Sviluppo Economico," in Cassone, 1979.

Gobbo, F., and R. Prodi. "Le Imprese Minori in Regioni di Recente Industrializzazione." Mimeographed. Convegno CNR-University Bocconi, 1980a.

——— eds. *Per Una Ristrutturazione e Riconversione dell'Industria Italiana*. Bologna: Il Mulino, 1980b.

Grassini, F. "Le Imprese Pubbliche," in Grassini and Scognamiglio, 1979.

———. "I Trasferimenti dello Stato all'Industria Pubblica," in Gobbo and Prodi, 1980b.

Grassini, F., and G. Scognamiglio, eds. *Stato e Industria in Europa: l'Italia*, AREL. Bologna: Il Mulino, 1979.

Graziani, A., ed. *L'Economia Italiana: 1947-1970*. Bologna: Il Mulino, 1972.

———. *Crisi e Ristrutturazione dell'Economia Italiana*. Roma: Einaudi, 1975.

Graziani, A., and E. Pugliese. *Investimenti e Disoccupazione nel Mezzogiorno*. Bologna: Il Mulino, 1979.

Grilli, E. "Italian Commercial Policies in the 1970s." World Bank Staff Working Paper, No. 428. Washington, D.C., October 1980.

Grilli, E., and J. Kregel. "Lo Sviluppo Economico Italiano nel Dopoguerra: Una Reinterpretazione." Mimeographed. Convegno CNR-Univ. Bocconi, 1980.

Guerci, C.M. "Piani di Settore al Difficile Collaudo." *Mondo Economico* No. 31, 1978.

———. "Crisi Industriale ed Evoluzione del Concetto di Settore," in Cassone, 1979.

Guizzetti, P. *Stato Padrone, le Partecipazioni Statali in Italia*. Milano: Mondadori, 1977.

Italian Government, Ministry of Budget. "Piano Vanoni-Schema di Sviluppo della Occupazione e del Reddito in Italia nel Decennio 1955-65," in *Mondo Economico* No. 3, 1955.

Italian Government, Ministry of Budget, "Nota Aggiuntiva," in *Mondo Economico* No. 22, 1962.

Italian Government, Ministry of Budget. "Programma Economico Nazionale 1965-69." Roma, 1965.

Italian Government, Ministry of Budget. "Piano Pieraccini—Programma Economico Nazionale 1966-70," in *Mondo Economico* 9 (Settembre 1967).

Italian Government, Ministry of Budget. "Progetto 80–Rapporto Preliminare al Programma Economico Nazionale 1971–75," in *Mondo Economico* 26 (1969).

Italian Government, Ministry of Budget. "Piano Triennale 1979–81," in *Mondo Economico* No. 35 (1978) and No. 4, No. 5 (1979).

Italian Government, Ministry of Budget. "Piano Triennale 1981–83." Mimeographed. Proposed to the prime minister, January 1981.

Italian Government, Ministry of Industry. "Relazione Sullo Stato dell' Industria in Italia." Roma, 1979.

Italian Government, Ministry of Industry, "Piano Energetico Nazionale 1980–90," in *Energia* No. 1, (January 1981):92–101.

Italian Government, Ministry of State Holdings. "Relazione Programmatica." Roma, 1980.

Lutz, V. *Italy a Study in Economic Development.* Oxford: Oxford University Press, 1962.

Mancinelli, E. "Industria Locale e Concorrenza Esterna nell'Area della Grande Industria," in Graziani and Pugliese, 1979.

Marotta, G., and F. Schiantarelli. "A Note on Tax and Credit Incentives in Italy and the Effective Price of Investment Goods." Mimeographed. London School of Economics, 1981.

Marzano, A. "Credit Subsidies and Efficiency." *Review of Economic Conditions in Italy* No. 2 (June 1980):305.

Momigliano, F. "Ristrutturazione e Riconversione Industriale, Politica Industriale e Programmazione Economica." *Rivista di Economia e Politica Industriale* 5, No. 1 (1979*a*):51–90.

———. "Politica Industriale per L'Elettronica e L'Informatica in Europa." *Economia e Politica Industriale* No. 23 (1979*b*):59–91.

———. "Problemi di Economia e Politica dell'Innovazione negli Anni 70 nei Paesi Avanzati e in Italia," in Gobbo and Prodi, 1980*b*.

Monti, M., and B. Siracusano. "The Public Sector's Financial Intermediation, the Composition of Credit and the Allocation of Resources." *Review of Economic Conditions in Italy* No. 2 (June 1979):223.

———. "In Reply to Narozzi and Onado." *Review of Economic Conditions in Italy* No. 2 (June 1980):373–386.

Nardozzi, L., and M. Onado. "The Relations Between Banks and Enterprises and the Public Sector as Financial Intermediary." *Review of Economic Conditions of Italy* No. 2 (June 1980):355–372.

Onida, F. *La Bilancia dei Pagamenti Come Vincolo Alla Politica Economica.* Milano: F. Angeli, 1975.

Onida, F., et al. *Industria Italiana e Commercio Internazionale.* Bologna: Il Mulino, 1978.

———. "Il Potenziamento delle Esportazioni delle Piccole e Medie Imprese in Italia e Lombardia." Mimeographed. Milano: Associazione Industriale Lombarda, 1979.

———. "Specializzazione del'Industria Italiana nel Commercio Internazionale." Mimeographed. Convegno CNR-University Bocconi, 1980.
Pontarollo, E. "Le Politiche di Ristrutturazione Industriale in Italia dal 1961 al 1977." L'Industria-REPI, N.S.I., No. 3, (1980):369-394.
Posner, M., and S. Woolf. *Italian Public Enterprise.* Cambridge, Mass.: Harvard University Press, 1967.
Prodi, R. "The Italian Experience as Regards Public Sector Intervention in the Economy." *International Symposium on Industrial Policies for the 80's,* Madrid, May 1980a.
———. "Per Una Ristrutturazione e Riconversione dell'Industria Italiana," in Gobbo and Prodi, 1980b.
Ranci, P. "La Politica Industriale ei Piani di Settore." *Istituto Ricerca Sociale.* Mimeographed. Internal paper. 1980.
———. "Politica Industriale e Mercato del Lavoro," in Gobbo and Prodi, 1980b.
Rodgers, A. *Economic Development in Retrospect.* Washington, D.C.: Winston & Sons, 1979.
Rosenstein-Rodan, P.M. "Programming in Theory and in Italian Practice," in MIT Center for International Studies, *Investment Criteria and Economic Growth.* Cambridge, Mass.: MIT Press, 1955.
Savona, P. "La Struttura Industriale Italiana: Analisi dei Problemi e Prospettive." *Economia Italiana* No. 1 (1979):43-66.
———. "Costi e Benefici della Ristrutturazione e della Riconversione in Una Economia duale: Il Caso dell'Italia," in Gobbo and Prodi, 1980b.
Scognamiglio, C. "Strategia Industriale e Programmazione," in Grassini and Scognamiglio, 1979a. P. 29.
———. "Il Finanziamento delle Attivita' Industriale," in Grassini and Scognamiglio, 1979b. P. 115.
Ventriglia, F. "Sulla Ristrutturazione e La Riconversione Industriale." *Rassegna Economica* No. 6 (1977):1557-1576.
Visentini, G. "Le Piu' Recenti Agevolazioni Finanziarie all' Industria." *Rivista di Economia e Politica Industriale* 5, No. 1 (1979): 431-440.

Appendix 12A: List of Relevant Acts for IP Intervention

Date	Number	Description
24.6.37	905	Foundation of IRI as a state holding for industrial development.
14.9.45	605	Encouragement of industrial development in the immediate postwar situation.
29.9.47	1,006	Public enterprise must give priority to southern undertakings for at least 17 percent of their purchases.
12.3.46	211	Control power over industrial investments granted to minister of industry.
8.9. '7 [changed by 12.10.50 n 840]	889	Fund for machinery industry to reconvert from war to civilian production administered by IMI (special fin Institution). This was transformed in EFIM in 1964.
11.9.47	891	Fund for industrial reconstruction, import of necessary inputs, and encouragement of exports.
14.2.47	1,598	Measures for industrial development in the South: tax-credit incentives.
29.12.48.	1,482	
15.2.47	1,419	Special fund to finance small and medium enterprises (SMEs) (275 million).
11.12.47	1,395	Increase in IRI endowment fund (20 billion).
15.9.47	896	Regulation of price control; power granted to CIP.

Source: *Raccolta Ufficiale Leggi e decreti della Repubblica Italiana,* Istituto Poligrafico della Stato, Roma, Various Issues.

Note: For clarity, I have reported the relevant features of each act in English, rather than the original Italian title. The amount in LIRA written in the text may have no reference to actual outlays. This fact stresses the bureaucratic and political difficulties existing in the policy-implementation phase.

The definition of south includes the five southern most regions in continental Italy and the two major islands. For brevity, the rest of Italy is defined as northern.

The date is written as day/month/year.

Date	Number	Description
6.10.50	835	Renewal of 17 percent purchase requirement from southern enterprises by public enterprise.
18.4.50	258	Fund for financing purchases of equipment and machinery (only SMEs) administered by IMI.
10.8.50	646	Special fund for industrial development in the South:cassa per il Mezzogiorno (CASMEZ) to finance infrastructure development (especially roads and public works in the period 1950–1960). Provides preferential loans for ten years at 4 percent and custom-duties exemption for machinery imports.
10.8.50	647	Infrastructural developments in underdeveloped areas in the North.
22.6.50 30.8.51	445	Foundation of regional special financial institutions to finance industrial undertakings.
22.12.51	1,575	Fiscal preferential treatment of undertakings that subcontract CASMEZ infrastructural works.
25.7.52	949	Measures to develop economy and employment: Infrastructure development in the South through CASMEZ (1952: 80 billion; 1953–1959: 90 billion/year; 1960: 110 billion; 1961: 100 billion). Infrastructure development in the North. Fund for financing agriculture-machinery investments. Foundation of long-term special financial institution (MEDIOCR).
10.2.53	136	Foundation of ENI: state holding for energy production and distribution.
11.3.53	159	Industrialization of the South: Infrastructures and regional financial institutions. Government interest subsidy: ten-year loans at 4 percent.
14.4.53	298	Industrialization of the South (funding up to 1956 and then to 1958): Special financial institutions for Sicily and Sardinia: preferential loans in cooperation with CASMEZ for three-ten-year periods, especially for SMEs.
22.12.53 22.3.54	955 172	Export-credits insurance administered by a special institution for trade (ICE).

Italian Industrial Policy

12.2.55	38	Measures to finance new industrial undertaking in the South, preferential loans at 5.5 percent.
4.2.56	54	Discretionary power granted to ICs as regards to government-financing policy. Confirmation of ten years funding to CASMEZ (1,000 billion in ten years).
3.12.57	1,196	Export financing to SMEs through MEDIOCR.
21.11.58	1,018	Preferential tax rates on electricity consumption in the South.
30.7.59	623	Coordination of financial assistance to SMEs for the period 1956–1967 (1,181 billion). Forecasted induced investment: 2,678 billion. Forecasted employment growth: 237,000 jobs. Interest subsidy up to 10 percent of total cost of investment.
29.7.57	634	Renewal of CASMEZ up to 1965. (6,900 billion of which is: 67 percent for financial incentives, and 33 percent for infrastructure development). Promotion of development poles. Public enterprise must carry 40 percent of their total investment in South, 60 percent of *new* investment in plants.
1.9.59	703	Export financing to agriculture and technology investment in machinery. Government interest subsidy up to three years for fifteen years (600 million).
29.6.60	657	Industrial development in the South: CASMEZ administers a loan in U.S. dollars.
11.8.60	933	Foundation of Nuclear Energy Agency (CNEN).
5.7.61	635	Export financing and insurance for various activities. State guarantee: 85 percent of short-term loans. 100 percent of long-term loans through special MEDIOCR fund (35 billion).
18.12.61	1,470	Assistance to industrial restructuring in the light of new international competition, especially SMEs through IMI Fund (5 billion). 15-year loans at 3 percent. Refinanced by:
28.3.68	342	10 billion
25.10.68	1,089	8
1.10.69	666	10

Date	Number	Description
18.12.70	1,034	30
22.3.71	184	10
18.5.73	274	40
4.8.75	403	30
26.1.76	4	40
24.5.76	350	30
6.12.62	1,643	Nationalization of electricity-generating companies under ENEL.
22.5.63	728	ENEL share participation to promote pure and applied research.
10.9.64	741	Tax on electricity consumption to increase ENEL's revenue for 1964.
5.11.64	1,176	Foundation of EFIM as a state holding for machinery industry.
18.3.65	170	Fiscal measures to promote mergers: tax credits on capital gains.
11.3.65	123	Special IMI Fund to finance SMEs (25 billion). Privileged loans and capital subsidies.
15.3.65	124	Financing SMEs investment in machinery through MEDIOCR and other regional financial institutions up to 85 percent of cost (10 billion).
26.6.65	717	Coordination of intervention in the South: CASMEZ extension to 1980 (1,640 billion for 1965-1969). 40 percent investment requirement for PE. 45 percent capital subsidy for restructuring. 20 percent capital subsidy for fixed investment. 30 percent capital subsidy for machinery. 30 percent purchase requirement for the South. Preferential loans for tourism developments plus 15 percent capital subsidy. Development contracts between government and private industries: the latter commits to carry large investment and the former carries on the necessary infrastructural developments.
28.11.65	1,329	(Nonselective) tax credits to investment in equipment (above 500 million).
9.10.67	973	Additional tax on electricity to increase ENEL revenue.
11.7.67	442	Additional funds for export financing (MEDIOCR) 6 billion.
5.6.67	422-423	Financing for aerospace programs.

Date	No.	Description
1967	1,523	Coordination of legislation concerning the South. Confirms 30 percent purchase from southern enterprises requirement for public enterprise.
25.10.68	1,089	Measures to promote new investment in the South (partial social-security contribution). Fund for applied research and development: ten-year loans at 3 percent repayable if successful (100 billion) (government share up to 70 percent of total).
5.11.68	1,115	Income guarantee for workers for industrial sector (80 percent of gross pay) (20 billion). Unemployment Compensation Fund: CIG. Short-term assistance to workers if enterprise needs restructuring. Indefinite assistance if job is lost.
21.4.69	167	Additional funds for export financing (MEDIOCR). Government guarantee of up to 500 billion/year (35 billion).
14.7.69	471	Financing for imports of high-technology equipment (IMI) (100 million $U.S.).
29.12.69	1,072	Increase in EFIM endowment fund period 1969–1972 (100 billion).
20.5.70	300	*Statuto dei lavoratori* (labor law). Regulations on labor mobility.
27.3.71	184	Fund for reconversion and restructuring through IMI (40 billion) fifteen-year loans at 3 percent in South. fifteen-year loans at 4 percent in underdeveloped North. ten-year loans at 5 percent elsewhere. Foundation of GEPI (state holding for temporary rescue) (60 billion initial-endowment fund).
25.6.71		Foundation of EGAM (state holding for mining industries) (344 billion initial fund).
4.9.71	588	Increase in IMI Fund for applied research.
4.9.71	594	Additional funds to promote new investment (MEDIOCR) and government guarantee to finance SMEs (50 billion).
4.9.71	589	Increase in social-security-contribution exemption in the South.
4.9.71	590	Increase in social-security-contribution exemption for SMEs.
6.10.71	853	Renewal of CASMEZ fund for period 1971–1975

Date	Number	Description
		(increase in investment requirement for PE to invest in South to 60 percent of total investment; 80 percent of *new* investment).
		Renewal of IMI Fund for applied research.
		End of philosophy privileging basic industries (steel, chemical, machinery) in the South.
1.12.71	1,101	Reconversions-and-restructuring intervention for textile industry, especially SMEs mergers (210 billion).
(Renewed in 1975		Fifteen-year loans at 4 percent Government share in total cost 70 percent .5 billion. 60 percent .5–3 billion. 50 percent 3–6 billion. Partial social-security exemption.
8.8.72	464	Reconversion-and-restructuring intervention extended from textiles to other industries (813 billion).
(Renewed in 1975)		If < 500 employees, same as 1,101 of 1971. If > 500 employees, need minister's approval. Extension of CIG intervention for workers displaced by reconversion-and-restructuring.
26.10.72	633	Introduction of VAT system.
18.12.72	842	Increase in government guarantee for export financing up to 750 billion/year.
7.5.73	243	Increase in EGAM endowment fund (215 billion).
7.5.73	253	Increase in ENEL endowment fund.
18.5.73	274	Special IMI section for reconversion-and-restructuring of SMEs (refinancing of 1,470 [1961]) (40 billion).
		More discretionary power to ICs to grant capital allowances to PE.
30.6.73	478	Institute for vocational training (100 billion).
4.8.73	496–494	Price control on goods produced by big enterprises and on necessary consumption goods.
27.12.73	878	Shipbuilding reorganization program (that is, rescuing) (159 billion).
7.6.74	216	Regulation of capital markets and tax credits to dividends.
		Foundation of CONSOB (equivalent to U.S. Securities and Exchange Commission).

24.12.74	713	Additional funds for export promotion and SMEs.
31.5.75	374	Additional funds for export promotion.
7.6.75	231	Additional funds to finance SMEs: 1975: 75 billion 1976–1980: 110 billion/year 1981–1983: 80 billion/year 1984–1989: 50 billion/year
16.10.75	492	Additional funds for export promotion (MEDIOCR) 1975–1977: Infrastructural development incentives (100 billion/year).
16.10.75	493	Financing new-equipment investment of SMEs (MEDIOCR). Special social-security-contribution exemption for female workers. Increase in CASMEZ endowment fund (1,000 billion).
2.5.76	183	Coordination of intervention in the South (14,500 billion). CASMEZ program for 1976–1980. Subsidies to investment: Government share. 　40 percent of .2–2 billion investment. 　30 percent of additional 2–7 billion. 　20 percent of additional 7–15 billion. 　15 percent of additional above 15 billion. National fund for preferential loans: 65 percent for the South. Increase in social-security-contribution exemption for the South.
5.5.76	206	Increase in ENEL endowment fund (2,000 billion).
16.3.76	71	Export-promotion improvement through ICE.
29.3.76	62	Emergency measures to absorb displaced workers laid off by undertakings in liquidation (through GEPI) (10 billion).
24.5.76	350	Emergency measures for reconversion and restructuring (last renewal of 1,470 [1961]) concerning preferential loans, export promotion, and GEPI intervention (30 billion). CIPE must approve preferential loans for invest-

Date	Number	Description
		ment above 500 million. CIPE must approve any investment above 10 billion.
30.4.76	373	Regulation of consumption of oil for heating and transportation usage.
30.4.76	374	Promotion of regional cooperation of SMEs and exports: tax credits for consortiums grouping more than five enterprises.
11.10.76	699	Proposed partial transformation of wage-indexation benefits into bonds of MEDIOCR to finance reconversion-and-restructuring.
9.12.76	902	Coordination of preferential loans to industrial sector (3,200 billion). Interest subsidy: 65 percent of total to South. 60 percent of total to underdeveloped North. CIPE must approve any *new* investment above 500 million.
1.6.77	285	Measures to solve youth-employment problem.
24.5.77	227	Export financing and insurance to SMEs through a special Insurance Agency of the National Insurance Company (20 billion).
8.8.77	501	Measures to ameliorate employment in the South. Partial social-security contribution and unemployment-compensation-fund contribution exemption. Extraordinary retraining programs and CIG for workers displaced in the South.
8.8.77	616	Coordination of industrial localization at regional level.
8.8.77	664	Acceleration of bureaucratic procedures for grants and loans below 15 billion in the South.
12.8.77	675	Coordination of industrial reconversion-and-restructuring and establishment of CIPI control:

	1977	1978	1979	1980	Total
Fund for reconversion-and-restructuring	535	700	740	655	2,630
Fund for research-and-development	100	235	265	—	600
Endowment fund to PE	750	(3,750 up	to 1982)		4,500
Endowment fund to GEPI	144	144	132	—	420

16.12.77	904	Tax credits to dividends (elimination of double taxation).
23.12.77	936	VAT modification on purchases and imports of new equipment.
22.12.77	1,258	Control on return of investment financed by Act 675 (1977): if return is less than 50 percent of expected, then financing is stopped.
15.6.78	279	EGAM liquidation (1,212 billion).
15.6.78	787	Coordination of financial restructuring of enterprises allows for bank consortiums up to five years to consolidate debts.
29.12.77	947	Special intervention for enterprises in difficulty in order to avoid bankruptcy and maintain employment
27.2.78	44	
5.10.78	602	
		State guarantee on loans to enterprises that have claims on public chemical and steel enterprises 300 billion
		Funds to IRI: 50 billion
		Funds to EMI: 26 billion
		Funds to EFIM: 25 billion
26.5.78	215	Regulation of labor mobility and CIG.
10.6.78	272	Acceleration of bureaucratic procedures for grants and loans below 15 billion to SMEs—even in exception of Act 902 (1976).
5.9.78	502	Measures to curb labor costs due to inflation: partial social-security-contribution exemption to counterbalance wage-indexation mechanism.
13.12.78	795	Priority in unemployment list granted to workers displaced by Acts 183, 902, and 374 (1976) and 675 (1977).
29.3.79	91	Extension of preferential loans measure of 902(1976) to large enterprises.
3.4.79	95	Measures to facilitate liquidation of big enterprises.

13 Industrial Policy in Japan

F. Gerard Adams and *Shinichi Ichimura*

The competitive success of the Japanese economy in world markets has focused attention on Japanese industrial organization and IPs. Can the success of Japan in building technologically advanced modern industries be attributed to public policy? What lessons can be learned from the Japanese experience that will be useful to the development of policies for industrial growth and competitiveness in the United States and in other industrial countries? This chapter summarizes the so-called *Sangyo-Seisaku* (IPs) in Japan from 1945 to the present. We consider the pros and cons of IPs as discussed in government and academic circles. We evaluate the role of policies in meeting the needs of the economy encountered at various points in the postwar period. Finally, we comment on the extent to which the success of this policy approach is unique to the Japanese economic-social environment and we delineate the dimensions of the Japanese approach that may be transferable to the United States.

Doubtless, the unprecedented speed of Japanese economic growth in the postwar period required an extremely rapid adjustment or restructuring of industrial composition. Since the Japanese economy is basically a free-private-enterprise system, this change of industrial composition has been brought about fundamentally as an achievement of free competition accompanied by policy guidance. This point deserves special emphasis because this chapter presents solely the arguments on the government policies toward business or industrial organizations and pays far less attention to the dynamic responses or positive actions of private enterprises, which made the government policies succeed or made the overall achievement of economic development better than expected.

The Japanese government, however, has also taken a number of public policies toward business, which were mainly attributed to the decision making of the ministry of international trade and industry. In addition, there are many policies for which other ministries are primarily responsible. For-

---

This chapter was adapted by F. Gerard Adams from Shinichi Ichimura's "Japanese Industrial Policies 1945–79," a paper presented at the Symposium of World Development and Restructuring the Industrial Economies, Varenna/Bellagio, Italy, September 1979.

eign-exchange control, for instance, is determined primarily by the ministry of finance. IPs may be defined in Japan as the governmental policies designed primarily to influence the behavior, the achievements, or the structure of private enterprises. The practice of policies differed in different stages of development. Therefore, the general characteristics of these stages are briefly sketched as a background to the specific IPs to be discussed later. Then the various types of IPs applied in Japan are explained with reference to the specific problems recognized by the government authorities in each period.

Four Stages of Development and Industrial Policy

The postwar development of the Japanese economy may be divided into four periods. This division is made not only for convenience but also to understand the general political-economic conditions in Japan for the past thirty-five years.

Period	Characteristics	Per Capita Product
1945–1952	Occupation period	(1950: 132 dollars)
1952–1960	Reconstruction period	(1955: 256 dollars)
1960–1970	Rapid-growth period	(1965: 891 dollars)
1970–1980	Trial period	(1975: 4,404 dollars)

The changes of industrial composition in the Japanese economy during this period are shown in table 13-1.

Table 13-1
Changes in Industrial Composition
(percent of total)

Year	Primary Industry	Secondary Industry	Tertiary Industry
1955	37.6	24.4	38.1
1960	30.2	28.0	41.8
1965	23.5	31.9	44.6
1970	17.4	35.2	47.4
1975	12.7	35.2	52.0
1980	10.6	37.3	52.1

Occupation Period: 1945-1952

The occupation was the period of recovery from wartime destruction and control and also a time for installing new institutional apparatus for democratic restructuring of the Japanese economy. Production levels of main manufacturing industries at the time of ceasefire were 10 to 30 percent of their highest prewar levels. Starvation was a real and imminent threat. Even before rampant inflation was under control by austerity programs under the supervision of U.S. advisers, the following measures were adopted: (1) dissolution of *Zaibatsu* (large financial combines); (2) enactment of antitrust and labor-union laws; (3) passing of the Foreign Exchange Control Act; (4) control of imports by requiring permits and certificates; (5) establishment of special quasigovernmental banks (Japan Development Bank, Japan Export Import Bank, Small Business Finance Corporation, and Reconstruction Finance Corporation).

All these measures were mobilized around the basic idea named Priority Production Formula (Keisha Seisan Hoshiki), which first tried to rebuild the production of coal, electricity, and steel. Scarce resources, foreign exchange, and imports were allocated to key industries like coal mining, steel mills, export industries, or for food imports or critical raw materials needed for the production of exportable goods. Similar priorities were given in financial loans. The loans provided by the previously mentioned financial institutions accounted for only a small portion of the total amount of loans given to private business, but they guaranteed that the industries supported by governmental, low-interest loans were given priority in obtaining other scarce resources and that they were credit-worthy. Private banks joined in supporting the investment of these industries. Thus the occupation period laid a ground and framework of the reconstruction period. The Korean War in 1952 changed the whole perspective of a dreamy future of the Japanese economy and gave rise to the realistic reconstruction more or less along the path of modernization since the prewar period. After the San Francisco Independence Treaty, Japan became bolder in pursuing its own policy decisions.

Reconstruction Period: 1952-1960

The momentum generated by the sudden increase in Japanese exports, especially Special Procurement by the U.S. forces, gave an enormous impetus to the reconstruction of the Japanese economy and set a new goal for Japanese economic development: namely, modernization and export promotion. The recovery of light industries and development of heavy-chemical industries were recognized as a basic strategy of industrialization in Japan at this stage. The popular slogan then was, "stability by savings; prosperity by exports." The constraint on industrial production was correctly recognized as set by the balance of payments. Government as well as private enterprise concentrated on breaking through the balance-of-payments constraint by modernizing Japanese manufacturing industries. Modernization meant, on the one hand, adoption of advanced, efficient technology, management know-how, or marketing systems in individual enterprises, and also interfirm cooperation in developing a more efficient industrial order (for example, joint investment, standardization of products, mergers, and exchange of information). Government played a somewhat active role in promoting the latter aspect of modernization.

The following measures exemplify certain aspects of Japanese IPs at this stage:

1. Antitrust law was modified (1953) to permit certain types of cartels, and the so-called rationalization cartels were formed to make joint purchases of raw materials or make quality control uniform.
2. Antirecession cartels were permitted under strict approval and supervision.
3. The Japan Development Bank, for example, started several special programs of loans to help some potential export industries modernize. The strategically chosen industries were the machinery, petrochemicals, and electronics industries.
4. The so-called overloan (loans extended from the Bank of Japan to private commercial banks) became prevalent, so that private commercial banks tended to be bullish in extending loans to new industries.
5. Some purchasing agents were established to buy the products of certain depressed industries and thereby reduce the serious impact on unemployment and management of potential export enterprise (for example, cotton textiles [1953], ammonium sulfate [1954], copper [1955], rayon staples [1957], and coal [1959]).
6. A new law was passed to promote the import of advanced technology and foreign capital associated with it in 1950. This policy was more actively pursued by the Ministry of International Trade and Industry (MITI). During this period, some industries established themselves as export industries and began to demonstrate the potential of Japanese exports. They were, for example, textiles, sewing machines, cameras, and telescopes. Some other new industries, which would later become stars of Japanese exports, were initiated as infant industries in this period (namely, automobiles, electronics, shipbuilding, and steel).

As early as 1955, the Japanese government adopted a program for the liberalization of foreign trade and exchange. The actual drive, however, because of postwar protectionism became intense only under the "Income Doubling Plan" in the next period.

Rapid Growth and Internationalization Period: 1960–1970

The ambitious plan to double per-capita income in ten years advocated by Prime Minister Ikeda actually achieved almost twice as much as the plan originally set. The strong incentives and motivation on the part of Japanese business to accomplish economic development on this resource-poor insular country were remarkable. Indeed, *rapid economic growth* became almost the national goal to be attained by the cooperation of government and business. The Committee of Industrial Structure established at MITI in 1961 became the most important advisory committee for IPs in Japan, and its members consisted of top goverment officials, top businessmen, and a few academic experts. The committee published practically every year a report giving a summary of the studies of the various problems facing Japanese industries and the indicative plan of IPs. Almost all the basic information of Japanese industrial-restructuring policies was contained in these reports. The reports were always best-sellers and gave insight about the direction of industrial development in Japan in each stage. Information offered by these reports to private enterprises was very detailed. In accord with these guideposts and other indicative plans of the government, private enterprise made an enormous effort in improving productivity and quality of products, developing new products, and increasing the amount of exports in many fields. The tempo of modernization accelerated, and most companies dared to invest in the new ventures even at the cost of deteriorating debt-to-capital ratios.

MITI was able to quicken the process of internationalization of Japanese key export industries through IPs. In particular, the problem was how to make the strategic industries, like automobiles, more competitive in the international market; they were small in scale, externally indebted, and technologically still behind U.S. or European companies in the same field. MITI contacted the private businesses frequently through official or unofficial routes and gave various forms of support (subsidies, low-interest loans) and suggestions, called *Gyosei Shido* (administrative guidance), to make mergers and joint investments, to specialize, and so on.

Liberalization of foreign trade became urgent, especially after the start of Kennedy round in 1962, and liberalization of capital transactions became a Japanese obligation after Japan became a member of OECD and IMF in

1963. A number of Japanese industries performed very well in increasing production and exports during this period. They were automobiles, electronics, computers, airplanes, and other machinery. Owing to the extraordinary performance of these new industries, Japanese exports increased so much that the constraint of the balance of payments disappeared in the latter half of the 1960s; this spurred unprecedented growth in the Japanese economy.

Rapid economic growth created several new problems: for example, pollution, extreme urbanization, and deserted villages, new types of consumer needs, a shift of the unemployed from declining industries like coal mining, and the need for modernization of small- and medium-size businesses. In addition, the increased dependence of the Japanese economy on the imported food, energy, and other natural resources began to worry government officials and experts. A number of IPs designed specifically to meet these problems were put into force. Needless to say, the problems were not solved easily and carried over to the following period. The new tasks of the Japanese economy were shaping up for three reasons: (1) the need to respond to demands for a higher standard of living; (2) the need for the Japanese economy to perform properly as a national economy ranking second in world trade and finance; (3) the need to develop the economy in better harmony with the natural environment. These were the assignments for the next period.

Trial Period: 1970-1980

The so-called Nixon shocks marked the beginning of this period: (1) abolishment of fixed exchange rate; (2) an embargo on soybean exports; and (3) U.S.-China rapprochement with no Japanese involvement. They were almost simultaneously or subsequently coupled with (4) the sharp rise of two and a half times of the import prices of major crops in the world market, mainly due to the abnormal climatic conditions in 1972-1973; and (5) the first oil crisis. The impact of these events awakened Japan to the fact that the Japanese economy was tightly integrated with the world economy through trade, capital, aid, knowledge, and human mobility and that interdependence between Japan and the rest of the world had to be taken into account for the purpose of policymaking in economic affairs. Many Japanese intellectuals felt that the Japanese economy was on trial and that more strenuous effort was necessary to overcome the difficulties of further industrialization of this resource-poor island. Many old policy measures toward business became unnecessary, but restructuring of industries was required in the light of new aims.

These aims had to be considered in view of the new problems in the late

1960s: that is, shortage of labor, secular trend to inflation, excessive urbanization, environmental pollution, bottlenecks caused by the import requirements of Japan's large economic size, the remaining technological gap between Japan and the United States–EC, insufficient capacity to develop large-scale technology, and inadequate social-overhead capital. To solve these problems, the following measures of IPs were advocated:

1. *Innovation in the industrial structure to meet the ever-improving needs of society:* (a) promotion of technological development; (b) encouragement of new (knowledge-intensive) industries; (c) promotion of a wider vista for an information-oriented society; (d) overcoming the bottlenecks due to the scarcity of critical factors of production; (e) elimination of low-productivity and stagnant industries.
2. *Harmony of industrial activity with nature and human life.* As the scale of economic activity expanded, the external diseconomies and the social cost of increasing material production began to pose many new noneconomic problems. Government intervention into the market mechanism was recognized as unavoidable. Measures were taken for the following purposes in the 1970s: (a) comprehensive utilization and regulation of land resources; (b) prevention of environmental pollution; (c) stabilization of prices (land, food, services, and consumer protection); (d) technology assessment; and (e) adaptation to social needs (housing, education, medical care, and other public services).
3. *Maintaining an appropriate social framework for effective competition at home and abroad.* Difficulties occurred in the industries with large-scale production and those facing competition from newly industrializing countries. The following were particularly relevant points in the 1970s: (a) consolidation of competitive conditions and prevention of damage from monopoly and oligopoly; (b) the government's active roles in some areas where competition and price mechanism alone cannot properly function (infant industries, stagnant industries, research and development, the information industry, special treatment of small business); and (c) assistance to international economic activities and establishment of new rules of conduct for trade and investment abroad.

Perspective on the 1980s

As we enter the 1980s the IP orientation is again undergoing changes. Japanese industry has been able to weather the pressures of the oil shocks with greater success than its trading partners. But many of these industries have encountered growing trade barriers—for example, limits on sales of Japanese automobiles to the United States and Europe, and economic stagnation of many of Japan's customers in the industrial world. MITI has reformulated its goals for the Japanese economy with such targets as the following:

1. contributing positively to the international community
2. overcoming the limitations of natural resources and energy
3. attaining coexistence of dynamism of the society and the improved quality and comfort of life

Recognizing the increasing difficulty of the international environment, MITI puts heavy emphasis on the development of a technology-based nation. Technological innovation and development of the knowledge-intensive industries are seen as a means of overcoming the energy-and-resource problem, of improving the quality of life, and providing products with continued markets in the world economy.

Obviously, the challenges of developing high-technology industry at or beyond the frontiers of the state of the art are greater than any encountered in building Japan's industrial power during the 1960s and 1970s.

Summary

Japanese industrial-restructuring policies were first adopted to protect infant industries and to modernize the traditional, small-scale enterprises. As the economy developed, policy became less protectionist, and now the economy is approaching the U.S. type of (fundamentally) free-enterprise system. The basic question in policymaking in these different historical stages is how the Japanese government authorities chose which industries were given priority in reconstruction and development.

Nature of Japanese Industrial Policy

So far, we have provided an historical outline of IP conducted largely by MITI. Good or bad, MITI plays an important role in guiding Japanese industrial development. But MITI is not the so-called headquarters of Japan, Inc. MITI's budget comprises only 1 percent of the national budget. As was described earlier, MITI's role is to offer a "vision" that serves as a policy target and to persuade industry in the chosen direction. In arriving at this view, however, MITI solicits the opinions of business, consumers, men of learning, and those with experience in various councils and committees; it is a process of mutual understanding and persuasion. So far the vision and the policies guided thereby have been very successful. The success in turn consolidated the trust and cooperation between government and private business. (This may be an extension of Japan's modernization since the Meiji era.) Vice-Minister Y. Ojimi called government and private enterprise "the two wheels of a cart," clearly a different conception of the relation between government and business than in the United States.

Policy Measures

Policy measures are based on: (1) legal regulations; (2) *gyosei shido;* or (3) other suggestive measures. The last measure is sometimes called *tsu-tatsu* (notification) and comprises many notifications issued from various ministries to private businesses. Their effectiveness depends on the availability of other policy measures when the notifications are not taken seriously. The wide use of *gyosei-shido* in Japan is well known, but a careful evaluation of its effectiveness needs further investigation.

The so-called visions of MITI have long played an important role in guiding public and private business planning. The visions are not formal plans nor are they meant to provide specific industrial targets; rather, they point out the priorities (the types of products and processes to be favored, the qualities to be sought, and so on). They are intended not only to guide the allocation of MITI's own resources but also to advise the business community.

Finally, in Japan there are numerous ways to provide financial support to business and industry in order to achieve IP objectives. Not all of these financial sources are in the control of MITI but, whether for allocation of subsidies, direct research support, low-interest-rate loans, or for tax and tariff matters, MITI plays a major role. Moreover, the financial aid is not only general or industry-wide; in many cases, it represents assistance to specific enterprises that have been selected to carry out the national effort in particular fields. Sometimes such aid is allocated to several companies, sometimes it is given separately, and sometimes for joint projects. The assistance to Fujitsu to develop computers is an example of substantial support for specific industrial-development proposals.

Choice of Strategic Industries

Ever since Japan's modernization began in the late nineteenth century, officials have recognized that Japan lacks land and natural resources and needs to export manufactured goods and import raw materials, food, and energy. Hence, it was obviously important to choose industries according to the principles of comparative advantage in international division of labor and cooperation. The need of allocating scarce productive factors not only by market mechanism but also supplementing it with public controls was widely recognized for the purpose of preserving public welfare, fair trade, and price stability.

An historically critical problem has been the allocation of production factors between more efficient large-scale enterprises and less-efficient, medium- and small-scale enterprises. This decision was not left to the market mechanism in many cases, partly to protect small businesses for employment and income-distribution purposes and partly to develop new export industries with the anticipation that they would eventually have a comparative advantage. In view of the problems of the deficit on foreign payments, it is only natural that the policy objective of the 1950s and 1960s was one of building international competitiveness, as we have already noted. But what was not clear and what evoked lively debate in the mid-1950s was that such competitive position could be achieved by emphasis on heavy capital-intensive industries. A static view of comparative advantage at that time would have suggested that Japan could rely on its still abundant and inexpensive labor force. Instead MITI opted to encourage the build-up of an integrated industrial structure complex (Shinohara 1980). MITI never took a short-term point of view in assessing the comparative advantage of Japanese manufacturing industries in international trade.

The criteria utilized by MITI in the selection of industries meriting encouragement were:

1. *The international-competitiveness criterion.* Industries might not only be import substituting at the beginning but later might be capable of competing in export markets. The cost of production of the selected industries must have a comparative advantage in Japan. But it is important to note that this selection took account of the potentials of technological progress as a means for obtaining an advantageous competitive position. This has been termed a *dynamized comparative-cost doctrine* (Shinohara 1980).
2. *The efficiency of capital criterion.* The idea here was to select industries whose products benefit from economies of scale and, as we noted earlier, could take advantage of the latest technology.
3. *The income-elasticity criterion.* This criterion measures the responsiveness of export demand with respect to world real income. The idea was to select industries in which the growth of world market could be expected to be relatively high.
4. *The employment criterion.* This criterion selected those industries that have many inputs from subsidiaries that offer good employment opportunities at small- and medium-size enterprises.

From these points of view, MITI selected a combination of highly technical and capital-intensive-but-basic industries like iron and steel, petroleum refining, petrochemicals and also, capital-intensive industries with many labor-intensive subsidiaries like automobiles, general machinery, electronics, and so on. This choice of strategic industries was not without controversy among top decision makers. This was particularly true of the development of the automobile industry. As early as 1949 the governor of the Bank of Japan and a number of academic economists insisted that Japan has little chance in obtaining a comparative advantage in this industry. MITI finally persuaded the government into developing that industry, thus achieving enormous exports in the 1970s; Such successes gave MITI a prestigious position in Japanese public policies. Private businesses took advantage of MITI's leadership in resolving rivalry among themselves and improving their public relations by giving the impressions that MITI's support implied the correspondence of their industries' development with the public interest.

Three Main Measures of Industrial Policies

One might say that the Japanese government had a clear idea of IP from the outset of postwar reconstruction and took positive measures in the following three ways:

1. Integration of industrial restructuring plan within the framework of a general economic plan. A typical example of this was the Income Doubling Plan in 1960 mentioned earlier. This plan had two aspects: One was the income plan, which was meant to get public support and give a well-defined objective to economic policies; another was more substantive in giving a detailed guidepost for developing heavy and chemical industries. This plan laid out the essence of Japanese economic policies in the 1960s, and it was used to justify various IPs adopted by MITI and other ministries.

The planning function was effectively carried out by using various quantitative methods of econometrics and predicting the future Japanese industrial structure. Interindustry tables and macroeconometric models were used extensively. In addition, a careful study of cost structure in each important industry was undertaken for different scales of production compared with the similar information on foreign competitors. (The MITI documents listed at the end of this chapter entitled, *The Long-term Vision of Industrial Structure,* include these studies and information. These documents offered excellent guidance for Japanese industrialists to obtain a perspective of the future of their industries relative to foreign competitors as well as in the framework of the developing Japanese economy. In these studies, policymakers paid attention to the income-elasticity criterion and competitive criterion, which were regarded as major guides for IP.

2. Preferential allocation of capital and financial resources to selected strategic industries. A number of governmental or semigovernmental banks

were used to supply low-interest loans to selected industries, whereas all commercial banks were strongly guided by the ministry of finance to coordinate their lending policies with MITI's IP.

3. Various policy measures were used to protect the strategic industries and to promote their development: (a) import restrictions by foreign-exchange control; (b) protective customs duties; (c) control of foreign capital investment; (d) commodity taxes favorable to domestic products; and (e) control of imports of foreign technology. The measures for promotion are: (a) preferential supply of low-interest loans from governmental and nongovernmental banks; (b) subsidies; (c) special depreciation allowances; (d) exemption from customs duties for special machine imports; (e) permits to import specific technology and know-how; (f) public-works expenditure allotted to some industrial locations; and (g) incentives given by MITI's administrative guidance.

Effect of Japanese Industrial Policy

We can evaluate the effects of Japanese industrial policy from several perspectives. On the one hand, it is certainly not correct to attribute all of the spectacular development of Japanese industry in domestic and foreign markets to IPs. Indeed, private enterprises, many operating with little or no governmental aid, are responsible for some of the greatest successes of Japanese industry. On the other hand, there is evidence in many directions that the policies achieved many of their objectives. For example, an analysis of changes in Japanese industrial structure shows clearly that the shift toward heavy industries and the chemical industries, which had been planned in the earliest revisions of MITI, occurred by 1970. We should note, however, that it took fifteen years to achieve such a shift, despite the government's deliberate efforts to achieve a higher stage of industrialization.

With regard to allocation of funds, the evidence supports the notion that funds went more heavily into the industries selected for development. Public-works investments were directed toward industrial infrastructure investments. Government investment kept pace with private fixed-capital formation, whereas investment in consumer-oriented public works did not grow as fast as investment in industrial infrastructure. Only in the late 1960s, and increasingly in the 1970s, did public expenditures toward consumers increase relatively in response to desires for rising standards of consumption.

Emphasis in allocating public funds was placed on: (1) strategic industries like machinery and metal products; (2) protection and modernization of primary industries; (3) expansion of basic industries like electric power, transportation, and construction industries; and (4) protection and modernization of small commercial businesses. The general direction of the supply of funds can also be traced by the records of loans from the Japan Development Bank which is the leading government bank and the industrial composition of loans from private commercial banks; thus the supply of loanable funds in Japan was controlled by the Bank of Japan. The level and system of interest rates were tightly administered by the ministry of finance; the industrial allocation of the available funds was guided by the policies of governmental banks and followed by private commercial banks competitively in the effort of expanding their respective shares. The Bank of Japan always supplied the banks if the funds were demanded for strategic industries chosen by MITI or the Economic Planning Agency. The ministry of finance adopted a low-interest-rate policy unless the unfavorable balance of payments or inflationary pressures demanded restrictive policy.

Direct interventions of government into entry, pricing, production, sales, and investment on the basis of regulations were very wide. They may be classified as follows:

1. requiring official permits or certificates in new entry to the businesses
2. intervening into pricing
3. setting a standard price
4. direct controlling of price
5. controlling the amount of production
6. administering the amount of fixed investment
7. giving subsidies
8. allowing monopoly

A listing of policies indicated the full extent of interventions, access industries, and policy measures. These policy measures were directed to foster the strategic industries and modernize handicapped industries in the primary and tertiary sectors.

All in all, policies were successful in newly established manufacturing industries but not so in other sectors of the economy. The labor-productivity indexes are shown in table 13-2.

The labor productivity in the primary and tertiary sectors remained low, only one-seventh of the productivity achieved in the most efficient industry: the machinery industry. The policies directed toward these two sectors and toward the textile industry were primarily protective or remedial.

Finally, we may consider the question of whether the selected industries have successively become export industries. Japan gained 7.5 percent in world-market share over the period 1953 to 1970, a time when the United States and the United Kingdom suffered severe losses in their share of world markets. The rise in Japan's export price after 1967 suggests, however, the

Table 13-2
Annual Increase in Labor Productivity
(percent)

Sector	1955-1970
Primary sector	3.1
Tertiary sector	2.5
Chemicals	5.4
Metal and metal products	4.3
Machinery	7.2

end of the scale economies, labor shortages, and the rigidity of some goods prices due to the development of oligopolistic industrial organizations. Perhaps the end of the favorable effects of vigorous IPs pursued by MITI were at an end toward the later 1960s.

In the 1970s, however, a number of problems have emerged, seeming to indicate negative side effects of IP: For example, one is the pollution problem, and the other is price and wage rigidity caused by oligopolistic organization of Japanese industries fostered during the boom years. Pollution includes not only industrial pollution but also the social and other malaise due to too much urban concentration; these problems have recently attracted a great deal of attention from professional and government circles.

The increasing degree of oligopoly in a number of leading industries was well known in the early 1960s, but competition among the few was keen enough so that one could assume that effective competition prevailed up to the middle 1960s. However, while large corporations became more and more oligopolistic, they organized transactions with small- and medium-size enterprises as subcontractors. The productivity differential between large corporations became exaggerated. Large corporations often formed cartels, accused of illegality under antimonopoly law, during recessions. At the same time, IP to protect the primary and tertiary sectors and small- and medium-size enterprises created many types of associations called *Jigyo-Sha Dantae* (business associations or cooperatives). They are often the basis for cartel-like behavior or cooperation in business dealings; further, they often became the basis for administered pricing even among less-powerful businesses. They were frequently permitted in order to support smaller enterprises.

In recent years, however, the Japanese government has become increasingly conscious of restrictive regulations, and the execution of antimonopoly law is becoming stricter. The Fair Trade Commission is examining all laws, acts, and regulations related to governmental interventions; this will vastly alter the rules of business transactions in Japan. A new guideline announced recently (August 27, 1979) is as follows:

1. Any action concerning pricing or production level will be classified as legal, illegal, or undecided and will be regulated accordingly.
2. MITI's administrative guidance will be subject to regulations of the Fair Trade Commission.
3. Consultation will be permitted in advance.

Japanese business circles have welcomed this new direction of Japanese IP. MITI's policies toward business enterprises are bound to be influenced by the new guidelines, but the extent to which Japanese IP will change remains to be seen. It is certain, however, that the impetus will be to preserve or recover the competitive nature of Japanese industrial organization and private enterprise rather than the reverse.

As noted earlier, in the early 1980s the visions of MITI have so far emphasized the development of knowledge-intensive industries. Such IP direction presents challenges that earlier phases of development lacked. For example, can the selection of industries or activities to receive preferential treatment be made on the same basis and with the same confidence as in the past? Can financial support to specific research programs assure their ultimate commercial or competitive success? What is the role of public institutions in fostering computer-control systems, new materials, applications of electronics and information systems, development of small enterprises, and so on (all points covered in the discussions of MITI's latest vision)? These represent the challenges for Japanese IP in the 1980s.

Implications for Industrial Policy for the United States

Certain lessons can be drawn from the Japanese IP experience. First, the Japanese situation was and continues to vary in many ways from the U.S. situation. The clearest successes of Japanese IP came, as we have described, in the process of building modern high-technology and capital-intensive industry. For this, government direction, regulations, and financing proved very valuable, particularly in the context of MITI's ultimate aim. The case is far less clear for the redirection of Japanese IP that occurred in the 1970s and that is taking place in the 1980s.

Second, we must note that the Japanese industrial and commercial environment is entirely different from that in the United States. The spirit of cooperation evident in Japanese enterprises extends, at least in part, to relations between government and business. Business enterprises accept administrative guidance just as MITI emphasizes that its decisions are made on the basis of consultation with business. It is not likely that Japanese traditions or social organization can translate to the U.S. environment. Moreover, the absence of this spirit of cooperation may inhibit in the United States approaches that have worked in Japan.

Japanese policy has clearly been industry-specific during the 1960s and, perhaps to a lesser extent, during the 1970s. Yet there has been scope for private industry to operate, and many of the greatest successes were largely attributable to the initiatives of private enterprises. This dependence on private enterprises (perhaps with some government support) may be even more important in Japan as we move into the age of the knowledge-intensive industries. Similarly, for the U.S. public aid and encouragement, rather than intervention as occurred many times during the drive to curb pollution during the 1970s, may be helpful for heavy capital-intensive industries such as steel, automobiles, rubber, and so on. On the other hand, it is not clear that governmental assistance other than in the most general terms would be effective in accelerating the pace of development in such state-of-the-art industries as microcomputers. Indeed, evidence suggests that such a field is best left to small, independent enterprises, since even the largest firms find it difficult to compete effectively in the high-technology areas.

One important aspect of Japanese policy may, however, have transferability: This is the concept of the visions of MITI. These can be seen as planning only in the most general nonspecific sense. They represent a look at the status of the economy's industrial structure—at the prospects for future development—using the concept of comparative advantage in a dynamic sense. In this spirit, a periodic review of the national economy may provide a guide for public policies and for private decision making for the United States as it has for Japan.

References

Economic Planning Agency. (1979). "Basic Framework for the New Economic and Social Seven-Year Plan."

Imai, Kenichi. (1976). *Contemporary Industrial Organization*. Iwanami Shoten.

International Science Promotion Foundation, et al. (1979). *Report On the Present State of Japanese Heavy and Chemical Industries and Their Future Directions*.

Ministry of International Trade and Industry. (1969). *Twenty Years History of MITI*. Tokyo: M.I.T.I.

Ministry of International Trade and Industry. (1971). *Industrial and Trade Policies in the 70's*. Tokyo: M.I.T.I.

Ministry of International Trade and Industry. (1974). *Twenty-Five Years History of MITI.* Tokyo: M.I.T.I.

Ministry of International Trade and Industry. (1974, 1975, 1976, 1978). *The Long-Term Vision of Industrial Structure.* 1974, 1975, 1976, 1978 eds. Tokyo: M.I.T.I.

Ministry of International Trade and Industry. (1979). *Thirty Years History of MITI.* Tokyo: M.I.T.I.

Ministry of International Trade and Industry. (1979). *Industrial and Trade Policies in the 80's.* Tokyo: M.I.T.I.

Ministry of International Trade and Industry. (1980). *The Vision of MITI Policies in the 80's.* Tokyo: M.I.T.I.

Nezu, Risaburo. "Industrial Structure and Industrial Policies." Mimeographed. M.I.T.I.

Niino, Kojiro. (1978). "The Problems of Contemporary Industrial Policies," in *Economic Policies of Government and Industry,* eds. K. Kato, K. Goi, M. Komatsu, A. Takayanagi, and M. Noda. Tokyo: Keiso Shobo.

OECD. (1979). "The Impact of the Newly Industrializing Countries."

Ojimi, Y. (1970). "Basic Philosophy and Objectives of Japanese Industrial Policy." Statement presented at the Committee on Industry, OECD, in Tokyo, June 24, 1970.

Shinohara, Miyohei. (1976). *On Industrial Structure.* 2nd ed. Chikuma Shobo.

Shinohara, Miyohei. (1980). "Japanese-Type Industrial Policy." Occasional Paper No. 3, Tokyo, The Asian Club.

Ueno, Hiroya. (1975). "The Ideas and Evaluation of Industrial Policies." *Contemporary Economics (Gendai Keizai)* (Winter).

Ueno, Hiroya. (1980). "Industrial Policy," in *Encyclopedia of Economic Science (Keizai-Gaku Dai-Jiten).* Tokyo: Tokyokeizai Shimpo-sha.

Appendix 13A
Transformation of Industrial Structure and Economic Policies in Japan

What are the principal lessons of Japan's rapid progress from postwar devastation to its present state of global economic power?

Overall Integration of Economic Policies and Institutions

Economic policies can be effectively implemented when they conform with sociocultural conditions and institutions of the particular national economy. The unprecedented growth of the Japanese economy may be attributed to the following factors:

1. High rate of capital accumulation. This is particularly concentrated in private fixed-capital formation rather than overhead capital or housing; 30 percent or more of GNP is invested, half in industrial equipment.
2. High rate of saving. Such a high rate of capital formation was almost exclusively warranted by domestic savings, making the control of inflation manageable; the saving ratio kept rising with increasing per-capita income.
3. Borrowed and improved technology. Industry's deliberate effort of learning modern technology and superseding Western technology is proven by research-and-development expenditure in government and private enterprises, emphasis on engineering faculties in the top universities, and on-the-job training or technology or conscious management.
4. Industrious and well-educated workers. Despite the change in fundamental values in postwar education, thrift and industry remained the priority virtues. Workers are well educated: 90 percent finish high school; 40 percent graduated from colleges and universities. They are young. The interfirm mobility among small and medium enterprises is high, though the opposite is true with large corporations.
5. Agricultural productivity increases. Land reform, government support of agricultural prices, and rural investment released enormous numbers of workers—an estimated 22 million men from 1955 to 1977—to the manufacturing and tertiary sectors.

This appendix of S. Ichimura is a summary of Chapter 13.

6. Group loyalty and good human relations between labor and management. Japanese labor has been moderate and cooperative with management. Group loyalty, life-time employment, and profit-sharing (bonus) wage systems seem to have worked, except in some public enterprises. This is shown by the small number of working hours lost by strikes.
7. Flexible adjustment of industrial composition to the changing demand conditions and innovating technologies. This is clear by contrasting the changes in industrial composition of GDP and the changes in world-trade composition from one country to another. MITI's IP played a significant role.
8. Good relations between government and business. The whole-hearted determination of business circles, civil servants, and politicians alike to reconstruct the devastated nation bred the spirit of cooperation. The success of collaboration established trust and constant consultation: This was the true basis of Japanese IP.
9. Cooperation among commercial banks, the Bank of Japan, Ministry of Finance, and private business. Banks often played the role of business consultants, and the government (in particular, the Ministry of Finance) and the Bank of Japan jointly and adequately controlled the foreign exchange in the 1950s and 1960s and the money supply in the 1970s.
10. Political stability. Rapid growth often leads to social disorder. Postwar Japan did not remain perfectly immune to this malaise, but the Liberal Democratic party has been in power constantly and successfully guided the national economy. Land reform, protection of farmers, support of small and medium enterprises, early introduction of a social-welfare program, and an adequate taxation system to equalize personal income all contributed to the stability. Above all, the international environment has been unusually favorable for Japan.

In the 1970s, the shock period, the conditions favorable to rapid growth began to change. The Nixon shocks (revaluation of the yen, embargo of soybeans, and U.S.–China rapprochement *plus* the oil crises revealed the vulnerability of the Japanese economy vis à vis energy and food (mineral resources and land). Fortunately, these events occurred when Japanese industries were in a position to export sufficiently for imports of raw materials, food, and energy.

During the 1980s, the trial period, Japan must find its position in the world economy and succeed in integrating itself with the major trading partners. This will involve an adjustment of industrial structure vis à vis the older industrialized countries and the NICs.

Pressure on Japan comes from two contradictory sources: (1) the need to expand exports so that Japan can pay $30 billion extra for the same quantity of oil; (2) the difficulty of finding a market for $30 billion worth of exports without causing trade conflicts with other countries that are suffering from recessions and structural-adjustment problems.

Characteristics of Japanese Industrial Policy

Choice of Strategic Industries

Japan tried to develop myriad manufacturing industries: The motivation was to reduce the imports and overcome the chronic shortage of foreign exchange. Whenever possible, goods were produced domestically rather than imported. This was possible because the Japanese market was large, and the Tokaido megalopolis offered a compact market connected with the advantage of sea access.

Simultaneously, however, the Japanese government always chose to promote future industries that could eventually become major export industries. There was keen awareness of the future trend of demand and of production technology: As for demand, the U.S. pattern of consumption had already set a pattern so that it was not difficult to see the trend of diversification and fashion; as for production, Japan definitely chose input-saving (for primary materials) and more backward-linked technologies. The backward linkages was seen as creating employment and would serve to establish the industrial complex at home. Consequently, despite the clear emphasis of MITI's policies on basic industries, many other processing industries developed successfully.

Long-Term Vision, and Dynamic Change in Comparative Advantage

The Akamatsu-Vernon type of product cycle, or industrial adjustment in stages, was always considered in preparing the medium-term perspectives of Japanese industrial composition. Specialization in some industries was not considered permanent, although shifts in industrial composition were sometimes painful.

We can visualize industries moving through successive phases: imports, domestic production, exports, and, finally, direct investment abroad. Initially, protectionist measures were taken for the industries starting domestic production. For example, imports of heavy and chemical-industry products were restricted on the basis of the infant-industry argument. How long the old protective measures may be justifiably maintained is an important question to be studied from the viewpoint of the international division of labor.

The last stage of industrial development from the viewpoint of a single industry is direct investment abroad. Many textile companies in Japan have made direct investments in East and Southeast Asian countries, and their joint ventures are successfully competing in the world market. The extent to which this kind of technology transfer and transplantation of some industries abroad can be successfully performed depends on the success of achieving the transformation of industrial structure at home because the necessary foreign-exchange reserve must be earned by the exports of the products of other new industries.

In the late 1960s and 1970s, the growth rate of Japanese exports exceeded that of domestic production, and growth of overseas investment was even more rapid than that of exports. The oil crises stopped this trend temporarily, but as the Japanese balance of payments becomes steadily more favorable and as the exchange rate strengthens, overseas investment will recover.

One difficulty may be anticipated. After a certain stage of industrial development, further development of more technology-intensive industries may become increasingly difficult. The main reason is that the so-called boomerang effect causes a surplus of some industrial products in world markets, and yet the market for the products of next-stage industries may not yet be large enough. We must add, however, that the development of new industries in a NIC almost always increases its imports of complementary products from more-industrialized countries (shipbuilding and diesel engines, for example). The problem is whether the loss of a market by the older industry can be compensated enough by the new one. Competition between U.S. and Europe and Japan does not guarantee optimism, whereas competition between Japan and Asian NICs indicates optimism in this respect.

In order to forecast the future trend of demand and supply in the world market, collection of information has been essential. The role played by MITI and *Sogo sosha* (trading companies) in this respect can hardly be underestimated. Slightly more than half of Japanese foreign trade is handled by *Sogo-shosha:* 48.7 percent of exports and 56.0 percent of imports in 1980. The main function of MITI's IP was to offer such information and vision. The *White Papers* on trade and various reports on long-term perspectives of industrial structure prepared by MITI staff are full of information on the world market and its future trend.

Limited Role of Government and Initiatives of Private Enterprises

Japanese IP has not given disproportionate protective support and enormous subsidies to industries like automobiles, electronics, or computers. Several characteristics of the government's role are not widely recognized.

Appendix 13A

1. Various protective measures taken for a certain industry seldom lasted long. For example, the special allowance of accelerated depreciation for machinery was given only for the initial three years after 1951. The permit to regard some depreciation allowances as current cost for taxation purposes was granted only to favored industries, but the choice of industries has shifted, although somewhat belatedly, from iron and steel, shipping, or trading companies to pollution-preventing, airplane, computers, or atomic-power industries. The import quotas, custom duties and foreign-exchange control have been nearly eliminated. The specific exceptional commodities number only twenty now, including five in manufactured goods.

Special protective measures are permitted only on the basis of specific regulations. The most important industry to develop in the late 1950s and 1960s was machinery. Two laws were particularly important: the Temporary Law For Promotion of Machinery in June 1956; and the Temporary Law for Promotion of Electronic Industry in June 1957. On the basis of these laws, special-low interest loans were provided by public banks. The word *temporary* meant that these laws were limited in the coverage of industries and by time constraints. These laws were revised several times and then completely revised as Temporary Law For Promotion of Specific Electronics and Machinery Industries in 1971. The industries to be protected became more limited. The objectives were also expanded to suggest rationalization and expansion of production scale as well as to grant generous loans. This law was again changed to Temporary Law For Promotion of Specific Machinery and Information Industries in July 1978. The emphasis of promotion is now on electronification of all kinds of machines and development of software associated with it; this shows that the protective measures were only temporary. All the laws had deadlines when they became ineffective and were specific with regard to objectives and measures.

2. Japanese IP promoted both large-scale leading industries and the small and medium enterprises linked to them. Parallel development of large and small enterprises as well as key industries (for example, iron and steel) and processing industries (for example, electrical appliances) is a characteristic of Japanese industrial development. The vested interest of small- and medium-size corporations has always been protected. Indeed, the Agency of Small and Medium Enterprises is an important and powerful subagency of MITI.

3. IP also played a role in overcoming the difficulties facing some declining industries. One example is the shipbuilding industry: Here, the government adopted two policies; one is the short-term and another is the long-term policy. The short-term policy was based on the Shipbuilding Industry Law: The government sought to reduce the level of production to 72 percent (sixty-seven large companies in 1977), 67 percent (sixty-three large companies in 1978), and 39 percent (thirty-four large companies in 1980). Since the Fair Trade Commission complained that this was against

the Anti-Monopoly Law, the ministry of transportation requested the shipbuilding companies to form a depression cartel to control the level of production. The long-term policy was based on the Temporary Law For Stabilizing Specific Shipbuilding Enterprises of October 1978. A new association, Specific Shipbuilding Enterprises Association, was established; its function is to raise funds for purchasing the dockyards, equipment, and land from the shipbuilding companies and to close them down. The task required were about Y 96 billion; Y 1 billion was given by the government, and the rest was raised from the member companies and borrowed from Japan Development Bank and city banks. The loans were to be paid back over ten years by the remaining members of the association. The reductions had been largely completed as of 1980.

What is remarkable in Japanese economic growth is the fact that the Japanese manufacturers have shown an unusually high capacity to transform the industrial structure. But we must remember that such a capacity is an outcome of painstaking effort by private enterprises, only partly and temporarily assisted by government IPs.

4. We must also recognize the cooperation of labor unions. When they are ideologically oriented and inflexible in perceiving the needs of the national economy, serious conflicts can occur. The Miike Mining Company is a case in point. The severe difficulties of the Japanese economy in the 1970s have been recognized jointly by labor and management following the two oil crises. There has been a remarkable decline of labor disputes in Japan since the late 1970s. The unionization rate of Japanese workers is not particularly low compared to that of other countries: It is 31.6 percent in 1979 compared with 57.4 percent (United Kingdom), 41.9 percent (West Germany), and 23.4 percent (United States) but seems to have declined in recent years. But the nature of the unions, which are closely linked to the companies, is quite different.

These are limits to international specialization. Unless governments become aware of the development of similar commodities by competing countries, worldwide gluts and concomitant price declines will be unavoidable. (This has happened to the textile industry and is now happening in iron and steel, automobiles, and electronics.) Positive adjustment policies can only lead to protectionism. What is needed instead is trust in the price mechanism, supplemented by wise, future-oriented IP.

14 Industrial Policy in the United Kingdom

Michael Davenport

Almost one hundred years ago, the Royal Commission on the Depression of Trade and Industry (1886) deplored the noncompetitive state of British industry. The report cited lack of sufficient investment, small-scale and inadequately maintained plants, the lack of appropriate technical and managerial training, a failure to exploit new technology, poor labor relations, and even lack of fluency in foreign languages among sales representatives as contributing to this situation. The catalogue of industrial ills reads strangely as if it might have been written today.

The apparent incapacity of British industry—specifically, manufacturing industry—to respond to the challenge of competition, whether from the United States and Germany in the nineteenth century or Japan, Korea, Taiwan, and Hong Kong today, has been a continuous feature of British economic history. It has continued to inform the major areas of political economy—tariff policy, fiscal policy, credit policy, competition policy, and policy with respect to customs unions, and, most recently, entry into the EEC. While new interest in IP has recently emerged in the United States and some other countries, the characteristic attitude in Britain is close to cynicism. There, most approaches to IP, ranging from the establishment of propitious, broad macroeconomic conditions to detailed governmental control at the individual-firm level appear to have been tried and, at least as a recipe for ending relative industrial decline, found wanting.

Since the final quarter of the nineteenth century, British manufacturing has declined further in relation to its major trading competitors, whether measured in terms of fall in employment in manufacturing, loss of shares of world trade in manufacturers, or increased import penetration. The basic facts are not disputable. The appropriate IP for Britain is, however, an issue of considerable disagreement, even, at this time, within the cabinet. The controversy between laissez-faire and interventionism once again has been brought to a head by the seriousness of the recession in the summer of 1981. But this controversy has been critical to the history of IP throughout the century, as much an area of discord within the political parties as between them.

This chapter is concerned with the varying responses of policy in the United Kingdom to the worsening relative position of British manufacturers on world markets. It is more concerned with the story line of that policy, how it has developed over time, how successive administrations have reacted to academic theories or popular notions as to the sources of the problems and the role of political philosophy, rather than with a detailed enumeration of the institutional constructs or legalistic and financial arrangements designed to implement the policy.

Before proceeding, it is necessary to define that set of administrative measures which, for the purposes of this chapter, shall constitute IP. One might argue that the present predicament of the British economy follows essentially from the lack of international competitiveness in the manufacturing sector and that all policy action designed to face the double-headed monster of stagflation, that is more or less the total spectrum of economic policy, is responding to that predicament. IP may be narrowly considered to encompass only those policies directly aimed at speeding up the rate of technical change or, somewhat more generally, aimed at raising the competitivity of industrial products (which usually means manufactured goods) on world markets. The broader definition seems more appropriate since it includes all those measures that may be construed as improving labor or capital productivity, using existing technology.[1] In Britain a slow rate of innovation has only been one of many factors to which the relative industrial decline has been ascribed.

In principle, then, as in other chapters in this book, measures designed to mop up unemployment due to enterprise failure or sectoral or regional decline are excluded from our compass of IP. As will be seen, industrial policy instruments, though not originally intended for that purpose, have been so used. This redirection of instruments to new policy goals is not peculiar to Britain but has been taken somewhat further in Britain than elsewhere.

For a century, economists and others have endeavored to explain Britain's poor performance. As suggested earlier, the arguments have not changed dramatically, although certainly different factors have been stressed at various times. It does not seem necessary for this chapter to attempt an evaluation of the various arguments. There are a number of studies that attempt such an evaluation.[2] However, the arguments are relevant insofar as they bear on the nature of the IP instruments developed at different times. Until recently they tended to evoke a panacea approach to industrial policy. Now the emphasis is more on the multicausal nature of the problems and the need for a multipronged attack.

More Investment Panacea

In general, the response of policymakers has reflected contemporary views on the causes of Britain's industrial motives. One particularly widely held explanation has been the inadequacy of capital investment in manufacturing, despite the absence of any clear empirical evidence that productivity has suffered relative to other countries from particularly out-of-date capital or excessive intensity of capital use.[3] Nevertheless, the importance attached to a high rate of investment and the acceptance of the view that the marginal social rate of return exceeds the marginal private rate of return is demonstrated by the widespread, if not universal, presence of fiscal incentives to investment throughout the market economies.

In Britain from 1945 onward, various schemes for accelerating depreciation for tax purposes have been available. The original scheme consisted of so-called initial allowances, whereby a certain proportion of the value of the investment would be used to reduce tax liabilities in the first year. In 1954 a system of investment allowances was added such that it was very often possible to set more than the total value of the investment against tax, which meant in effect that an investment subsidy was being made available. Since the Finance Act of 1972, the whole of any capital expenditure in plant and equipment can be written off against profits for tax purposes in the first year. In addition, there is a 54 percent initial allowance on new industrial buildup and an annual writing-down allowance of 4 percent thereafter. Under this new system, governments have foresworn the use of accelerated-depreciation schemes for demand management purposes—a very common practice before 1972.

Such purely fiscal incentives to investment may be considered as a general IP. Investment subsidies that are contingent on certain technological innovations or industrial reorganization to increase productivity more clearly represent selective or conditional types of IPs. These will be discussed later in this chapter.

No survey of IP in Britain can ignore regional policy. Regional policy may be primarily aimed at regenerating areas of declining industrial activity and increasing unemployment, but, in doing so, it uses the techniques and shares the goals of IP on a regional basis. British approaches to IP have been to some extent molded by approaches to regional policy, which were, in fact, defined earlier.[4]

From the 1920s, observers have expressed concern about the impact of declining industries on particular regions: textiles in Lancashire and shipbuilding and coal mining in the North-East and Scotland. In 1934 the Special Areas Act was passed. In 1940 the Barlow Committee made a strong plea for much greater government intervention.[5] Other considerations had priority at that time and action did not come until the Distribution of Industry Act in 1945. That act designated certain development areas—much later, after complaints and the Hunt Committee report (1969) supplemented by grey or intermediate areas—in which a whole range of incentives to investment was made available. The boundaries of these areas have been changed from time to time but they are essentially those areas with above-average unemployment. The incentives have varied over time with Labour administrations tending to be more generous than Conservative ones. Investment grants (up to 45 percent of the value of the investment), low-interest loans for investment, subsidized or free factory space, and sites in industrial estates at low rents and well supplied by transport, power, and water have all been used. However, it is interesting that the availability of financial incentives has not on the whole been conditional on employment creation. The most powerful means of encouraging investment in the development areas has been the negative sanction of refusing the necessary Industrial Development Certificate (IDC) for establishing a plant elsewhere.

In 1967 a Regional Employment Premium was established by the Labour government in an attempt to supplement the impact of the voluntarist system of investment incentives and the sanction of the IDC. It was also justified by the argument that investment subsidies in the development areas were distorting the capital-labor rate. It consisted of a direct subsidy to encourage employment in the development areas and was terminated by the Heath government in 1974. Studies show that it had a positive impact on employment in the regions although there is disagreement on the extent of that impact.[6]

It is useful to mention here the Selective Employment Tax (instituted in 1965 and discontinued in 1971), which was more a general IP instrument but did have an associated subsidy for employment in manufacturing in the development areas. The tax ranged from $1.25 per employee per week in 1966–1967 to $2.40 in 1969–1971. It was returned (after several months) to firms in manufacturing, together with a subsidy (at least between 1968 and 1970) to manufacturing firms in the developing areas. The tax was generally unpopular, particularly with small businesses, and a committee was established to investigate its economic impact. The Reddaway report (1973) suggested that the effects of the tax were to some extent possible to those intended, in that its major impact on productivity was in wholesaling and retailing, where cuts in employment brought about by the tax were greater than losses in output. This finding has been challenged by other writers, however.[7]

We could not argue that regional policy has done more than slow the process of industrial decline in the designated regions. Even if investment and employment has been higher in the development areas that it otherwise would have been, it is not clear to what extent this has been at the expense of investment and employment elsewhere.

Education and Training Panacea

One factor behind Britain's poor industrial performance often mentioned in the 1960s and 1970s was the educational system. The argument was sometimes expressed in terms of the shortage of scientifically trained persons leaving British schools and universities; later, the lack of business schools seemed more important. There has, of course, been the more general argument that industry has suffered from the rigidities, inequities, and class bias of the educational system as a whole.

In respect to the last of these arguments, it would be wrong to suggest that educational policy has been strongly influenced by industrial considerations; political dogma has been paramount. But the gains to industrial performance have always been featured in any polemics regarding educational reform. The Labour government virtually succeeded in abolishing the grammar-school system between 1974 and 1979. Previously, the grammar schools would accept only pupils who had passed the notorious eleven-plus examination. Thus at an early age most pupils were selected for intensive, academic studies in the grammar schools or more-vocational, less intellectually demanding curricula at the secondary modern schools, from which entry to the universities or other higher education was well-nigh impossible. Besides being socially reprehensible to the Labour party, the system was held to be detrimental to standards in the secondary moderns since all the more-able pupils and teachers were said to be creamed off by the grammar or private schools. In any event, the gradual elimination of grammar schools was a tremendous boost to the private-school system—indeed, many became private—while the present Conservative government has reprieved most of the few grammar schools still extant in 1979. The long-standing Labour threat to the private educational sector is still no more than that.

The 1951 Tory government was more concerned with the supposed inadequate supply of applied scientists and engineers entering the labor market. In 1953 the government expanded numbers of students at technical colleges and the following year financed a major expansion of technological facilities at selected universities. In 1956 a five-year plan was implemented to develop the technical colleges and increase the number graduating by 50 percent as well as to double the number of trainees under day release from their jobs. A diploma in technology ranking with an honors degree was created, and nine technical colleges were made colleges of advanced technology; in later years, these and several other technical colleges were granted university status. The Finniston report, however, argues Britain is still very short of university-trained engineers.[8]

As Turner (1969) relates, by the 1960s the emphasis had switched to the need for business schools (of which there were none in 1960), some eighty years after the first U.S. graduate business school was established and despite the fact that as early as 1920 there were business schools at fifty U.S. universities. In a rush of enthusiasm, thirty-seven university business schools and university management departments, five independent business colleges, and a plethora of business courses in technical colleges and other colleges of further education were instituted, with many people genuinely convinced that it would lead to a renaissance of British industry. The problems of identifying and attracting competent teaching staff from the business world who would find academic salaries and attitudes compatible were enormous. The question of the appropriate curricula is still extremely controversial.[9]

Business schools and management courses have been instrumental in transferring U.S. business practices to the United Kingdom but have hardly transformed business attitudes. There is still much valid criticism of the inflexibility, lack of imagination, inassertiveness, remoteness, lack of dedication, and sheer incompetence of the upper management of British industry. There is still a preponderance of the middle-class, privately educated coterie for whom business—as opposed to the professions—is still not quite respectable, new business practices are slightly unsavory, and, indeed, the profit motive is considered a necessary evil. Many people, not only from the Left, would argue that radical change toward a more-egalitarian society with more openness of opportunity is the sine qua non for a new approach to business in an increasingly competitive world. That is why the move to comprehensive education has found considerable support in the now-more-business-oriented Conservative party and why the Thatcher government has not tried to undo the comprehensivisation of the educational system undertaken by the previous Labour administration.

Better Industrial Relations Panacea

In the explanation of Britain's industrial woes, another recurrent theme—but one with much sharper party political differences—is that of the poor state of industrial relations. Caves found that disruptive industrial relations (as measured by the numbers of strikes or working days lost) had an impact on productivity differences between industries in Britain.[10] We may draw the inference that Britain's productivity as a whole suffers from strike activity, but we must bear in mind that some countries with much higher productivity in industry have worse strike records. More generally, some observers argue that labor-restrictive practices and sheer trade-union obstructionism often inhibit innovation in technology or work practices, lead to overmanning, and to the expenditure of substantial managerial time and effort in the resolution of sometimes-petty disputes.

The innate conservatism, even deep-rooted fear of change, that characterizes the trade-union movement stems from its traditions in the organization of skilled craftsmen. These workers were exclusive, proud of their unique skills, jealous of their interests, and conscious of the importance of solidarity. In wage negotiations, the craft unions set the pace; the large amorphous, less-sophisticated general unions of unskilled workers followed. The craft workers saw capital equipment as their tools of trade and never as a possible substitute for their skills. Thus the ideas of actually negotiating working methods and the introduction of new technology along with pay are anathema to the trade-union movement, and in that respect it is quite unlike its U.S. counterpart. Furthermore the obstructionism of the British trade unions can be particularly damaging because they are typically organized and negotiate on an industry-wide basis.

Over the last decade two major trade-union issues have been raised—both with implications for labor productivity, and both have served as important political battlegrounds between the major parties. In 1969 the Labour government produced a *White Paper* outlining its proposals for trade-union reform, including mediation-and-arbitration procedures.[11] These were bitterly resisted by the unions and did not reach legislation. In 1971, however, the newly elected Conservative government pushed through much stronger legislation, outlawing the closed shop and establishing registration procedures such that unless a union had registered it would lose its immunity against breach-of-contract proceedings in the event of a strike. The closed shop was once again legalized and the registration procedures abolished whan a Labour government was returned in 1974. The following year, in a further bid for union compliance with government wage policy, the Employment Protection Act established procedures to narrow the ground under which workers could be dismissed, as well as establishing the Advisory, Conciliation and Arbitration Service to attempt nonmandatory resolution of disputes, especially regarding pay and union recognition. Finally in their 1980 Employment Act, the Conservatives imposed some limitations on the closed shop, notably to the effect that it could not be imposed on workers who had started their employment before closed-shop arrangements had been agreed on. The Conservative administration is now under pressure from various groups in the party to go further in outlawing the closed shop again, to make dismissal for incompetence or noncompliance easier, and to outlaw secondary picketing (that is, picketing by those not directly party to the dispute).

The direct impact of such legislation on productivity would probably be limited. It would not do much to weaken the power of unions in resisting change, though of course the closed-shop issue has important individual-rights and freedom-of-conscience aspects. The problems are more deeply seated, but certainly neither the cozy relationship between the unions and the Labour party with all their philosophical, financial, and personal links, nor the belligerent relationship between the unions and the Conservative party appears to have done anything to modify the unions' obstructionist attitude to change. If there are some signs that over the last two years strike activity has diminished and labor productivity has responded to a reduction in overmanning, it is the result of record levels of unemployment and bankruptcies.

Research and Development Panacea

As early as 1948 the National Research Development Council (NRDC) was formed, mainly to exploit, by licensing arrangements, inventions coming out of British universities and government laboratories. It also provides financing to individuals or small firms wishing to implement new inventions in return for royalties. Its resources are very limited but it has managed to get certain technologies off the ground.

In 1964 the Labour government placed great emphasis on technological change and established a ministry of technology (which for the period of the ministry's existence absorbed the NRDC). It initially selected four critical industries—machine tools, computers, electronics, and telecommunications—that it aided, largely by ordering and paying for new products before they had been produced or tested. To some extent, they were then made freely available to users in the private sector.

The ministry as a separate entity was discontinued when a Conservative government was elected in 1978. Harold Wilson's grandiose plan to bring about a "white-hot technical revolution" had shown some modest gains in terms of innovation in a few selected industries. According to Pavitt (1981), although the 1970 Conservative administration did not have the same zeal for sponsoring research and development—and, indeed, there was an absolute decline in the volume of research-and-development expenditure between 1969 and 1975—even by 1975, civilian research and development as a proportion of GDP was not particularly low by OECD standards. Freeman (1981) shows that it continued to be concentrated in a limited number of industries—for example, aircraft, chemicals, and chemical-related industries[12]—and those industries tended to be those in which the United States was concentrating its research and development and where economies of scale were particularly important.

The Heath government did, however, establish the Research and Development Requirement Boards, of which there are some twelve today, each for a different industry. These boards still have responsibility for allocating public funds for research and development.

Pavitt estimates that government expenditures on research and development were equivalent to about 1.1 percent of GDP in 1978, about the same as France and Germany and somewhat more than the EEC average. However, more than half of that expenditure was on defense research and development and when that is excluded the U.K. government spent some 0.5 percent of GDP on civilian research and development against 0.7 percent in France, 1 percent in Germany, and 0.75 percent in the EEC as a whole.

Government encouragement of invention and innovation has concentrated—whether through the twelve Requirement Boards or the NRDC—on specific industries. Within these industries it has been project-oriented although the NRDC has recently taken to financing small innovative companies as well as specific projects. Daly (1981) undertook a case study of the Machine Tool Industry Scheme. She reports that the industry's reactions were that only the preproduction ordering scheme was a clear success. It did seem to encourage both the industry to produce new products and potential users to try them out. Other mechanisms—for example, whereby the government guaranteed the repurchase price of numerically controlled machine tools that users might buy and then find unsatisfactory—were not judged particularly useful by the industry. On the whole, Daly concluded, the rather dismal record of the machine-tool industry might have been worse but for the subsidies it has received for innovation; but that even so, the £ 100 million spent on these might have been better spent on improving training and apprenticeship schemes for school leavers entering the industry.

Big and Little Neddies

The arguments about an overall apparent lack of investment, with questions of technical and managerial training, with labor relations and the resistance to technological change by the trade unions, and with the inadequacy of research-and-development expenditure are clearly not independent one from another. They all have some element of validity, and none alone can explain the poor performance of British industry. No single approach to industrial performance seemed adequate. Somehow the major actors—government, management, and the unions—had to get together in mutual confidence to thrash out these problems at an industrial level, and attack them from several sides at once.

Among the declining industries in the interwar period, various attempts were made to link subsidies to industrial reorganization, to scrap excess capacity and, in some cases, to reequip with up-to-date machinery. The major examples of this were the Cotton Industry (Reorganization) Act of 1939, the Coal Mines Act of 1930, and the 1936 scrap-and-build plan for shipbuilding. There were more dirigiste attempts to go further. Harold MacMillan and his group of conservative center-progressives introduced an Industrial Reorganization (Enabling) Bill in 1935, which would have given statutory powers to the majority of producers in an industry to force any recalcitrant minority into accepting plans for reorganization.[13] The arguments of this so-called planning movement were not presented very coherently and had little impact. They are of interest in that they constituted a unique case of advocacy of a strong element of compulsion in industrial reorganization—compulsion not by the government but by fellow entrepreneurs. IP in Britain has on the whole been characterized by its liberal, voluntarist, and cooperative approach.

In the early 1960s Britain was experiencing another of its periodic bouts of self-criticism. Successive balance-of-payments crises and continuing inflation had led to credit squeezes, restrictive-demand management, and occasional wage-and-price freezes, none of which seemed to give more than the most temporary respite. Such policies were harmful to growth, and in Britain politicians were being increasingly reproached for a poor growth performance. Much was made of the comparison with the German miracle, which was the object of bewilderment, envy, and no small resentment.

France also seemed to be performing much better in terms of economic growth and that was particularly galling, for while the Germans enjoyed a reputation of industriousness and managerial competence, the British viewed the French as quite the opposite. However, the apparent success of the French system of indicative planning was the inspiration for the Tory government which set up in 1962 the National Economic Development Council (NEDC) or Neddy. This was intended to act as a forum for discussion by management, unions, and the government. Assisted by a number of sectoral working parties or little Neddies (there are now twenty-nine), the NEDC was expected to establish consistent targets for input for each major sector and for each major product. By establishing such industry-specific targets much of the risk and uncertainty would, it was argued, be eliminated from product-planning and investment decisions. Each sector would gear up to fulfill its part of the plan, knowing that other sectors would be ready to buy the targeted output. In 1963 the NEDC came out with an overall GDP growth-rate target of 4 percent per year.

Though the early achievements of the NEDC in the planning field were not all that significant, the establishment of the institution was important, largely because it continued to serve as the principal forum for discussion between government, industry, and the trade-union movement; the significance of such a forum is now recognized at both ends of the political rainbow. Its establishment in a sense added a new element to government responsibility. The government, besides explaining and justifying its economic policies to Parliament, is generally expected to do so before the representatives of industry and the trade-union movement at successive meetings of the NEDC. The establishment of the NEDC also was a watershed in the role of economic analysis and economists in policy formation. When it was set up with twenty economists on its secretariat staff, the number of economists in the government service was increased threefold. Apart from two in the ministry of agriculture, it was the first time that economists were employed to deal with sectoral or industrial policies. Some concern for these problems permeated for the first time into the Treasury, mainly through

English Industrial Policy

contacts between economists. The number of economists in government service rose rapidly again with the establishment of the Department of Economic Affairs in the following Labour administration.

After the election of 1964, Harold Wilson appointed George Brown as the first minister for economic affairs. A year later he presented Parliament with The National Plan, Britain's first and last effort at detailed economic planning.[14] We need not discuss it; it was doomed before it started and the government knew it. It set a target of a 25-percent increase in national output over six years. This required an annual rise in productivity of 3.8 percent, but with no clear indication as to how this would be achieved.

Richard Crossman (1975, p. 30), then-minister of housing, wrote in his diary on August 3:

> Cabinet. And the main item was George Brown's National plan. We had four key chapters in front of us, including the summary at the beginning and the question was whether, in view of the deflation Callaghan (Chancellor of the Exchequer) launched in his statement last week, we should still publish the Plan next September as we has intended. Tony Crosland (Minister of Education, shortly before Junior Minister to George Brown) had this in mind when he asked how we could talk about a plan based on a 4 per cent growth rate when we now knew perfectly well that for the next eighteen months at least production wasn't going to rise by anything like that - in fact when the government was actually cutting back production by its deflationary measures . . .

Any possibility of the plan serving any other purpose than pedagogic was killed by successive sterling crises, culminating in devaluation and severe deflationary policies in November 1967.

After the ill-fated National Plan was launched in 1965, the formal indicative planning activities of the NEDC ceased and have not been revived. Nevertheless, the NEDC remains an important focus of IP today. Its tripartite working parties cover 40 percent of manufacturing output. These working parties make recommendations concerning such matters as product design, use of new technology, standards and specifications, marketing techniques (particularly in foreign markets), training, and so forth. An important function is preempting the negative trade-union response to technological or managerial change. Also, the exchange of information and discussion of common interests between the working parties aids in the formulation of company plans and objectives.

The various NEDC development committees and working parties look in detail at the problems of their industries and have produced a number of excellent reports. Beyond the reports, there has often been a lack of effective follow-up. Where the authorities have been asked to meet a specific need, perhaps in export credits or in government procurement standards or as regards launching-finance schemes, the board of trade or, later, the ministry of industry, has typically responded quickly and generously; witness the market-entry-guarantee scheme or the product-and-process-development scheme. It is where the onus for further progress lies with the industry that achievements are more difficult to pin down. No doubt the very presence of both sides of industry around the same table is helpful to achieving changes in technology or working practices, yet as Silberston (1981) puts it, "a fundamental problem is that, although they may not find it difficult to agree on the factors making for poor performance as compared with competitive firms overseas, it is likely to be much more difficult to agree on remedies. The union side is likely to wish for more investment in modern equipment, while the management side advocates more flexible working practices. The old conflicts arise, therefore, and cannot easily be resolved" (p. 48).

One area where the working parties have failed to make many inroads is the orderly elimination of overcapacity in their sectors. This is apparently beyond the limits of what can be obtained by voluntary agreement embracing the trade unions, and the working parties have not been seriously pushed in this direction (though it is unlikely that the present administration would consider this a desirable activity).

The working parties have persuaded the government to establish a number of sectoral investment-subsidy schemes—for example, the Microprocessor Applications Project (MAP) and the Micro-electronic Industries Support Programme (MISP). Of general relevance is the Product and Processors Developments Scheme (PPDS). These facilities, while not very heavily funded, have been retained by the current Conservative administration.

MAP is a good example of what is generally considered a well-thought-out, comprehensive industry-specific scheme. It has four principal parts: a program of seminars and publicity to generate interest in the potential applications of microelectronics; a program of accelerated courses for various skills; grants to defray consultancy costs; and a contribution of 25 percent of the development costs of new applications. As Northcutt (1981) reports, in the first two years of the scheme some 130,000 have attended seminars; over 30,000 attended short training courses in 1980; over 1,600 feasibility studies have been sponsored; and support has been approved for over 300 projects. All in all over £25 million has been spent. Northcutt offers various criticisms—inadequate advice concerning consultants, delays in vetting procedures, and so on—that suggest a greater degree of discrimination between one proposal and another, but on the whole MAP seems to have succeeded as far as the beneficiaries are concerned. The scheme incorporates various new and imaginative ideas, such as the publicity program and payments to consultants, which, if successful, could be used in other industry-specific schemes. It is still too early to tell whether taxpayers are getting a good return for their money.

English Industrial Policy

Under the 1972 and 1975 Industry Acts specific financial assistance for particular investment projects has been available in key industries, in many cases in response to requests from NEDC working parties. The present government has allowed these schemes to run until their date of termination. Industries benefiting from such assistance have included wool textiles, where the elimination of excess capacity has been an important criterion; the iron and steel foundry; the drop-forging and the nonferrous-foundry industries; the machine-tool and electronic-component industries, where efforts to develop new products have been stressed; and the clothing and footwear industries where reorganization into larger, more-efficient units has been stressed. The total amount offered under these schemes in the financial 1979–1980 was $17 million.[15] These schemes are now generally being wound up, with only two still open for applications. These are also a number of more general schemes left over from the previous administration for which the present government has tightened the criterion. Under the Selective Investment Scheme, now closed for applications, only $14 million had been paid out by the end of the 1979–1980 financial year, although over $100 million had been committed. The scheme has a high leverage, with government support only counting for some 10 percent of total outlays. The support-for-major-projects scheme has been reprieved by the present government but the criteria for support—with considerable but unquantified emphasis on improved productivity—have been tightened. Seventy-five projects are presently under consideration, but only a handful have been approved to date.

These various investment support schemes that fall under section 8 of the 1972 Industry Act have clearly not been accepted enthusiastically by the incoming Conservative government. To some extent, they have been instituted in the past as a liberal response to demands for protection from particular industries. But they have been too limited in scope to effect the major changes in productivity and nonprice competitiveness and, hence, trade performance that would be necessary to counteract these demands.[16]

Picking the Winners

The Conservative government also abolished the Industrial Reorganization Corporation (IRC). This was set up in 1966, with a brief to encourage international competitiveness, and particularly to exploit economies of scale through structural reorganization, mainly by arranging mergers and financing takeovers. It also helped firms in temporary difficulty (notably, Rolls Royce) and in some industries (again, machine tools was one), it lent money to speed up the production of new products, or, in the case of textiles, to modernize equipment. The IRC was a precursor, although on a much-smaller scale, of the National Enterprise Board (NEB), which was established by the second Wilson government in 1975 and later abolished by the Thatcher government in 1979.

Like the IRC, the NEB was given many jobs. Its establishment followed the department of industry's *White Papers* on *The Regeneration of British Industry* (1974) and *An Approach to Industrial Strategy* (1975). Silberston (1981, p. 47) sums up the goals of the industrial strategy succinctly:

> The aim was to provide a framework in which the prospects of the most sections of industry could be considered over a period of five or more years, an analysis would be made of the past performance of individual sectors of manufacturing industry, and the implications of alternative medium-term growth assumptions would be worked out. Those sectors most important for achieving the government's economic objectives (the "winners") would be selected as follows:
> (i) industries intrinsically likely to be successful judged by past performance and current prospects;
> (ii) others which had the potential for success if appropriate action was taken;
> (iii) industries whose performance has most effect on the rest of industry. An attempt would then be made to tackle the problems affecting their performance. Tripartite committees were to discuss in detail the problems and opportunities of particular sectors. The government would help to see that these committees were set up and would try in various ways to promote their main recommendations; it also made two important commitments. The first was to give priority to industrial development and to see that its own policies were consistent with this. The second was to help ensure that industry was able to earn sufficient profits on its investment.

In practice, until recently, the NEB has spent far more money on supporting lame ducks than on picking winners. The lamest of these has been British Leyland, for which the NEB has recently been relieved of responsibility although British Leyland is still kept going by massive periodic infusions of Treasury funds. Another duck of a different breed was ICL. International Computers Ltd. was established by an IRC-brokered merger in 1968 with substantial research-and-development aid. Inadequate earnings to allow international survival required a further substantial public loan in 1973. In 1975 the government transferred its 10.1-percent holdings to the NEB, later sold off in 1979 by the Conservative government at a time when ICL's outlook looked promising. Since then, with the company's fortunes again at a low ebb, the government has given limited temporary support.

Until 1980 the ICL story looked relatively successful. Government financial support appeared to have established the company as a middle-size mainframe computer manufacturer with 35 percent of the British market and substantial export sales. Other established companies, in which the NEB have had substantial holdings transferred to it after government rescue operations, have included Ferranti, Albert Herbert, and Cambridge Instruments; only the last of these remains in the NEB pond.

The more important role originally foreseen for the NEB, however, was as a sponsor of innovation in fields of advanced technology, either alone or in association with the private sector. The guidelines have been tightened up by the present government to avoid any duplication with the private sector and to ensure that the NEB's investments be turned over to the private sector as soon as they are commercially viable. Since the NEB is supposed to operate according to commercial principles, its investments cannot be justified on the grounds that their private rate of return understates their social rate of return. Clearly, the risks of investment in these areas are considerable and the private capital market may be unwilling to make venture capital available or, for lack of experience, impose unrealistically tough conditions. Moreover, there may be problems of lethargy, inherited commitments, structural inflexibility, or lack of imagination on the part of existing companies that inhibit investment in new technologies.

This last argument is the crux of the concept of picking winners. W.B. Willott (1981, p. 142), Chief Executive of the NEB, puts it this way:

> The skeptic is entitled to ask why, given the imperfections of human nature, the NEB can succeed where others fail. Part of the answer is that the NEB is an organization whose objectives are specifically to identify, appraise and seize opportunities for the UK. The attitudes of the staff and the culture of the whole organisation are, therefore, geared to making things happen that would not otherwise happen. In other words, its function is to question the received wisdom in British industry and financial institutions and to act as catalyst for change. The obverse of the coin, of course, it that the NEB lacks the accumulated experience and knowledge of any good, established firm about the industry, its customers and the behaviour patterns of the other competitors. Experience can lead a company automatically round the most obvious open manhole covers. The NEB has, in a sense, to work harder and more analytically. It also needs to compensate for in-house experience by finding ways of drawing on outside experience, and it has developed the practice of seeking a range of outside advisers, in addition to Board members, to participate in and criticize projects as they develop. The lack of experience is also one of the fundamental reasons why the NEB itself seeks private sector participation from the outset, to provide an independent cross-check on the merits of an investment, on the way it is set up and the people selected to run it (and, ultimately, to facilitate divestment).

The NEB has initiated companies in such areas as microelectronic components, electronic office systems, computer peripherals, underwater-engineering equipment, and, recently, genetic engineering. It has clearly made a specialty of electronics and within electronics it has aimed at the application of new technology. Many of the technological ideas have come from close working relations with university and research laboratories. None of the NEB-bred companies has yet made a profit. The NEXOS word processor and the INMOS microchip are coming to the market in 1981. These companies cannot expect a very warm welcome from the Thatcher government if they find that their funding is inadequate and they come back for more. Moreover they can expect to find ample competition in world markets from other manufacturers of similar technologically advanced products, some of which have also benefited from advanced-technology aid provided by their home governments.

Neo-Conservative Macrostrategy

When the present administration was returned to power in 1979, the emphasis of IP was switched from the public support of research and development, of investment in new innovations, and public enterprise as such. Rather, the new government stressed the importance of establishing the right macroeconomic environment, which included a tax system more sympathetic to entrepreneurial risk and imagination and fewer regulations and restrictions concerning products or manufacturing processes. The new approach was, of course, consistent with the dominant view that there were no single causes for Britain's lack of international competitiveness, that a major sociological seachange was required, and that public policy was limited in its impact. Indeed, all that the government could do was to make the conditions for free enterprise as propitious as possible and trust that human nature and the invisible hand would do the rest. The market was to choose the winners.

Of course the main preoccupation of the new administration was to reduce the rate of inflation, which it thought could only be achieved by strict control of the money supply over a period of years. For this monetary control to be possible, a steady reduction in the public-sector borrowing requirement (PSBR) was considered necessary. It was and is the strong belief of the government that investment—particularly, by small- and medium-size companies and in risky or innovative projects—is particularly damaged by inflation.

The government did not abolish NEDC or the NEB and its clutch of high-tech companies. Initially the role of NEDC was downplayed, but it was retained to avoid grievously offending the trade-union movement, which had no other focus of contacts (formal or informal) with the government. More recently, however, since the government has found that a total hands-off policy with regard to the going level of wage settlements is not practicable, NEDC has been used as a lecture room for instruction on the importance of wage restraint. Meanwhile the sectoral working parties have continued their useful work as before.

Throughout the electoral campaign the Conservatives condemned the practice of shoring up such derelict firms as British Leyland or British Steel.

In practice realpolitik, the political cost of adding to already-rising unemployment; the cost to the PSBR of redundancy payments and further unemployment benefits; the cost to the balance of payments of allowing such critical firms, which virtually constitute the motor-car and the crude-steel industries, to go under; and finally considerations of national security have persuaded the government to keep these firms alive. On the other hand, the NEB has divested itself of its holdings of other earlier bail outs.

Certain members of the incoming administration were, at least at the time, impressed by the work of Bacon and Eltis (1978). They argued that the rapid growth of nonmarket expenditures, particularly by the local authorities, was diverting resources, (notably skilled labor) from the manufacturing sector. Certainly the local authorities have grown rapidly, both in terms of their real expenditures and in terms of numbers of employees. Also there is some evidence that in periods of higher-than-normal unemployment, the local authorities have raised their labor forces particularly rapidly, serving as a sort of employer of the last resort. Nevertheless, much of the increase in public-sector employment as a whole has been in female employment and over the 1970s the female-participation rate has increased rapidly. Second there is little evidence from CBI surveys or elsewhere that a shortage of skilled labor has been a key element in inhibiting greater output in the manufacturing sector.

Bacon and Eltis's more general argument was that the government has increasingly preempted labor and capital resources, resulting in a distortion of output toward nonmarketed goods and services away from marketed goods and services, especially manufactured goods. They further argue that this has caused wage inflation as workers have tried to maintain their share of marketed output, lower profits and investment, and a lower exportable surplus of marketed output.

The argument is in fact more subtly presented than this. But in the end, they take a number of phenomena—rising public-sector shares of employment and output, higher taxes, wage inflation, falling share of exports of manufacturers—and construct a parable of cause and effect. Other parables could equally well fit the facts, and in any event it is not clear what is particularly peculiar to Britain about their explanation. Other countries have experienced similar shifts in sectoral output without the same dire consequences.

In any event, the idea that the private sector is being squeezed out by the public sector frequently surfaces in discussion of the present government's strategy. In recent evidence to the Parliamentary Committee on the Treasury, the Treasury insisted that even at the present high level of unused capacity, an increase in public-sector investment would squeeze out private-sector investment. This broad suspicion also explains resistance in the Cabinet to the latest proposals for joint public-private investment initiatives in the derelict riot-prone inner cities. The alternative favored by the chancellor is to press ahead with the proposal for low-tax, minimal-regulatory-control, free-enterprise zones in the depressed urban areas. This idea was raised at the election but so far has met with little enthusiasm by the local authorities. Indeed, in the whole area of deregulation, apart from the abolition of exchange controls and certain other banking procedures, nothing much has happened.

Response of the Left

One could argue that there are factors specific to the British economy that support the argument that Britain should practice a more vigorous IP than its principal competitor countries. The most obvious is that U.K. industry is both far behind and falling further behind its competitors as measured by loss of market shares at home and abroad. Any catching up must follow a major effort to reverse the deteriorating trend. As Stout (1979) has pointed out, the general macroeconomic explanations of Britain's poor performance are typically directed toward explaining the low level of productivity—which should make growth relatively easier—rather than the decline in Britain's relative level of productivity. He suggests some reasons why there may be vicious circles in relative industrial decline. In any event, spontaneous combustion does not look probable. Any reversal of the decline would seem to necessitate a major governmental initiative.

A more specific argument for an active government role has been increasingly heard recently. It concerns North Sea oil and the so-called Dutch disease. The argument is that the current and expected impact of oil on the balance of payments will sustain an overvalued effective rate of exchange from the point of view of exports and imports of manufactures. This will cause oil to increasingly displace exports of manufactures while imports of manufactures rise in response to their relative cheapness. Any efforts to reduce the exchange rate—for example, but a more lax monetary policy or pegging it within the EMS—will eventually bring about the same result as the consequent higher rate of price of inflation will have an impact on exports and imports of manufactured goods in the same way. No one can defeat the law of comparative advantage, and the manufacturing sector is inexorably set to decline. In other terms, as long as the exchange rate is allowed to move over the long-run in the direction required to bring the balance of payments toward equilibrium, other components must move so as to offset the effects of rising oil exports.

However, this analysis is far too static; other developments are possible. For example, if the exchange rate is temporarily held down—say by outward capital transfers—the increase in economic growth associated with higher total exports of goods may, if accompanied by a rise in productivity, make it possible to prevent a higher inflation rate. In that case a new equilibrium can be achieved with increased exports of both oil and manufactures, increased inputs of manufactures, and possibly continued higher capital transfers abroad.

Nevertheless the impact of North Sea oil on the balance of payments increases the importance of rapid gains in price competitivity, if the manufacturing base is not to be further eroded. Furthermore, since it is generally accepted that oil production will level off within a decade and thereafter decline, it is essential that an active, up-to-date manufacturing base be at hand and capable of supplying manufactured goods to replace the ultimately dwindling exports of oil.

As has been suggested, the present administration emphasizes the importance of establishing the appropriate macroeconomic environment, especially as regards reducing tax burdens and containing inflation. Recently one of the more outspoken members of the Cabinet, John Biffen, has spoken of the positive aspects of high unemployment. As Stout (1981, p. 70) puts it: "the most interesting supply-side aspect of the monetarist approach to policy—and perhaps its one potentially dramatic effect—is the one least mentioned openly by the government. This is that the very depth and duration of the de-manning of industry will work a sea-change in the attitudes and values of both workers and management, permanently 'de-rigidifying' industrial structure by removing the assumption of occupational security."

At the other end of the political spectrum, the left-wing members of the Labour party advocate the return of protectionism, along with a vigorous expansion of public-sector investment. Much influenced by the Cambridge Economic Policy Group, they see a high tariff wall as the only way of securing the domestic market for domestically produced manufactures and turning around the secular upward trend in unemployment. Their vicious circle is one of declining market shares at home and abroad and declining profits and investment, all of which prevent the exploitation of economies of scale and other productivity gains.

North Sea oil is no alternative because it protects the balance of payments and allows deindustrialization to continue or even accelerates it. A once-and-for-all devaluation would not be sufficient to reverse the trend, though left-wingers favor this as a (very) second-best alternative. Only protectionism, they argue, provides any sort of medium-term strategy. In this respect they are throwbacks to Chamberlain and the tariff reformers of the turn of the century.[17] As for the Tariff Reform Movement, their IP is protection.

Conclusions

From between the polar extremes of neo-Conservatism and left-wing protectionism, from the middle ground shared by most Conservatives and Labourites along with the Liberals and Social Democrats, little new in the way of ideas for IP has emerged in recent years. There is talk of a more activist role for government, more and wider-spread financial assistance and tax incentives for research and development, increasing the role of public purchasing, and more funding for the National Enterprise Board—in other words, more of the same 1975 industrial-strategy approach. With the Thatcher administration bogged down in the mire of problems of short-term fiscal and monetary management, we have not heard much of a more activist role for the markets that used to be the cornerstone of its IP and so far has hardly been given a serious trial.

The general arguments in favor of IP have been well rehearsed and are summarized in chapters 3 and 4 of this book. Williamson's work (1975) suggests that at least in the United States the most innovative firms are in the upper-middle-size group. Beyond that size the comforts of market domination, or worries about provoking antitrust investigation, deter innovative activity. Below that size the costs of trying to protect the innovation from exploitation by one's competitors, together with the risk that any competitive gain will be lost if this protection fails, serve as significant deterrents.

In the United Kingdom the relatively large share of the public sector in the GDP probably helps to sustain the level of innovative activity. First, the argument that monopoly power discourages research-and-development expenditure may not hold if an industry is, or nearly is, a state monopoly. Crude-steel production, coal mining, and shipbuilding might be cases in point here. Second, certain publicly owned sectors may explicitly use social rather than private rates of return as investment criteria: the health service, for example. Third, there is relatively heavy dependence of certain industries on defense contracts and willingness of government to finance defense-related research and development. These factors may help explain why, despite lower growth rates and a lower rate of fixed investment to GDP in the United Kingdom than in the OECD area as a whole throughout the 1960s and 1970s, research-and-development expenditures have on Pavitt's (1981) evidence not been especially low. In Britain, however, the commercial exploitation of technical and managerial innovation seems to be the weak point.

The prognosis is not encouraging. Exasperation with constantly declining relative labor productivity and the apparent inadequacies of IP, as it has developed over the last three decades has led important sections of the two major political parties to adopt radical macroeconomic credos: faith in supply-side forces and in protectionism on the Conservative and Labour benches, respectively.

Certainly traditional British IP has suffered from a lack of breadth, a lack of finance and, most important, a lack of urgency. Compare the U.K. experience with France, where Le Plan has been forcefully reestablished since the first oil crisis as the overall structure through which a vast panoply of ISPs and FSPs are focused on precise goals, such as on outdoing German or Japanese productivity rates in specific sectors, quantified reductions in foreign-oil dependence, gaining a certain share of the European computer market, or whatever.[18]

The comparison with French IP suggests two further more specific criticisms of the British approach that perhaps can be met without vast changes in the social or industrial structure. First, British policy needs to be more firm specific. Up to now the government has only dealt with large individual firms as terminal patients, though NRDC has recently taken to supporting small firms with a range of high-technology projects. The fast-expanding sectors of microelectronics, scientific instruments, bioengineering, mining equipment, medical equipment, and so on will, like computers, aerospace, and household-electronic equipment in the past, be increasingly dominated by global oligopolies. In these areas small firms may play a useful innovating role, but as long as they remain small they cannot present serious competition to the international giants.

Another major weakness of British IP is its lack of continuity. This chapter's theme has been the switches from one panacea to another in response to the sociopolitical preoccupation of the moment. Now the only new offerings are nineteenth-century laissez-faire policies or nineteenth-century protectionism. Until IP is made less of a political football and industry is convinced that it can reasonably assume continuation of the institutions and instruments of IP over the typical planning horizon, they will fail to meet even their present limited potential. Some of the sectoral schemes that the present administration has retained are imaginative and seem to be working well. Even these schemes could work better if they clearly enjoyed the administration's full-hearted support and were immune from the next round of budget cuts.

Notes

1. In terms of the taxonomy presented in chapter 2 of this book, general or nonselective IPs as well as ASPs, SSPs, and ISPs are all included. Regional-specific policies, it is argued, cannot be entirely disqualified, although for them competitivity may be a secondary consideration.

2. See in particular, Caves and Krause (1980), especially pp. 1-20 and 135-198.

3. For some recent empirical work see Caves, in Caves and Krause

(1980), pp. 135-198, and references cited therein, particularly Bacon and Eltis (1974).

4. See the related study by Glickman (1981).

5. See Royal Commission on the Distribution of the Industrial Population (1940).

6. See various papers in Department of Industry (1976).

7. For a useful critical summary, with many references, of the entire taxation system in the United Kingdom, see Pechman (1980).

8. See Department of Industry (1980).

9. See Turner (1969), chap. 3, for a discussion of the early problems of the business schools.

10. Caves (1980). Because of the structural form of Caves's equations it is not clear whether the reduction in output per man is greater than proportional to the number of days of strikes. Caves does show, however, that firms tend to hold higher inventories relative to their U.S. counterparts to cope with uncertainties in rates of output in industries where strikes are more frequent relative to the U.S. industry.

11. See Department of Employment and Productivity (1969).

12. These include food, drink, and tobacco; textiles and footwear; and rubber and plastics.

13. See Winch (1970).

14. See Department of Economic Affairs (1965).

15. See Department of Industry 1980 (*a*).

16. See Stout (1979).

17. This is except that they are associated with the wrong university. In the late nineteenth and early twentieth centuries, Marshall and the Cambridge economists were supporters of the Free Trade Campaign. In 1895 the London School of Economics was founded, inter alia, to give intellectual support to the Fair Trade movement, the predecessor of the Tariff Reform Movement.

18. See chapter 10 of this book.

References

Bacon, R.W., and W.A. Eltis. *The Age of US and UK Machinery*. London: National Economic Development Office, 1974.

———. *Britain's Economic Problem: Too Few Producers*. 2nd ed. London: Macmillan, 1978.

Blackaby, F., ed., *Deindustrialization*. London: Heinemann, 1979.

Carter, C., ed., *Industrial Policy and Innovation*. London: Heinemann, 1981.

Caves, R.E. *Productivity Differences Among Industries,* in Richard E.

Caves and Lawrence Krause, eds., *Britain's Economic Performance.* Washington, D.C.: Brookings Institution, 1980. Pp. 135-190.

Crossman, R. *The Diaries of a Cabinet Minister.* Vol. 1. London: Hamish Hamilton and Jonathan Cape, 1975.

Daly, Anne. "Government Support for Innovation in the British Machine Tool Industry: A Case Study" C. Carter, ed., *Industrial Policy and Innovation.* London: Heinemann, 1981.

Department of Economic Affairs. *The National Plan.* Cmnd. 2764, London: HMSO, 1965.

Department of Employment and Productivity. *In Place of Strife: A Policy for Industrial Relations.* London: HMSO, 1969.

Department of Industry. *The Regeneration of British Industry.* Cmnd. 5710, London: HMSO, 1974.

———. *An Approach to Industrial Strategy.* Cmnd. 6315, London: HMSO, 1975.

———. *Economics of Industrial Subsidies.* London: HMSO, 1976.

———. *Engineering Our Future.* Cmnd. 7794, London: HMSO, 1980.

———. *Industry Act 1972, Annual Report.* London: HMSO, 1980a.

Freeman, C. "Technical Innovation and British Trade Performance," in F. Blackaby, ed., *Deindustrialization.* London: Heinemann, 1979.

Glickman, N. "Regional Policy and Industrial Policy." Mimeographed. Philadelphia: University of Pennsylvania, 1981.

Hunt Committee. *The Intermediate Areas.* Cmnd. 3998, London: HMSO, 1969.

Northcutt, J. "Policies for Micro-electronic Applications in Industry," in C. Carter, ed., *Industrial Policy and Innovation.* London: Heinemann, 1981.

Pavitt, Keith. "Technology in British Industry: a Suitable Case for Improvement," in C. Carter, ed., *Industrial Policy and Innovation.* London: Heinemann, 1981.

Pechman, J.A., "Taxation," in Richard E. Caves and Lawrence Krause, eds., *Britain's Economic Performance.* Washington, D.C.: Brookings Institution, 1980, pp. 199-260.

Reddaway, W.B., and others. *Effects of the Selective Employment Tax, Final Report.* Cambridge University Press, 1973.

Royal Commission on the Depression of Trade and Industry. *Report.* Cmnd. 4715, London, 1886.

Royal Commission on the Distribution of the Industrial Population (the Barlow Commission). *Report.* Cmnd. 6153, London: HMSO, 1940.

Silbertson, A. "Industrial Policies in Britain 1960-80" in C. Carter, ed., *Industrial Policy and Innovation.* London: Heinemann, 1981.

Stout, D.K. "Deindustrialization and Industrial Policy," in F. Blackaby, ed., *Deindustrialization.* London: Heinemann, 1981.

———. "Macrostrategy for British Industry in 1980's," in *World Economic Review* 3, No. 3 (Philadelphia: Wharton Econometric Forecasting Associates, 1981).

Turner, G. *Business in Britain.* London: Eyre and Spottiswoode, 1969.

Williamson, O.E. *Markets and Hierarchies.* New York: Free Press, 1975.

Willott, W.B. "Industrial Innovation and the Role of Bodies like the National Enterprise Board," in C. Carter, ed., *Industrial Policy and Innovation.* London: Heinemann, 1981.

Winch, D. *Economics and Policy.* New York: Walker, 1970.

Appendix 14A: List of Principal Institutions and Support Schemes of Industrial Policy in the United Kingdom

1. *National Economic Development Committee (NEDC).*
   Established 1962. Chairman: Chancellor of the Exchequer.
   Membership: Government, Confederation of British Industries (CBI) and Trades Union Congress (TUC).
   Economic Development Committees and Sectoral Working Parties: first established in 1964 to study problems of particular industries or services and make recommendations to NEDC, now over forty.
2. *National Research and Development Corporation (NRDC)*
   Established 1948 to stimulate invention and innovation and market license rights to invention resulting from public research. Outlays: about £15 million per annum statutory obligation to balance revenue and expenditure.
3. *Research and Development Requirements Boards*
   Established 1973, to allocate government funds for research between research institutes, universities, and government laboratories. Now twelve boards covering specific industries.
4. *Other Research and Development Schemes*
   Product and Process Development Scheme: contributes development assistance (launching aid) in form of 25 or 50 percent contribution to costs with levy on sales. Outlay: about £26 million per annum.
   The Micro Processor Applications Project: provides programs of seminars, trainings, finances consultancies, and contributes 25 percent in development costs. Outlays (including Micro-electronics Industry Support Programme): about £110 million per annum.
5. *National Enterprise Board*
   Established under Industry Act 1975. Public corporation and major stockholder or outright owner of a number of high-technology companies in high risk fields. Run as a commercial organization.

Main NEB Investments, 1980 (£ million)

Aregon (viewdata systems)	4.5
British Underwater Engineering (underwater-engineering equipment	7.0
Cambridge Instruments (scientific and medical instruments)	15.0
Data Recording Instrument Company (peripherals)	15.0
Inmos (microelectronic components)*	21.0
Insac Products Ltd (computer software)	4.0
Monotype (printing machinery)	3.5
Nexos (electronic office systems)	16.0
Q1 Europe (microcomputer office systems)	2.0
United Medical Enterprises (medical-equipment exporter)	6.0
Wholesale Vehicle Finance (motor-distributor finance)	11.0

Source: W.B Willott in C. Carter, (1981), p. 140.
* £ 50 million committed.

6. *Regional Industrial Development Boards*

   South West Industrial Development Board.

   Northern Development Board.

   North West Industrial Development Board.

   Yorkshire and Hamberside Development Board.

   Scotish Industrial Development Advisory Board.

   World Industrial Development Advisory Board.

   These boards make grants Regional Development Grants and Loans under parts 1 and 2 of the 1972 Industry Acts. Payments in the 1979/1980 fiscal year totalled £ 330.8.

7. *General Investment Support Schemes*
   The regional boards also administered the following general-support schemes:
   a) Accelerated Projects schemes (a counter-cyclical scheme with payments of assistance approximately equivalent to 10 percent of project outlay-payments of $49.1 million by end of fiscal 1980).
   b) Selective Investment Scheme (closed for applications 30 June 1979—payments of $14.1 million and offers of $106.5 million to end of fiscal 1980).

Appendix 14A

- c) Support for Major Projects Scheme (no payments made to end of fiscal 1980. One grant of $0.85 million offered).
- d) Energy Conservation Scheme (closed for application 30 June 1980 payments totalling $2.1 million and offers of $12.8 million to end in fiscal 1980).

8. *Sectoral Diversement Support Schemes*

   The regional boards also administer the following sectoral schemes, all of which are closed for application except the final three: Wool Textile, Ferrous Foundry, Machine Tool, Clothing, Paper and Board, Nonferrous Foundry, Instrumentation and Automation, Footwear Manufacturing, Assistance to Manufactures of Printing Machinery, Assistance to Manufactures of Textile Machinery, Poultry Meat Processing, the Offshore Supplies Interest-Relief-Grant Scheme, Redmeat Slaughterhouse, Microelectronics, and Drop Forging. Total payments made from dates of introduction (mostly 1976 and 1977) to end of fiscal 1980 were $129.7 million.

9. *Special Assistance to Shipbuilding and Associated Industries*

   Under part 2 of the Industry Act 1972, payments were made in 1979/1980 under the Cost Escalation Insurance Scheme of $3.6 million against premiums of $3 million, and grants have been offered of $35 million to secure orders under the Shipbuilding Intervention Fund.

15 Developing-Country Experience with Industrial Policy: Korea, Venezuela, India, and Brazil

*F. Gerard Adams,
Jere Behrman,
Jaime Marquez, Brian Pinto,
and Theophilos Priovolos*

The range of experience with IP in the developing world is large, but certain themes reflect the common denominators of the underlying problems. As noted in chapter 7, these principally involve import substitution, export promotion, nationalized enterprises, and the role of multinational enterprises. Questions of planning (its scope, specificity, and effectiveness) also arise in many developing economies. Since the developing economies are greatly concerned with infrastructure investment and since their domestic markets are usually relatively small IPs tend to have industry- and even project-specific focus even when their orientation is economy-wide or general.

In this chapter, we present overviews of IP in a select sample—Korea, Venezuela, India, and Brazil—of the many developing economies. These four countries are fairly representative, however, of those of the developing countries that have chosen the path of industrial development. Korea is one of the Pacific Basin super exporters, although perhaps the development path here has been somewhat more focused on heavy industry than in the other Pacific Basin export-promoting countries. Venezuela is representative of the resource-rich but limited-domestic-market economies. India represents another typology of policy, since this country continues to focus on import substitution and on promoting an autarkic type of development. Brazil, on the other hand, has a large market, and, to some extent, domestic resources, but it lacks the energy reserves of Venezuela. Also, Brazil, partly as a result of a natural shift from import substitution toward export promotion, has had considerable success in its development. Our discussion of IPs

---

F. Gerard Adams and Jere Behrman wrote the section for Korea; Jaime Marquez wrote the section for Venezuela; F. Gerard Adams and Theophilos Privolos wrote the section for Brazil; and Brian Pinto wrote the section for India.

in the developing world omits only representation of the so-called LDCs—the poor countries, particularly of the African continent, that are not yet in a position to carry on a successful industrial-development policy.

Korean Experience with Industrial Policy

The Korean experience in the past two decades is of considerable interest for at least two reasons. First, in a number of dimensions Korea has been among the most successful of the developing countries. For the period 1960–1978, for example, the World Bank (1980) ranks the Korean average annual exponential growth rate of real per-capita GNP of 6.9 percent second only to Singapore's 7.4 percent among the ninety included developing countries.[1] Manufacturing has grown even faster so that manufacturing as a percentage of GNP has increased from 12 to 24 percent. Overall real exports have increased at an average annual exponential rate of 32.3 percent, with exports as a percentage of GNP increasing from 3 to 34 percent. Manufactured exports have risen even more rapidly at 42.3 percent per year, with their share in overall exports rising from 14 to 85 percent. Real wages in manufacturing and mining rose at 7.2 percent per year in 1960–1979, which reflects almost a fourfold increase in less than two decades. Economic-distribution equality increased. Second, the developing countries are more conscious of the Korean experience than of that of many other developing countries, in part because of the rapidly growing and currently relative large Korean manufactured imports into their markets.

Because of the many impressive aspects of the Korean experience, it has been subjected to fairly intensive analysis. We briefly summarize the results of these studies with regard to the general Korean experience, possible unique factors, and the role of IPs.[2]

General Korean Development Experience

During the Japanese colonial period from the early 1900s through the Second World War, agriculture was extensively developed in the southern half of the Korean peninsula, but there was only a small modern manufacturing sector. Until the mid-1950s adjustments due to partition and to the Korean War dominated the economy. Therefore the economic structure in 1955 was much the same as it was at the end of the Japanese occupation, with 48 percent of GNP coming from primary sectors and 8 percent from manufacturing. Exports were almost entirely from the primary sector and totaled only 1.6 percent of GNP. Investment was 10 percent of GNP.

During the last half of the 1950s and the start of the 1960s, IPs were of a typically import-substitution variety, with an overvalued multiple-exchange-rate system, induced in part by its role in generating foreign-exchange earnings from the resident U.N. military establishment. The government responded to current balance-of-payments problems by a series of ad hoc measures, including increasing use of quantitative restrictions to supplement high tariffs on consumer goods as the domestic currency became more overvalued. Some export incentives were provided by a free-market premium on foreign-exchange certificates gained from export sales and modest cash subsidies. In 1959 explicit export-incentive mechanisms were introduced with tariff exemptions on raw materials used in exports. Between 1955 and 1960 real exports grew at 16.3 percent per year and manufacturing value added at 10.3 percent per year. But essentially these high growth rates only represented catching up to more normal levels from the unusually low 1955 proportions, which reflected the regional colonial specialization and the subsequent partition and Korean War disruptions. As a result the percentages of exports and of manufacturing real value added in real GNP rose to 2.4 and 10.8 percent, respectively. Between 1957 and 1960 real wages in manufacturing and mining increased at a 5.1 percent annual rate. But there were some problems: Between 1955 and 1960 real GNP per capita grew only 0.7 percent per year, the GNP deflator increased at 12.0 percent per year, the current account deficit averaged 9 to 10 percent of GNP, and total domestic savings and gross investment fell from 3.7 to 1.6 percent and from 11.9 to 10.9 percent of current GNP. Thus there were a number of negative features of the economic performance.

The first half of the 1960s was characterized by considerable economic, social, and political instability—in part because of the economic shortcomings just outlined. There were also efforts at policy reform and liberalization of the foreign-sector regime as a result of these shortcomings and the spreading perception that import substitution had run its course. Partially because of major reforms introduced in the two years after the election of President Park (who remained in power until he was assassinated in late 1979) in early 1964, the rates of growth of real exports, real manufacturing value added, and real GNP per capita all accelerated to annual averages of 24.0 percent, 11.8 percent, and 3.6 percent for 1960–1965. Within the same period the ratio of real exports and of real manufacturing value added to real GNP rose from 2.4 to 5.2 percent and from 10.8 to 13.9 percent. As a percentage of current GNP, total domestic savings and gross domestic investment rose from 1.6 to 7.7 percent and from 10.9 to 15.1 percent, and the current-account deficit fell from -9.3 to -7.4 percent. The average annual rate of growth of real wages in mining and manufacturing fell to a still-positive 1.1 percent, but the rate for agricultural labor was slightly negative -0.1 percent, which probably was unequalizing. The GNP deflator accelerated, with an average annual inflation rate of 19.3 percent.

The reforms introduced in the mid-1960s included: fiscal revisions to assure more government revenue; monetary reforms and interest-rate increases to encourage savings and more efficient allocation of investment; the unification of the exchange rate coupled with the second major devaluation in three years in 1964; and relaxation of import controls (culminating in the switch in 1967 from a positive list of eligible imports to a much less restrictive negative list of ineligible imports) with maintenance of tariffs and some selected additional incentives as well as further expansion of export incentives so that by 1967 exporters operated in almost a free-trade regime with export performance as a criterion for granting import licenses and a system of export targets for individual firms (in particular, production and destination markets). These reforms reflected the acceptance of the general strategy of adopting much more outward-looking policies, predicated on the views that consumption-import-substitution options had been exhausted, that the domestic market was too small to permit further import substitution with appropriate scale economies in intermediate and capital-goods production, and that the poor natural-resource base did not permit dependence on natural-resource-based exports to generate sufficient foreign exchange for a high-growth economy.

The economy responded with very high growth rates and large structural changes in many dimensions. Real GNP per capita grew at average annual exponential rates of 8.8 percent in 1965–1970, 7.5 percent in 1970–1975, and an estimated 8.9 percent in 1975–1979, despite the major shocks in the 1970s for oil importers and for exporters to depressed-developed-country markets. Real manufacturing value added grew at average annual rates of 21.3 percent in 1965–1970, 18.5 percent in 1970–1975, and 15.7 percent in 1975–1979. Total real exports increased at average annual rates of 36.5 percent in 1965–1970, 25.0 percent in 1970–1975, and 18.0 percent in 1975–1979. Real wages in manufacturing rose at average annual rates of 7.1 percent in 1965–1970, 8.4 percent in 1970–1975, and 13.4 percent in 1975–1979. Real agricultural wages rose at average annual rates of 8.2 percent in 1965–1970 and 1.5 percent in 1970–1975. Employment in manufacturing grew at average annual rates of 10.7 percent in 1965–1970, 11.4 percent in 1970–1975, and 8.7 percent in 1975–1979. Total employment grew at 3.5 percent in 1965–1970 (exceeding the 2.9 percent growth in the economically active population), 3.9 percent in 1970–1975 (equaling the growth in the EPA), and 3.6 percent in 1975–1979 (exceeding the 3.5 percent growth in the EPA). Real exports as a share of real GNP rose from 5.2 percent in 1965, 14.7 percent in 1970, 28.3 percent in 1975, and finally to 38 percent in 1979. Real industrial value added as a share of real GNP rose from 13.9 percent in 1965, 21.6 percent in 1970, 31.9 percent in 1975, and finally to 33 percent in 1979. Total domestic savings as a share of GNP rose from 7.7 percent in 1965, 21.6 percent in 1970, 31.9 percent in 1975, and finally to 33 percent in 1979. Total domestic savings as a share of GNP rose from 7.7 percent in 1965, 17.1 percent in 1970, 17.7 percent in 1975, and to 28 percent in 1978. Gross investment as a share of GNP rose from 15.1 percent in 1965, 27.2 percent in 1970, 27.1 percent in 1975, to 38 percent in 1979.

This available list of percentage growth rates and shares in GNP is probably numbing to the reader. But the point is that Korean growth and structural change in this decade and a half has been spectacular, with accompanying increases in employment and equalizing tendencies in income distributions.[3] Most developing countries would be delighted with sustained changes half of the Korean magnitude. Also, the dominant source of the growth and structural changes has been the export expansion of labor-intensive (more skill-intensive over time) manufactured goods in line with Korea's comparative advantage and in response to the outward-looking orientation with a slight export bias.

Unique Factors in the Korean Experience

Of course, every developing country's experience is unique. But at times the Korean experience is dismissed in regard to its lessons for other developing countries because of a number of alleged special features. Krueger (1978) and Westphal (1978) both challenge this claim, however, after considering these so-called unique factors.

One allegation is that the Korean experience merely reflected catching up with other countries from the relatively low position in the mid-1950s due to the disruptions of two wars, decolonization, and partition in the previous one and one-half decades. Undoubtedly there is some merit to this claim for the late 1950s and perhaps for the early 1960s. But by the late 1960s Korea had caught up with international Chenery-type patterns, and yet the changes continued at a fast pace for more than another decade.

A second contention is that Korean exports benefited from unusual integration into the Japanese and U.S. markets, with the Japanese connection growing quickly. Again, there may be some truth to this contention, but the share of Korean exports to *other* markets grew from 30 to 49 percent between 1960 and 1979, which does not seem to be consistent with overemphasis of these two trading partners. Moreover, between these two countries the composition shift was away from faster-growing Japan to the slower-growing United States. (That is, Japan received 63 percent of all Korean exports in 1960 and only 22 percent in 1979; in contrast, the U.S. share increased from 7 percent in 1960 to 29 percent in 1979.) Finally, with the exception of offshore military procurement by the United States during the Vietnam War, neither Japan nor the United States has granted Korea any special preferences that were not available to other developing countries (although Westphal notes that there *may* have been subtle preferential treatment in regard to such policies as the allocation of textile import quotas by the United States).

A third belief is that Korea has benefited from other dimensions of commercial contacts, such as direct foreign investment and subcontracting, that have been fostered by its close ties with the United States and Japan. Again, this probably is not a major explanation. In regard to direct foreign investment, for example, Westphal (1978) estimates that no more than 5 percent of the total capital stock in manufacturing was financed by foreign direct investment in Korean manufacturing. In the 1970s foreign direct investment increased, but still averaged less than one-fifth of the increment. Although in some industries (notably electronics) wholly owned foreign subsidiaries accounted for a majority of exports, for all manufacturing exports their shares in the early 1970s were only 15 percent. The timing of much of the foreign direct investment, in fact, suggests that it was *in response to* the attractive conditions created by the Korean export boom, not the *cause* of the boom.

A fourth assertion is that Korea received very large reconstruction- and military-related-aid flows that facilitated economic development. Such inflows indeed were quite large in the 1950s, but that was not a high-growth era (although such inflows may have helped to satisfy the preconditions for later growth). Moreover, as noted earlier, in certain respects the U.N. military expenditures may have been counterproductive by encouraging overvaluation and too much of an inward orientation. In any case, the really high growth rates of the late 1960s and 1970s occurred after such aid had largely ended.

A fifth suggestion is that a very strong government made possible the continuity of export-promotion policies and prevented undue wage increases that would have made Korean exports noncompetitive. Certainly in recent years the Korean government has appeared very strong and repressive in regard to civil liberties. It also has long maintained continuity in regard to export promotion. But again, the story, is not that simple. In the initial years of export expansion, the government was not nearly as strong as is the case currently. Moreover, mentioned earlier, real wages in Korea have increased much more rapidly than they have in most of the world. Finally, a number of other developing countries have had very strong growth-oriented governments, but few have matched Korea's success.

Finally, some imply that other special factors inherited from the past (most notably, the highly educated population and the relatively equal distribution of assets [most importantly, land]) make the Korean experience very special. Again, there probably is some validity to this, but such an assertion is far from comprehensive. Indeed, Korea (and the other East Asian super exporters) does have a well-educated population and an even land distribution as compared with many developing countries; But one or both of these characteristics are shared with many other countries that have had far less economic success. Sri Lanka is a good example. The southern cone of Latin America probably long has had an equally or more-educated population as well.

In summary, many of these special factors probably have some relevance, but no single facet nor combination (although it always is difficult to be sure about the interaction effects that Adelman, 1980, suggests are quite large) seems to explain away the very important role of the outward-looking export-biased policy stance in explaining the Korean economic success of the past two decades.

Korean Experience and IPs

What has the role of IPs been in this experience? As we have noted, there have been a number of IPs in Korean policy. At the extreme, imports of some items have been precluded. State enterprises have functioned as well in some areas. Infant-industry arguments have been used to justify special treatment for particular industries.

But there are several striking dimensions to the Korean experience with IPs. They generally have been very export-oriented. Even very new infant industries have been encouraged to expand quickly into export markets,[4] and exporters have been given special access to the domestic market. As a result, one may view the somewhat complex Korean IPs more as a package of activity-oriented policies directed toward exporting than as truly industry-specific.

Because of this outward orientation, strong inducements for efficiency improvements to meet world competition in order to expand into new markets have accompanied the IPs rather than the protection of inefficiencies by IPs. The outward orientation also has limited the divergence in incentives across industries by limiting rents and by lessening the duration of erroneous policies. The variance in estimated effective protection rates used in the multivariate analysis of table 7-2 is relatively small for Korea. Thus the outward orientation of the general Korean policies has permitted the use of IPs for particular purposes without incurring the high costs due to inevitable mistakes and the creation of vested interests that so frequently have resulted from using IPs in developing countries.

Industrial Policy in Venezuela

Venezuelan industrialization plans have emphasized growth rather than distribution. The industrialization strategies have been limited by insufficient capital and market use. Increases in this factor have largely been met by imports of capital goods, and these imports have been financed by oil-export revenues.

Prior to the 1970s the need for foreign exchange, the almost-complete control of oil production by foreign oil companies, and the growing demand for oil in developed economies, placed Venezuela as a leading producer and exporter of oil. The nonrenewable nature of oil reserves favored the approach of rapid capital accumulation to create a large and diversified industrial base. This process of using foreign-exchange revenue to finance capital imports was denoted as *sowing the oil*.

The lack of concern for distributional matters led to an unequal income distribution[5] and, as a consequence, nutritional and educational provisions were far from sufficient for a large segment of the population. Moreover, this limited the access of a large part of the labor force to the industrialization process because of lacking skills, and to the products market because of too little income.

The emphasis given to production and growth over distribution has resulted in a relatively poor human-capital stock that has deepened the dependence on foreign supplies of skilled workers. The relevance of distributional issues has been explicitly recognized in recent plans, although it remains to be seen whether the Venezuelan IP will maximize production growth subject to a minimum of social achievements or vice versa. For more details see Merhav (1980) and Palma (1976).

Venezuelan Economic Structure and Development

On the economic-demographic front Venezuela is an oil-exporting country and a member of OPEC. The state owns the oil and the government manages the revenues derived from it. Oil revenues have enabled the government to carry out ambitious industrialization plans. However, the same oil revenue has allowed the existence of foreign competition in a relatively small market. According to U.N. reports, the Venezuelan population in 1980 numbered around 14 million persons, with an average annual growth rate (1950–1980) of 3.2 percent with approximately 40 percent of the population under 14 years old.

The history of industrialization efforts is short. Initial efforts were made during the Second World War due to cuts in foreign supplies of manufactured goods. However, this initial impulse was not longlasting because the accumulation of reserves during this period made possible the acquisition of foreign goods as soon as the war ended. The second attempt to industrialize Venezuela was during the 1950s and consisted of the substitution of imports for food-processing, beverage, and textile products. The policy instrument used was tariff protection for these products and reduction in tariffs for their intermediate and capital inputs. This policy resulted in high economic growth until 1958, when the military dictatorship, ruling since the early 1950s, was deposed.

After 1958, the growth rate of the economy slowed down due to the political chaos and to the weakening of the oil market. As a result, the new democratic government felt the need for more effective coordination of economic activity. Planning was seen as a way to achieve higher growth rates, and to this end, a central planning agency, CORDIPLAN, was created in December 1958. This date can be considered the starting point for serious efforts in industrialization policy in Venezuela. The main objective of CORDIPLAN is the formulation of a rational plan for the allocation of government resources. Although the government does not dictate private-sector policy, this plan indicates to the private sector how its main customer, the government, will function for the next five years.[6]

Before describing the policies that have been carried out, we shall explain briefly how the government implements its policies. Oil revenues are administered by the government; increasing government control over the oil industry gave the government great financial power. Thus the government can stimulate planned activities by lending money to private entrepreneurs, giving subsidies, and by purchasing goods and services from the private sector. In addition, the government participates directly in certain industries such as oil, iron ore, electricity, and water. Beyond its financial power, the government uses its legal power to give stimulus to key activities by building tariff walls, giving tax incentives, and preventing the development of activities contrary to the desired pattern of industrial growth.

Evaluation of Past Experience in Industrial Policy

The industrialization process, as suggested previously, has had as a main goal the rapid diversification of the productive structure of Venezuela. The achievement of this goal depends on three broadly defined factors: (1) low-cost mineral resources, cultivable land, and a large market; (2) capital equipment; and (3) human capital. Venezuela possesses low-cost mineral resources and cultivable land.[7] It does not have a large market given the relatively small population, however. Unequal income distribution and ability to import reduce even more the size of the market for domestic products. Capital equipment and human capital have been below the necessary levels to achieve a rapid rate of industrialization. Naturally, these last two elements have played a key role in understanding IP in Venezuela.

With respect to the need for capital goods in the industrialization process, government policy has consisted of: (1) tariff exemption for imported capital goods and intermediate goods (Palma 1976, Allen 1977, and Hassan 1975); (2) provision of financial support to firms through the Fondo Industrial de Crédito (Industrial Credit Fund). Funds are channeled to the private sector through several financial institutions at 9 percent (in 1974) and with three moratorium years. In addition, the Banco Industrial (Industrial Bank) makes short- and medium-term loans for activities related to production, transportation, storage, and so on. Other aspects of policy have been (3) disincentives for foreign investment for fear of further dependence as a result of more than fifty years of control by the oil companies over production and prices (Hassan 1975); and (4) tariff protection for manufactured goods. For example, the ad-valorem tariff for imported cars has been as high as 300 percent; more recently this high tariff applies to noncompetitive models. Tariff protection helped to expand the industry in its initial stages (Allen 1977, and Hassan 1975); in recent years, however, frequent tariff exemptions for manufactured goods coupled with licenses given to existing producers resulted in a very concentrated production structure and higher imports (Merhav 1980). This policy, coupled with insufficient human capital, resulted in an industrial structure dependent on modern, foreign techniques and production methods following the product characteristics and quality of competing imports.

The relevance of human capital was not seriously considered by the government until the 1960s. Centuries of Spanish tradition and agrarian activity conditioning the social structure and cultural orientation did not result in the development of human resources. Beginning in 1960, the government began a sizable educational program as well as technical schools and training programs such as the internship program (in which science students spent time working in industries). Nevertheless, the late start of these programs resulted in a lack of skilled labor and limited the achievement of higher growth rates of production in the industrial sector.[8] The result has been more capital-intensive techniques (foreign supplied) in production activities, thus reducing market size. This process prevented higher growth rates in domestic capital-goods industries.

We turn now to a comparison of the differences between targets and achievement for the growth rate of manufacturing as shown in table 15-1. Hassan (1975) attributes the difference between the actual growth rate and the planned growth rates to insufficient demand. As we will show, a radical change has occurred since the increases in oil prices in the fall of 1973. Table 15-2 shows the difference between planned and actual industrial diversification.

In table 15-2, Hassan (1975) says that the industrialization process has not been successful. He argues that the national plan is also a political document reflecting the government's philosophy and that there is little disagreement in Venezuela about the fundamental goals of the plan. Therefore the

Table 15-1
Percent Average Annual Growth Rate of Manufacturing under the Four Five-Year Industrialization Plans

	First Plan	Second Plan	Third Plan	Fourth Plan
Years	1960–1964	1963–1966	1965–1968	1970–1974
Planned growth	14.4	13.5	10.8	9.4
Actual growth	9.2	7.9	5.4	6.4

Source: Hassan (1975).

policy criterion is not an adequate evaluation criterion; thus one is left with the goal-achievement criterion.

An alternative criterion, suggested by Allen (1977), although not measurable, is the degree of improvement in economic decision making. Although actual growth rates are short of planned ones, planning and IP in Venezuela are successful in the sense that the plans not only improve economic decisions made by the public sector but the help in continuous self-improvement.

In summary, a main goal of Venezuelan IP has been an increase in the living conditions of the population; this has been sought by increasing the rate of growth of the manufacturing sector as a way to reduce the dependence of future growth on oil activity. This industrialization process has employed low-cost materials, and it has been possible to finance the purchase of capital goods by the foreign exchange generated by oil exports. The availability of foreign exchange coupled with unequal income distribution, however, slowed down the growth of the domestic market. Tariffs for manufactures were a useful policy instrument in the early stages of industrialization. Recent experience shows a negative balance for this policy due to poor implementation by the government. In addition, investment in human capital has been scanty. Human resources, economic nationalism, foreign competition, and attitudes toward industrialization and foreign products have been the limiting factors in achieving a higher rate of growth in the industrial sector.

Industrial Policy Plan for the Period 1981–1985

The ultimate goal of the plan for 1981 to 1985 does not differ from previous plans insofar as it stresses the improvement of the living conditions of the population through diversifying manufacturing activities away from oil production. However, Venezuela experienced significant changes during the 1970s. The large increases in the price of oil gave the government huge

Table 15-2
Diversification Achievement
(percent share in GDP terminal years)

Industry	1964 Target	1964 Actual	1966 Target	1966 Actual	1968 Target	1968 Actual	1974 Target	1974 Actual
Agriculture	6.5	7.1	7.2	7.3	6.4	7.2	6.6	7.6
Petroleum	21.7	27.0	19.2	24.9	18.8	24.2	14.1	14.5
Mining	2.6	1.2	1.3	1.2	1.4	1.0	1.2	1.0
Manufacturing	15.4	14.4	20.0	14.7	19.8	14.9	23.2	21.1
Construction	5.2	4.6	6.6	4.8	6.2	5.3	6.5	4.8
Commerce	15.6	15.1	14.3	16.3	15.4	16.0	18.7	11.7
Services	33.0	30.6	31.4	30.8	32.0	31.4	29.7	39.3
Total	100.0	100.0	100.0	100.0	100.0	100.0	100.0	100.0

Source: Adapted from Hassan (1975).

financial power, which was used to stimulate the economy, during the late 1970s to the point that the excess demand for manufactures had to be met by increasing volumes of imports, obviously financed with oil revenues. This partially impaired the possibilities of reducing the relevance of oil in the industrialization process.

Problems of the Industrial Sector. According to the plan of 1981-1985, the main reason for sluggish growth in the manufacturing sector are the following:

1. Full-capacity utilization with no incentives to expand. The lack of incentives to invest in the manufacturing sector is due to rigid price ceilings for manufactured final goods but not for intermediate goods and labor. The absence of price controls in sectors of the economy such as services resulted in rates of return unfavorable to manufacturing. In addition, insufficient labor with adequate quality for both top managerial positions and research activities dampened the possibilities to grow at a faster rate.
2. The incentives to stimulate manufactured exports are outdated. Furthermore, high labor costs and domestic prices have reduced export possibilities. In addition, the increasing amounts of imports of capital goods have prevented the development of a domestic industry to produce these capital goods.
3. Reduced market size and minimum size for a plant have resulted in production concentrated in a small number of firms with monopolistic price-setting behavior, in spite of the demand increase experienced in 1973-1978 that would have allowed more firms.[9]
4. Inefficiencies in the manufacturing sector arising out of the overprotection given by the government in the form of tariff walls. Similarly, although not specifically mentioned in the plan, protective labor laws resulted in no motivation to self-improvement by the workers.
5. Price ceilings were put most emphatically on massive consumption goods. These goods experienced sluggish growth as mentioned earlier, resulting in a deterioration of living conditions for the majority of the population.

Industrial-Policy Targets

Now that the government's perception of the problems of the industrial sector has been pointed out, the IP targets as follows are understandable:

1. higher growth rate for the nonoil-manufacturing sector (diversification target)
2. increases in productivity
3. greater technological independence
4. import substitution of capital goods and export promotion of manufactured goods
5. development of a more active financial market

In addition to the targets, the IP plan has established higher priorities for certain sectors. These priorities are determined partly by the government's perception of the most pressing social problems. Nationalism and economic viability are also taken into account. The sectors with highest priorities are those whose production is subject to massive consumption—namely, food processing, building materials, and pharmaceuticals. The industries providing capital goods, intermediate goods, and chemical products also have high priority.

Policies and Policy Instruments

The goal of a higher growth rate for the nonoil-manufacturing sector can be achieved only to the extent that some of the other goals are also achieved. In this sense, the diversification of the economy becomes an ultimate goal and the remaining targets become necessary conditions to be met in order to achieve the diversification target.

Among the various policies to achieve higher technological independence and higher productivity are:

1. Creation and stimulation of links among research centers to generate increasing domestic research.
2. Government financial support to firms employing technology developed in the country and to firms engaged in research-and-development activities. This government support takes the form of tax exemption on profits reinvested in research-and-development activities as well as profits arising out of this kind of activity.
3. Discouragement of simple technological transfers from abroad as in turnkey projects and more emphasis on cooperation among members of the Andean Pact.

The import-substitution policy will be based on the use of the effective tariff protection (to value-added) to protect industries producing capital goods. In regard to the export-promotion policy, the government will give financial support (in the form of lower interest rates, availability of funds, and flexible periods of maturity) to firms engaged in exports of capital goods and chemical products.

The policies just mentioned deal directly with their respective targets. There is another kind of policy that tries to achieve the targets in an indirect way; for the Venezuelan case we find, among others, the following:

1. Human-resource policy. The purpose here is to expand the number of programs designed to increase human capital, such as training programs and tax credits on such programs.
2. Foreign-investment policy. This policy's main objective is to control the amount and type of foreign investment subject to national interests and to the regulations of the Andean Pact.
3. Pricing policy. This policy ensures that there will be price regulation in sectors with a large concentration of production in a few private firms.
4. Public-investment policy. According to this policy, there will be more government participation in sectors with a monopolistic production structure or in sectors with large capital requirements.
5. Commercial policy. This policy is designed to expand the number of wholesalers in conjunction with small and medium enterprises. In addition, the government will build the infrastructure needed to stimulate commercial activity such as harbors, roads, and storage and distribution centers.

Although the Sixth National Plan recognizes the increasing importance of income distribution, it follows the traditional pattern of placing the highest priority on growth.

Conclusions

The Venezuelan plans call for information that is unavailable and that makes evaluation difficult. Hassan points to the lack of statistical information as one of the causes of failure in achieving the targeted growth rates.

The underlying philosophy of the plans and their objectives has been clear: the plans have been traditional in their import-substitution orientation. This is perhaps understandable in view of Venezuela's resources and capital availability, although the lack of a highly skilled labor force and an insufficiently large domestic market have stood in the way of achievement of the plans' objectives. Indeed, the problems associated with import-substitution policies in a small country (discussed in chapter 7 of this book) are clearly apparent in many aspects of the Venezuelan experience.

Industrial Policy in India

IP in India has been far less triumphant than the success stories of Taiwan and Korea. There are, nevertheless, important lessons to be gained by reviewing the progress of IP in India. This section sketches India's IPs' evolution from 1956 onward and comments on its role in India's economic development.

It is important to view India's IP in the context of the general philosophy of economic planning adopted by the state. Nehru (1960), India's first prime minister, wrote of Britain's colonization of India, that the economy of India had thus advanced to as high a stage as it could reach prior to the industrial revolution but foreign political domination led to a rapid destruction of the economy India had built up, without anything positive or constructive taking its place. When India became independent in 1947, one of the goals that occurred to its leaders was to accelerate the process of growth and simultaneously in order to make it socially more purposive. IP was a natural outgrowth of this, and with the Second Five Year Plan (1956–1961), became especially important in controlling the pattern of investments. This was because, in contrast to the First Five Year Plan (1951–1956), which concentrated on agriculture and was based on a Harrod-Domar type model that emphasized savings and required investment, the second plan was *structural* and was industry-specific in nature and emphasized certain basic, heavy industries. Officials believed that the long-run rate of growth would be a function of investments in the heavy, capital-goods sector (Bhagwati and Desai 1970). The second plan consequently set in motion two components of policy that were to have a strong impact on the economic efficiency of the state in India: (1) industrial targeting and licensing and (2) exchange control and the licensing of imports of capital goods, intermediates, and consumer goods (Bhagwati and Srinivasan 1975).

Industrial Policy Resolution, 1956

India remains something of an enigma to westerners, as this quotation from *The Economist* (1981) indicates:

> ... image ... most westerners have of the Indian economy [is] ... like this: on the one hand, surprisingly advanced industry ... which has launched a space rocket, produces its own computers and imports virtually no consumer goods. On the other hand, backward agriculture, where millions of peasants scrape an inadequate living from parched earth ...[9]

To a hardheaded Indian economist or political analyst, however, the fabled land of contrasts presents a somewhat less romantic image. The problem is ultimately a question of ends and means. It is with this attitude that the progress of IP will be examined. The Industral Policy Resolution of 1956 (IPR-56) had the following objectives:

1. enlarging the role of the public sector and government
2. preventing monopoly and the concentration of economic power
3. promoting small-scale industry and balanced regional development
4. increasing industrial output and employment opportunities in industry

Other important objectives have included reducing self-reliance on foreign capital and encouraging import substitution (implicit in the desire to increase the importance of capital goods and intermediates in industrial production). There are three levels at which these objectives can be examined:

1. To what extent have they been achieved? This is discussed in the following text.
2. Are they consistent? If not, what kind of trade-offs are desirable? For example, intermediate-goods industries such as steel, aluminum, soda ash, caustic soda, petrochemicals, and so on, are very capital-intensive. They are also marked by pronounced economies of scale. Consequently, there is a conflict between larger plants and the need to conserve scarce capital on the one hand and preventing concentration of economic power on the other. At the same time, by recognizing comparative advantage, one could resort to foreign trade and combine this with domestic production to achieve scale economies. The involvement of foreign technology is often unavoidable, but foreign technology and foreign capital tend to go together, and foreign collaborators may be reluctant to team up with any but a large industrial house. This conflicts with goal of self-reliance.[10] Thus trade-offs are inevitable, making it necessary to *recognize* the need for trade-offs and to plan for them.
3. Are they the *right* objectives? This is, of course, a normative question and cannot be dissociated from political consideration, a classic example being afforded by the devaluation of the Indian rupee in 1966.[11]

Toward its objectives, IPR-56 classified industries as follows:

1. Schedule A named industries that would be the exclusive responsibility of the state, including atomic energy, defence equipment, shipbuilding,

air and rail transport, important mineral resources, iron and steel, and so on.
2. Schedule B listed industries in which the state would progressively expand its ownership, with private enterprise expected to supplement the efforts of the government in these industries. These included sea and road transport, antibiotics and essential drugs, fertilizer, synthetic rubber, and so on.
3. All other industries would generally be left to the initiative and enterprise of the private sector.

Clearly IP in India has seldom been spelled out in terms of ISPs. An important exception is the case of sick textile mills, where legislation was specifically enacted to aid or take over such mills, with the formation of the National Textiles Corporation (NTC); but apart from crises in specific industries or complaints directed against them, IP has been geared to provide general guidelines and protection. In general, it has not been based on the principles of neoclassical economic theory. Only in recent years has specific project evaluation been prescribed for large, public investments (for example, by the Project Appraisal Division of the Planning Commission, which uses cost-benefit analysis). Although reducing the concentration of economic power has been cited as a major objective, the quagmire of industrial licensing red tape, and the corruption it has caused—a natural consequence of trading off opportunity loss with the payments necessary for speeding up processing—has in many cases helped create oligopolistic or monopolistic structures, a prime example being automobiles.

Two reports examining the impact of industrial licensing and policy were prepared at the instance of the government. The principal findings of the Hazari Committee (1967) and Dutt Committee (1969) were:

1. Concentration of economic power had increased, with a few large industrial houses getting a disproportionately large share of the licenses issued. The same was true of foreign collaborations.
2. The majority of licenses had been granted to a few states, with excessive concentration in metropolitan areas, thus aggravating imbalances in regional development.
3. *Capacity* targets were overemphasized at the cost of *output* targets.
4. A few large industrial houses tended to preempt capacity by applying for licenses that were sometimes not implemented, thereby strengthening monopoly power.

Later Policy Pronouncements

The government announced a new IP in 1970, following it up with a major announcement in February 1973 and the Foreign Exchange Regulation Act of 1973. The policy had two essentially new features:

1. It went into an elaborate classification of industries. The core sector and the export-oriented-industries sectors are relevant. The first consisted of a list of industries prepared in consultation with the planning commission, which were considered of basic and strategic importance to the economy. Core industries would be the ones where large industrial houses and dominantly foreign companies would be permitted to participate with the minimum of red tape and with several concessions, the most important being priority allocation of foreign exchange. The reason was that these industries are seen as having important linkages with the rest of the economy and therefore are considered basic to the process of economic growth. The second consisted of those industries that are primarily geared for export. These involved attractive concessions (for example, a foreign company exporting 100 percent of output need not issue any equity locally).
2. It enlarged the role of the private and foreign sectors, which is contrary to what was envisaged in 1956.

Policy with Respect to Multinational Companies

Multinational companies (MNCs) have been an important factor both for foreign-exchange-related issues and the acquisition of technical know-how. The operation of MNCs and their subsidiaries in India may be indicatively (though not exhaustively) classified as follows:

1. Those engaged in producing consumer goods and cosmetics. The bulk of these products is aimed at the relatively well-off metropolitan or big-town resident.
2. Those producing antibiotics and drugs and pharmaceuticals. Allegations against such companies have included:
   a) exorbitant prices
   b) concentration on exotic formulations, cough syrups, and multivitamins, which are aimed at the already well-nourished segment of society; and relative neglect of vaccines and essential life-saving drugs;

c) operation in a manner irrelevant to the Indian social and economic context.
3. Those engaged in services (for example, banking, insurance, travel agencies, and so on).
4. Those engaged in the transfer of sophisticated technology. An important point here is that the extent to which an LDC is willing to tolerate, and even encourage, the presence of an MNC is positively related to the perceived benefits from its operations. As an extreme example, contrast a company that uses the latest in engineering technology with one engaged in making chewing gum or a carbonated drink.

There are obvious gains on both sides: a large, diverse market for the MNC, and access to both sophisticated technology and equipment on the part of the LDC along with the attendant managerial skills. The government therefore needs to balance three conflicting, but nonetheless compatible, objectives:

1. conserve and build up scarce foreign exchange and put it to the socially most advantageous use
2. give MNCs, especially those that could contribute to export earnings and the transfer of know-how, sufficient incentive to operate within the country
3. ensure that the MNC is not using the country as a dumping ground for obsolete equipment or luxury goods aimed at the upper-income strata

As an attempt to conserve foreign exchange and optimize its social use, the government passed the Foreign Exchange Regulation Act 1973 (FERA). Section 29 of FERA effectively defines a foreign company as one in which the nonresident interest is more than 40 percent. All companies satisfying this definition would find it extremely difficult to expand or diversify unless they diluted foreign equity holding to less than 40 percent. Concessions would be made to predominantly export-oriented companies. Further, guidelines were set for the Indian component of the cost of an expansion relative to the extent of foreign holding, (for example, companies with foreign holdings exceeding 75 percent are required to raise 40 percent of the estimated cost of expansion by issuing additional equity capital to Indians).

MNCs and their subsidiaries reacted differently to the restrictions on their activities and the repatriation of foreign exchange. Some diluted their capital and went into export-oriented industries or even diversified into totally unrelated businesses (for example, from tobacco to hotels), financing all expansion by locally raised equity. Others, like one engaged in computers and another in manufacturing a soft drink, opted to get out of business. The computer company, despite being extremely advanced, confined its manufacturing activities to card punches and the overhauling of obsolete data processors brought from abroad. The soft-drink company, apart from being an insignificant foreign-exchange earner, spent considerable foreign exchange in importing a concentrate for its soft drink from abroad.

Concluding Remarks

A rational economist's evaluation of India's experience with planning and IP is perhaps typified by the summing up of Bhagwati and Desai (1970, chap. 23). The authors conclude that Indian planning concentrated excessively on detailed "targets down to the product level, and a wasteful physical approach to setting and implementation thereof, along with a generally inefficient framework of economic policies designed to regulate the growth of industrialisation." They concede, however, that toward the end of the 1960s, "India was beginning to learn the basic lesson that costs mattered. cost-benefit calculations had to be increasingly made, alternative projects needed to be weighed against one another, and the framework of trade, exchange rate, and investment policies had to be carefully designed to exploit India's advantages in the availability of enterprise, efficient administration, education, and a tradition of growing industrialization (over a century)."

One cannot help speculating what might have been had the government placed greater reliance on market forces of if they had adopted export promotion instead of import substitution. A simulation regarding this latter aspect was done by Bhagwati and Srinivasan (1975, chap. 14). Their conclusion was that additional exports would have paid for themselves by increasing investment and growth in the future and that a policy of promoting exports more energetically would have produced better economic results.

In conclusion, we should state that while a numbers-game approach to evaluating the role of IP is valid and necessary, it is also essential to look at certain social and cultural factors, such as the power structure prevalent in Indian society and its linkages with economic and political processes. This is particularly true of the rural areas. Thus as a recent economic survey of India (*The Economist,* 1981) concluded: "Romantics say that India's past lies in its villages; shorn of romance, so does its future."

Industrial Policy in Brazil

The Brazilian government has played an extensive and innovative role in Brazilian economic growth through development policies, investment in infrastructure, and through state enterprises. As in most developing economies, IPs in Brazil have been closely interwined with other aspects of policy, particularly balance-of-payments policy. Instead of one consistent policy path in the postwar period, one can observe adaptation of policy directions to the needs of the economy so that the policy experience must be summarized in a number of distinct phases. This chapter summarizes the main elements of IP in Brazil during the postwar years.

Economic Setting and Development Perspective

While the outside world until recently has seen Brazil on the brink of economic development, the growth experience in Brazil goes back considerably further than is generally appreciated.[12] Yet the development of Brazil into a modern industrial country remains largely a postwar phenomenon. While government policy participated actively in fostering this development, it is clearly as much a result of the economic environment as of the policies.

Industrialization Period: 1945-1961. In the post-World War II period Brazil moved to a new industrialization phase shaped by an explicit strategy. In contrast to earlier Brazilian industrial progress, this industrialization resulted from encouraging key sectors: consumer durables, basic intermediate products, and eventually capital goods. These were sectors where, at least from a static point of view, Brazil's comparative advantage was not clear, but where there were prospects for dynamic comparative advantage as the industries moved down the learning curve and as scale economies were achieved.

The initial policy steps toward import substitutions were largely motivated by balance-of-payments problems. Beginning with import licensing, then turning toward a multiple-exchange-rate system, and finally in 1957 with heavy tariff protection, import substitution was based on the so-called Law of Similars, which prohibited or restricted importation of goods for which domestic substitutes were available.

The early part of the period also saw increasing government activity including planning, though on a very aggregate and minimal basis: the five-year SALTE Plan in 1948; the cooperation with the United States in the Joint Brazil-United States Technical Commission and the Joint Brazil-United States Development Commission known as the Comissao Mista; the setting up of national and regional development banks; and finally, the start of some resource-development enterprises under national auspices, the most notable of which is Petrobras.

The development impetus reached its strongest pace under government encouragement in the administration of President Kubitschek beginning in 1956. This period saw the development of a Target Program by the National

Development Council and of Executive Groups for specific industrial sectors. These steps were clearly industry-specific. The Target Program was concerned with the industries that would be the basis for further rapid industrialization. Specific targets were set for basic industries including steel, aluminum, cement, cellulose, automotive, heavy-machinery, and chemicals. Infrastructure investment focused on elimination of actual and projected bottlenecks. There was also concern with education, particularly training of technical manpower. The executive groups were charged with reorganizing the development of specific industries. The clearest example of this was the setting up of a wholly indigenous automobile-manufacturing industry. Other examples include major expansions of cement, paper and pulp, starting of the shipbuilding industry, steel, heavy-mechanical, electrical-equipment, and tractor production; much of this industrial development was done with foreign assistance. The tariff program was used to protect the growing domestic industries and to block importation of equivalent products from abroad; there were substantial incentives to encourage foreign investment.

The most striking monument to this era of rapid development is undoubtedly the new capital city of Brasilia. This represents a highly project-specific effort, intended to refocus the energies of the country from the coastline to its interior. It turned into a crash program, undoubtedly highly wasteful of resources, and a source of many of the economic difficulties that were to follow. But looking back—and particularly not checking too carefully on what else could have been achieved with the same resources—Brasilia appears as an important focus for Brazilian energies and a step in the direction of organizing government activities around a new center. This represents an important intersection between regional development and IP.

The ending of this period of rapid development showed the Brazilian economy with a vastly accelerated inflation rate and with increasing difficulties on the balance of payments.

Mid-1960s: Period of Slow Growth. One can argue that the slower period of growth that followed in the mid-1960s was a natural outcome of the overheating and of the emphasis on import substitution industrialization that preceded it.

As import-substituting industries reached full potential, they did not quickly produce goods as efficiently nor in as great variety as the world market. Moreover, import substitution reaches a natural limit when products that can be produced domestically, at least with reasonable efficiency, are produced domestically. But the sources of slower growth probably lie more in the need to restrain the economy to control inflation, which was tackled with aggregate economic policy and with the innovation of indexing.

An important aspect of this period, which was not to pay off until later, was the turn toward export promotion and more realistic foreign-exchange policy and renewed encouragement of foreign investment under the administration of President Branco. This period can be seen as one of retreat from industry-specific development policy and a time (if not a successful one) of stabilizing with a turn toward traditional monetary and fiscal aggregate-stabilization tools.

Second Growth Period: Late 1960s to Mid-1970s. The next period of growth follows the switch in policy in the late 1960s under the economic-growth strategy of Delfim Netto and lasts to the problems associated with the high cost of petroleum and the growing burden of the foreign debt in the mid-1970s. After the years of slow economic growth and fairly conventional anti-inflationary policy of the 1960s, under the government of General Costa e Silva the new finance minister, Delfim Netto, sought a new growth strategy. On the one side, restraining aggregate-demand policies were eased, with improvement in the availability of credit, more complete indexing of the minimum wage to the increases in the price level, and tax reforms to provide the government's growing revenue needs. The extension of policies of credit and wage indexing as well as the policy of minidevaluation made possible the expansion that seemed to stimulate real growth more than inflation. Another important feature was the increasing emphasis on a growth strategy based on foreign trade and, specifically, a drive to increase and diversify exports. This was not so much an ISP as it was a sector-specific, providing important tax and credit incentives to the export industries based in large part, of course, on the industries that earlier had had encouragement for import substitution. Another feature of this period was further large investments in infrastructure and in housing.

During this period, state-owned enterprises assumed a very important role. In 1971, for example, of the top twenty-five firms in Brazil ranked by assets, seventeen were government companies. Among the one thousand largest companies in Brazil as of 1973, state-controlled companies represented 50 percent of net book value and 17 percent of total sales.[13] While these enterprises are government controlled, they maintain considerable autonomy and in many cases they retain a minority private-ownership interest, some of which is traded actively in Brazilian stock exchanges.

The public enterprises have become dominant in the infrastructure fields, electricity, communications, and so on, but they have also moved aggressively into conventional large-scale business fields such as banking, steel, petroleum (Petrobras), petrochemicals, and mining. In banking, the government has a controlling interest in Banco do Brasil, which engages in commercial-banking activities as well as other activities carried out by a central bank and by many of the regional development banks. In steel, government enterprises play a major role, as they do in mining and other natural-resources development.

Brazilian policy with respect to foreign enterprises has also been an important consideration. With the exception of certain fields such as minerals and petrochemicals, these firms have not been required to form joint enterprises with local firms, but many of them have significant local-equity participation. Their operation has been supervised closely—for example, by the industry commissions—and these firms have developed in accord with Brazilian IP objectives, in many cases contributing an important dynamism and a high level of skill to Brazilian industry. Examples of the types of rules applied have been the traditional local-content requirements, which succeeded in bringing the automobile industry to self sufficiency, the incentives for stimulating foreign companies to export from the Brazilian market, and more recently, efforts to persuade them to do research and technical development in Brazil.

But this period was to come to an end finally on the sharply increasing rate of inflation, the prodigous growth of foreign debt and the balance of payments deficits associated with petroleum imports and debt service.

Post-Oil-Crisis Period. As for other developing countries that are on balance petroleum consumers, the rise in oil prices has been a heavy burden for Brazil. This has been intensified, since Brazil has developed an extensive automobile fleet and since transportation is heavily dependent on trucking and buses. Nevertheless, Brazil has managed (until 1980) to survive without a serious recession. Economic performance in the late 1970s must be characterized as a stop-go policy, and finally, 1981 saw a serious recession episode.

There had been resistance to application of the traditional antiinflationary tools of monetary and fiscal policy in 1979, leading to the transition of the planning ministry from Simonsen to Delfim Netto, who was considered the economic wizard behind the earlier period of expansion. Delfim announced a supply-side policy that aimed to stimulate agriculture, a sector with huge potential in Brazil but that had been allowed to lag in the growing effort toward industrialization. New financial incentives were provided for agriculture in the form of minimum prices and credits, and these have had the effect of substantial growth in agriculture in general and in export crops such as soy, sugar, coffee, cocoa, and, lately, frozen orange juice in particular. This represented a new IP focus. It also relates to agricultural development's focusing on improved utilization of the Matto Grosso lands.

At the same time, additional incentives to exports and the slowness of domestic demand due to aggregate economic policy, have stimulated the export performance of the Brazilian economy to a point where in the early 1980s exports of manufactures have accounted for more than half of the Brazilian export earnings. It is interesting to note that export-promotion policies have not supplanted import-substitution policies. Insofar as possible, import substitution has been extended to capital goods as well as consumer products, and Brazil is making explicit efforts to achieve transmission of new technologies and development of advanced industries such as aircraft and small computers.

Energy policy, in response to high petroleum prices, has been a particular focus of IP. Brazil announced and put into place a policy of rapidly expanding alcohol production based on sugar to supply a significant fraction of domestic automotive needs by 1985. At the same time, efforts have been made by Petrobras to expand production of petroleum, hydroelectric development schemes have been undertaken, and coal development is planned. Nuclear-power plants under construction may turn out to take longer and be more costly than had been originally envisioned.

In other industries—particularly those connected with available resources—Brazilian government policy has been active in large part with cooperation of foreign investors. Pressures from the debt burden and the need to continuously refinance the outstanding debt and the problems associated with the high inflation rate have led to macropolicies of restraint which represent the proximate cause of the 1981 and 1983 recessions. The effort at outward-oriented export-promotion development both in industry and agriculture can be considered part of Brazilian policy into the 1980s.

Role of Industrial Policy

What, then, has been the role of IP in Brazilian economic development? And what will be the role of IP in the future?

It is apparent from the foregoing discussion that in Brazil IP must be seen in a very broad perspective. Policies have evolved, reflecting the priorities of the broader policy approaches of which they have been a part. Thus emphasis on import substitution came when balance-of-payments considerations were dominant and as opportunities for import substitution were exhausted, efforts were made in the direction of export promotion. Similarly, as the lag in Brazilian agriculture became seriously apparent more recently, with the need to import foodstuffs, increased efforts were made to stimulate agriculture.

Brazilian IP thus aimed at economic development and at the balance-of-payments problems with policy measures that are sector-specific rather than industry-specific. But it also incorporates some narrowly industry- or project-specific public intervention. Among these have been the organization of privately controlled industries like automobiles as well as the actions of semiautonomous public corporations (Petrobras and others) in resource development and public utilities and transportation and communication.

The mixture of policy mechanisms used in Brazil is typical of the innovative policy approach taken in this country. Import quotas, tariffs, deposit schemes, price controls, and credit adjustment have all served at one time or another to limit imports and to stimulate the domestic production of import substitutes. Administrative measures to achieve domestic production strategies have also been applied, although, as in the case of the motor-vehicle industry, with the cooperation, willing or unwilling, of the foreign-owned private firms. Export promotion has similarly been achieved with a mixture of mechanisms such as subsidies, tax concessions, preferential credits, import schemes conditional on exports, minidevalutaion, and so on.

A variety of measures have also been used more recently to encourage agricultural production and exports. These schemes have involved increasing agricultural minimum prices and, to a very substantial extent, providing preferential credits to agriculture. There is also substantial public participation and direction in the huge resource development and hydroelectric projects now in construction, Carajas and Itaipu, for example. Overall, Brazil presents a very complex picture of regulations and incentives, varying over time, which are intended to achieve the objectives of development and balance-of-payments equilibrium.

How can one evaluate whether these policies have been successful? From the point of view of aggregate economic performance, Brazil has done very well over the postwar period, even though there have been periods of interrupted growth, balance-of-payments disequilibrium, and rapid inflation. From the point of view of economic performance at the industrial level, there is again at least superficial evidence of good performance. With the advantage of a large market, Brazilian industry has made the country largely self-sufficient in consumer goods and in many capital goods as well. A massive automobile industry has been developed that appears to have substantial gains from economies of scale. On the other hand, it is not possible to make a quick judgment on whether this industry will be technically innovative, whether it will produce a sufficient mix of vehicles, or whether it will be able to profitably participate in world-export markets. On the other hand, recent success of Brazilian export industry suggests that, at least with the types of direct incentives and exchange-rate-policy support provided, Brazilian exports can be competitive in world markets. The success of Brazilian industry in developing new markets, particularly in the LDCs, is worth noting.

Finally, with respect to ISP and, particularly with respect to Brazilian public or semipublic enterprises, the questions are somewhat more serious. The record of Petrobras in finding and developing oil resources is not as good as had been hoped, although it is difficult to say whether this reflects the lack of oil resources, the difficulty of locating oil formations under Brazilian geologic and geographic conditions, or simply the problem of large publicly owned and managed enterprises. Problems associated with other large enterprises under public ownership raise similar issues. The recent problems of the nuclear-power program, similar though they are to those encountered in other countries, nevertheless point to the difficulties of public enterprise where decisions are sometimes dominated by political considerations. The alcohol program is another instance where it is difficult to reach conclusions on purely economic grounds.

What then are the prospects for the future? In the current period of stabilization and retrenchment, dominated by the difficulties of the balance of payments and foreign debt and the high inflation rate, IP becomes all the more important. The success at stimulating agricultural output and the effectiveness of Brazil's manufactured-goods exports are positive signs for sectoral policies that use the carrot rather than the stick. Also, there are ample opportunities for such policies to move agricultural output and industrial production still further. On the other hand, the growing competitiveness of world markets and the growing barriers will pose a challenge—one that is all the more serious as a result of the high level of technological development and product quality being achieved by Brazil's export competitors in the Far East.

Notes

1. In more recent years (1980-1981) Korea was, however, subject to severe recession.

2. Among the numerous studies of interest are Adelman (1969, 1974); Adelman and Robinson (1978); Balassa (1971); Brown (1973); Cole and Lyman (1971); Frank, Kim, and Westphal (1975); Hsing (1975); Hassan (1976); Hong and Krueger (1975); Hong (1976); Kim (1970); Lee (1980); Ranis (1980); Renaud (1976); Rao (1978); Wang (1975); Westphal (1971, 1978); and Westphal and Kim (1977). I draw particularly on Westphal (1978).

3. Economic problems remain. For example, inflation has remained high (an annual average increase in the GDP deflator of 13.7 percent in 1965-1970, of 15-3 percent in 1970-1975, and of 17.3 percent in 1975-1979) which may be attributed to less monetary discipline than in the also-spectacular experience of Taiwan. (Nevertheless, Korean rates have declined relative to the rest of the world.) Also, Ranis (1980) rates the Taiwanese experience higher in regard to income distribution, in part because of relatively more rural investment.

4. Although some seem to assume the contrary, there is nothing in legitimate infant-industry arguments that necessarily favors import substitution over export promotion.

5. According to a recent study (Merhav 1980), the poorest half of the population has only 15 percent of total family income. For commercial purposes, the market is constituted by the richest third of the population, which holds 75 percent of total family income.

6. For instance, the decision to expand the electrical network led to an increase in the private production of transformers, cables, and poles to meet the demand for these products (other examples can be found in U.S. (1976) and U.S. (1979).

7. Besides oil reserves, Venezuela has 912,050 square kilometers of which only 1 percent was used for crops in 1960 (Allen 1977).

8. This lack of skills cannot be easily solved. It is not only a matter of more schooling. Around two-thirds of the labor force had deficient infant nutritional levels, possibly leading to mental damage (Merhav 1980).

9. In 1961 there were 7,531 enterprises, of which 1 percent were large, 1,119 medium size, and 6,216 small (by Venezuelan standards). In 1970 the number of firms declined to 5,945 with more than 325 large enterprises (Allen 1977, and Merhav 1980).

10. For an interesting comment on IP in India, see Desai (1974).

11. See Bhagwati and Srinivasan (1975, chap. 10).

12. For a detailed discussion, see Robock (1975) and Baer (1965).

13. See Baer, Villela, and Kerstenetsky (1973).

References

Adelman, Irma. (1969). *Practical Approaches to Development Planning: Korea's Second Five-Year Plan.* Baltimore: Johns Hopkins University Press.

Adelman, Irma. (1974). "South Korea," in Hollis Chenery, et al., eds., *Redistribution and Growth.* London: Oxford University Press, for the World Bank and the Institute of Development Studies, University of Sussex.

Adelman, Irma, and Sherman Robinson. (1978). *Income Distribution Policy in Developing Countries: A Case Study of Korea.* Stanford: Stanford University Press.

Allen, Loring. (1977). *Venezuelan Economic Development: A Politico-Economic Analysis.* New York: Jai Press.

Baer, Werner. (1965). *Industrialization and Economic Development in Brazil.* Homewood, Ill.: Richard D. Irwin.

Baer, Werner. (1979). *The Brazilian Economy: Growth and Development.* Columbus, Oh.: Grid Publications.

Baer, Werner, Annibal V. Villela, and Isaac Kerstenetsky. (1973). "The Changing Role of the State in the Brazilian Economy." *World Development* 1.

Balassa, Bela. (1971). "Industrial Policies in Taiwan and Korea," *Weltwirtschaftsliches Archiv* 114, pp. 24-61.
Bhagwati, Jagdish, and T.N. Srinivasan. (1975). *Foreign Trade Regimes and Economic Development: India.* New York: Columbia University Press, for NBER.
Bhagwati, Jagdish, and Padma Desai. (1970). *India: Planning for Industrialization.* Oxford: Oxford University Press.
Brown, Gilbert T. (1973). *Korean Pricing Policies and Economic Development in the 1960s.* Baltimore: Johns Hopkins University Press.
Cole, David C., and Princeton, N. Lyman. (1971). *Korean Development: The Interplay of Politics and Economics.* Cambridge, Mass.: Harvard University Press.
Desai, Nitin. (1974). "Industrial Policy," in Sandesara, ed., *The Indian Economy: Performance and Prospects.* Bombay: University of Bombay.
Dutt, S. (1969). *Report of the Industrial Licensing Policy Inquiry Committee.* New Delhi: Government of India, Ministry of Industrial Development.
The Economist, March 28, 1981.
Frank, Charles R., Jr., Kwang Suk Kim, and Larry E. Westphal. (1975). *Foreign Trade Regimes and Economic Development: South Korea.* New York: National Bureau of Economic Research.
Hasan, Parvez. (1976). *Korea: Problems and Issues in a Rapidly Growing Economy.* Baltimore and London: Johns Hopkins University Press for the World Bank.
Hassan, Mostafa. (1975). *Economic Growth and Employment Problems in Venezuela: An Analysis of an Oil Based Economy.* New York: Praeger.
Hazari, R.K. (1967). *Industrial Planning and Licensing Policy: Final Report.* New Delhi: Government of India, Planning Commission.
Hong, Wontak. (1976). *Factor Supply and Factor Intensity of Trade in Korea.* Seoul: Korea Development Institute.
Hong, Wontak, and Anne O. Krueger, eds. (1975). *Trade and Development in Korea.* Seoul: Korea Development Institute.
Hsing, Mo-Huan. (1975). "The Development Experience of Taiwan and South Korea: A Comparison." *Academia Economic Papers* 3, pp. 1-19.
Kim, Seung Hee. (1970). *Foreign Capital for Economic Development: A Korean Case Study.* New York: Praeger.
Krueger, Anne O. (1978). *Foreign Trade Regimes and Economic Development: Liberalization Attempts and Consequences.* (Cambridge, Mass.: Ballinger for NBER).
Lee, Kai-Cheong. (1980). "Macroeconomic Studies on Foreign Trade and Economic Growth—The Cases of Taiwan and South Korea." Unpublished Ph.D. dissertation. Philadelphia: University of Pennsylvania.

Merhav, Meir. (1980). "Un Perfil de la Política Industrial, 1980-85." Mimeographed. Caracas.

Nehru, Jawaharlal. (1960). *The Discovery of India*. New York: Meridian Books.

Palma, Pedro. (1976). "A Macroeconometric Model of Venezuela with Oil Price Impact Applications." Unpublished Ph.D. dissertation. Philadelphia: University of Pennsylvania.

Ranis, Gustav. (1980). "Challenges and Opportunities Posed by Asia's Super-Exporters: Implications for Manufactured Exports from Latin America." Mimeographed. New Haven: Yale University.

Rao, D.C. (1978). "Economic Growth and Equity in the Republic of Korea." *World Development* 6, pp. 383-396.

Renaud, Bertrand. (1976). "Economic Growth and Income Inequality in Korea." World Bank Staff Working Paper, No. 240. Washington, D.C.: The World Bank.

Robock, Stefan H. (1975). *Brazil: A Study in Development Progress*. Lexington, Mass.: Lexington Books, D.C. Heath and Company.

U.S. Department of Commerce. *Venezuela*. Washington, D.C.: Government Printing Office.

U.S. Department of Commerce. *Venezuela: A Survey of U.S. Business Opportunities*. Washington, D.C.: Government Printing Office.

Wang, Yen-kyun. (1975). "A Macroeconometric Analysis of the Balance of Payments of Korea and Policy Implication." Unpublished Ph.D. dissertation. Philadelphia: University of Pennsylvania.

Westphal, Larry E. (1971). "An Intertemporal Planning Model Featuring Economies of Scale," in Hollis B. Chenery, et al., eds., *Studies in Development Planning*. Cambridge, Mass.: Harvard University Press.

Westphal, Larry E. (1978). "The Republic of Korea's Experience with Export-Led Industrial Development." *World Development* 6, pp. 347-382.

Westphal, Larry E., and Kwang Suk Kim. (1977). *Industrial Policy and Development in Korea*. World Bank Staff Working Paper, No. 263. Washington, D.C.: The World Bank.

World Bank. (1980). *World Development Report, 1980*. Washington, D.C.

Part III
Criteria

16 Criteria for U.S. Industrial-Policy Strategies

F. Gerard Adams

IP, like most other policy issues, is a question of choosing between alternative courses of action. Typically, no single path leads from where the economy stands to where the policymaker wants it to go. Even when there is broad agreement on the aims of policy, there is frequently little consensus about the alternative policy strategies. Differences in philosophical and economic views about the operation of the market system and about the efficacy of government intervention often constitute disagreement. IPs are particularly prone to such policy disagreements since, directly or indirectly, they are likely to have an impact on specific industries and sectors. They do so, not through the disembodied invisible hand of market forces, but through explicit government regulations or incentives.

The policymaker should face the question of how to select an IP and how to do so with a maximum of objectivity. What are the criteria that apply to such choices? Such is the topic of this chapter.

The principal questions to be considered here can be summarized as follows:

1. What criteria are relevant to the issue of whether IP should be used to stimulate economic growth and productivity or whether the economy's performance should be left to market forces supplemented by aggregate-demand management?
2. What criteria should determine the choice between general industrial policies (GIPs) versus policies targeted to specific industries (ISPs) or even to specific projects or firms (PSPs or FSPs)?
3. Assuming an IP effort, what criteria should guide the selection of policy mechanisms?
4. Assuming targeted policies, what criteria should be used in the selection of the industries, projects, or firms supported?

In the first section of this chapter we consider the goals of economic performance, both from an economy-wide macro perspective and from the point of view of individual industries and regions. At this point, we consider how the U.S. economy has performed in recent years with respect to these objectives and, perhaps more importantly, with respect to hopes or expectations. In the following section, we summarize the relevant conclusions of the theoretical studies and surveys of the practice of IP presented in earlier chapters in this book. In the remaining sections of this chapter, we return to the questions about criteria to establish guidelines for research on IP and for the policy decisions themselves.

Policy Objectives and Performance

Dissatisfaction with the performance of the U.S. economy in recent years derives naturally from the United States's failure to fulfill expectations. The pace of economic expansion has slowed; productivity has failed to grow. Many U.S. industries are in trouble, with profound technical and financial difficulties and with an apparent lack of competitiveness in world markets. Inflation has accelerated sharply and growth of per-capita purchasing power has slowed; indeed, there have been years of significant decline as wages have failed to keep pace with increases in the price level. We will examine the external perception and the realities of U.S. economic performance in greater detail in the following sections.

First we must stress that evaluation of the performance of the economy must recognize the multidimensional nature of social objectives. The aims are not only on the aggregate measures of economic well-being, but are also in some respects microeconomic, focusing on the health of particular industries and particular regions.

Economic Growth and Productivity

Beginning with the principal macroeconomic aims, increasing aggregate real output (or its close parallel, per-capita real purchasing power) is a primary objective. The almost-unique preoccupation with this goal of the 1950s[1] has given way to a recognition that other objectives are also important and, indeed, that because of the undesirable externalities, growth of output may not be synonymous with increased welfare.[2] Yet as the growth rate of productivity of other industrial countries systematically exceeds our own and as the absolute level of per-capita income in many of them approaches ours, there is again concern with the growth dimension (table 16-1). One might add that such concern also is based on the stagnation of growth of real per-capita income as compared to, for example, earlier in the postwar period and the consequent failure to satisfy rising expectations and increased emphasis on how the total income is distributed.

Table 16-1
Growth of Productivity, Leading Industrial Countries
(GDP per employed person)

Country	1960–1970 Percent per Year	1970–1979 Percent per Year	1973–1979 Percent per Year
United States	2.0	1.1	0.3
Canada	2.3	1.3	0.4
France	4.9	3.4	2.9
Germany	4.4	3.4	3.1
Italy	6.4	2.6	1.7
Japan	9.5	4.5	3.4
United Kingdom	2.7	2.0	1.1

Source: Congressional Budget Office (1981).

Employment

This discussion leads naturally to a second goal: employment, the central aim of the Employment Act of 1946. As we see in table 16-2, with respect to employment the performance of the U.S. economy has been somewhat more favorable than that of many industrial economies. Over the past ten years, some 20-million jobs have been created; indeed, that is part of the problem. These job opportunities have, in many cases, taken the form of low-productivity jobs and, consequently, they are one of the explanations for the slowdown in the productivity dimension of economic performance. Nevertheless, in cyclical troughs unemployment rates have reached highs not previously encountered in the postwar period.

Inflation

A third macroeconomic dimension of performance that evokes considerable concern is, of course, the rate of inflation. It goes almost without saying that performance has deteriorated in this regard as inflation rates in the 1970s have been significantly higher than earlier in the postwar period (table 16-3). But it is also important to recognize the role of external factors such as the increase in petroleum prices and the heating up of demand pressures associated with the Vietnam War in the late 1960s and the world-business cycle in the early 1970s. The phenomenon of accelerating inflation cannot be separated from the slowdown of productivity, a factor that would help to

Table 16-2
Employment and Unemployment, U.S. Economy

Year	Civilian Labor Force (millions)	Employment	Unemployment (percent of labor force)
1960	69.6	65.8	5.5
1970	92.6	84.8	8.5
1980	104.7	97.3	7.1

Source: Economic Report of President, 1981.

Table 16-3
Inflation

Year	GNP Deflator (1972 = 100)	CPI (1967 = 100)	Producer Price Index Finished Goods (1967 = 100)
1960	68.7 (2.9)	88.7 (2.7)	93.7 (1.6)
1970	91.4 (6.6)	116.3 (6.7)	116.3 (8.2)
1975	125.6 (7.2)	161.1 (9.1)	163.4 (8.4)
1980	178.6 (9.3)	246.8 (13.3)	247.0 (13.5)

Source: Economic Report of President, 1981.
Note: Numbers in parentheses are annual percent rates.

offset the upward movement of wage rates. If the real economy could function without regard to the movement of the price level and if the inflation did not have significant distributive consequences, we might be able to downgrade this dimension of economic performance.[3] But the evidence is that inflationary pressures have serious impact on real economic performance in many parts of the economy: the reduction in investment incentives, and the consequences for income distribution, for example. Some of these outcomes may well stem from the institutional and legal environment (the historical cost-depreciation regulations, for example) or the strategy of economic policy (the heavy emphasis on monetary policy as a tool of economic stabilization). Nonetheless, they represent real impacts from inflation on the other dimensions of economic performance.

Table 16-4
International Data
(billions of $)

	Merchandise Trade			Balance on Goods and Services	Balance on Current Account
Year	Exports	Imports	Balance		
1966	19.6	14.8	4.8	5.1	2.8
1970	42.5	39.9	2.6	5.6	2.3
1975	107.1	98.0	9.1	22.9	18.3
1980 (estimate)	220.9	249.2	−28.3		

Source: Economic Report of President, 1981.

Balance of Payments

A fourth relevant dimension of macroeconomic performance is the balance of payments and the international value of the dollar. A critical issue in this regard is the competitive performance of U.S. industry in world markets (table 16-4). During much of the 1970s, the international performance of the U.S. economy was not favorable, with substantial trade deficits and a gradual and significant decline of the U.S. dollar from the parity at which it was stabilized under Bretton Woods. This compares (until recently) to the strength of the Japanese yen and of the European currencies. On the one hand, the decline of the dollar was, of course, closely related to the rate of inflation and the failure of U.S. industry to maintain its international competitiveness. On the other hand, it is important to stress the high burden imposed by growth of imports of oil and the far greater increase in their cost per unit as a result of the oil shock. Looking at the other parts of the balance of payments, U.S. economic performance has been far more satisfactory. But the fact remains that we have been unable, until very recently, to offset the burdens imposed by the high cost of imported petroleum; consequently, the trade balance has been adverse and, until very recently, the dollar had declined sharply in comparison to other currencies.

Microeconomic Industrial Issues

The concern abut the U.S. economy and the emphasis on general and specific IPs derives not only from deficiencies of macroeconomic performance. The microeconomic dimension is very important, not simply because it points out the industries and regions with problems, but also because it indicates the nature of the difficulties that the economy has encountered. The first dimension of microeconomic performance is the performance of specific industries. In the evolution of any economy, some industries will be expanding and others may be contracting; some will be healthy and others will be unhealthy, as indeed, some firms prosper while others encounter difficulty. While this would suggest looking at the economy from a microeconomic industrial perspective, the diversity of experience among the industries and firms is not in itself a sign of trouble.

The concern recently is in the difficulties being encountered by certain major industries—particularly steel, automobiles, consumer electronics, and rubber. These industries, which have been mainstays of U.S. economic progress, have encountered severe difficulties. Some major enterprises have been threatened with bankruptcy unless they receive government bailouts. For example, in the steel industry,[4] we find a pattern of failure to modernize: Old plants operate with outmoded equipment, thus bearing high costs relative to the costs of modern technology and relative to the best modern plants of our foreign competitors. U.S. steel companies use old-fashioned processes with high requirements for fuel inputs and with excessively high needs for labor (that is, the open-hearth process as contrasted to continuous-casting techniques that are widely used in Japan). It is not surprising as a result to see the threat of increasing inroads into domestic markets by foreign steel producers, although there may be some justification to the argument that foreign producers achieved their high level of efficiency and their low cost with government assistance.

The situation of a number of other industries is similar though the problems may have a different origin. The U.S. auto industry, for example, was slow to respond to the change in the market toward small, fuel-efficient vehicles. One can argue that this represents a lag in technological adaptation, but one may also see it as a misreading of the signals of the market. In any case, the U.S. auto industry persisted in the production of large cars when consumers were turning to the purchase of smaller, fuel-efficient vehicles, many of which were produced abroad. At the same time, the industry clung too long to old-fashioned plants that were still usable but that lacked the equipment to match foreign-car factories in automation and in product quality.

The consumer-electronics industry, a field in which the United States was long a technological leader, suffered from the so-called product cycle.[5] Initial technological breakthroughs have almost all originated in the United States. The industries have developed advanced-technology products only to find serious competition from foreign producers when the product reached the mass-market stage. This pattern has been observed in the case of various types of consumer electronics and now appears to be repeating itself in copiers, integrated circuits, and computer-related products. Nevertheless, there is little evidence to suggest that the scientific vitality and development pace of U.S. high technology has been impaired.

Microeconomic Regional Issues

The other microeconomic dimension is regional.[6] The regional economic situation is closely related to industrial well-being as a result of geographic concentration of industry. In the United States, the development of regional disparities is particularly apparent between the older industrial areas of the Northeast and the North Central states and, particularly, of their urban industrial areas. These urban areas have fallen behind severely in terms of rate of growth, both of income and population, and in terms of unemployment, largely as a consequence of the industrial problems discussed earlier. But some regions—notably, the Southeast and the Southwest, the Mountain States, and to a lesser extent California—continue to have rapid growth. There are also disparities between rural areas, the suburbs, and the center cities. Regional disparities are even more important directly from the point of view of welfare than of industrial disparities. Few people will agree with the view that we should simply allow the urban areas of the Northeast to decline in favor of the new areas of the South and West. In a system of political organization based on regional constituencies, regional disparities become a matter of political as well as social concern.

Summary

On the basis of the foregoing discussion, what can be said about the performance of the U.S. economy and its need for policy? There is little doubt that the results of the 1970s have been mixed at best, if not downright unsatisfactory. This does not mean that the 1980s must be a repeat of the 1970s, even in the absence of remedial policies. Indeed, some signs of transition and adaptation are apparent in the restructuring of the automobile and steel industries and in the reduced use of petroleum and in improved export performance. On the other hand, the adjustment of the economy has been slow and painful so far, and competitive pressures from foreign producers, some of them in the LDCs, have been increasing. We must, accordingly, search for policies that will accomplish an industrial restructuring or will ease the transition.

Principal Conclusions of the Surveys of the Theory and Practice of Industrial Policy

We summarize here the relevant conclusions of the previous chapters. The issues to be considered involve questions raised by the theoretical survey as well as the principal guidelines of the work on philosophy and experience with IPs in the United States and in other parts of the world.

Theoretical Discussion

The theoretical survey provided a number of criteria that would provide support for intervention in the operation of the market. These criteria can be summarized as follows:

1. imperfections in the operation of the free-market mechanism
2. dynamic approaches to comparative advantage
3. product cycle and international competition
4. sources of technical progress

In practice these points may not be readily separable; in many respects they overlap. But they represent distinct strands of approaches to the relevant issues. We will consider them here in greater detail.

Imperfections in the Operation of the Free-Market Mechanism. If the underlying assumptions about competitive market structure and behavior are met, there is only limited room for intervention into market processes. In the static case, only in instances of externalities, public goods, and so-called declining-cost industries can it be argued that market processes will not lead to optimal resource allocation. From this point of view, one might be led to suppose that the case for market intervention is a narrow one and that IP is, by and large, unnecessary or inadvisable. As is noted in chapter 3, this is not a realistic conclusion. Even in the static framework, the imperfections in competitiveness, and the widespread existence of externalities of various kinds (positive as well as negative) suggest that there is scope for improving the optimization of resource use through various kinds of policy. It is not clear, of course, that this means that policies should be applied. We point to the need to examine the costs of such policies as well as the need to make a realistic evaluation of their benefits in the following discussion.

The added consideration is that of second best. Broadly interpreted, this means that the case for avoiding market interventions assumes that there are no interventions anywhere. The presence of intervention in the market—either in the domestic economy or in the economies of our international competitors—changes the conclusions about optimization derived from the competitive-market model. Thus if there is market intervention with respect to one industry, one cannot assume that operation of the free market will automatically lead to an optimal solution with respect to all others. In the case of foreign competition, such an observation is all the more important since we may not be seeking primarily overall optimization between all countries but rather only that which affects our own. For example, subsidies or other assistance to the steel industry by our foreign competitors may call for a defensive IP in favor of our own industry.

Dynamic Approaches to Comparative Advantage. The preceding discussion is based on a static view of comparative advantage. A dynamic view, which argues that future comparative advantage may be different from that being encountered currently, is an important part of the theory of economic development. The critical issue in this view is the recognition that the relevant consideration is not the comparative advantage in a static sense but rather a future-oriented view. Comparative advantage is a dynamic and multidimensional phenomenon. This means that policy measures can change comparative advantage-development of a skilled labor force, achievement of economic scales of production, linkages between different types of symbiotic industries, and so on—and are in some sense the result of dynamic evolution, one in which policy has in the past played an important role in some countries. Policies based on a dynamic view of comparative advantage lie behind Japanese IP and appear to have been one of the important factors in the recent success stories of economic growth in the Southeast Asian countries.

Product Cycle and Competitive Aspects. The product-cycle view follows naturally from the dynamic conception of the international comparative advantage. It argues that the process of international division of labor produces a natural evolution of production. In recent years evidence of a product-cycle phenomenon has been seen in the process by which new, initially high-technology products are mass produced in the developing countries. In effect the comparative advantage of the product changes as the technology is perfected and as the size of the market increases to justify mass-production activity. This phenomenon raises serious questions for IP in the United States. On the one hand, it is tempting to attempt to protect the markets impacted by foreign competition or to provide them with aid so that they can continue to produce. On the other hand, traditional comparative-advantage arguments would suggest that competitive market forces should be allowed to operate and production should be switched to products that we can produce most advantageously.

For reasons of difficulty of adjustment and transition (high unemployment, for example), few countries are willing to sit by while the product-cycle shift takes place. The impacts on the foreign balance, on employment, and on welfare of the industry itself and its suppliers frequently lead to efforts to salvage the industries that are imperiled by the growing foreign competition. Whether the policy of supporting the losers is optimal must be considered, probably on a case-by-case basis. Alternatively, one may ask whether policies can accelerate the favorable aspects of the product cycle either in the sense of supporting the new industries or of easing the transitions that are involved.

Technical Progress. The theory of technical progress is another justification for various types of IPs. Basic research has externalities that are frequently difficult for private industry to capture. Similar externalities apply to many aspects of applied research and development. While patent laws are intended to enable industry to capture the gains from new technology, in many instances they are only a very imperfect mechanism for this purpose. In many countries, basic research and, to some extent, development expenditures are heavily supported by public bodies. Some of this work is carried on in universities, which appear to be a substantial source of high technology in the United States, and in research institutes. But it is important to note that particularly in the United States, much of the development and commercialization of the new product is done in the private sector, often by small-scale entrepreneurs rather than by the large integrated corporations. Implications for optimal public policy toward the high-technology industries need further consideration.

Philosophy and Experience with Industrial Policies

As earlier chapters in this book show (see particularly chapters 5, 6, and 7) the approaches to IP and the experience in various countries are diverse. We cannot adequately summarize this rich record here, but a number of conclusions relevant to the formulation of criteria for guiding IPs are particularly important.

  1. *In most countries the philosophy and strategy of IP reflects closely the traditional relations between business and government.* Looking across the historical record for many countries, it is striking, but not surprising, to see how much the differences in policy approaches to industry reflect the traditional view in each country of the relations between government and industry, although these must be seen as evolving and adapting over time. Thus in the United States the emphasis has been on macro stabilization rather than industrial structure. While efforts are being made to aid particular industries in accord with long-standing traditions, there is not a for-

mal plan of industrial restructuring or, for that matter, something that might be called an IP. In contrast, in France for example, we find continued examples of ISP focusing on particular industries (electronics, autos, steel, and nuclear power) despite, until the election of the Mitterrand government, the shift away from planning and toward greater freedom for private enterprise decision making.

2. *The great divergence of IP between countries and its relationship to the long-lasting aspects of business and government relations suggests that IP strategies are not easily transferred from one country to another.* For example, it would be difficult for the United States to adopt the Japanese approach, which is so much dependent on a relationship of mutual support between business and the relevant government agencies. For a U.S. version of MITI to be successful, basic changes in the way in which government agencies regulate and in the way in which business responds would be required.

3. *Domestic political considerations have played an important role in the formulation and implementation of IPs.* The importance of domestic political issues, particularly those relevant to employment and regional discrepancies, have persistently influenced IPs in almost all countries and have been dominant in some cases (the Mezzogiorno policies in Italy, for example). It is interesting also to observe that domestic political considerations have been a continued barrier not only to full European economic integration but even to the formulation of a coherent European approach to IP.

4. *However, IPs are generally intended to be responsive to the requirements of the economy and of particular industries as perceived at the time by policymakers.* It is not suprising that policy philosophy and implementation should be greatly influenced by the economic setting in which it takes place. Thus the immediate postwar needs of reconstruction in Europe and Japan called for rebuilding the manufacturing industry; the need for foreign exchange called for building up the international competitiveness of industry in Japan; and currently, the concern with inadequate growth and international competitiveness in the United States has brought forth various proposals for economic revitalization or recovery. Policy in general and IP, in particular, respond to the needs of the economy and even to the needs of particular industries, regions, and firms.

5. *In many instances (perhaps in most cases) IP has been of an ad hoc nature.* This has been particularly true of rescue operations, but it is also characteristic of many other efforts at picking the winners—policies that have focused, for example, on specific high-technology ventures without fully evaluating their role in an overall industrial framework.

6. *On the other hand, there have been ex-ante planned IPs based on a comprehensive analysis of industrial perspectives.* The Japanese case is the clearest example of comprehensive IPs based on a broad vision of the needs

and prospects of the Japanese economy and its possibilities for establishing comparative advantage in international markets. At least on the surface, there appears to be a close relationship between planning, which has been prevalent in many countries, and IPs. But the evidence does not show always that formal indicative planning procedures have served as an effective basis for IP, even in countries (like France) that have had a tradition of planning.

7. *The specific measures of industry assistance have differed greatly among countries.* In some cases the emphasis has been on bolstering private industry, with tax incentives, preferential access to financial capital (as for the Japanese steel industry), tariff protection, and so on. In others we have seen the formation of national or quasinational companies to carry on heavy industrial activities, a pattern that was particularly apparent in the less-developed economies. In some cases the opposite instruments have been used with same intent. Compare for example, the antitrust policies in the United States with the policies of industrial rationalization in France. Most countries have supported scientific research, but there has also been broad diversity with regard to the mechanism of aid to research and development—some of it going to private firms directly, some of it in the form of tax concessions, and some of it targeted to research institutes or to joint private and government projects. This diversity of mechanisms again seems to reflect the long-standing arrangements typical of each country. Consequently, while in an international perspective, no one instrument is clearly more effective than others; each country may well find some instruments more effective or suitable than others.

8. *On the other hand, the selection of the industries for aid has not been as diverse as other aspects of IP.* To the extent that countries have been relatively free to select the beneficiaries of IP, they have frequently sought to develop the same industries. Of course, with regard to aid directed to industries in difficulty, there is little or no choice. But in so-called picking-the-winners IPs, there is considerable freedom of choice among potential beneficiaries. Which are the industries for which prospects are brightest and that can benefit from IP? The country surveys suggest that in many cases aid has been directed at the same industries in many countries? Efforts by the Japanese and French to develop high-technology industries and support for basic research and for applied research and development represent parallel approaches. Assistance has frequently also gone to heavy industries like steel or petrochemicals—fields that are thought to be prestige or leading industrial sectors. This pattern is typical of many LDCs or NICs.

In view of the diversity among countries, it is difficult to reach a conclusion about the experience with respect to the criteria that have guided the formulation of IP and the selection of beneficiary industries, and the implementation of such policies. It would be difficult, moreover, to conclusively evaluate the experience of various countries from the point of view of the effectiveness of IPs. Obviously, some IP experiments have been more successful than others. But it is not always clear to what extent the degree of success is a reflection of the particular target chosen, the mechanism used, or even to what extent it reflects a fortunate combination of circumstances. In many cases it is difficult even to determine whether the policy *was* a success. The evidence of the failure of policy is frequently more clear than is the evidence of success. That an industry *appears* to have developed successfully is not sufficient, since the industry may be operating inefficiently or at low return on capital or it might well have developed even in the absence of policy. On the other hand, competitiveness in industrial markets in the case of industries that are no longer receiving subsidies or other form of aid does suggest a measure of success.

The guidelines for IP that have worked successfully in one country may not consequently work in a different political, social, and economic environment. The foreign experience may be suggestive, but it is advisable to review the needs for a U.S. policy and its potentials carefully (perhaps on a case-by-case basis) in the light of conditions that prevail in the United States.

Criteria for Industry Policymaking

General Guidelines

What then are the appropriate criteria to guide industrial policymaking? We turn here to some general principles.

Inadequate Economic Performance Is Not Sufficient Condition for Justifying Industry Policy. Our earlier discussion of the record of the U.S. economic performance is suggestive of the fact that countries are likely to turn to IPs when the economy in general or particular industries or regions appear to be performing less well than might be desired. Planning or other interventions with the operation of the free market are designed to improve economic performance and to direct it toward attainment of the economy's goals. However, these goals are multiple and achievement of one objective may mean sacrificing another. In effect, the society establishes a preference function that weights the various objectives and seeks to achieve maximum well-being. That free-market forces do not automatically achieve the desired goals has frequently been used as a justification for policy, although not necessarily IP.[7] But where policy focusing on supply-side or industrial targets might appear to be appropriate, the question is not so much whether the economy has been working satisfactorily but *whether a strategy of IP* can achieve a better result than can free-market forces without intervention. This leads naturally to our next observation.

Policy Alternatives Must Be Considered from a Cost-Benefit Standpoint. Criteria for policy evaluation are that the policy offers a net benefit as compared to not having a policy at all, and/or as compared to all other policy alternatives. This suggests a comparison between the society's benefits with the costs. This is not a straightforward matter, however.

On the benefit side, the evaluation of the multiple objectives may be difficult. The benefits may be indirect in the sense that an improved industrial structure may lead to improved productivity and international competitiveness. But exactly what makes up an *improved* industrial structure is not at all clear. Such an improvement has static implications in terms of the utilization of the available labor force and plant and equipment, but its most important implications are dynamic. This aspect will be discussed in the following section.

On the cost side, too, the definition of costs and their measurement is difficult. It is often possible to measure the cost of various types of government programs in terms of revenues foregone in the case of tax-incentive programs or in terms of financial subsidies paid. These may not, however, measure accurately the full cost since the diversion of resources from other use is the true measure of the economic cost rather than simply its financial burden on the Treasury. But other considerations, some of a dynamic nature, may also be important. As we will discuss further, the implications of focusing resources into particular activities or sectors of the economy may not be costless in terms of impacts on incentives in other parts of the private sector. On the other hand, the assumption that such costs necessarily dominate the benefits is without foundation.

Industrial Policy Must Be Evaluated from a Dynamic Perspective. The shaping of an economic or industrial structure is a dynamic process. Just as the development of economic structure takes place gradually over time, the responses of industries to market forces or to IP actions have a time dimension. The evaluation of IP strategies must take into account the dynamic aspects of economic development. Consequently, IPs must look ahead to the time when the policies will be effective. Frequently, this will be far into the future, when the situation of the economy may be considerably different from what it was at the time the policy was formulated. At that time too, other competitors in the world market may also have undergone considerable change.

We are concerned here with criteria for evaluation of IPs that are intended directly to improve the economy's production potential. While a broad definition of IP might include various supply-side policies (encouragement of savings, for example) as well as various types of demand stimulus, it is helpful to avoid some of the controversies recently associated with a discussion of these issues. Consequently, as we have indicated, our discussion of criteria for policy evaluation will be limited to IPs intended to influence productivity and competitiveness directly. Thus we maintain a broad but nevertheless conventional definition of IP.

It is also well to acknowledge from the start that we bring to the discussion a preference toward use of the market mechanism. IPs represent, inevitably an intervention with the market. But they may be implemented in a variety of ways, some of which are more and others less consistent with private decision-making. Our following appraisal assumes that whenever possible, the market mechanism will be used to implement policy—that private decision making will be supplemented by public policy only where such policy is essential and that incentives are preferable to administrative interventions.

Should There Be Industrial Policy?

Once the failure of the economy to achieve its potentials is recognized, it is difficult to avoid the conclusion that there is a need for policy. The notion that the best policy is no policy requires the belief that policy is inherently likely to do more harm than good. Only the most stalwart supporters of laissez-faire would argue against any remedial policy, in the form of separate measures or a coherent strategy, general or specific, demand-side or supply-side. But little more can be said without a more specific statement as to the nature of the policy alternatives being considered.

The issue of whether there should be IP is a somewhat narrower one. The question is whether policy should be limited to the conventional aggregate policy tools or whether policies should be aimed more directly on factors influencing the economy's productivity and competitiveness. Even conventional fiscal and monetary policies may have consequences for productivity. Thus the impact of a demand stimulus can be traced through to greater incentives for investment, and a policy to increase saving may, under appropriate conditions, facilitate a higher level of investment and productivity. But conventional aggregate policies, if they work to boost productivity at all, are likely to be quite inefficient for this purpose. Policy measures aimed directly at improving productivity and competitiveness—for example, incentives for investment that lead to greater capital intensity or support for research and development to improve technology or financial guarantees for industrial rejuvenation—are likely to yield far more so-called bang for the buck and far more quickly. This makes the question largely an economic one. Can the objectives be achieved at lower cost with IP? In this regard, the specifics of such policy are an important consideration. We will consider them in greater detail in the following discussion.

General versus Industry Specific Policies

The central question in the recent debate on reindustrialization has been whether IP should be industry-specific or general. This is not an issue concerning impact, since few policies are likely to be neutral across the economy, but rather it is a question about implementation. Should the incentives be targeted to particular industries, or should they be available generally across all sectors of the economy? Selection of particular industries is at the heart of the so-called picking-the-winners proposals. It is equally central, also, to the rather different aims of providing support to the losers or of establishing mechanisms to aid specific industries in a transitional phase. The criteria for decision making turn out to be rather different depending on the nature of the policy objective.

General Industrial Policies

Behind the proposition that IPs should be general rather than industry-specific lie several basic hypotheses. The first is that once an IP stimulus is provided, the market is the optimal mechanism for determining which industries should take advantage of the policy. Such a philosophy lies behind many of the arguments in favor of GIPs—for example, the study by Krugman (1980). The argument here is that intervention with the operation of the market by establishing ISPs would result in allocation decisions that are contrary to market signals and, consequently, likely to be less than optimal. Krugman argues that this will mean diversion of investment resources and that increases in investment in the preferred industries must be at the expense of other industries. This presupposes that total investment remains fixed, which may not apply at all stages of the business cycle. Carrying the free-market argument to its extreme, one might argue against any and all IPs, whether general or specific.

The second postulate is that even if it were desirable to aid particular industries, government agencies would be unable to make the proper choices. Again, Krugman (1980) provides support for this proposition. His examination of the experience in various countries (the steel industry in Japan, the Concorde experience in Europe, and the French efforts with computers, for example) can be interpreted to mean that the allocative decisions made by public authorities generally have failed.

But these propositions cannot be accepted without discussion. Even the strongest supporters of free enterprise will recognize that reality is far from the idealized system of the economics textbooks. Much of the industrial world is competitive but in a sense very different from that required for the optimum-resource-allocation theorems to hold. The dynamics of new technology and of the enterprises that introduce it are an important positive attribute of allowing private enterprise to make choices. But it is not clear that the private enterprise mechanism operating without intervention provides an optimal solution. Numerous interventions by governments regulations—some intended to allow for market failures but others with very different purposes—apply. Foreign competitors to domestic industries frequently have public support and operate in very different ways from the competitive free-enterprise paradigm.

With regard to the selection of particular industries, the difficulty of choices made by the public sector is widely recognized and has been noted in some of the country studies in this book. On the other hand, some writers—notably, Shinohara (1980), and Ichimura (1979)—point to the success of IPs in Japan, particularly in a framework of the comprehensive forward-looking evaluations of dynamic comparative advantage, the so-called visions of the Ministry of International Trade and Industry (MITI) to which we have referred earlier.

An added consideration at this point is the fact that GIPs are not likely to be neutral in their effect on industrial structure (Adams and Duggal 1982). Even if a GIP is formulated in the most general way possible, so that it is available to any industry or enterprise in the economy, it is likely to be more advantageous to some enterprises than to others. Picture, for example, the impact of an investment-tax credit on equipment. Such a tax credit is likely to be more advantageous to business with heavy needs for eligible equipment, for those constrained by financial considerations, and for those who have profits and are paying income taxes against which the credit could be offset. The so-called safe-harbor leasing provision of the 1981 tax law adds a refundable feature to the investment-tax credit that benefits the auto, steel, and rubber industries and many smaller business enterprises and nonprofit organizations that were unable to take advantage of the tax credit. The lack of neutrality of most GIPs also extends to the regional dimensions; not only because of the differential industrial impact of such policies but also because they may stimulate new investments in the developing areas of the country at the expense of the older regions (Glickman 1982). It would be very difficult to design GIPs that would be on the one hand, effective, and on the other, totally neutral. If in fact the impact of GIPs is after all industry-specific, it is difficult to ignore their specificity in the design of the policy measures. Indeed, it will not be ignored in the inevitable bargaining of the legislative process. Under those circumstances, it would probably be wise if the industry-specific impacts of alternative GIPs were recognized and taken into account explicitly.

This yields a somewhat equivocal conclusion. On the one hand, private enterprise as the decision-making mechanism in a framework of GIPs has significant merits that must not be underestimated. On the other hand, it is not clear whether GIPs alone, allowing the private sector to make all the choices, are generally neutral with respect to industries or regions nor whether they will accomplish the desired structural changes.

Industry Specific Policies

The pros and cons of ISPs have already been considered. We turn here to an examination of alternative aims of ISPs, those that are intended to develop the winners, those that are intended to help industries in trouble, and those that are transitional in nature. Unavoidably, many ISPs turn out to be firm-specific or even project-specific as well.

Aiding the Potential Winners. As has been noted in earlier chapters in this book, various countries (particularly Germany and France but to a lesser extent many others) have followed a policy of aiding what have been termed *potential winner industries*. In the Japanese case, the approach has been designed and orchestrated by MITI, which has tried to identify those fields where Japanese industry would have a dynamic comparative advantage. In the 1960s, this meant the development of a modern steel and auto industry. In the 1970s, it meant adjustment to the problems of energy cost and pollution and to the restructuring required by the problems of textiles and shipbuilding; in the 1980s, this will mean development of the knowledge-intensive industries (MITI 1980). Government aid and private financing directed by administrative guidance have been aimed to build technologically advanced industry that is competitive in world markets.

The concept of dynamic comparative advantage as a guide for selecting the winner industries is a promising one, recognizing that such industries should ultimately be able to compete effectively in world markets—that is, to meet a market test without government assistance. This suggests selection of industries with important economies of scale and industries where gains in efficiency can be captured by use of advanced technology. To a lesser extent, it may mean simply advanced high-technology industries, but the barriers to effectively selecting such industries are high; the returns are not yet in whether, even in Japan, the selection and development of such industries can be done effectively by government agencies.

It is not clear, moreover, that government assistance is necessary to develop these industries. Could the private market have developed them without assistance? Again, the Japanese experience points to industries such as automobiles where government help has not been necessary, but also to others such as computers where government aid appears to have made an important contribution (Gresser 1980). Arguments based on the theory of externalities associated with research-and-development expenditures and the theory of technological change can be brought to advance the idea that public support can make a net contribution to the new high-technology industries.

A critical question, moreover, is how narrowly specific the choices must be. Selection of broad industrial categories (microelectronics, for example) is a very different matter from selecting a particular product or process. The more narrow or specific the selection, the greater the interference with the operation of the competitive-market mechanism. Yet when public funds are being expended, it is difficult to avoid establishing criteria for selecting eligible recipients even if this means making choices among different research endeavors, processes, or even firms. In the European experience (particularly in France) and in Japan this has meant public funding, and frequently, intervention in the operation of specific enterprises. This may be avoidable only by establishing broad eligibility rules so that all eligible firms could claim industrial assistance and by deliberately encouraging multiple alternative approaches to the same technological-development problem. The financial participation by private enterprises in the development efforts, bearing some of the risk and cost, is also a means to utilize private enterprise decision making.

Aiding the Losers. Unfortunately, much direct assistance in the United States, the United Kingdom, Italy, and elsewhere has gone to ailing industries. Financial aid and loan guarantees have gone to industries that have lost competitiveness, and frequently to firms whose bankruptcy would have impacts on other related industries, on employment, and possibly on national defense. Such policies are clearly selective of particular industries, even of particular enterprises, the cases of Lockheed and Chrysler come to mind. Justification for such ISPs or FSPs are dramatically different from that involved in selecting the winners. Rationalization lies in the loss that the society would suffer if the declining industry or firm were allowed to disappear. It is easy to exaggerate these losses, but there are indeed some real losses such as those involved with employment and the costs of transition to other activities, potential losses for other industries that have provided inputs or that have relied on the industry as a supplier, the risks associated with national defense, and possibly, the balance-of-payments impacts. While it is important to recognize the costs associated with dislocation as a consequence of phasing out declining industries, they must not be confused with long-run costs of maintaining uneconomic industries (Finnel 1981, p. 102). The criteria for aid should involve a comparison of the losses that would occur with the costs of government assistance. One difficulty is the question of how long such assistance should be provided. Temporary aid to an industry that has the potential of modernizing and of reestablishing its competitive position is a very different matter from helping an industry that will remain noncompetitive. But experience teaches us that it is very difficult in advance to gauge whether assistance is truly temporary or whether long-run government assistance will be required.

Transitional Aid. Finally, we turn to transitional aid, which has already been referred to. The arguments for transitional aid overlap considerably with those for aiding the losers. But the economic arguments for providing transitions are considerably stronger than for simply helping the losers. Moreover, transitional aid may involve more than assistance to the losers. It may call for assistance to the new industries that will take the place of the declining industry. The Japanese have been notably successful, for example, with finding alternative employment for the shipyards that once produced the very large tankers. The criteria guiding transitional aid are again considerations of cost and benefit, whether the benefits from transitional aid justify the costs involved. As we noted earlier, it is difficult to establish in advance how large the cost will be, but the justifications for transitional assistance are considerably stronger than those for long-term aid to declining industries.

Selection of Industries

Selection of industries is greatly influenced by the aims of the IP as the preceding discussion suggests. Focusing here on the winners or on the transitional industries (which can presumably be transformed into winners) by what criteria should be beneficiary industries be selected? This is not an easy question to answer since it involves not only the characteristics of the industries themselves, but the likely response of market forces to IPs and their behavior in the absence of policy. For example, we might ask whether special aid should be provided to the following:

1. heavy industries whose equipment needs modernization
2. high-technology industries where there are important externalities but where the private sector is already active
3. industries that are heavily influenced by foreign competition, but that eventually might be able to compete effectively in foreign markets
4. industries that have high employment or supplier-industry linkages throughout the domestic economy
5. investments which can be justified only with a very long-time perspective or which involve very large risks.

Theoretical discussions in earlier chapters of this book provide some guidelines. Some of the primary factors to be considered are the following:

1. *The externalities in a static and dynamic perspective.* There is a clear case for government aid to industries where positive externalities indicate that the private sector would not allocate sufficient resources. A broad range of possibilities follows from this position. High-technology industries, particularly those where there is a need for basic research, are a prime prospect for assistance. Interestingly, the fact that the private enterprise may already be active in high-technology fields is not an argument against further policy stimulus since the rationale for IP in this case depends on recognizing the externalities that the private sector is not able to capture. In the case of basic research, there is frequently prima facie evidence that the payoff from public support of various types (subsidization of research, support of research centers in the universities, write-offs of research spending, and so on) is high. But even development expenditures that carry the industry down the learning curve have a payoff that extends considerably beyond the enterprise making the expenditure, and there are frequently payoffs from achieving a critical scale of operation as well. On the other hand, we should note that much of the progress in new technology has been contributed by small enterprises and that public intervention should not stand in the way of the entrepreneurial spirit that has been a source of much technological improvement.

2. *Competitiveness in world markets.* The criterion of present or future competitiveness in world markets is not, as it may appear, simply a mercantilistic view. Competitiveness is a difficult market test. If the industry can meet that test, we can presume that resources are being allocated efficiently. This is a strong rationale for export promotion rather than import substitution in LDC development policies. The world-market test must be applied with a dynamic view since industries presently in need of assistance may ultimately be competitive. On the other hand, the test cannot be applied irrespective of the amount or duration of the assistance that is required. Perhaps the infusion of aid required is so great or the prospect of meeting the competitiveness test is so uncertain that a policy of industrial assistance cannot be justified. Moreover, competitiveness in world markets must be gauged in light of the exchange rate. An overvalued exchange rate may make it impossible for economic firms to compete while undervaluation may permit even inefficient firms to compete successfully in world markets.

3. *Linkages to other parts of the domestic economy.* In some instances, linkages to the domestic economy represent a valid rationale for industrial assistance. The most common argument is that of employment, but this is also the one most fraught with confusion. Just because an industry employs a large number of workers who are threatened with unemployment is not

sufficient reason to provide it with continued support. The issue is whether the social cost of unemployment can justify support to a declining industry. Other instances of linkage may, however, be important to recognize. For example, industries that represent an essential link in an integrated industrial structure cannot well be judged on their own separately from the other industries with which they interact.[8] Industries that service other sectors may be essential to the sector being serviced and that sector would lose competitiveness if the service industry disappeared. There are many cases where this argument has a substantial degree of validity, but it should not be used to say that certain industries (like steel) are inherently important to national industrial welfare and, consequently, deserve IP support. Nor does it inevitably justify the development of processing industries as extensions of primary-commodity production in the developing countries—that is, the resource-based industrialization concept (Adams and Behrman 1981).

4. *Time perspective and risk.* The notion that private investors have too short a time perspective and too little willingness to accept risk is not an unequivocal basis for aiding industries which are risky or which require long gestation periods. Even if it can be demonstrated that public authorities have a longer time perspective and a better ability to handle risks than private businessmen—by no means a foregone conclusion!—the question is what degree of risk taking and time perspective are socially optimal. Can ISPs favor industries that require a longer time perspective and greater risk than the private sector is willing to bear without exceeding optimal limits? Perhaps the strongest argument with respect to these questions is that ISPs can be used to create options: to develop new technologies, to advance industries along the learning curve, and to expand the pool of trained workers, for example. Such options offer externalities in that they represent opportunities that can ultimately be exploited by the private sector.

5. *Industries affected by domestic regulatory policy.* One of the widely recognized problems of the 1970s has been the impact of regulatory policy on many U.S. industries. In an effort to reduce pollution and to improve safety on the job, a variety of regulations have been imposed. These regulations have an important payoff in cleaner air and water and greater safety, but they have increased industrial operating and capital costs in comparison with our competitors elsewhere. One can argue that the public, which benefits from the regulations, should also bear some of their cost. This is particularly true in cases where the industry has been unable to meet regulatory guidelines except at the cost of becoming noncompetitive as compared to foreign producers who may bear less stringent restrictions. A case for industrial assistance or protection can be made in these circumstances. On the other hand, it is possible to argue that if our standards for clean air and water are higher than elsewhere, heavy polluting industries should better be located where the restrictions against pollutions are less stringent.

6. *Foreign industrial assistance.* In numerous cases foreign countries have provided assistance of various kinds to their industries, often precisely with the aim of making them competitive in world markets. One might be reluctant to suggest countervailing measures of IP. Nevertheless, where foreign industries are beneficiaries of special aid or where dumping occurs, some type of assistance or protection for the corresponding domestic industries may well be justified.

7. *Noneconomic considerations.* Appeal to noneconomic considerations—national defense, national prestige, questions of regional equality, or even political motives—have been a frequent basis for industrial support, as our specific-country studies indicate. It is difficult, of course, to counter the national-defense rationale as a basis for IPs, except to note that it is clearly a more valid argument when it is applied to the steel industry than when it is used to protect the cheese industry in the United States or the leather-boot industry in Sweden. The national prestige motive, which has motivated European policies in several instances (note the Concorde, for example), has frequently produced economically disastrous results as has the motive to provide regional equalization (the noncompetitive industries constructed under the Mezzogiorno policy in Italy, for example).

Conclusion

Clearly, there are a number of valid rationales for ISP, which can serve as criteria for selecting the industries that should benefit from IP. We have noted, however, that in many cases it is difficult to implement the criteria because the costs and benefits are uncertain; because it may be difficult to avoid giving long-term support to declining industries; and because IP opens a Pandora's box of noneconomic motives for industry support.

Selection of Industrial-Policy Measures

At this point, we turn to the criteria that might be used to distinguish between alternative mechanisms of IP. A scale of priorities for various degrees of market intervention developed by Corden (1974) has been discussed earlier. We indicated previously that there are strong arguments in favor of maximum utilization of market mechanisms. When there is a choice between administrative measures or incentives operating in a market environment, experience and theory tend strongly to support market incentives. But there are significant questions with regard to which mechanisms to use and with regard to the criteria that might apply. The various types of policies to be considered fall into the following broad categories:

1. direct investment and financing, public enterprises
2. preferential financing
3. protectionist measures
4. tax or subsidy incentives
5. guideline measures

Most specific IP measures can be accommodated in one of these five categories. They are presented here in order of the degree of direct intervention that they imply from the most to the least direct.

1. *Direct investment.* Direct public participation through public enterprises, investment, financing, loan guarantees, and similar means is the most direct form of public intervention. We noted in earlier chapters that in many cases, government or quasi-government corporations have been the means to achieve IP, particularly in Brazil and in France. While this represents direct participation in industrial development, it is not necessarily the most direct means of intervention since government corporations have frequently been allowed a substantial measure of free decision making and participation in the market mechanism. The essential point is that direct investment and/or financing decisions by the public sector involve it directly in allocation decisions. This applies whether there is public ownership, whether there is financing of private enterprises, or (sometimes) when there are only loan guarantees.[9] Public decision making in these cases may go down to the level of approving individual projects (PSP policies).

2. *Preferential financing.* Preferential financing, either in terms of availabilities of funds or of special favorable financing terms, offers possibilities for influencing industrial development with modest intervention in actual business investment. Since funds may be made available on the basis of eligibility rules, where the ultimate decision on the use of funds is made by the private entrepreneur who frequently shares the risk, this means relatively moderate intervention. But there are risks of linking capital financing with detailed regulations on the choices and performance of the borrower.

3. *Protectionist measures.* Tariffs and other forms of protectionist measures like trigger-price mechanisms, orderly marketing agreements, quotas, and so on, represent intervention with the operation of the international competition aspects of the market mechanisms. In this sense the allocative decision is left to the private entrepreneur under the umbrella of the protection from foreign competition established by the protectionist measures. A tariff, or a trigger price that does not directly interfere with the volume of imports, represents a smaller intervention in market mechanisms than does a fixed quantitative quota, but it also frequently a less effective barrier to competition from foreign concerns.[10] Exchange-rate policies, overvaluation, or undervaluation constitute another approach that has been used, particularly in some of the developing countries (for example, Brazil).

4. *Tax or subsidy incentives.* Typically, tax incentives or subsidies are more general policies than are the preceding policy approaches. While in principle tax-incentive schemes (investment-tax credits, current expending of research expenditures, and so on) may fall into the category of nonindustry-specific policies (GIPs or ASPs), in fact they may have specific targets. The extent to which they affect specific industries depends on the type of concessionary policy followed, from ones that may be quite neutral in impact to others that may represent tax concessions or subsidies to specific types of industrial activities.

5. *Guideline measures.* This is a broad category that includes the range of activities from indicative planning to quite detailed administrative interventions. The Japanese visions and the Japanese policies of administrative guidance are good examples of both extremes. The visions represent simply a broad (and, it appears, useful) perspective on prospects and opportunities for future economic development. They point out to the participants in the economy the direction in which a dynamic appraisal of comparative advantage might lead. Seen simply in that light, the visions do not represent intervention; rather they contribute to the operation of the private sector by offering additional information. The administrative-guidance approach, on the other hand, represents an explicit intervention with the operation of market mechanisms. While the extent to which such measures have actually been effective is not certain, the objective is to intervene directly with private-sector decisions, frequently at the level of the specific project or firm (PSP and FSP).

Conclusions

What does economic theory and experience suggest with regard to the choice among the mechanisms of IP? It is not useful at this point to say only that one seeks optimal decision making and that such decision making can be achieved through market or nonmarket mechanisms. On the contrary: We have indicated our preference for market mechanisms. Market mechanisms take advantage of market-based cost-benefit calculations and of individual initiative and risk taking. They avoid the rigidities and political considerations that have been known frequently to affect decision making by the public sector. Recognizing that IP in general and ISPs in particular can play an important role in achieving an economic *renaissance,* the criteria that should influence the formulation of specific IP measures should be those that maximize the use of advantageous market mechanisms and incentives and minimize the influence of administrative decisions and market interventions.

Notes

1. See Denison (1962).
2. See Nordhaus and Tobin (1973), for example.
3. For a discussion, see Thurow (1980). The phenomenon of a growth slowdown has occurred to some extent in almost all countries worldwide, in part as a consequence of the oil shock and the need to restructure the industrial economies. But it is most felt in the United States (and perhaps Britain), which was so long the leader among the world's advanced industrial countries.
4. See Crandall (1981). For an econometric study of steel, see Adams, and others, (1982).
5. See Vernon (1966).
6. For a discussion of the regional dimensions of the industry problem, see a study in process by N.J. Glickman, also see Bell and Lande (1981).
7. An example is the income-distribution goal, which may not be achieved by free-market forces, and toward whose achievement we use the tax system as a redistributive device.
8. Thus it is probably not wise to evaluate the experience with respect to the Japanese steel industry without considering its links to other Japanese industries.
9. The extent of government participation in the decision making of Chrysler Corporation, a beneficiary of loan guarantees, is quite astonishing. A board including the Secretary of the Treasury and the Chairman of the Federal Reserve were expected to approve even relatively minor aspects of Chrysler management in a way similar to a bankruptcy trustee.
10. Orderly Marketing Agreements are really quotas, despite their seeming voluntariness.

References

Adams, F. Gerard, and Jere R. Behrman. (1981). "The Linkage Effects of Raw Material Processing in Economic Development: A Survey." *Journal of Policy Modeling* 3 (October):279-294.

Adams, F. Gerard, and Vijaya Duggal. (1982). "General Versus Industry-Specific Industrial Policy Incentives." *Journal of Policy Modeling* 4 (June):161-174.

Adams, F. Gerard, and Lawrence R. Klein. (1980). "Evaluation of Industrial Development Policies: Overview." Mimeographed. Philadelphia: Economics Research Unit, University of Pennsylvania.

Adams, F. Gerard, et al. (1982). "Industrial Policy Analysis for the U.S. Steel Industry: An Econometric Study of Policy Alternatives." Report prepared by the Economics Research Unit, University of Pennsylvania, for the U.S. Department of Labor. Philadelphia: University of Pennsylvania, Economics Research Unit.

Bell, M.E., and Steven Lande. (1981). *Industrial Policy: Regional Dimensions.* Lexington, Mass.: Lexington Books, D.C. Heath and Company, forthcoming.

Congressional Budget Office. (1981). "The Productivity Problem." Working Paper. Washington, D.C.

Corden, W.M. (1974). *Trade Policy and Economic Welfare.* Oxford: Clarendon Press.

Crandall, R.W. (1981). *The U.S. Steel Industry in Recurrent Crisis: Policy Options in a Competitive World.* Washington, D.C.: Brookings Institution.

Denison, E.F. (1979). *Accounting for Slower Economic Growth.* Washington, D.C.: Brookings Institution.

Denison, E.F. (1962). *The Sources of Economic Growth in the United States and the Alternatives.* U.S. Supplementary Paper 13. New York: Committee of Economic Development.

Finnel, Arthur. (1981). "Legislatively Mandated Industry Transitions: What Are the Total Costs?" in Wharton Applied Research Center, *Analysis of Consumer Policy.* Philadelphia: Wharton. Pp. 81-106.

Franko, Lawrence G. (1980). *European Industrial Policy: Past, Present and Future.* New York: The Conference Board.

Glickman, Norman J. (1982). "Regional and Industrial Policy." Study prepared for the Economic Development Authority, U.S. Department of Commerce, forthcoming.

Gresser, Julian. (1980). *High Technology and Japanese Industrial Policy.* U.S. House of Representatives, Subcommittee on Trade of Committee of Ways and Means. Washington, D.C.: U.S. Government Printing Office.

Ichimura, S. (1979). "Japanese Industrial Restructuring Policies 1945-79." Mimeographed. Paper presented to the Symposium on World Development and Restructuring of Industrial Economies, Varenna/Bellagio, Italy, September 10-16, 1979.

Klein, Lawrence R. (1980). "Industrial Policy." Mimeographed. Philadelphia: University of Pennsylvania, Economics Research Unit.

Krugman, Paul. (1980). "Foreign Experience with Industrial Policy: A Critical Review." Mimeographed. Cambridge, Mass.: M.I.T.

Ministry of International Trade and Industry. (1980). *The Vision of MITI Policies in 1980's: Summary.* (Provisional translation.) Mimeographed. Tokyo: MITI.

Nordhaus, W., and James Tobin. (1973). "Is Economic Growth Obsolete?" in NBER, Fifteenth Anniversary Colloquium, *Economic Growth*.

OECD. (1971). *Industrial Policies in 14 Member Countries*. Paris.

OECD. (1974). *The Industrial Policy of France*. Paris.

OECD. (1971). *United States Industrial Policies*. Paris.

Pinder, John, T. Hosomi, and W. Diebold. (1979). *Industrial Policy and the International Economy*. Washington, D.C.: Trilateral Commission.

Shinohara, M. (1980). *Japanese-Type Industrial Policy*. Occasional Paper A-3. Tokyo: The Asian Club.

Thurow, L. (1980). *The Zero Sum Society*. New York: Penguin Books.

Vernon, R. (1966). "International Investment and International Trade in the Product Cycle." *Quarterly Journal of Economics* 80 (May).

Author Index

Abernathy, W.J., 42, 45
Adams, F., and V. Duggal, 409
Adelman, I., 365
Albert, M., 230
Albrecht, D., 68
Allan, R.H., et al., 199
Allen, L., 368, 369
Antonelli, C., and F. Momigliano, 264
Arrow, K.J., and G. Debreu, 21

Bacon, R.W., and W.A. Eltis, 347
Bagnasco, A., 264
Balassa, B., 52, 53, 65, 71, 75, 168
Baldwin, R.E., 27
Baratta, P., 279
Behrman, J.R., 172
Bergsman, J., 182
Bergsten, C., 70, 137
Bettencourt, A., 244
Bhagwati, J., 168
Bhagwati, J., and P. Desai, 374, 379
Bhagwati, J., and T.N. Srinivasan, 173, 182
Biffen, J., 349
Bilson, J., 93
Bischoff, C., 117
Bishop, C., 91
Blackaby, F., 68, 288
Borkakoti, J., 36
Brimmer, A., and A. Sinai, 117
Brooks, H., 113
Brown, George, 341
Bywater, M., 75

Camagni, R., 270, 279
Capron, W., 99
Cassese, S., and G. Graziosi, 271
Castellano, C., 270, 279
Caton, C., et al., 117
Caves, R., 336, 352
Caves, R., and M. Uekusa, 130
Cazes, E., 66

Chamberlain, E., 162
Chipman, J.S., 28
Choksi, A.M., 158, 174, 175, 176–177, 178
Clement, B., 130
Cline, 142
Coen, R., 117
Colonna, M., 283
Comanor, W.S., 45
Cooper, G., and J. Denton, 51
Corden, W.M., 32, 33–35, 158–159, 161, 178, 194, 195, 196, 415
Cotta, A., 53, 65, 221, 240
Crawford, J., et al., 192–194
Crossman, R., 341

Daly, A., 339
Daly, D.J., and Globerman, 214
Daly, D.J., et al., 206
D'Antonio, M., 283
Davidson, B.R., 197
De Bandt, J., 81
Debreu, G., 21
De Cormay, G., 67, 70
Dell'Oro, A., et al., 270
Denison, E., 99–100
Denton, G., 56, 73
Dixon, P.J., 196
Dobson, J., 133
Donges, J.B., 168, 171
Dutt, S., 376

Edwards, G.W., and A.S. Watson, 197
EEC, 59, 60, 68, 73, 74, 75
Eisner, R., and P. Lawler, 117
Ekstrom, J., 50
Ethier, W., 28, 29, 36, 37
Evans, H.D., 196
Ezekiel, M., 92

Faini, R., 281, 283
Faini, R., and F. Schiantarelli, 283

Fame, J., 75
Feldstein, M., 118
Filippi, E., 279
Finger, J.M., 29
Finnel, A., 411
Franko, L., 52, 53
Freeman, C., 338
Friedlander, A., 100
Fua, G., 264

Galbraith, J., 44, 124
Gantt, A., and G. Dutto, 175-176
Giraud, A., 230
Glickman, N.J., 409
Glynn, D., 71
Grassini, F., 264
Gravelle, J., and R. Wescott, 121
Grazer, H., 117
Graziani, A., 268, 274, 283
Greer, R.D., 45
Gresser, J., 411
Griliches, Z., 111, 112
Grilli, E., 268, 270
Grilli, E., and J. Kregel, 280
Gruen, F.H., 196
Guerci, C.M., 270, 279
Gunder-Frank, A., 153
Gunnerson, T.H., 196

Hall, R., and D. Jorgenson, 117
Hamberg, D., 113
Hamilton, A., 32, 91
Harkness, R., 27
Harris, S.F., 196
Hassan, P., 368, 373
Hazari, R.K., 376
Hiemenz, U., and K. Rabenau, 62
Himmelberg, R., 92
Hirsch, S., 29, 30
Hirschman, A.O., 163
Holland, 52
Hough, J.R., 37

Ichimura, S., 409

Jacquemain, A., 68
Jenny, F., and A. Weber, 53

Jewkes, J., et al., 45, 113
Johnson, H.G., 33, 35

Klein, L., and P. Taubman, 117
Komiya, R., 50
Kopcke, R., and R. Syron, 118
Kregel, J., 268
Kreinin, M., 133
Kreps, J., 99
Krueger, A.O., 168, 170, 171, 182, 363
Krugman, P., 80, 408
Kuester, G., 53

Leibenstein, H., 165, 166
Leontief, 27
Lewis, J.N., 197
Lewis, W.A., 159, 162
Linder, S.B., 29
Lipsey, R.G., and K. Lancaster, 35
Little, I.M.D., et al., 168
Lloyd, A.G., 196, 197
Lloyd, P.J., 35
Longworth, J.W., 197
Lutz, V., 264

MacAvoy, P., 97, 100, 101
Machlup, F., 14
Maier, H., 43
Majumdar, B.A., 31
Mancinelli, E., 283
Mansfield, E., 43, 45, 99, 105, 111, 112, 113, 132
Martin, R., 93
Mathias, P., 209
Maunder, P., 52
May, J.D., 216
McArthur, J., and B. Scott, 223
McKenzie, L.W., 21
McKie, J., 94-95
Meier, G.M., 153
Merhav, M., 366, 368
Meyer, F., 70
Momigliano, F., 270, 273, 279
Monti, M., and B. Siracusano, 285
Moussis, N., 76

Nardozzi, L., and M. Onado, 285

Author Index

Negishi, T., 29, 33
Nehru, J., 374
Norman, N.R., 196
Northcutt, J., 342

OECD, 54, 61-70 *passim*
Ohlin, B., and P. Hesselborn, 50
Ojimi, Y., 315
Onida, F., 269, 270
Oppenlaender, E., 66

Palma, P., 366, 368
Parker, J., and E. Zieha, 118
Pavitt, K., 113, 338, 350
Peck, M., 111
Peltzman, S., 100
Phillips, A., 98, 99
Pinder, J.H., et al., 61, 63, 64, 76, 94
Posner, M.V., 29
Posner, M.V., and S. Woolf, 264, 265, 267-268
Prodi, R., 15, 19n, 51, 53, 64, 69, 269, 288
Pryor, F., 102
Pursell, G., and R.H. Snape, 196

Ranci, P., 279, 280
Ranis, G., 181
Rea, K.J., and J.T. McLeod, 205
Rees, M., 67
Reisman, S., 212
Rosenstein-Rodan, P.M., 264
Ruggiero, R., 75

Samuelson, P., 26
Saunders, C., 65
Savona, P., 268, 269, 270
Scherer, F.M., 45, 113, 125-126, 129, 131
Schmitt, P., 72
Schultz, T.W., 197
Schumpeter, J., 44, 66
Scognamiglio, C., 266, 268, 279, 288

Scott, B., 230
Scott, W.D., 196
Servan-Schreiber, J.-J., 224
Shepherd, J.J., 217
Shinohara, M., 316, 409
Silberston, A., 342
Simon, H.A., 165
Smith, A., 28, 91
Smith, T., 52
Solustri, A., 70
Stegemann, K., 215
Stern, I., 127
Stoeckel, A.B., et al., 193
Stoffaes, C., 15, 53, 63, 68, 221, 224, 225, 240
Stoleru, Lionel, 233, 240
Stout, D.K., 348
Suleiman, E., 50, 52, 63, 65

Tannenwald, R., and W. Farb, 117, 118
Tullock, G., 171
Turner, G., 335

Vaccara, B., 135
Varian, H.R., 22
Venceslai, 74
Ventriglia, F., 279
Vernon, R., 29, 52, 67, 103
Vinsentini, G., 279

Warnecke, S., 50, 71, 76
Warr, P.G., 196
Watson, A.S., and J.H. Duloy, 197
Weidenbaum, M., 99
Westphal, L.E., 180, 363, 364
Wilcox, C., and W. Shepherd, 102
Williamson, O.E., 350
Willott, W.B., 345
Wittenbach, J., 118
Wonnacott, R.J., 206

Young, S., and A. Lowe, 50

Subject Index

Act to Regulate Commerce (1887), 97
Activity-specific policies (ASPs), 15, 90, 115
Aeronautics industry: Canada, 213, 218; France, 224, 225, 227, 232; Germany, 251, 254; U.S., 139, 140, 145
Agache-Willot (France), 224
Agreement on Guidelines for Officially Supported Export Credits, 140
Agricultural Export Trade Expansion Act (1978), 142
Agricultural policies: Australia, 142, 197–198, 201; Brazil, 385; Japan, 325; U.S., 89–90, 141, 142, 144
AIDC (Australia), 199
Air Canada, 217
Air France, 238
Airbus, 4, 66, 227, 240, 254
Albert Herbert (U.K.), 344
Alberta, Can., 208
Albert's theorem, 230
Alcoa, 143
American Challenge (Servan-Schreiber), 224
AMTRAK, 103
Anglo-Iranian Oil Company, 102
Antitrust policies, 37, 65, 75; Germany, 62, 77, 130, 252; Italy, 65, 77; Japan, 320–321; U.K., 52, 77, 81, 129–130; U.S., 88, 94, 113, 128–131, 145. *See also* Monopoly power
Argentina, 143
Ariane rocket, 232, 240
Armco, 143
Arrow-Debreu-McKenzie model, 21–26
AT&T, 119
Australia, 189–203
Automobile industry: Brazil, 385; Canada, 212; France, 229, 230, 233;

Japan, 229, 311, 317; U.S., 119–120, 144, 398
Averch-Johnson effect, 98, 99

Banks: Australia, 199; France, 70, 140, 224; Italy, 265; Japan, 309, 310, 319, 326, 330; Venezuela, 368
Barlow Committee (U.K.), 333
Barre government (France), 227, 228, 230, 238, 245
Barrier-to-exit phenomenon, 273
Basel Agreement (1972), 80
Belgium, 52, 53
Berliet-Saviem (France), 224
Bidding consortia, 132
Bilateral agreements (Canada), 212–213
Boeing, 126, 127, 139
Branco government (Brazil), 382
Brasilia, 381
Brazil, 143, 154, 170, 171, 181, 359, 379–386, 416
Bretton Woods, 397
British Columbia, 208
British Leyland Motor Corporation, 102, 344, 346
British Petroleum, 102
British Steel Corporation, 102, 346
Business schools (U.K.), 335–336

Cambridge Instruments (U.K.), 344
Canada, 140, 142, 205–220
Canadair, 218
Canadian National Railway, 217
Canadian Pacific Railway, 207
Capacity restrictions (Germany), 252
Capital formation, 69–70; Germany, 252; Japan, 317–318; U.S., 115–119; Venezuela, 366, 367–368
Cartels, 65, 88; Germany, 65, 66, 252; Japan, 130, 309, 310, 320, 330
Carter administration, 132

425

CASMEZ (Italy), 265, 281
CEA (France), 227, 232
Cellar-Kefauver Act, 130
CERD (EEC), 75
CES (France), 230
Chaban-Delmas government (France), 238
Chemicals industry: France, 224
Chile, 170, 172, 182
China, People's Republic of, 142
Chirac government (France), 227, 228
Chrysler Corporation, 104, 144, 411, 418
Ciasi (France), 227-228, 242
Cidise (France), 228, 229, 242
CII (France), 227
CII-Honeywell-Bull, 66, 233
CIPE (Italy), 264, 268
CIPI (Italy), 264
CIRC (Italy), 264
Clayton Act (1914), 128
CNET (France), 232
Coal industry: France, 223, 226; Germany, 69, 252, 253, 254, 255; U.K., 339
Codis (France), 228-229, 242
Cogema (France), 232
Colombia, 170, 171
Colonna Memorandum (1970), 73
Combustion Engineering, 140
Commodity Credit Corporation (USDA), 141, 142
Common Market. *See* European Economic Community
Communications Satellite Corporation (COMSAT), 103
Communist bloc, 141
Compagnie des Machines Bull (France), 225
Compagnie francaise des petroles, 102, 232
Compagnie générale d'electicité (France), 224
Comparative advantage, 401
Competition-promoting policies, 64-65, 75, 413; Australia, 198-199; Japan, 313, 316

Computer industry: France, 225, 227, 233, 240, 242, 408; Germany, 250-251, 254-255; U.K., 342, 344, 345-346; U.S., 145. *See also* Electronics industry
Concorde, 4, 66, 225, 227, 408, 415
CONRAIL, 103
Consumption preferences, 165-166
Cooperation (EC), 74-75
Corporate-income-tax rate (U.S.), 116
Costa e Silva government (Brazil), 382
Costs/benefits (private/social), 23-24, 33, 34, 158-162, 166, 167, 269, 313, 406
Cotton industry (U.K.), 65, 339
Cotton Textile Agreement, 71
Crawford Report (Australia), 192-194, 200
CREST (EEC), 75

Daimler-Benz (France), 233
Data Resources, Inc., Model, 117
Datar (France), 226, 241, 242
Decision-making process, 16-19; Italy, 264-268
Defense industry: Canada, 211, 212-213; U.K., 338; U.S., 91, 112-113, 124-127, 144, 145
DeGaulle government (France), 224
Delfim Netto (Brazilian Planning Minister), 382, 383
Depreciation allowances: Japan, 329; U.S., 90, 94, 115, 116, 117, 118, 119, 144
Depression of 1930s, 92, 169, 182, 208
Developing countries, 153-182, 359-360, 416
Development banks: Australia, 199; Canada, 209, 213, 214; France, 228-229, 242
Development contract (France), 228, 242-243
Dillon (U.S. Treasury Secretary), 116
Direct investment, 416
DISC (Domestic International Sales Corporation) Program, 88, 121, 143

Subject Index

Distortion-correcting policies, 34–35, 159
Dominion Steel and Coal Company (Canada), 208
DREE (Canada), 214
Dutt Committee (India), 376

Economist, The, 374, 379
Ecuador, 154
EDF (France), 223, 227, 232
Edge Act (1919), 141
EDP (Canada), 210, 218
Education: Japan, 325; Korea, 364, 365; U.K., 334–336
EFIM (Italy), 265
EGAM (Italy), 265
Egypt, 171
Electricity: France, 223, 224, 232
Electronics industry: Canada, 213; France, 224; Germany, 250–251; Japan, 329; U.K., 342; U.S., 145, 398–399
Elf-Aquitaine (France), 232, 238
Elf-Erap (France), 224
Employment Act (1946), 114
Employment policies, 26, 69, 413–414; France, 241–242; Italy, 269–270; Japan, 316; U.K., 334; U.S., 144, 395. *See also* Labor *entries;* Unemployment
ENEL (Italy), 265
Energy policies: Brazil, 384; Canada, 216, 218; France, 223, 227, 232
ENI (Italy), 69, 102, 265, 267–268
Entrepreneurship, 162–163
Environmental policies, 99, 100, 146, 160
Equity funding (France), 228–229, 242
EURATOM, 66, 72, 73
EURONORM, 75
European Coal and Steel Community (ECSC), 72, 73, 75, 76, 133
European Communities (EC), 51, 52, 71–76, 82. *See also* European Economic Community
European Company Law, 72, 75
European Economic Community (EEC), 51, 56, 58–59, 64–65, 70, 71–76 *passim,* 133, 331, 338
European Investment Bank, 74
European Monetary System, 71
European Payments Union (EPU), 133
European Regional Development Fund, 74
European Social Fund, 74
Exchange-rate policies: developing countries, 169, 170, 416; France, 70, 71, 223, 227; Japan, 309; Korea, 170; U.K., 71; U.S., 80, 143, 312, 397
Experimental Technology Incentives Program, 107
Export policies, 70; Australia, 192–194, 200; Brazil, 383–384; Canada, 140, 142, 213–214; developing countries, 153–157, 170–171; EEC, 59; France, 225–226, 238; Germany, 70, 139, 140, 143; India, 171; Italy, 140, 270, 274, 285–288; Japan, 328; Korea, 364; U.K., 137, 138–139, 140; U.S., 88, 89, 90, 94, 121–123, 126–127, 131–133, 135–144
Externalities, 159–160, 313, 402, 413

FDES (France), 223
Federal Trade Commission, 129
Federal Trade Commission Act (1914), 128
FERA (India), 377, 378
Ferranti (U.K.), 344
Financial instruments, 66, 68–70, 416; Australia, 199; France, 228–230; Germany, 68; Italy, 70, 140, 265, 271; U.K., 70
FIRA (Canada), 207
Firm-specific policies (FSPs), 15, 159, 229
Foreign Agricultural Service (USDA), 137, 142
Foreign Credit Insurance Association (FCIA), 139
Foreign investment: Australia, 199–200; Canada, 207; France, 224; Korea, 364

Fortune's 500 list, 125
France, 56, 70, 78, 79, 102, 103, 140, 143, 221–245, 416; cartels/mergers, 65, 69, 81, 130; IP, 52, 53, 62–63, 87, 403, 404; R&D/innovation, 66, 77, 81, 209, 242, 338; and U.K., 340, 351
Francolor (France), 102
Free trade (Canada), 216–217
FSAI (France), 230
Fujitsu (Japan), 315

GDP: developing countries, 154; EEC, 58–59; Korea, 154, 386; U.K., 350
General Agreement on Trade and Tariffs (GATT), 71, 134, 207, 213
General Dynamics, 104, 144
General Electric, 121
General industrial policies (GIPs), 5, 15, 408–410; France, 222, 228, 229, 240; U.S., 90
General-industry studies, 8–9
General Sales Tax system (EC), 64
General System of Preferences, 71
GEPI (Italy), 265
Germany, Federal Republic of (West Germany), 52–53, 56, 65, 68, 69, 247–262, 330, 340, 410; antimonopoly policy, 62, 77, 130, 252; export policy, 70, 139, 140, 143; public ownership, 102, 146; R&D, 66, 67, 81, 109, 112, 114, 121, 209, 249, 250–251, 338
Ghana, 176
Giscard d'Estaing government (France), 244
Glomar Explorer, 107
GNP: developing countries, 154–157, 170; Germany, 247; Italy, 264; Japan, 154; Korea, 154, 360, 361, 362; U.S., 154
Government bailouts. *See* Rescue-the-loser policies
Government intervention, 25–26, 32, 33, 56–57, 61–64, 65, 67, 77–79, 134; France, 62–63, 78; Germany, 62, 79; Italy, 64, 78, 265–268, 270–274; U.K., 63–64, 78; U.S., 96–104, 134, 145–146, 414
Government procurement policies: Canada, 215; U.S., 89, 124–127, 144
Greece, 154

Harrod-Domar model, 374
Hazari Committee (India), 376
Heath government (U.K.), 334, 338
Heckscher-Ohlin model, 27–29, 30
Hermes (Germany), 70
High-technology industries, 9–10
Honeywell, 227
Hong Kong, 154, 170, 179, 181
Hoover Dam, 103
Hudson's Bay Company, 206–207
Hughes Communications, 140
Human capital, 33, 160; Venezuela, 367, 368. *See also* Labor *entries;* Training programs
Human rights, 136, 141, 143
Hunt Committee Report (U.K.), 333

IAC (Australia), 191–192, 194–195, 200, 201
IBM, 88, 94, 126, 128, 145, 146, 225, 233
IBRD, 168
IDC (U.K.), 334
IDEA (Canada), 211
IERD (Canada), 210
Ikeda government (Japan), 311
IMF, 311
IMI (Italy), 66, 265
Import policies, 70–71; Brazil, 380, 381, 384; developing countries, 169–170; India, 181; Venezuela, 372, 373
Income distribution, 418; Venezuela, 365–366
India, 171, 176, 177, 181, 359, 374–379
Indonesia, 154, 179
Industrial-concentration-promoting policies, 65–66
Industrial Expansion Plan, 92

Subject Index

Industrial organization and size, 44–46; France, 224; Italy, 274–279
Industrial Planning in France (McArthur and Scott), 223
Industrial policies (IPs), 3–5, 13–14, 15, 16–19; and innovation, 46–47
Industry-specific policies (ISPs), 3, 5, 15, 159, 165, 166, 410–412; France, 222–234 *passim*, 242, 243, 403, 410; Germany, 247, 248, 254–255, 410; Italy, 411; Japan, 410, 412; U.K., 411; U.S., 87, 90, 97–99, 119–123, 134–135, 144, 411
Industry studies, 8–10
Infant-industry model, 32–33, 161; Germany, 250; U.S., 91
Inflation, 118–119; France, 227; Korea, 386; U.S., 395–396
Information systems, 166–167, 252
Infrastructure development: developing countries, 164–165; France, 223; Korea, 164
INMOS (U.K.), 345
Innovation, 23, 31–32, 36, 41–47, 61, 66; Canada, 210–211; EEC, 75–76; France, 77; Germany, 62, 77; Italy, 279; Japan, 31, 32, 313; U.S., 32, 91, 100, 111–112, 132. *See also* Research and development
International Banking Act (1978), 141
International-competitiveness studies, 9
International Computers Ltd., 344
International demonstration effect, 165–166
International relations, policies affecting, 70–71
Interprovincial Steel and Pipe Corporation (Canada), 208
Interstate Commerce Commission (ICC), 99
Investment-tax credit, 409; France, 229; U.S., 115–116, 117, 118, 119, 120–121
Iran, 179
IRAP (Canada), 210
Iraq, 143, 179
IRC (U.K.), 52, 63, 65, 66, 130, 339, 343

IRI (Italy), 265, 267, 268
Israel, 154, 171
Italian Tobacco Monopoly, 73
Italy, 52, 53, 66, 70, 78, 79, 80, 140, 263–305, 411; antimonopoly policy, 65, 77; Mezzogiorno, 19, 51, 64, 268, 269, 273–274, 280–283, 403, 415; public ownership, 64, 65, 69, 102, 264, 265, 279
Iveco (France), 233

Jackson-Vanik Amendment (Trade Act of 1974), 141
Japan, 76, 87, 132, 134, 140, 144, 154, 229, 237, 307–330, 363, 412, 417; MITI, 130, 138, 307–328 *passim*, 409, 410; R&D/innovation, 31, 32, 109, 110–111, 112, 113, 114, 209, 313
Johnson administration (U.S.), 225
Joint Research Center (EEC), 66, 75
Joint ventures, 107

Kennedy Round, 71, 213, 311
Kiel Institute of World Economics, 168
Korea, Republic of (South Korea), 132, 164, 170, 176, 359, 360–365; GNP/GDP, 154, 171, 172, 180, 360, 361, 362, 386
Korean War, 309, 360
Kubitschek government (Brazil), 380

Labor-adaptation policies, 69, 81; Germany, 252; Italy, 264, 270, 279–280
Labor costs: France, 223, 227
Labor productivity: Japan, 319; U.K., 336, 337; U.S., 99–100
Labor skills, 23
Labor unions, 330; Japan, 309, 326; U.K., 336–337
Land distribution: Korea, 364, 365
Learning-by-doing economies, 23–24, 29, 31–32, 36, 161
Leasing arrangements, 115, 119–120, 409
Lesotho, 154, 179
Libya, 179

Linder model, 29, 31
LINK model, 7
Lobbies, 166
Lockheed Aircraft, 104, 126, 127, 140, 144, 411
Lomé Convention, 71
Luxury items, 165-166

Macdonald government (Canada), 207
Machine-tools industry: France, 233-234; Japan, 329; U.K., 339
MacMillan government (U.K.), 339
Macroeconomic model, 6-7
Malaysia, 181
Manitoba, Can., 208
MAP (U.K.), 342
Marginal cost pricing, 160-162
Marginal trade-offs, 158-159
Market characteristics, policies affecting, 64-71
Market fragmentation, 162
Market mechanism vs. market intervention, 400-401, 405-406, 407
Marshall Plan, 222, 248, 268
Massachusetts, 91
McDonnell-Douglas, 126, 127, 139
McKinley Tariff Act (1890), 92
Mergers, 65, 66, 69, 75, 81, 88, 130-131
Mexico, 177, 181
Michelin Tire Company, 214
Miike Mining Company (Japan), 330
Military-industrial complex, 124. See also Government procurement policies
Mineral exports: Australia, 189
Minimum-wage laws, 25, 69; France, 223
MISP (U.K.), 342
MIT Center for Policy Alternatives, 112
MITI (Japan), 130, 138, 307-328 *passim,* 409, 410
Mitterrand government (France), 403
Monetary policy: France, 227
Monitoring costs, 166-167
Monnet Plan (France), 222

Monopoly power, 37, 44, 65, 131, 198, 376. See also Antitrust policies
Monory government (France), 229, 238
Morrill Tariff Act (1861), 92
Multi-Fibre Agreement, 71, 81, 229
Multinational corporations, 163; and India, 377-379

NASA, 107, 126
National-champion policies. See Picking-the-winner policies
National Highway and Transportation Safety Administration, 100
National Industrial Recovery Act (1933), 92
National prestige, 250, 415
National Research and Development Assessment Program, 107
National Science Foundation, 107
National Textiles Corporation (India), 376
Nationalization. See Public ownership
NBER, 168
NEB (U.K.), 63, 343-345, 346, 347, 355
Netherlands, 52, 53
New-products-promoting policies, 67; Canada, 210-211
Newfoundland, 208
NEXOS (U.K.), 345
Nigeria, 176
Nixdorf Computer AG (Germany), 255
Nixon administration, 321, 326
North Sea oil, 348-349
Nuclear energy policies: France, 225, 227, 230, 232, 240; Germany, 251; U.S., 140, 143, 145
Nuclear Nonproliferation Treaty, 136, 143, 145

Occupational Safety and Health Administration (OSHA) (U.S.), 100, 146
OECD, 93-94, 168, 311
Oil crisis (1973-1974), 170; France, 227, 235-236; Japan, 312; U.S., 397, 418

Subject Index

Oil industry: Brazil, 380, 384, 385; Canada, 208, 216; France, 224, 232; U.K., 348–349; Venezuela, 366
Old-age pension (France), 223, 243
Ontario, 207, 208, 211, 212, 216
OPEC, 170, 179, 366
Output adaptation policies, 68–69
Overloan (Jap.), 310

Pakistan, 181
Pareto optimum, 22, 34
Park government (Korea), 361
Patents system, 23, 46, 107, 240, 402
Pechiney-Ugine-Kuhlmann (France), 224
Pecuniary externalities, 32, 33, 161
Petrobras (Brazil), 380, 384, 385
PetroCanada, 208, 218
Picking-the-winner policies, 61, 62, 63, 67, 79, 88, 404, 410–411; Australia, 190–191; Germany, 62, 79; U.K., 343–346; U.S., 127, 140, 145
Planning: developing countries, 163; France, 52, 222–223, 224, 230, 241; Italy, 270–271
Policy ranking, 33–35
Pompidou government (France), 224, 227, 238
Portugal, 154
Posner model, 29
PPDS (U.K.), 342
Price controls: France, 223
Product cycle, 29–32, 270, 327; U.S., 398–399, 401–402
Production Insurance Corporation, 92
Productivity, 394–395; France, 224, 227, 228, 238–240
Project-specific policies (PSPs), 15, 159, 166
Protectionism. *See* Tariffs and nontariff barriers
Public ownership: Australia, 199–200; Brazil, 382; Canada, 208–209, 213, 217; developing countries, 174–178; EC, 65, 102; France, 65, 69, 102, 222–223, 243; Germany, 102, 146; India, 176, 177; Italy, 64, 65, 69, 102, 264, 265, 279, 283–285; U.K., 102; U.S., 88, 102–104
Public utilities, 119
Pulp and paper industry (Canada), 208

Quebec, Can., 207, 208

Railroads: Canada, 207, 217; France, 223; U.S., 97, 103, 119
RDIA (Canada), 214
Reagan administration, 93, 101, 107, 137, 139
Recession: Brazil (1981), 383, 384; Germany (1967), 248
Reconstruction Finance Corporation (RFC), 92
Region-specific policies (RSPs), 15; Canada, 214; France, 70, 225, 226, 229; Germany, 62, 70; Italy, 19, 51, 64, 268, 269, 273–274, 280–283, 403, 415; U.K., 70, 333–334, 356–357; U.S., 119–120, 399
Renault (France), 102, 233, 234, 238
Rent seeking, 166
Reorganization Program (EEC), 74–75
Rescue-the-loser policies, 411–412; France, 230, 410; Germany, 410; Italy, 64, 79, 411; Japan, 410; U.K., 63, 79, 411; U.S., 104, 135, 144, 411
Research and development, 43–44; Canada, 209–213, 218; EC, 66–67, 81, 109, 113; France, 209; Germany, 66, 67, 81, 109, 112, 114, 121, 209, 249, 250–251, 338; Italy, 66, 279, 285–288; Japan, 109, 209; U.K., 66, 67, 81, 109, 112, 338–339, 355; U.S., 89, 91, 100, 104–114, 120–121, 132, 209, 402
Resources, mobility of: Germany, 252; Italy, 264
Restructuring intervention, 61–62
Revenue Act (1962), 115, 116, 117
Revenue Act (1971), 121
Revenue Act (1981), 115, 117, 119, 120, 409
Rhode Island, 91

Rhône-Poulenc (France), 224
Ricardo model, 27, 236
Risk, 24–25, 414; Germany, 249–250
Rolls Royce (U.K.), 63, 343

Sacilor (France), 236
SAGE air-defense contracts, 126, 145
Saint-Gobain-Pont-à-Mousson (France), 224
SALTE (Brazil), 380
San Francisco Independence Treaty, 309
Saraceno Report (Italy), 266
Saskatchewan, 208
"Satisfising behavior," 165
Saudi Arabia, 179
Saving ratio: Japan, 325
Scale economies, 160–162
"Second best" theory, 35, 37–38, 158
Sector-specific policies (SSPs), 15, 159; U.K., 357; U.S., 119–120, 127, 144
Set-Aside Program, 89–90
Sherman Act (1890), 128, 129
Shipping subsidization, 81; France, 229; Germany, 253, 254; Japan, 144, 329–330; U.K., 339, 357; U.S., 143–144
Shoe industry: France, 229; U.S., 135, 144
Sidbec (Canada), 208
Siemens (Germany), 233, 255
Simonsen (Brazilian Planning Minister), 383
Singapore, 154, 170, 181, 360
SNCF (France), 223
SNIAS (France), 224, 234
Social-welfare function, 69, 158, 163, 165, 166
South Africa, 141
Southern Mediterranean Cooperation Agreement, 71
Soviet Union, 109, 143, 145
Space research: France, 232; U.S., 91, 112–113, 124–127
Spain, 154, 170, 171, 181
Spinelli Report (1973), 74
Sri Lanka, 158, 365

State holding companies, 66, 69. *See also* Public ownership
Steel industry, 75; Canada, 208; France, 224, 229, 230, 234–237, 241; Italy, 267, 268; Japan, 398, 404, 408, 418; U.S., 119–120, 144, 398
STEPEX (Canada), 210
Structural adaptation policies, 67–68; Germany, 62, 248–253; Italy, 66, 270, 279, 283–285; Japan, 317; U.K., 52, 63, 65, 66, 130, 339, 343
Substitution effect, 131
Sullivan Principles, 141
Supply-side economic theory, 117
Sweden, 53, 67, 68, 70, 79, 415
Switzerland, 137
Synthetic Fuels Corporation, 90, 104
Sysco (Canada), 208

Taiwan, 154, 158, 170, 171, 386
Tanzania, 158
Tariff of 1789, 133
Tariffs and nontariff barriers, 25, 70–71, 75, 142, 416; Australia, 195–197; Canada, 207, 213–214, 216–217; developing countries, 172–174; EEC, 70, 71, 133; France, 223; Germany, 62; Japan, 134, 311, 329; U.K., 349, 352; U.S., 91–92, 132–133, 134, 135, 142
Tax policies, 35, 417; Canada, 215–216; Germany, 121, 253–254; U.S., 107, 114–123
Technical Assistance to Import Injured Industries, 107
Technology model, 30–32
Telecommunications industry: France, 223, 227, 232; U.S., 119, 139, 140, 145
Temporary National Economic Committee (TNEC), 92
Tennessee Valley Authority (TVA), 93, 103
Textile industry: France, 224, 229, 230; India, 376; U.S., 135, 144
Thailand, 154
Thatcher government (U.K.), 344, 350

Subject Index 433

Thomson-Brandt (France), 224
Togo, 154, 179
Tokyo Round, 71, 134
Trade Act of 1974, 107, 134, 141
Trade-adjustment assistance programs, 134, 144
Trade balance: Canada, 212, 213; France, 227, 233; Japan, 310, 328; U.K., 348–349; U.S., 397
Trade Expansion Act (1962), 90, 133, 134
Trade Opportunities Program (TOP), 137
Trade policies. See Tariffs and nontariff barriers
Trading companies, 132, 328
Training programs, 23, 32–33, 69, 81, 160; Germany, 252
Transportation: Canada, 217
Treaties: EC, 72–73
Treaty of Paris (1951), 72
Treaty of Rome (1957), 65, 70, 71, 72–73, 223
Trewarbeit (Germany), 70
Trilateral Commission Report (1979), 94
Tunisia, 154
Turkey, 154, 170, 176

Uganda, 176
Unemployment, 413–414; EEC, 59; France, 227–228, 241–242; U.S., 144, 395. See also Employment policies
Unilateral Declarations (1976), 140
United Kingdom, 32, 53, 56, 58, 63–71 passim, 78, 79, 102, 319, 330, 331–357, 374, 411; antimonopoly policy, 52, 77, 81, 129–130; export policy, 137, 138–139, 140; R&D, 66, 67, 81, 109, 112, 338–339, 355
United States, 87–151; agricultural policy, 89–90, 141, 142, 144; antitrust policy, 88, 94, 113, 128–131, 145; and Brazil, 380; and Canada, 211, 212–213; defense and space, 91, 112–113, 124–127, 144, 145; employment policy, 144, 395; exchange-rate policy, 80, 143, 312, 397; export policy, 88, 89, 90, 94, 121–123, 126–127, 131–133, 135–144; government regulation/ownership, 88, 96–104, 134, 145–146, 414; inflation, 395–396; and Japan, 309, 312, 321–322; and Korea, 363–364; labor unions, 330; procurement policy, 89, 124–127, 144; regional issues, 119–120, 399; R&D, 32, 100, 104–114, 120–121, 132, 209, 251; tariff policy, 91–92, 132–134, 135, 142; tax policy, 107, 114–123; winner-loser policy, 104, 135, 144, 411; world-market share, 319
U.S. Air Force, 126
U.S. Army Corps of Engineers, 164
U.S. Commerce Department, 137
U.S. Congress: Joint Economic Committee, 94, 99, 137, 140
U.S. Department of Agriculture, 137, 141, 142
U.S. Department of Transportation, 107
U.S. Export-Import Bank (Eximbank), 88, 90, 136, 137, 139–141
United States Industrial Policies (OECD), 94
U.S. Internal Revenue Code (1954), 116, 117
U.S. Justice Department: Antitrust Division, 128, 129
U.S. Public Law 480, 141, 147
U.S. State Department, 137, 141
U.S. Treasury Department: ADR system (1971), 116–117
Usinor (France), 236

Value Added Tax (VAT): EEC, 64–65; France, 223, 240, 243
Venezuela, 359, 365–373
VIAG (Germany), 66
Vietnam War, 363, 395
Volkswagen (Germany), 80, 102
Voluntary agreements, 65, 81

Wage policies: Australia, 198, 201; France, 223, 227; Korea, 360, 364; minimum wage, 25, 69
Webb-Pomerene Act (1918), 90, 131-132, 143
Western Electric, 140
Westinghouse, 140
Wharton Long Term Industry model, 7
White Paper on Manufacturing Industry (Australia), 190-192, 200
Wilson government (U.K.), 338, 341, 344
Windfall profits tax, 107
World-market share, 319
World Traders Data Report, 137

"X-inefficiency," 165, 166, 177

Yaounde Convention, 71
Yugoslavia, 154, 181

List of Contributors

Jere R. Behrman, University of Pennsylvania
C. Andrea Bollino, University of Pennsylvania
Martin Cherkes, University of Pennsylvania
Michael Davenport, Wharton Econometric Forecasting Associates, Philadelphia
Francois DeWitt, L'Expansion, Paris
Shinichi Ichimura, University of Kyoto
Jaime Marquez, University of Pennsylvania
William J. Milne, University of Toronto, Scarborough
Brian Pinto, University of Pennsylvania
Theophilos Priovolos, United Nations Conference on Trade and Development (UNCTAD), Geneva
Peter Urban, Bureau of Agricultural Economics, Canberra
Gerhard Wagenhals, University of Heidelberg
Robert F. Wescott, Wharton Econometric Forecasting Associates, Philadelphia

About the Editors

F. Gerard Adams received the doctorate from the University of Michigan. Since 1961, he has been at the University of Pennsylvania, where he is professor of economics and finance and director of the Economics Research Unit. He is also senior consultant of Wharton Econometric Forecasting Associates, Inc. Dr. Adams has served as a business economist in the petroleum industry and as a forecaster on the staff of the Council of Economic Advisers and the OECD. He is a consultant to numerous government agencies and business corporations. His work has ranged widely in the areas of macroeconometric model building and forecasting, energy economics, regional modeling, and international economics. He is coauthor of *An Econometric Analysis of International Trade* (1969), *Commodity Exports and Economic Development* (Lexington Books, 1982), *Modeling the Multiregional Economic System* (Lexington Books, 1980), and of numerous other publications.

Lawrence R. Klein, Benjamin Franklin Professor of Economics and Finance of the University of Pennsylvania, is chairman of Wharton Econometric Forecasting Associates, Inc., and principal investigator of Project LINK, an academically oriented research project linking econometric models of various national and regional economies. He is past president of the American Economic Association, Econometric Society, and Eastern Economic Association. He serves as consultant to various private corporations and national and international agencies. He is the author of many books and research papers, as well as an active member of several scientific or scholarly societies. He was awarded the Nobel Prize in economics in 1980 for his work in developing econometric models and their application to forecasting and policy analysis.